£10-67+

ALBAN BERG

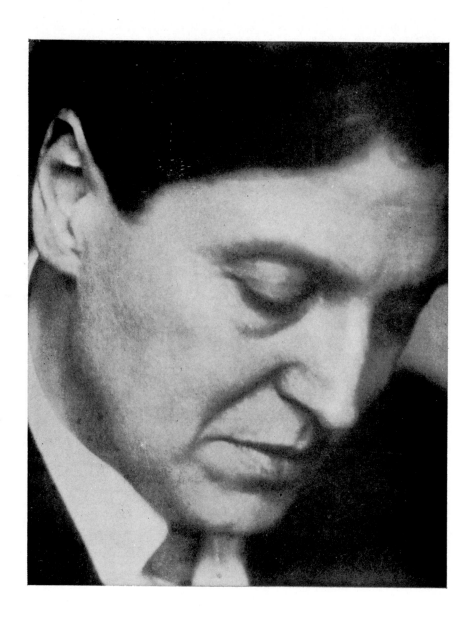

Berg in 1935

MOSCO CARNER

ALBAN BERG

The Man and The Work

DUCKWORTH

Y CAR

First published in 1975 by
Gerald Duckworth & Co. Ltd.
The Old Piano Factory,
43 Gloucester Crescent, London NW1

Completely revised and reset 1983

© *1975, 1983 by Mosco Carner*

ISBN 0 7156 0769 3 (cased)

Photoset in Wales by
Derek Doyle and Associates, Mold, Clwyd
Printed in Great Britain by
Redwood Burn Limited,
Trowbridge, Wiltshire

For

FELIX and HEDI SALZER

IN LONG AND AFFECTIONATE FRIENDSHIP

CONTENTS

ILLUSTRATIONS

PREFACE TO THE SECOND EDITION

Much water has flowed under the bridges of the Thames since the first publication of this book in 1975. In the meantime three important events have occurred concerning Berg's life and work. The first was the revelation in spring 1977 of an episode in Berg's private affairs which to some extent affected his relationship with his wife, but was of crucial import for the genesis and character of his Lyric Suite. Secondly, Helene Berg died on 30 August 1976, at the age of ninety-one. While she was alive, a responsible biographer was forced to impose on himself a large measure of discretion and caution in order not to offend the susceptibilities of Berg's somewhat eccentric but noble and high-minded widow. With her death this is no longer necessary, and it is the biographer's duty to tell the truth about her extraordinary conduct over the matter of the autograph score of the Lyric Suite and about the circumstances that led her in 1969 to impose a total embargo on the material of the third act of *Lulu*, left unfinished by her husband. Thirdly, the orchestration and filling of some compositional lacunae of that act have now been done by Friedrich Cerha, thus restoring the missing dramatic and musical balance and symmetry of the opera and allowing us to see, at long last, the heroine in her true perspective. This was impossible with the torso of the work as it was staged until 1979. I attended the first production of the complete *Lulu* which was staged at the Paris Opéra on 24 February 1979, with a hand-picked cast under the direction of Pierre Boulez, produced by Patrice Chéreau. The first English production with the resurrected third act was given at Covent Garden under Colin Davis, Götz Friedrich producing, in February 1981.

All these events necessitated a radical revision of the relevant chapters of my book, which I first prepared for its French edition (Paris, 1979) when I also expanded and reformulated other sections of it. In this second English edition I have incorporated some further new material that has come to hand since, and made a few more improvements.

In conclusion I would like to add that in spite of the two important source books mentioned in the Preface to the first edition, and in spite of the new material that came to light, I still consider that the time has not yet come to attempt a fully comprehensive definitive 'Life' of Berg. For one thing, I believe that Helene Berg did not publish *all* the letters addressed to her by her husband and that in those letters she did publish, some of the content was suppressed by her. I have seen a copy of the original edition of her book, now a collector's item, in which on virtually every other page whole sentences and long paragraphs were blacked. Nor am I absolutely certain that what Helene published corresponds accurately to what Berg had in fact written to her. These letters must therefore be read with circumspection. For another thing, a standard biography of Berg must await, not only the publication of the authentic text of Berg's letters to his wife, but also of numerous other letters to and from Berg, in particular the large correspondence exchanged between Berg and Anton Webern. To judge from published excerpts, this will undoubtedly provide a mine of interesting new information. The publication of this correspondence has long been promised by the Universal Edition but has so far not materialised.

August, 1982   M.C.

PREFACE TO THE FIRST EDITION

Although intended as a full-length study of Alban Berg, the man and the artist, my book lays no claim to be a strictly comprehensive treatment of the subject. To take its second and more important part, The Work, first. I have concentrated on Berg's published compositions and devoted but little space to his unpublished juvenilia, among them the seventy-odd songs. In my brief general discussion I have used the findings of Nicholas Chadwick, who personally inspected the manuscripts of these songs at the Österreichische Nationalbibliothek in Vienna. By the same token I have treated the third act of the opera *Lulu* with less attention to detail than I would have done if Berg had lived long enough to finish its orchestration or if we saw the whole of this act in someone else's completion. As regards the method I applied to this second part of the book, I have, in contrast to Berg's two foremost biographers, Dr Willi Reich and the late Dr H.F. Redlich, treated Berg's works not chronologically but by genres. Both methods have their advantages and disadvantages. In a chronological treatment, the reader is made aware of the gradual evolution of a composer's style, but he will have to bear with a deal of tiresome repetition. A treatment by genres avoids this, but cannot show the development of style in its continuity. I have tried to take account of this in the biographical part of my book. The reader may be surprised to find the discussion of the Chamber Concerto not in the chapter on chamber music but in that dealing with orchestral works. My reason for this is twofold. I consider any combination going beyond a nonet as nearer to the orchestral than the chamber music sphere. Moreover, the work is a concerto for piano, violin and thirteen wind instruments: not only is it treated with virtuosity, but from it run links to the Violin Concerto of some ten years later.

In my analyses I have tried, wherever possible, to relate them to the imaginative content of a work. Hence the Goethe quotation at the head of Part II of my book. In the songs and the operas this was none too difficult since the words were a guide to the poetic intentions Berg realised in the music. But this was much harder in the purely instrumental compositions where I could merely guess at their content from the character of the music and Berg's personality as I see it. The reader is free to disagree and see a different content in such works as, for instance, the Three Orchestral Pieces, op. 6 and the Lyric Suite. Similarly, with such complex, multi-layered compositions as Berg's, their formal design cannot always be defined in clear, unambiguous terms and here again there is room for disagreement with my suggestions. The same holds true of my derivation of certain themes and motives from a given twelve-note series as, for instance, in *Lulu* and the finale of the Lyric Suite.

One more word on my analyses. I have pursued in them two aims. The first was the normal, traditional one – to examine Berg's formal design, texture, melody and so on and also draw attention to what seemed to me points of special interest in a given work. My second aim was directed to his use of twelve-note technique. Schoenberg once said something to the effect that the serial method of composing was a 'family affair' and, hence, should be kept private. The listener was to concern himself solely with the What of a composition, that is, its imaginative content. This ought to be his attitude in actual performance. But in a serious discussion of dodecaphonic works the How becomes as important as the What. How a note-row is built and how it is treated in the course of the music determines to a large extent the work's character. The listener may not be conscious of it but it affects his aesthetic judgment subliminally. I submit that not even the most acute of ears will, unaided by study, be able to discover how Berg arrives for instance at the half-series in his Lyric Suite, or that the *Lulu* series is the matrix of virtually the whole material of the opera. Not that this knowledge is at all necessary in order to enjoy the music. What matters to the listener is the purely aural aspect, the sound image. (And that goes also for *Wozzeck* with its underlying instrumental forms.) Yet I maintain that, if he has been forewarned, as it were, or if intellectual curiosity has prompted him to occupy himself with the technical aspect of this music, then his aesthetic pleasure will be much heightened. In order to assist him in this I have devoted considerable space to the divulgation of Berg's 'family affair' in the Lyric Suite, the Violin Concerto and *Lulu*.

As to the biographical part of my book I may, with some justice, be accused of too cursory a treatment of Berg's early years before he began his studies with Schoenberg. But I found this part of the composer's life not interesting enough to be the subject of a detailed account. In my view it was not until he started to study with Schoenberg that the man and composer in Berg began to acquire substance and strength. As to my source material, two collections of letters have been of outstanding value to me. The first is Helene Berg's *Alban Berg. Briefe an seine Frau* (Vienna, 1965; London, 1971), the opening letter dating as far back as the spring of 1907. My second source is Berg's largely unpublished correspondence with Schoenberg, which spans a period of twenty-four years (1911-34), and which is now deposited by Schoenberg's heirs in the Library of Congress, Washington. This most voluminous correspondence represents a mine of new information on the composer's life and work, and it also sheds fresh light on the unique relationship between a teacher and his former pupil, between a fatherly mentor and guide and his disciple. I wish to express my deeply felt gratitude to Frau Helene Berg and to Mr Ronald R. Schoenberg for their extreme kindness in giving me permission to have photostat copies of the original letters made and to quote large excerpts from them in my book. To avoid unnecessary footnotes, I state that all quotations from the composer's letters to his wife and his erstwhile teacher derive from these two collections. (The translations are all mine.) Moreover, Frau Berg has been most helpful in clarifying for me certain biographical points and in allowing me to reproduce a number of illustrations. I am also indebted to the heirs of Frida Semler Seabury for kind permission to quote from Berg's letters to her, now at the Library of Congress; to Mr Louis Krasner, Syracuse (New York) for important information on the genesis of Berg's Violin Concerto; to Mr Barrie Gavin and the BBC Television Service for the loan of photographs; to Miss Miriam Miller and the BBC Music Library for their help with scores; to Mr Harold Spivacke, Chief of the Music Division of the Library of Congress for his ready assistance in the provision of photocopies; to Berg's publishers, Universal Edition, Vienna, for their kind permission to quote from the composer's music, to the Royal Opera House, Covent Garden, and to the German and Austrian Institutes of Culture, London.

For generous help in various details my grateful thanks are also due to Dr Willi Reich, Zürich; Mr George Perle, New York; Prof. Fedele D'Amico, Rome; Dr Maximilian Spaeth, Nuremberg; Mr Nicholas Chadwick, Dr Douglas Jarman, Mr Peter Stadlen, and Miss Hazel Sebag-Montefiore. Last but not least, I wish to express my gratitude to Lord Horder and my publishers for taking so much interest and care in the production of my book. It only remains for me to add that, when I visited the late Gian Francesco Malipiero at his home at Asolo in the autumn of 1970, the Maestro was kind enough to let me have copies of a number of Berg letters addressed to him of which I have made use in the book.

January 1971   M.C.

INTRODUCTION

To an age such as the present, when the turnover of new compositions has become enormous, and when the plurality of techniques and styles as well as their short life and swift changes have come to be considered a matter of course – to such an age atonality and twelve-note music have ceased to be a problem. Indeed, what to the generation to which I belong appeared at the time a true *ars nova* opening up entirely new vistas, the *avant-garde* of today dismisses as 'old hat' – outdated and *passé*. Has not Boulez the composer declared that 'Schoenberg est mort', while Boulez the conductor continues to perform his music and that of his two great disciples with remarkable zest and frequency? Is it of course part of the birthright of every creative artist to forge ahead and in the process alter the physiognomy of his art. To that extent Boulez's dictum about Schoenberg is certainly legitimate and acceptable. But music is not only a matter of styles and techniques. What matters in the last resort is what lies behind the notes – what causes them to be written in just this order and not another. A Haydn quartet, a Mozart opera, a Beethoven symphony and a Schubert song are, in point of style, wholly dated. What renders them timeless masterpieces is their imaginative content or, if you like, their spirit and ethos expressed in a particular language. And, equally important, there seems to exist a correlation between imaginative strength and technique. No composer, great in the metaphysical sense, was inept in his technique. In fact, it is part of his greatness to be such a perfect craftsman. Imagination and technical excellence are also the landmark of the so-called Second Viennese school. It too can boast unquestionable masterpieces, masterpieces subject to the same aesthetic laws as govern tonal music, but requiring a kind of analytical listening in order to arrive at a full appreciation of them.

My own interest in the Schoenberg school dates back to my student days in Vienna in the mid 1920s. By this time the activities of the Society for Private Musical Performances had ceased, so that occasions to hear truly contemporary music in Vienna, especially that of Schoenberg, Berg and Webern, were few and far between. I recall the envy I felt whenever I read reports in the *Musikblätter des Anbruch* about frequent performances of works by the Schoenberg school in Germany, while the Vienna musical Establishment, faithful in adhering to a time-honoured tradition, applied its policy of *Totschweigen*, of completely ignoring its three most famous composers, with almost unqualified success. It was not until I settled in Britain in 1933, when my musical horizon began to widen in the direction of contemporary music of many lands, that I heard fairly frequent performances and broadcasts of the music of the Holy Viennese Trinity and was prompted to familiarise myself with it.

The dominant figure of this Trinity is of course Schoenberg, one of the three great musicians – the other two being Stravinsky and Bartók – to have influenced music in the first half of our century in the most radical manner. Schoenberg's seminal importance both as composer and teacher cannot be exaggerated. Of his two eminent disciples, Webern is the unrivalled master of the musical aphorism, carrying his master's twelve-note method to a *ne plus ultra* of concentration, and in the early 1950s becoming, posthumously, the point of departure for the serial method to be applied to every constituent or, to use the now fashionable expression, parameter of music. And what of Berg? Since his death half a century will soon have elapsed which, I believe, is a time span long enough to enable us to see him in the round and place him in historical perspective. Stravinsky, so partial to Webern who for him was a 'perpetual Pentecost', likened Berg's music, if compared with Webern's, to an old woman about whom one says: 'How beautiful she must have been when she was young'.[1] I must confess that the meaning of this remark wholly eludes me. Did Stravinsky consider the early Berg better than the later Berg? The composer of the String Quartet, op. 3, and the Three Orchestral Pieces, op. 6, to be preferred to the author of *Wozzeck*, the Lyric Suite and *Lulu*? However, for purely temperamental reasons Berg appeals to me more strongly than the other two members of the Second Viennese school. No value judgment is here involved, but simply the fact that the ethos of his music speaks to me with a particular eloquence. With Berg I feel I am in the presence of a great humanist whose creations are all 'about' something which in the last analysis has to do with life and life's bitter experiences. It is, I suggest, the humanity emanating from his music that links him so closely to his much adored Mahler and, as with Mahler, it is Berg's strong lyrical vein, a vein sensitive, soft-grained and most pliable, to which I respond immediately. His detractors were not slow in seizing on this paramount feature and declared Berg 'the Puccini of twelve-note music'. (Whether this passes as a defect today I very much doubt.) Moreover, Berg's lyrical outpourings are balanced by a strong dramatic instinct, to be felt not only in his songs and, of course, his two operas, but in all his instrumental works, from the early Piano Sonata, op. 1, to his swan-song, the Violin Concerto. This equilibrium is one of the most characteristic traits of Berg's style, just as is the right distribution of contrapuntal and more homophonic writing in a work. There is, moreover, his perfect sense of formal proportion and his

---

[1] Igor Stravinsky and Robert Kraft, *Memories and Commentaries*, London, 1960, pp. 104-5.

ability to control and discipline an overwhelming wealth of ideas in a way resulting in an organic whole in which, so to speak, every note has its right place. This gift was probably inborn, but it needed the hand of his great teacher to bring it fully out of him and develop it to perfection, as witness, for instance, his early String Quartet of 1910.

There are, in addition, several other characteristics which eloquently attest Berg's individuality. I mention in the first place his symbolic use of musical forms in the service of dramatic characterisation and action in his two operas, and his treatment of the row as a dramatic means such as, for instance, the absorption of Dr Schön's series into the main Lulu series at his death in Act II, scene I. No less characteristic is Berg's number symbolism to which, as we shall see, he was much given, and in which the numbers 3 (Chamber Concerto), 7 (*Wozzeck*) and especially 10 and 23 (Lyric Suite) and their multiples, are the extra-musical determinants of diverse aspects of his music. Yet it is a sign of Berg's compositional mastery that his mathematical *jeux d'esprit* are merged into the free play of his creative imagination to such an extent that even the best informed listener remains unaware of any constriction, just as he remains unaware of the restraint Berg imposes on himself by the employment of 'automatic' devices such as canon, inversion, retrograde (palindrome), rigid formal symmetries and cryptograms. All of which Berg seems to have erected as a kind of intellectual bulwark or dam against an overflow of music of a most highly charged personal, subjective content.

As for his handling of Schoenberg's twelve-note method of composition, Berg goes his own and highly original way by making a series and its derivatives the symbols of the *dramatis personae* and their relationships with one another (*Lulu*); or by successively altering certain notes in the row in order to represent an evolving inner programme, such as 'submitting to fate' (Lyric Suite). Also, in marked contrast to his teacher and Webern, Berg increases the thematic potential of a series by dividing it into so-called half-series and/or splitting it into segments to be used independently (Lyric Suite). Altogether, Berg proves far more enterprising and adventurous in his serial technique than either Schoenberg or Webern.

Berg was the only member of the Holy Viennese Trinity, who, after the adoption of the dodecaphonic method of composition, continued to preserve a link with his own past through the assimilation of the major-minor tonality with serial technique. He used to boast that he could conceal the twelve-note manner of his music so that no listener would be able to notice it. This was, he said, 'das Kunststück' – 'the master trick'. That this mixture makes for an 'impurity' of style is clear, and to that extent Berg was an eclectic who tried to make the best of both worlds. Schoenberg and Webern made no such concession. But is the marriage in Berg of the tonal and the twelve-note system really a concession? I do not think so. I am rather inclined to see it as a psychological compulsion, an inner necessity that forced Berg to maintain a bridge between the traditional and the new. Schoenberg and Webern were radical revolutionaries – Berg was the advocate of gradual transformation, in short, of evolution. But such a distinction has nothing to do with aesthetics. There are masterpieces in both the pure and the 'impure' twelve-note style.

THE MAN

ONE

INFANCY AND EARLY YOUTH
1885-1904

Alban Berg was descended on both the paternal and maternal side from non-Austrian forebears. His father hailed from Wöhrd, a suburb of Nuremberg, and the family tree of his mother had its roots in Baden-Würtemberg and southern Bohemia. Berg believed that his father's ancestors were high Bavarian officials and officers, with the aristocratic 'Freiherr' or 'Baron' as handle to their name, which his grandfather was wise enough to drop.[1] Yet researches carried out by the Nuremberg music critic, Maximilian Spaeth (the results of which Dr Spaeth kindly placed at my disposal), as well as investigations I caused to be made at the Nuremberg Stadtarchiv, show that Berg was mistaken. His great-grandfather was in the service of the Bavarian court, first in a menial capacity and then as a minor official attached to the Königliche Hauptkasse or Royal Finance Department. His son Joseph was a drum-major and subsequently corporal in the Bavarian Army and led a somewhat adventurous life. He was married twice – the second time to Kunigunde Koerper, the daughter of a tiler at Wöhrd who bore him six children, the fourth of whom, Konrad, was Berg's father. In Konrad's birth certificate the occupation of his father is entered as *Fabrikarbeiter*, factory worker.

Konrad Berg (1846-1900) was originally a commercial traveller who, after settling in Vienna in 1867, opened an export and import business. He acquired Austrian citizenship and in 1871 married, apparently above his station, Johanna Maria Anna, *née* Braun (1851-1926), the daughter of a Vienna court jeweller, who later ran a shop near St Stephen's Cathedral selling devotional articles for Catholics.

The Bergs had four children – Hermann (1872-1921), who emigrated to America, where he became a successful businessman and at one time invited Berg to settle there; Carl or Charly (1881-1952) who, like his father, was in the export and import trade and was a gifted amateur singer; our composer Alban Maria Johannes, who was born on 9 February 1885 and died on 24 December 1935; and Smaragda (1887-1953),[1a] who seems to have been the black sheep of the family. She was a lesbian, made an unsuccessful marriage,

[1] Letter to his future father-in-law, of July 1910, in Helene Berg, *Alban Berg. Briefe an seine Frau*, p. 160.

[1a] The rare names 'Smaragda' and 'Alban' were chosen at the suggestion of the Greek Consul in Vienna, a friend of Berg's father. In Berg's birth certificate his Christian names were entered as 'Albano Maria Joannes'.

and after her divorce tried in 1908 to commit suicide, just as Alban did in the autumn of 1903 after an unhappy love affair. The reason for this was the birth of an illegitimate daughter, the outcome of Berg's affair with a Carinthian peasant girl, Marie Scheuchl. The eighteen-year-old father had no money of his own to support the child and was therefore forced to disclose this, for its time, most shameful event to his family. Berg never got in touch with his daughter, but after his death a photograph was found among his papers showing a girl of seven or eight, with features very similar to Berg's. Did Berg remember this youthful affair when he came to compose *Wozzeck* where there is another Marie who is the mother of an illegitimate child? Berg began his composing career at the age of fifteen with songs for which the musical set-up in his family may have been an additional incentive. One imagines that no sooner would he write a song than his brother Charly would try it out, with Smaragda as accompanist. She was a competent pianist, a pupil of the famous Theodore Leschetitzky, with a particular interest in contemporary music, notably Debussy and Ravel, and it seems that it was through Smaragda that Berg made his first acquaintance with the French impressionists. It is probable that the Berg children inherited their musical talent from their maternal grandfather who, though unable to read music, played the piano by ear and also showed a marked facility for drawing and the designing of jewellery, which repeated itself in Berg's gift for the graphic arts. Thus it was Berg who designed the *Jugendstil* cover for the first edition of his Piano Sonata, op. 1 and the Four Songs, op. 2, not to mention the calligraphic neatness of his autograph scores, which is in marked contrast to the near-illegibility of many of his letters.

The resemblance between father and son was striking. Both were very tall and sparsely built, and both showed features in which a nervous tiredness and even melancholy were prominent. Berg's feminine face is strongly reminiscent of Oscar Wilde's, a fact of which he was aware, and like Wilde, Shelley and Raphael, he retained his youthful looks until a few weeks before his death at the age of fifty. The mother, on the other hand, seems to have had a pronounced extravert nature, with both feet firmly planted on the ground. She was robust and energetic, and all sentimentality and extravagant behaviour were alien to her. That there was a strong egocentric streak in her make-up, emerges from Berg's letters to his wife. Johanna or, as Berg sometimes referred to her in these letters, Jeanette, was well read and, according to people who knew her, showed an appreciation of music, painting and architecture.

Life at the 'Schönbrunnerhaus', Tuchlauben 8, in Vienna's first district, was a pleasant one for the children. They had a governess from the Alsace, Ernestine Gotzlick, who taught them French and the piano, and who on special occasions would arrange for plays, musical charades and *tableaux vivants* to be performed by the children before the parents and their guests, and it may be that Berg's remarkable sense of the musical theatre was first awakened by these performances. In the spring of 1898 the Bergs moved to the seventh district, as the house at Tuchlauben was to be pulled down. As long as the father was alive, the family lived in *gutbürgerlich* or comfortable circumstances, with an estate on the Ossiacher See in Carinthia – the Berghof – acquired by Konrad Berg in 1894, where Alban spent many a summer until 1920, when it was sold. Yet even afterwards he would frequently stay there as a paying guest of the new owner.

The Berghof, the surrounding country and the whole sunny atmosphere of this southern Austrian province held Berg in thrall all his life, not least because he found it so conducive to creative work. A vivid picture of the young Berg at Berghof has been drawn by Frida Semler Seabury, the young daughter of an American business friend of Konrad Berg, who spent the summers of 1903 and 1904 at the estate which Berg's mother, after her husband's death in 1900, ran as a kind of boarding-house for paying guests during the summer season. Frida describes the eighteen-year-old youth as being always in high spirits, full of fun and a most pleasant companion. They used to go swimming together in the lake which Berg, a very good swimmer, would cross from one end to the other. This was, incidentally, the only form of sport which he was able to practise, because of his small heart. In the afternoon or evening there would be play-reading with divided roles, notably of Ibsen's dramas, or music when Smaragda would sing Alban's latest songs or the two would play piano duets. Berg would often go through volume after volume of poetry in search of suitable verses to be set to music. Frida, a girl of sixteen and a student at Wellesley College, Massachusetts, had literary ambitions,[2] and Berg would find her a most responsive partner with whom to discuss literature and music. Already then Berg was familiar with Wedekind's dramas, among them *Erdgeist*.

After Frida left for America they corresponded with each other up to about 1908. Berg's letters cover pages and pages and suggest that his heart was perhaps not entirely uninvolved in this friendship. It is amusing to read in a letter of July 1907 that this youth of twenty-two fancied himself to be

> a judge of human nature in general and the soul of woman in particular, and I derive this knowledge not so much from books as from my own experience. And I can state that despite being young for these things, I have never been deceived in these judgments – on the contrary, I have always been right.

Typical of the introspection of a growing-up youth is a letter of 18 November 1907 in which, in referring to Frida becoming president of the students' union at her college, Berg writes:

[2] The verses of Berg's early song, 'Traum', are by her, and a play of hers was performed at her college.

I am hardly able to think myself into your position as president which is undoubtedly an honoured one. For I have become, if anything, more shy of people, even less capable of occupying a leading position in life, and feel only happy if I can devote myself quietly to my work, untouched by the hustle and bustle of the outside world. Only then can I find the strength and joy to create. Only then life becomes for me satisfactory and tolerable!

Turning to musical matters, Berg writes of his great enthusiasm for Strauss's *Salome*, the first Austrian production of which he attended, together with Mahler, Schoenberg and Zemlinsky, at Graz in the spring of 1906 and which he saw again at the Dresden Musikfest in the same year. Berg's reason for mentioning this opera to Frida was its production at the Vienna Volksoper by a Breslau ensemble to which he went no fewer than six times.[3] 'How I would like', he writes, 'to sing to you *Salome* which I know so well' so that Frida could take in all its beauties. Ten years later Berg found both this opera and *Elektra* uninteresting and tedious. Berg tells her of three Schoenberg concerts in 1907 at which Mahler was present and the rehearsals of which Berg, then a pupil of the former, attended. Referring to the uproar which followed the performance of Schoenberg's first Chamber Symphony, op. 9, he writes to Frida the prophetic words: 'It will probably be a long time before Schoenberg is recognised at least as much as Strauss, but his day will come and America also will experience it'. Mahler's Sixth Symphony with its 'magnificent mountain atmosphere and cow-bells' leaves him deeply moved and he is disgusted that the 'Viennese have at last succeeded in driving Mahler out ... who is really irreplaceable'. Of Mahler's successor at the Hofoper, Felix von Weingartner,[4] he speaks with scarcely veiled contempt, and he urges Frida to go to all opera productions and concerts that Mahler would be conducting in New York.

Turning to literature, Berg expresses to Frida his immense admiration for Oscar Wilde (always more highly appreciated in central Europe than in England) and compares him favourably with Bernard Shaw – 'nowadays everybody is sarcastic!' For the young Berg, the truly modern writers of his time were Strindberg, Altenberg, Maeterlinck, Hauptmann and Wedekind. What Berg says to Frida about Wedekind is particularly interesting in view of his later choice of *Erdgeist* and *Die Büchse der Pandora* for his opera *Lulu*:

Wedekind – this whole new movement – the emphasis on the sensual in

---

[3] Owing to fierce opposition on the part of the Catholic Church, *Salome* could not be given at the Vienna Hofoper until October 1918, less than a month before the collapse of the Habsburg Monarchy.

[4] From Berg's letter to Frida of 14 January 1908 one gathers that, for a new production of *Fidelio*, Weingartner reverted to the original 1805 version of the opera, the final act of which plays in Florestan's dungeon throughout.

modern works!! There is such a strong current in all modern art. And I believe this is good. At last we have arrived at the realisation that sensuality is not a weakness, not a yielding to one's own desire but an immense strength in us – the pivot on which all our being and thinking turn! Yes, all our thinking!! With this I declare firmly and decisively the great importance which sensuality has for everything spiritual. Only through an understanding of sensuality, only through a profound insight into the 'depths of mankind' (or should it be rather 'heights of mankind'?) does one arrive at the true idea of the human psyche.

Berg seemed at this time much preoccupied with sensuality in art, as he wrote in the same vein to his future wife.

The death of Konrad Berg on 30 March 1900, aged fifty-four, was a profound shock for the family and especially for the young Berg. A few months after, on 23 July, he had his first attack of the asthma from which he was to suffer all his life. The number '23' in the date is important, for from that moment it began to assume for Berg a very special and even fateful significance. The shop near St Stephen's had to be sold and, in order to ensure a regular income for the mother and the younger children, the Vienna houses she had inherited were heavily mortgaged. With their administration the mother entrusted Charly and, from 1908, Alban, much to the latter's dislike, as it later greatly interfered with his creative work. It was soon after his father's death that Hermann in America invited Alban to join him, but it seems that a wealthy aunt came to the rescue and enabled him to continue at the *Realschule*. Berg was a most intelligent pupil, but his exclusive interest lay in literature, poetry and music – like Schumann he first wanted to be a poet – and so he failed his sixth form, which he had to repeat, and did not pass his *Abitur* or matriculation until the summer of 1904 when he was nineteen. Berg later confessed that it was a complete mystery to him how he succeeded in passing his final exams.

In October Berg entered the Niederösterreichische Statthalterei or Administrative Authority of Lower Austria as an unpaid official on probation, in preparation for a career as K.K. Staatsbeamter or imperial and royal civil servant. Berg discharged his duties with exemplary conscientiousness and thoroughness, as he did later those of secretary to Schoenberg's Verein für musikalische Privataufführungen; but he did his figures and calculations – he was in the accounting department of the Statthalterei – with his mind on composing. Fortunately he worked only two years as a civil servant, for in November 1905 his mother came into a large inheritance from her older sister (Julie Weidmann) consisting of eight blocks of flats in Vienna and a villa in Hietzing-St. Veit into which the Berg family moved. Alban resigned from his post in the Statthalterei in October 1906 (in the previous August he had been confirmed in it as a paid official), and, much against his mother's initial resistance, decided to devote himself entirely to composition. Like a number of Austrian writers and artists who for material reasons were forced to accept a career as civil servants and did their creative work in their spare time – Franz Grillparzer is perhaps the outstanding example – Berg felt at the Statthalterei like a square peg in a round hole. The chief reason for this was that exactly at the time when he had become a civil servant, an event occurred which was of the most decisive and crucial importance for his career as composer – he had become a pupil of Schoenberg.

TWO

PUPIL OF SCHOENBERG
1904-10

Berg began as an autodidact, though he himself resented this term, considering everything he had written up to the time of his studies with Schoenberg as the work of a bungler. In a letter to Schoenberg, written as late as 4 December 1930, he says that he strongly objected to a reference in the article 'Berg' in Riemann's *Musiklexikon* which stated that he was self-taught up to the age of fifteen 'which is in so far idiotic as before I came to you (when I was twenty), I taught myself nothing but "composed" in a bungling [*stümperhaft*] manner, and it was only through you that I came to realise that one can also *learn* something'. As mentioned before, Berg started composing at the latest in 1900. At any rate his first songs date from that year, and up to 1908 he wrote some eighty songs which have remained in manuscript,[1] except for the Seven Early Songs and the Storm song 'Schliesse mir die Augen beide'. He considered the large majority of them immature and wanted to destroy them, but at his wife's request allowed her to preserve them, on condition that they were never to be published.[2] The songs are remarkable for the literary taste and discrimination displayed by the young composer in his choice of the verses. According to Schoenberg, they showed real talent in spite of being modelled on Wolf and Brahms.[3] Redlich, who inspected them, declares with the hindsight of *Wozzeck* and *Lulu* that they are 'veiled operas'[4] which, to judge from the many excerpts quoted in a recent thesis,[5] is, I feel, reading far too much into them.

It was Smaragda who in October 1904 saw in the *Neue musikalische Presse* Schoenberg's announcement of composition classes, and induced her brother Charly to go and see Schoenberg and take, without Alban's knowledge, a number of his songs to Schoenberg, who found them so

---

[1] They are now deposited in the Österreichische Nationalbibliothek in Vienna.

[2] But 'An Leukon' (Gleim, 1908) was published by Willi Reich in his *Alban Berg. Mit Bergs eigenen Schriften und Beiträgen von Theodor Wiesengrund-Adorno und Ernst Krenek*, Vienna, 1937.

[3] See Schoenberg's short article on Berg, 1949, published in H.F. Redlich, *Alban Berg. Versuch einer Würdigung*, Vienna, 1957, London, 1957, p. 328. (Page references to Redlich's book are to the German edition.)

[4] ibid., p. 42.

[5] Nicholas Chadwick, *A Survey of the Early Songs of Alban Berg*, Oxford University, 1971, unpublished.

promising that he accepted Berg as pupil.[6] In the following I quote from Schoenberg's article on Berg written in 1949 in his own English:[7]

> When Alban Berg came to me in 1904, he was a very tall youngster and extremely timid. But when I saw the compositions he showed me – songs in a style between Hugo Wolf and Brahms – I recognised at once that he was a real talent. Consequently I accepted him as a pupil, though at the time he was unable to pay my fee. Later his mother inherited a great fortune and told Alban, as they have now money, he could enter the conservatory. I was told that Alban was so upset by this assumption that he started weeping and could not stop weeping ere his mother allowed him to continue with me.

Schoenberg was a teacher of genius. He had an intuitive understanding for the particular needs of a given pupil and urged him only to listen to his inner voice – 'to thine own self be true'. The pupil was not to fill his manuscript with notes anyhow, but to regard his composing as something exceptional which was to convey only what was inborn and natural in him, and sprang from artistic truth. Indeed, artistic truth was the alpha and omega of Schoenberg's own aspiration as a composer. What he tried to inculcate in his pupils was the principle of 'integral composition', in which the notes were not accidental products but the result of inner laws peculiar to the pupil's own style, and an organic extension, as it were, of his personality. Moreover, Schoenberg never based his teaching on his own works, but on those of the great classical composers from Bach to Brahms. His aim was to develop the pupil's composing tools to such a degree that he should be able to tackle successfully any kind of problem. There is an interesting letter about this written by Schoenberg on 5 January 1910 to Emil Hertzka, the founder and first director of the Vienna music publishing firm, Universal Edition, in which, in referring to his two pupils Berg and Stein,[8] he says:[9]

> What I have achieved with these two in particular could so easily be convincing. One (Alban Berg) is an extraordinarily gifted composer. But the state he was in when he came to me was such that his imagination apparently could not work on anything but *Lieder*. Even the piano accompaniments to them were song-like in style. He was absolutely incapable of writing an instrumental movement or inventing an instrumental theme. You can hardly imagine the lengths to which I went

[6] Reich, *Alban Berg*, p. 8.

[7] Redlich, *Alban Berg* (1957), p. 328.

[8] Erwin Stein (1885-1958) began his career as a conductor in various German theatres, and in 1914 became an editor (Universal Edition), critic and writer on music. He was one of Schoenberg's most ardent champions and did much to propagate the cause of the Second Viennese School. He later settled in London where he died in 1958.

[9] *Arnold Schoenberg: Letters*, ed. Erwin Stein, London, 1964, no. 1.

PLATE 1: Family Group. Left to Right, Front Row, Third: Berg's Mother. Back Row, Third and fourth: Berg and Helene

PLATE 2: Left to Right, Charley, Smaragda and Alban Berg as Children

PLATES 3 & 4: Berg as Schoolboy

in order to remove this defect in his talent. As a rule teachers are absolutely incapable of doing this, because they do not even see where the problem lies, and the result is composers who can only think in terms of a single instrument. (Robert Schumann is a typical example.) I removed this defect and am convinced that in time Berg will actually become very good at instrumentation.

But there is something else one cannot fail to observe about these two men. The fact is, their things aren't at all like 'exercises' but have the maturity of 'works'. And these young men can, *with complete success*, tackle problems of whose existence other people have no notion or which – to say the least – they would not know how to deal with.

About the time that Berg became Schoenberg's pupil, Anton Webern began to study with him, and between the two men – Webern was Berg's senior by two years – an intimate friendship sprang up which lasted uninterrupted till Berg's death. Similarly, the teacher-disciple relationship developed into a lifelong bond as important for Schoenberg as it was for Webern and Berg. 'I never let an occasion pass without emphasising with pride that you are *the* teacher of my life', wrote Berg to his former master in December 1930. Schoenberg seems to have exerted an almost hypnotic power on his pupils, and perhaps on no one more strongly than on the highly sensitive and impressionable Berg, for whom – fatherless as he had been since the age of fifteen – his master seems to have become a towering father-figure. The extent to which both Berg and Webern held Schoenberg in awe, even after they had finished their studies with him and had become composers in their own right, emerges from a remark made by Berg to Adorno that they hardly ever dared to speak to him in statements but mostly in questions. Moreover, up to about the time (1917) when Schoenberg offered Berg the brotherly *Du*, the latter spoke in his correspondence with him always in terms of humble modesty and utter respectfulness. There was nothing Berg would not do for Schoenberg either in propagating his ideas or rallying to his aid when his master found himself in precarious material circumstances, as happened in the autumn of 1911. A year before, Schoenberg had been allowed to hold a course in theory and composition at the Vienna Music Academy outside the official curriculum and only after great difficulties.[10] It was an unremunerative appointment and after it ended Schoenberg was thrown back on his own scanty resources. Berg, without Schoenberg's knowledge, drafted an appeal in which he said that the composer's friends and pupils considered it their duty to bring his extremity to the notice of the public, a step to which they had been prompted by the

[10] There were even interpellations in the Austrian Parliament criticising Schoenberg's appointment. See also Schoenberg's two applications to the President and the Governing Board of the Music Academy, of March 1910, in Stein, *Arnold Schoenberg: Letters*, nos. 5 and 6.

'thought of this artist coming to grief for lack of the common necessities of life. Catastrophe has overtaken him with unexpected speed and help from a distant source would be too late.' This appeal was sent to patrons of the arts with a view to a money collection and obtained some forty signatures, but Berg's rescue action proved unnecessary, for in the meantime Schoenberg's financial circumstances had improved with his move to Berlin.

Berg took charge of all the paraphernalia connected with the move. He negotiated with the transport firm, informed Schoenberg of every detail of his negotiations and, together with Webern, packed all his paintings ready to be sent to Kandinsky in Munich.[11]

Schoenberg must have admonished him to take care and not to throw away things when packing, to which Berg in an engaging schoolboy vein replied:

Throw away! How could I throw away a piece of paper which has a word or a brush-stroke or a note of yours on it! I would rather take it home with me as indeed I keep everything of yours, be it only an envelope. So don't worry! Nothing will be lost! [Autumn 1911].

A factor must be mentioned which greatly contributed to making the bond between Schoenberg and his pupils so strong. This was the situation in which the whole Schoenberg circle found itself in Vienna before the First World War. To belong to this circle was tantamount to belonging to a small army of revolutionaries who, under their leader, were besieged on all sides and against whom the most violent attacks were constantly launched by the Establishment. Schoenberg could never quite forget the bitter hostility shown to him in his native city and such traits in his character as aggressiveness, intolerance and authoritarianism must largely be seen in the mitigating light of a defence mechanism erected against his many detractors. As for Berg, he too had little good to say about Vienna, yet, harnessed as he was to the city by an ambivalent love-hate relationship, he never left it, unlike his master; though in the middle 1920s and early 1930s there were

[11] Schoenberg, who was also a gifted painter, began painting about 1908 and continued with it, on and off, until 1935. As painter he was closely associated with a group of Munich artists founded in 1911 by Vassili Kandinsky and Franc Marc, in whose inaugural exhibition he was represented by three of the paintings mentioned above. The group published in May 1912 an almanach, *Der blaue Reiter*, the purpose of which was to publicise the new movement, to emphasise its relationship with the new music and to reveal the true quality of hitherto underrated art such as folk art, primitive art and the art of children. Although this almanac was intended as the first of a series, it was the only issue to be published.

Among the paintings reproduced in it was Schoenberg's famous *Self-Portrait* (1911), which shows him walking with his back turned to the observer, his hands crossed behind and holding a walking-stick. Other reproductions included, in addition to those by Kandinsky and Marc, Picasso's *La Femme à la mandoline*, Kokoschka's *Bildnis*, Matisse's *La Musique* and Cézanne's celebrated *Nature morte*. Moreover, the almanac contained facsimile reproductions of the score of Schoenberg's *Herzgewächse*, an early song of Webern's, 'Ihr tratet zu dem Herde', and the first of Berg's three Mombert songs, op. 2.

opportunities when he could have accepted a teaching appointment at the Berlin Hochschule für Musik. Berg called his native Vienna a 'godforsaken city', 'this city of song which one cannot hate too much', 'a museum of coffeehouses'; and Austria was for him 'the enemy country', while America, Germany, England, France and Holland where his music was performed, were the 'friendly countries'. Neither he nor Webern was ever offered a teaching post at the Music Academy and they were by-passed in favour of such mediocrities as Franz Schmidt and Julius Bittner, whose music conformed to the conservative criteria of the Establishment. As Berg wrote to Schoenberg on 6 April 1931, in connection with an official appointment at the Music Academy: 'There were interpellations in the Nationalrat demanding an explanation why they "let me go" (as if they had ever *asked me*!) which remained unanswered.'

Berg's treatment by 'official' Vienna is one more example of this city's traditional behaviour towards their living great, in whom it glories only after they are dead. Schubert, Grillparzer, Wolf, Mahler, Freud, Schoenberg and Webern — they all experienced what it meant to be outstanding amid mediocrities who, always in an overwhelming majority, feel genius to be a most irritating and disturbing quality whose possessor must be first attacked, then silenced and finally ignored. No one has defined this typical Viennese attitude more succinctly than Grillparzer in his epigrammatic verse:

Auszeichnung hier erwarte nie,	Honour never expect here,
Denn das System verbeut's.	For the system forbids it.
Man hängt das Kreuz nicht ans Genie,	One appends no cross to genius,
Nein, das Genie ans Kreuz.	But genius to the cross.

We have anticipated, and must return to Berg's studies with Schoenberg. His teacher took him systematically through the disciplines of harmony, counterpoint, form and instrumentation to lead him to 'free composition', of which Berg gave an account to Frida Semler towards the end of July 1907; by then he had been with Schoenberg for nearly three years:

This year I completed my counterpoint lessons with Schoenberg, and I am very happy to have earned his approval (as I found out by chance). Now next autumn comes 'composition'. This summer I have to work hard, partly composing away (I am writing a piano sonata for my own benefit), partly repeating the counterpoint studies (six- to eight-part choruses and a fugue with two themes for string quintet and piano accompaniment). Naturally, I enjoy it all very much — and this is necessary; for if I did not enjoy it, I would not be able to do it. And Schoenberg's immense ability [*Können*] affords one, to be sure, a grandiose panorama of the whole literature of music, and a sound and accurate judgement into the bargain.

During his six years with Schoenberg Berg wrote, in addition to a number of unpublished compositions,[12] the Seven Early Songs (1905-8), the Piano Sonata, op. 1 (1907-8), Four Songs for Voice and Piano, op. 2 (1909) and the String Quarter, op. 3 (1910). Three of the Seven Early Songs (*Liebesode, Traumgekrönt* and *Die Nachtigall*) and the Quintet (with Berg playing the piano) were first heard at a concert of works given by Schoenberg's pupils at the Hall of the Gremium der Wiener Kaufmannschaft on 7 November 1907, when also the first movement of Webern's unpublished Piano Quintet (1906) was performed. The concert brought Berg his first press notices, two of which I reproduce to show the contradiction in the critics' assessments. Strangely enough, the writer in the *Neues Wiener Journal*, a conservative and even reactionary paper, expressed himself wholly favourably, while the critic in the *Neue Zeitschrift für Musik*, a periodical regarded as progressive and supporting the new music, took a most damning view of the concert:

> Eight different talents – what they have in common is the rare seriousness of their aspirations. All matters to do with the craft of composition, rules of harmony, polyphonic part-writing are handled with impressive sureness and by some with real virtuosity. The feeling for the character of sound effects is always on the alert; in some composers one notices a remarkable talent for the logical construction of the forms. There is conspicuous resistance to superficial effects. The valuable results of good training are respect for art, purity of feeling, sureness of style. It is wonderful how Schoenberg's powerful and original personality guides the talents of these pupils strongly and surely in this way. [*Neues Wiener Journal*]

> Students' concerts are not normally reviewed here. In this case there is something so unusual that I feel I must say something about it. Arnold Schoenberg's school of composition can rightly be called the 'high school of dissonance', since hair-raising things are achieved by both master and pupils in this field. As far as I can judge from short pieces, of the eight pupils there were two whom I felt to have talent. These were Alban Berg and Dr A. von Webern. As with all the pupils, the ruinous influence of Schoenberg's compositions made itself felt with these two. [*Neue Zeitschrift für Musik*]

A year later, on 8 November 1908, a similar concert was given by Schoenberg's pupils at the Grosse Musikvereinsaal in which Webern's Passacaglia op. 1 and Berg's Twelve Piano Variations were performed. Here again, there were completely contradictory notices. One critic wrote that 'after only eight bars the variations got tangled up in a maze of indescribable

---

[12] A Piano Quintet; Twelve Variations and Finale on an Original Theme for piano (1907-8) (published in Redlich, *Alban Berg*), and a great number of songs.

modulations. No theme but twelve variations on it.' Another critic gave it as his opinion that 'Berg's Variations, fine and rich in melodic invention, excellently written for the instrument, show a strong talent for composition. Technically, he has obviously learnt a lot from Brahms.'[13] As, indeed, Berg had, under the guidance of Schoenberg, for whom Brahms was the unsurpassed master of musical structure and logic.

The spring of 1910 saw the termination of Berg's studies with Schoenberg, the ripe fruit of which was the String Quarter, op. 3, the last work to be written under the eyes of his teacher. Schoenberg himself has given us a picture of Berg's last years under him, in an article (1936) originally intended as preface for Willi Reich's first biography of Berg and reproduced in Reich's English biography (1965), from which I quote the following excerpt.[14]

> The instruction in composition ... proceeded effortlessly and smoothly up to and including the Sonata. Then problems began to appear, the nature of which neither of us understood then. I know it today: obviously Alban, who had occupied himself extraordinarily intensively with contemporary music, with Mahler, Strauss, perhaps even Debussy, whose work I did not know, but certainly with my music – it is sure that Alban had a burning desire to express himself no longer in the classical forms, harmonies, and melodic forms and their proper schemata of accompaniment, but in the manner in accordance with the times, and with his own personality which had been developing in the meantime. A hitch was apparent in his creative activity.
>
> I cannot remember what he worked on with me afterwards. Others can report more reliably on this point. One thing is sure: his string Quartet (op. 3) surprised me in the most unbelievable way by the fullness and unconstraint of its musical language, the strength and sureness of its presentation, its careful working and significant originality.

With Schoenberg's move to Berlin in the autumn of 1911, personal meetings between him and his former pupil became rare. But Berg remained in frequent correspondence with his guide and mentor, informing him about his artistic plans and details of his private life.

---

[13] Quoted in W. Reich, *The Life and Work of Alban Berg*, London, 1965, pp. 24 and 27. This is the English edition (1965) of Reich's *Alban Berg. Leben und Werk*, Zurich, 1963.
[14] ibid., pp. 28-9.

THREE

ALBAN AND HELENE
1911-14

On 3 May 1911 Berg married Helene Nahowski. It was the most important event in his private life. Helene was the daughter[1] of an Austrian civil servant and she was studying singing with the intention of taking up an operatic career. Berg had first met her in the winter of 1906-7 at the Hofoper – both were assiduous opera goers – and by Easter 1907 a passionate friendship had sprung up between the two young people, who were of the same age. Berg soon felt that in Helene he had found a true soulmate and companion for life, yet, blissful and wholly absorbing as their courtship was, the four years that passed before they could marry were for the two, especially Berg, a most wretched and miserable time. For Helene's parents, notably her father, most strongly objected to a union, on the grounds of Berg's unstable health, his asthma, his taking of drugs against it and against insomnia, and his lack of any real profession. These and other reasons made Berg a most unsuitable son-in-law in the eyes of Herr Nahowski. In one of the few letters Helene contributed to her collection of Berg's letters to her,[1a] she writes:

> These last few days I've been very unhappy about all this. I had to think that you are always writing of your great love for me, but don't you reflect that our future depends on whether your health improves or doesn't? From their point of view, my parents are not altogether wrong if they turn you down. They think I would be constantly worrying about you and so would not be happy with you. Any woman who loves is bound to wonder whether her love is going to bring her suffering, even though it may be her destiny to suffer. But won't *you*, Alban, have one more try to get well? It will take some sacrifices, I admit, but surely you will want to do it for my sake – no, *our* sake.
>
> I've had a bad night because I knew that my letter would hurt you, saying harsh things to you, as if I were no longer interested in you and your health. But no, Alban, I am not giving you up. Perhaps you will still achieve something 'great' one day, and I want to help you with it, so that

---

[1] Persistant rumours in Vienna had it that Helene was the natural child of the Emperor Francis Joseph.

[1a] *Alban Berg. Briefe an seine Frau*, p. 85.

you can do your work unimpeded by physical frailty and enjoy life without having at once heart trouble and asthma.

So that's a monstrously long sermon and a confession, too. Take it as it is meant, and please: be patient. [23 July 1909]

Berg, convinced in his heart of hearts that Helene was the only woman for him, fought for her as persistently and indefatigably as did Schumann for his Clara. This fight reached its epistolary culmination in a twelve-page letter (July 10)[2] to his future father-in-law, in which Berg refutes point by point and in the greatest detail all the objections which Herr Nahowski must have raised against the marriage in a letter to Berg. The latter's missive has four long sections headed by the captions: My 'Intellectual Inferiority'; My 'Impecuniousness'; My 'Shattered Health'; The 'Moral Depravity of Members of my Family'. Berg tries to demolish Herr Nahowski's arguments by eloquent but sometimes rather far-fetched counter-arguments, to which he gives a certain edge by the slightly ironical tone of his language. What is notable in this letter is the openness with which Berg speaks about his sister's perversion (Herr Nahowski's 'depravity'), arguing that there is hardly any family in which there is not a black sheep causing the parents sorrow and shame; what he says about homosexuality shows for its time (1910) an astonishingly tolerant and advanced attitude, just as in a previous letter to Helene he exculpates prostitution and defends it against the hypocritical morals of bourgeois society. It is probable that, in his progressive opinions on subjects which were then still taboo, Berg was influenced by the views of his much adored Karl Kraus, which were partly responsible for his later choice of the two Wedekind dramas, in which the heroine sinks down to the level of a common prostitute, while her devoted woman friend is a lesbian. Another point worth noting in this letter is that Berg, stung by Herr Nahowski's evident assumption that music was not a real profession from which a living could be made, abandons his usual modesty and for once indulges in exaggerated self-praise. Thus he writes of the 'extraordinary musical talent' which showed already 'in the compositions of my infancy' ['als ungelehrtes Kind'] and adds that the works he has already published, as well as those which will be performed in the coming season, 'are better than many of the songs, piano pieces and chamber music which one hears', which fully justifies his expectation of 'a great future'.[3]

The letter is a remarkable document attesting Berg's power of reasoning, his tenacity in pursuing an aim he had set himself, and also his great literary fluency. Unfortunately, it never reached its addressee – Herr Nahowski placed it unopened in Helene's room. When eventually Alban and Helene married, her father had made it a condition of his consent that the two, who

---

[2] *Alban Berg. Briefe an seine Frau*, pp. 160-72.
[3] It is in this letter that he mentions his descent from aristocratic ancestors.

were Catholics, become Protestants so as to facilitate a divorce! Yet in the summer of 1915, shortly before Berg joined the Army, he and his wife returned to the Catholic faith and went through a second marriage ceremony at a Catholic church in Hietzing. They had their flat in this Vienna district, at, Trauttmansdorffgasse 27, where Frau Berg continued to live until her death on 30 August 1976, at the age of 91, preserving her husband's study just as he had left it on that fateful December day in 1935.

The Bergs were a most devoted couple. Indeed, their union seemed to be that rare thing – an ideal marriage. Helene, whom Alma Maria Mahler describes in her memoir as 'a creature of seraphic loveliness inside and out',[4] was an exceptional woman. Of a noble character and endowed with *Fingerspitzengefühl* or immense tact, she tried to smooth out things for the hypersensitive and vulnerable composer as far as possible and thus make his professional life run with the minimum of friction. As he once wrote to her: 'There are only three things for me – you, Nature and music (Schoenberg)'. In one of his first letters to her written in the spring of 1907, he sounds the ground-bass of his feelings for her which was to reverberate for most of his life: 'I finally want to tell you that I do no longer possess the strength to renounce you because I know that you have become indispensable to me'. Again, on 9 July 1918: 'If I did not have you, my only one, I would kill myself'. And after eleven years of married life: 'All paths with you are paths to heaven'. Berg's dependence on his wife was total. She was as necessary to him as the very air he breathed. When away from her he would write her practically every day and sometimes twice a day, and was deeply upset and even desperate when she did not reply at once.

Helene was his Egeria, his tutelary spirit, who, he felt, watched over him and without whom his creative work would suffer. In a letter of 27 May 1922 he writes: 'Pferschi,[5] to whom do I owe *Wozzeck* but you? If was you who gave me *outer* and *inner* peace for five years, that peace without which I could not compose a single note and which no one but you could give me or take away from me.' How closely Berg associated her with some of his compositions emerges from a letter of 11 July 1914, in which he speaks of his Three Orchestral Pieces, op. 6, which were suggested by Schoenberg and dedicated to him on his fortieth birthday. Berg then continues: 'So if I don't *officially* dedicate these three pieces to Pferscherl, there is yet in all three a good bit of Pferscherl, and even if Pferscherl should not like them straightaway, I know she will one day love them as she loves me ...'. While it is difficult to link the *Marsch* of op. 6 with Helene, the *Praeludium* and notably

---

[4] *And the Bridge is Love*, London, 1959, p. 132

[5] They had an inexhaustible fund of pet names for each other. Berg's favourite for Helene was 'Pferschi' or 'Pferscherl', meaning 'little peach'. It is only in his letters to his wife that Berg reveals a most engaging, almost child-like naivety, so much in contrast to the considerable intellectual powers evinced in his public *persona* as composer, writer and teacher.

the *Reigen* with its suggestion of a Viennese waltz seem to conjure up her personality in the same way in which, twenty-one years later, Manon Gropius is portrayed in the first two movements of Berg's Violin Concerto. About the D minor Interlude in the last act of *Wozzeck* he writes on 27 May 1922: 'I owe it to you and *you alone. You composed* it and I only wrote it down. *That is a fact.*' Finally, after the String Quartet, op. 3, had been performed at the Salzburg Festival of the International Society for Contemporary Music on 2 August 1923, which brought Berg the first great success of his career, he wrote to his wife suggesting that she join him there, so that 'people should see what you look like, you to whom the Quartet belongs and who brought it into being'. Yet this blissful state of affairs, which Berg outwardly preserved until his death, completely changed in May 1925 when the forty-year-old composer fell deeply in love with Hanna Fuchs-Robettin, the wife of a wealthy Prague industrialist, and sister of the playwright, Franz Werfel who was the third husband of Alma Maria Mahler. We shall return to this event in a later chapter.

There seem to have been two sources from which Berg drew his inspiration for his compositions. One was the living presence or vivid recollection of persons with whom he was linked in love and friendship – Helene (opp. 1 to 6), Schoenberg and Webern (Chamber Concerto), Hanna and Alexander von Zemlinsky (Lyric Suite) and Manon, Alma Maria Mahler's young daughter (Violin Concerto). Berg shared this with Schumann, the Schumann of the great piano cycles, and it is this which in my opinion accounts for the quivering life and humanity emanating from his music which at first made it more accessible to the public at large than the more abstract 'absolute' compositions of Schoenberg and the hermetic Webern.

The second source of Berg's inspiration seems to have been his compassion for the underprivileged and the social outcast, as seen in his two operas. Whether his was genuine compassion or compassion in the sense in which Simone Weil once defined it – 'Compassion is the recognition of one's own misery in the other' – it would be difficult to say. But a most revealing remark Berg made to his wife in a letter of 7 August 1918 inclines one to assume the second kind. In speaking of Wozzeck he writes:

> There is a bit of myself in his character, since I have been spending these war years just as dependent on people I hate, have been in chains, sick, captive, resigned, in fact humiliated.

Reading this, one cannot avoid the impression that Berg, half consciously and half unconsciously, felt what I would call a 'second-class citizen'. What with his chronic ill-health, the condescending behaviour of his own utterly philistine family (notably his mother) during the early years of his carrer, the humiliation suffered by the offensive conduct of his future father-in-law and, last but not least, his great and overpowering teacher – all this may have combined to exert an immense pressure on his highly sensitive and vulnerable personality – hence perhaps his ability to identify himself so completely with the protagonists in *Wozzeck* and *Lulu*. According to Alma Maria Mahler, both the Berg and Nahowski families were 'overbred and slightly degenerate'.[6] These are unscientific and very elastic terms used by the layman to describe certain oddities and abnormalities of behaviour, the exact cause of which is often extremely difficult to establish. I merely relate the fact that Helene's brother Franzl, the youngest of the Nahowski children, suffered from schizophrenia; in the autumn of 1930, at the age of forty-one, he committed a Van Gogh-like act[7] and for a time was in a mental home at Rekawinkel near Vienna. As for the Bergs, the two youngest children – Alban and Smaragda – showed a high degree of nervous sensitiveness;[8] in Berg's own words, he was 'highly strung, excitable and extremely sensitive'. But, given Berg's nature, his complaints to his wife about the treatment he suffered during the war prompting him to write those words about the hero of *Wozzeck* and himself, must not be taken at their face value. Moreover, he displayed a most intense concern for the health and well-being of his wife in which there seems to have been an element of neurotic anxiety, just as there was in the meticulous scruple and conscientiousness, even pedantry,[9] with which he attended to his private and professional affairs. In his early years he had a horror of travelling in a train and was plagued by an irrational fear of missing it which prompted him to arrive at the station at least an hour before its departure.[10] And of thunderstorms he had a child-like fear.

As regards his physical state, Berg suffered from chronic ill-health. True, most of his illnesses were of a minor and passing nature, but they occurred so frequently and in such close succession that he could be described as 'illness-prone'. With the years, he became something of a hypochondriac much concerned with his health. Apparently under Schoenberg's influence he came to regard his various ailments as psychosomatic, including his asthma which, as he wrote to his master in 1914, he was completely unable to explain on physical grounds. Typical of his view that the cause of his illnesses was largely psychological is a letter to his wife of 12 August 1916. He had an inflamed throat and wondered

> where on earth I could have picked it up, stupidly thinking of all sorts of possible infections and colds, when I suddenly had a brainwave: don't look for *physical* reasons ... there must be some psychological ones. How could I have forgotten that? In the last ten or twenty years, perhaps thirty

---

[6] *And the Bridge is Love*, p. 132.
[7] He cut off the little finger of his left hand as a form of 'sacrifice'.
[8] Personal communication from the late Helene Berg.
[9] In a letter to Schoenberg of 8 June 1921 he speaks of 'my tendency to pedantry'.
[10] Sigmund Freud suffered from the same anxiety.

even, a complaint in any part of my body has almost invariably followed immediately after some emotional disturbance or distress ...

The scourge of his life was asthma, with which he was afflicted, like his contemporary Proust, from fairly early years. Yet for this illness there was a physical cause. This was his small heart, a so-called *Kinderherz*, and his thorax, which was too narrow in proportion to his height (which made him walk slightly bent forwards) so that the lungs pressed against heart and stomach.[11]

Psychologists, however, may see some significance in the fact that it was just after his father's death that Berg had his first attack of asthma. The letters to his wife, to Schoenberg and Webern, contained innumerable references to this affliction, to the sleepless nights it caused him and the mental and physical exhaustion the following morning. The most acute attacks would occur when the Bergs moved at the beginning of summer from Vienna to his in-laws' estate at Trahütten in Styria,[12] and were apparently caused by the change of air and climate from low-lying Vienna to the Styrian mountains. Berg liked to take an ironic view of his asthma, as when he wrote to his master on Good Friday 1914, saying that the *Marsch* of his Three Orchestral Pieces was the 'march of an asthmatic, which I am and which, it seems, I shall always remain'. A good-natured self-irony was indeed a trait of his character often directed at his own composing. Thus, he once said to his pupil Adorno: 'When I compose I always feel I am like Beethoven; only afterwards do I become aware that at best I am only a Bizet.'[13]

Berg fought against his chronic ill-health with a steely determination to prevent it interfering with his creative work, to which he applied himself with all the energy at his disposal. But there cannot be much doubt that, apart from the fact that he was a slow worker,[14] highly self-critical and a perfectionist, his various illnesses, above all his asthma, seriously impeded his composing. This may explain why Berg wrote a comparatively small number of works, though these, it is true, include two full-length operas. There are altogether fourteen published compositions of Berg, and it was due to his fear that their grand total might not be high, that after *Wozzeck*, which

[11] Personal communication from the late Helene Berg.

[12] Before the purchase of their villa, the Waldhaus, on the Wörthersee in 1931, they would spend most of the summer at Trahütten, partly because they could live there at little expense, but largely because the place afforded Berg the quiet and solitude he needed for his creative work. A great deal of *Wozzeck* was written at Trahütten, where he could work far better than in Vienna. 'In Vienna', he wrote to Schoenberg in August 1927, 'things do not progress properly, what I write there is more the product of my head than my heart'.

[13] Theodor W. Adorno, *Alban Berg, Der Meister des kleinsten Übergangs*, Vienna, 1968, p. 18.

[14] In a letter to Schoenberg of 12 August 1921 Berg, after expressing his regrets that the former had not been able to work during the last few weeks, writes: 'With your rapid production a few weeks' delay won't make much difference. But with *me* this is of great importance, for I work very slowly and therefore every lost day counts.'

is his opus 7, he ceased giving them opus numbers.

I have mentioned Berg's self-irony. This seems to be mirrored in his compositions in the suggestion of a certain ambiguity of feeling and perception, *e.g.* the first two of the Altenberg Songs, the finale of the Chamber Concerto, the Captain and the Doctor in *Wozzeck*, and Alwa, Schigolch, the Athlete and the heroine of *Lulu* (Act II). Was this irony perhaps a stance Berg adopted as part of his *persona* behind which he concealed an essentially tragic, pessimistic view of life? True, there is nothing in his letters to substantiate this assumption, but it seems to me that the majority of his works deal with a larger underlying theme, the theme of existential menace and death. Adorno speaks of Berg's 'complicity with death', and it seems no mere coincidence that Berg's choice of operatic subjects should have fallen on *Wozzeck* and Wedekind's two *Lulu* dramas – *des sujets troubles* in which suicide and murder of the most violent and brutal kind bring about the final solution of the tragic conflict. There is much truth in what Flaubert wrote: 'One is certainly not free to write on any subject. One does not choose one's subject but is chosen by it'. There is a chasm gaping between Berg's outward *persona* – the handsome scion of a Viennese bourgeois family, slightly languorous and epicene, given to comfortable living, a known appreciator of gastronomic delights, always friendly and obliging to the people around him – and the world of his imagination which revolved around extreme human suffering, death and destruction. Schumann's profound remark springs to mind: 'Wir würden schreckliche Dinge erfahren, wenn wir bei allen Kunstwerken auf den Grund ihrer Entstehung blicken könnten'[14a] In this context I venture to suggest that what may have contributed to forming Berg's tragic view of life was the terrible dread of suffocation attendant on the most severe of his asthmatic attack.[15]

To anticipate. When Schoenberg criticised Berg so severely in Berlin in June 1913, his strictures appear to have extended to the pervasive sadness of his music. For Berg, after his return to Vienna, wrote him a letter in which he promised to take his words very much to heart, adding significantly: 'As soon as I am in the country I shall begin with the Suite [the Three Orchestral Pieces, op. 6]; perhaps for once I shall be able to compose something *cheerful.*'

This seems a convenient place to say something about Berg's attitude towards Freud and psychoanalysis. According to Reich, who became his pupil in 1928, Berg used to emphasise the relation of music to Freudian depth-psychology in the sense that it was the function of music to be the

---

[14a] 'We would learn terrible things if in all works of art we were able to see into the root of their origin'.

[15] It is interesting to learn that in recent experiments carried out on asthmatic children, they were asked to invent stories of their own. Most of these turned out to be sad and full of tension and conflicts, whereas the normal 'control' children told stories of a happy, cheerful and, altogether, optimistic character. See Lindy Burton, *Vulnerable Children*, London, 1958, p. 208.

representation and illumination of the unconscious.[16] Berg seems to have accepted Freud's concept of an unconscious as such, but, to judge from letters to his wife and to Schoenberg, completely rejected the theory of wish-fulfilment and repression of sexual drives. True, at one time he himself had sought cure for his asthma from Freud's famous disciple, Dr Alfred Adler, since, as we have seen, he believed that this illness, despite his organic disposition, was of mainly psychological origin. The treatment, however, had no beneficial effect.

It is probable that Berg took his cue for his negative view of psychoanalysis from Karl Kraus, who was a declared enemy of it (though Freud greatly admired Kraus) and once wrote that 'psychoanalysis is the mental illness of which it pretends to be the cure'. In the summer of 1913 Webern had some psychological difficulties and consulted an analyst. Berg, in a letter to Schoenberg of 9 August, expressed his doubts as to whether this treatment had any sense: 'What can a psychoanalyst know unless he happens to be a genius?' Yet in the following months Berg appears to have changed his opinion to some extent. Writing to his mentor on 10 October, he says that the many things Webern told him about his treatment struck him as 'very plausible and sympathetic – it seems totally different from what Kraus attacks'. Nevertheless, his fundamental objections persisted, at any rate up to the early 1920s. In the autumn of 1923 Helene underwent some psychoanalytical treatment at Bad Gastein. When Berg learned of it, he was much disturbed and urged her to stop it and inform the doctor that, if she had been in need of such treatment, Berg would have consulted 'Professor Freud or Dr Alfred Adler whom we have known very well for many years'.[17] He begs her not to be upset: 'in a week we shall be laughing at the confidence trick of this "psychoanalysis", with all its explanations of unfulfilled desires, sexuality etc. A single day in the snow and woods of the Semmering will wash away all the inner dirt poured into your poor clean little soul', and he closes with yet another reference to 'all the filthy aids of this beastly science "psychoanalysis" ' (letter of 29 November 1923).

We return to the year 1911, when an event occurred that greatly saddened Berg and the entire Schoenberg circle. This was the death on 18 May of Mahler, at whose funeral they turned up in force to pay their last homage. It was Schoenberg and his two disciples who were among the first to recognise in Mahler the great creative musician, while most of Vienna's musical

---

[16] Reich, *The Life and Work of Alban Berg*, pp. 117-18. Freudians may be tempted to see a sexual symbol in the fact that both Marie and Lulu are killed by means of a knife.

[17] Berg met Freud as a young man somewhere in the Dolomites when he became ill with influenza, and consulted him as the only doctor at the moment available at the hotel. Berg was much amused at Freud's inability to cope properly with this trivial illness. See Adorno, *Alban Berg*, p. 25.

Establishment saw in him, very largely, only the eminent conductor and
opera director. It is true that up to about 1909 Schoenberg was on the whole
not sympathetic to Mahler's music, for reasons he himself summed up in his
letter to Mahler of 5 July 1910,[18] but this changed completely in the following
years. He dedicated his *Harmonielehre* to Mahler's memory, made a memorial
speech in Prague in 1912 and wrote a long appreciative essay on the
composer.[19] Berg, on the other hand, was from the beginning an ardent
Mahler enthusiast who regarded him, next to his teacher, as the greatest
composer of his time. Berg's favourite Mahler symphonies were the Third,
Sixth, Ninth, and *Das Lied von der Erde*, for the first performance of which
under Bruno Walter he travelled specially to Munich in November 1911.
There was indeed a certain affinity between the two musicians which
showed, on the human side, in their intense concern and compassion with
suffering man – Mahler, one feels, would have been most deeply stirred by
Wozzeck – and in a tender, infinitely sensitive lyricism which they shared in
common. Mahler's influence is clearly felt in Berg's early songs written
before he began his studies with Schoenberg.[20] It then gradually disappeared
under the teaching of his master, who was orientated towards Brahms, to re-
emerge with redoubled force in his Three Orchestral Pieces, op. 6, and the D
minor Interlude in the final act of *Wozzeck*, which in its turn partly derived
from an abortive symphony of 1912-13.

This is perhaps the place to mention a little-known fact about Berg's
association with the sketches of Mahler's Tenth Symphony, which was
brought to my knowledge by the late Deryck Cooke, author of the admirable
performing version of the symphony. In October 1924 Franz Schalk, the
director of the Vienna Opera, gave an orchestral concert in which he
included the Adagio of the Tenth which is the only movement Mahler left in
a more or less finished orchestration. Whether Schalk played this movement
as it stood or in the performing version made by Krenek, I was unable to
establish. But the fact is that in 1925 the Universal Edition gave Berg the
score of Krenek's version in order to check it against Mahler's original. Berg
filled nine pages of music manuscript paper a photostat copy of which was
kindly placed at my disposal by Mr Cooke. Apart from pointing out errors
Berg also made suggestions for alteration in the scoring which for some
reason Krenek did not enter in his score. Erwin Ratz, the editor of the critical
edition of Mahler's works[21] remarks in the Preface to the Adagio of the Tenth
that Schoenberg, Berg and Krenek knew these sketches but always refused to

---

[18] Stein (ed.), *Arnold Schoenberg: Letters*, no. 263.

[19] It is contained in Dika Newlin (ed.), *Arnold Schoenberg: Style and Idea*, New York, 1950, pp. 7-
36.

[20] See Nicholas Chadwick, 'Berg's Unpublished Songs in the Österreichische Nationalbibliothek', in *Music and Letters*, April 1971.

[21] Publ. by Internationale Gustav Mahler Gesellschaft (Vienna, 1964).

complete them. In view of the above, this statement is incorrect.

Apropos of Berg's own symphony. It was designed in one continuous movement comprising the four movements of the classical symphony, and was to have ended with a boy soprano singing from the gallery words from Balzac's mystic novel, *Seraphita*, which Schoenberg was intending to use as a subject for an operatic trilogy. The whole concept of Berg's symphony, with its vocal finale, was of course Mahlerian. But the time of the big romantic symphony had passed with Mahler (Schoenberg significantly wrote a *Chamber* Symphony), and the odds are that Berg, whose bent was not for large-scale symphonic writing, would not have completed the symphony even if Schoenberg had not dissuaded him from it and, instead, suggested writing something gay to combat his inclination for the sad and tragic. But Berg was at first firmly decided on carrying out his idea of a symphony, and in a letter of 9 July 1913 to his former teacher, he writes:

> Unfortunately, I must confess to you that I have not made use of your various suggestions for what I should compose next. However much I felt attracted by your suggestion for an orchestral suite (with 'character' pieces) and no matter how often I thought of it, it did not materialise. I found myself forced to give way to an older desire, namely, to write a symphony. And when I tried to compromise with this desire and wanted to compose a suite to begin with a prelude, this, on working on it, turned again into the beginning of this symphony. I shall go on with it ... But the plan for a suite will surely mature one day to such an extent that I shall really be able to write it and realise your kind suggestion. I hope with all my heart that you will not be cross with me because I postponed the fulfilment of your wish and will not regard this as *wilfulness* on my part. You know yourself, dear Mr Schoenberg, how I am always conscious – I could never be conscious of anything else – of being your pupil who obeys you in every respect and knows that anything he might do *against* your wishes, would be wrong. If in the last few weeks I have thought so much and so intensely of the symphony, this was largely because I wanted to catch up with all that I would have written *under you if you had stayed in Vienna*, since I wanted to follow your remark that 'Every one of my pupils should also have written a symphony.'

Yet in the end Berg discarded this symphony of which he seems to have written an appreciable amount, part of which he worked into the *Praeludium* of op. 6.

Three compositions belong to the period after the String Quartet up to the First World War – the *Five Orchestral Songs after Picture Post-Card Texts of Peter Altenberg*, op. 4, the Four Pieces for Clarinet and Piano, op. 5, and the first and third of the Three Orchestral Pieces, op. 6. Of the Five Orchestral Songs, two – nos. 2 and 3 – were first performed in a concert at the Grosse

Musikvereinssaal on 31 March 1913, under the direction of Schoenberg. The complete cycle was not heard until much later, in 1952, when also the full score was published.[22] Berg, after submitting his songs to Schoenberg, was overjoyed when the latter chose two for performance and informed him that, though they were intended as a cycle, they could very well be done separately. In reply to Schoenberg's letter of 14 January 1913, Berg wrote back on 17 January expressing his immense delight that he had found them

> not too bad, especially their scoring where, recalling my wretched beginnings, I feared to have written nonsense with every bar, including things which I *heard* with my inner ear as intensely as possible. Even Webern's view to the contrary (he saw only two songs) could not silence my doubts until I read your kind words.

He then goes on to speak at length of the 'new means' he employed in the songs – means which at the time of composing seemed to him quite natural to use, but which afterwards struck him as disagreeable because of their accumulated use – 'not because I found them *superfluous* but because I was afraid they might give the impression of showing off [*protzen*] – "there you are: everything that is good and expensive!"' Berg then goes into the reason why he used these new means which Schoenberg had not liked:

> It was only quite recently that I began to listen to an orchestra with *real understanding* and comprehend full scores. And these are always the scores of the newest works.[23] In the last few years I have scarcely seen a score by Wagner, to say nothing of the classics (certainly a great mistake!). I now have a greater understanding of the new sounds created by the new means. I hear them even where one could do without them and employ them because I cannot help it. The way I express myself resembles perhaps that of a child who hears at home so many foreign words that it constantly employs them, even when it cannot yet speak German properly. But I hope that this child knows at least how to use foreign words correctly ... or does here the saying apply: 'don't use new means! You never know how they will sound!'

One feels behind these words Berg's anxiety to explain and justify his use of new devices, since the Altenberg Songs were his first orchestral score. This comes out particularly clearly in his delight that Schoenberg was pleased with 'especially their scoring', and in his stressing the fact that he heard the effect of these devices in his inner ear.

---

[22] No. 5 came out in a supplement to the magazine *Menschen*, Dresden, 1921.
[23] Schoenberg, Strauss, Debussy, Dukas and Ravel.

For the concert on 31 March[24] Schoenberg had chosen a programme representative of the modern Viennese school:

Webern	Six Orchestral Pieces, op. 6
Schoenberg	Chamber Symphony, op. 9
Zemlinsky	For Orchestral Songs
	(to poems of Maeterlinck)
Berg	Two Alternberg Songs from op. 4
Mahler	Kindertotenlieder

The audience, already restless and noisy during the Webern and Schoenberg pieces, could no longer contain itself in the Berg songs. After the first, a voice was heard above the vociferous turmoil shouting: 'Silence! Now comes the second post-card!' When in the second song the singer (Julius Boruttau) sang the words 'Plötzlich is alles aus ...' ('Suddenly all is over'), another member of the audience exclaimed 'Thank God!'. There followed an incredible scene, with the whole hall in uproar, so that the concert was broken off and police had to intervene. These incidents led to a court case in which one of the witnesses, a doctor, declared that the music had such an 'enervating and detrimental effect on the nervous system that many listeners already showed signs of a nervous depression'.[25] Schoenberg later said to the conductor, Hermann Scherchen, that on that occasion he would have wished to have had a revolver with him. (Incidentally, the uproar at this Vienna concert was matched by the riotous scandal that broke out at the first performance of Stravinsky's ballet, *Le Sacre du Printemps*, in Paris two months later.) Wellesz was of the opinion that what was partly responsible for the uproar was the public's reaction to the discrepancy between the shortness of Altenberg's verses and the colossal and extravagant orchestra employed by Berg. Indeed, under the impact of this scene the composer for a time toyed with the idea of re-scoring the songs for a smaller orchestra.

There were two things which incensed Berg in particular. One was a notice by the critic of the *Mittagszeitung* which stated that Altenberg's verses were '*Afterpoesie*' or a 'sham', that Berg's settings were a 'joke, hypermodern *Gestanzeln*' or 'ditties', and that the music was probably 'music of the spheres', which was an ironic dig against Berg's friend, the architect Adolf Loos, who was hard of hearing. The second thing to arouse the composer's indignation was a notice in *Die Zeit*, to the effect that he had assisted Schoenberg financially. Berg wrote a letter to the editor saying that this was completely untrue and that, on the contrary, Schoenberg had given him lessons for years without payment. This letter was never published, and the

---

[24] It was promoted by the Akademischer Verband für Kunst und Literatur, a society comparable in its aim to the London Institute of Contemporary Art. At a previous concert of this society (April 1911), Berg's Piano Sonata and his String Quartet were first performed.
[25] Egon Wellesz, *Arnold Schönberg*, Vienna, 1921, p. 44.

paper had even the insolence to ask Berg for a photograph from which to make a cartoon. The same paper bruited it about that Schoenberg had told Hertzka of Universal Edition not to publish works by Berg and Webern because he considered them not satisfactory. The upshot of this concert, which involved Schoenberg and Berg in, perhaps, the greatest scandal of their careers, was that Julius Korngold, the first music critic of the influential *Neue Freie Presse* and musical pope of Vienna, let it be known that he and his assistant (Josef Reitler) decided to stay away from any concert which had works of Schoenberg, Berg and/or Webern in the programme.

After the concert Berg wrote to Schoenberg expressing his heartfelt gratitude:

> Even the various distortions in the press and the scandal at the Musik-vereinsaal could not diminish my happiness that you conducted my songs. Your decision to do them, the great trouble you took with them, the chance of hearing my things on the orchestra and – under your direction, their actual performance and in the company of works by you, Mahler and Webern – in short, I am happy about everything. (3 April 1913)

It is, incidentally, interesting to learn from Berg's letters to Schoenberg that his first intention to compose an opera dates from the year 1912, when he was about to complete the fifth and last of the Altenberg Songs. Writing on 6 November, he says that after finishing that song

> I would like to tackle something else for the stage if I had a suitable text. I thought ... of Strindberg's *Kammerspiele* and now that you have suggested Strindberg to me, the idea naturally appeals to me all the more.

Strindberg was, together with Wedekind, Berg's favourite modern playwright; he described him as 'of gigantic stature compared with Keller, Hamsun, Hesse and others'. What seems to have attracted him so strongly to the Swedish dramatist was his power to reveal fundamental tendencies in human nature projected in a half-realistic, half-expressionist manner which was also the style of Büchner's *Woyzeck* and Wedekind's two Lulu dramas. Yet for the time being nothing came of this operatic idea, and Berg followed up the Altenberg Songs with his Four Pieces for Clarinet and Piano, op. 5 (summer 1913). Originally he seems to have had the intention of writing six pieces but finally decided on four, designed to represent the four movements of a miniature sonata. They were first performed in the Verein für musikalische Privataufführungen on 17 October 1919.

In early June 1913 Berg and his wife travelled to Berlin for a week's visit to the Schoenbergs. It was a visit full of stimulating experiences, among which was an 'unforgettable rehearsal' of *Pierrot Lunaire* and a performance of it.[26]

---

[26] Schoenberg's melodrama was first heard in Berlin in the previous year.

What impact this work made on Berg may be seen from a letter to Schoenberg about a year later (20 July 1914):

> I only know that on the two occasions when I heard *Pierrot* I was conscious of the most profound impression *ever* made on me by a work of art, and that the enigmatic power of these pieces has left *indelible* traces on my mind. But when I look at the score, the music still appears to me quite enigmatic and mysterious, and I cannot imagine that with my small technical ability (and my great shortcomings!) I shall ever be able to comprehend this work which seems to me like a miracle of nature.

Berg's Berlin visit would have been entirely unclouded but for the fact that on his last day Schoenberg discussed with him the two works written since he had left his master – the Altenberg Songs and the Four Clarinet Pieces, which he criticised so severely that the memory of it reverberated in Berg's mind for several years to come. In fact, the temporary estrangement between the two musicians, which was greatest in 1915 and lasted until 1916, may be said to have begun with that visit. Reich suggests[27] that it was the short aphoristic form of Berg's two compositons, with their absence of an extended thematic development, which may have been responsible for Schoenberg's strictures. I find this difficult to accept, since Schoenberg himself and Webern cultivated the miniature form in their period of free atonality.[28] Berg, to whom the aphorism was intrinsically alien, merely followed in their footsteps. We do not know the precise nature of Schoenberg's censure but, to judge from several of Berg's later letters to his former master, it was his leanings towards the French impressionists, his tendency to write sad, pessimistic music, the tailing off of his creative endeavours and, more generally, his 'lack of self-discipline' and 'unreliability' in private and professional matters which prompted Schoenberg to haul Berg over the coals. Evidence of how seriously the latter took these criticisms is provided by a letter to Schoenberg, written only a few days after his return from Berlin to Vienna (14 June 1913):

> You will surely understand, my dear Mr Schoenberg, that together with the loveliest memories of unclouded enjoyment, there is also the memory of that last afternoon with its depressing home-truths. Yet I have to thank you for your *reproof* as for *everything* I have received from you, knowing well that it was meant for *my own* good. I don't need to tell you that the great pain it has caused me, is proof of the fact that I have heeded your criticism. And, should I succeed in this intention for which I hope with an anxious heart (for the doubt of myself is always very strong and the slightest reproof from you robs me of almost *all* hope) – should I succeed

---

[27] *Life and Work of Alban Berg*, p. 41.
[28] Schoenberg's opp. 11, 16, 19 and 21, and Webern's opp. 5 to 10.

in my good intention, then this pain will lose its bitterness ... I hope to
show you by deeds what I am hardly able to express in words. As soon as I
am in the country, I want to begin with the suite. Perhaps one day I shall
succeed in writing something *cheerful*.

This 'something cheerful', however, was not to come until twelve years later,
in the Chamber Concerto. The suite became in the event the Three
Orchestral Pieces, op. 6, about which he wrote to his wife on 17 July 1914
that 'the *Marsch* is comparatively long. At last a long movement after so
many short ones! It is longer than the five orchestral songs put together.'
Berg took for his model Schoenberg's Five Orchestral Pieces, op. 16 (and also
Webern's op. 10) but, as he assured Helene (11 July): 'my pieces are *not*
derived, mind you, from them; on the contrary, they are utterly different', as
indeed they are. Since Schoenberg, by his suggestion for a suite of character
pieces, was the spiritual begetter of op. 6, Berg decided to dedicate it to him
on the occasion of his fortieth birthday, and was anxious to complete it in
time. But in the event he finished only the *Praeludium* and the *Marsch*, not
completing the *Reigen* until the summer of the following year. Here is Berg's
letter of 8 September 1914, in which with his usual modesty he gives his
reasons for the dedication:

> For years it had been my secret but persistent desire to dedicate
> something to you. The works composed under your supervision, the
> Sonata, songs and Quartet, do not count for this purpose since I received
> them directly from you. My hopes of writing something more independent
> and yet as good as these first compositons (something I could confidently
> dedicate to you[28a] without incurring your displeasure) have been
> repeatedly disappointed. Your kind suggestion of last spring (during the
> journey from Amsterdam to Berlin), gave me the courage to attempt a
> composition which I could dedicate to you without blushing. I cannot tell
> you today if I have succeeded or if the attempt has failed. Should the latter
> be the case, then, in your paternal benevolence, you will have to accept the
> good intention for the deed. I have really tried to give of my best and to
> follow your advice. In this endeavour the unforgettable experience of the
> Amsterdam rehearsals and the close study of your orchestral pieces [29] was
> an immense help and has sharpened my self-criticism more and more.
> *This* is the reason why I have not been able to complete the second of the
> three pieces, *Reigen*, in time and why I have had to leave it until later,
> when I shall probably succeed in changing what is wrong in it.

The *Praeludium* and *Reigen* were first performed in Berlin on 5 June 1923, as

---

[28a] Berg's Four Clarinet Pieces, op. 5 written a year before his op. 6, were not dedicated to his
former master until 1920.
[29] Schoenberg's Five Orchestral Pieces, op. 16. They had their first performance at a
Promenade concert in London in September 1912, under Henry Wood.

part of an Austrian Musikwoche, with Webern conducting. The complete work, whose scoring Berg revised in 1929, was first heard at Oldenburg in 1930.

We now turn to Berg's various other activities during those few years before the outbreak of the First World War. On 23 February 1913 the first performance of Schoenberg's *Gurrelieder* took place at the Grosse Musikvereinssaal under Franz Schreker. Berg was invited by Schreker, whom he seems to have first met in connexion with his work on the vocal score of the latter's opera, *Der ferne Klang* (see below), to take charge of some choral rehearsals, but at first had doubts about his ability to do justice to this task, and asked Schoenberg for his advice, which was encouraging. Berg replied on 31 December:

> Many thanks for your kind letter. It has given me immense pleasure, all the more since you encouraged me to take over the choral rehearsals, which, urged by Schreker, I had decided to do before your letter arrived, as otherwise Weigl[30] would have done it. But now that your letter came, I know that I have done right ... I had not only your advice but also the memory of *your own* choral rehearsals to guide me.[31] Also Webern ... gave me a few hints from his experience as conductor, so that it was hardly my merit if things went well ... Now that my first fears about the pure technique of conducting – in which, as you may remember, I showed much clumsiness and which, in my immodest opinion, has changed into something like a *little* routine (through practising at home) – now that I am at least no longer afraid of *this,* can really *hear* and hence make demands, in a word, can make music – I derive much pleasure from this activity.

Incidentally, Berg offered to study the part of the Narrator in the *Gurrelieder* with the well-known Viennese actor, Wilhelm Klitsch, and was at first greatly puzzled by the *Sprechstimme*[32] and asked Schoenberg for guidance as to how it should be treated.

Berg, in marked contrast to Schoenberg and, notably, Webern, was never a practising musician. These choral rehearsals were the only occasion on which he did some conducting. He was an indifferent pianist, and as such appeared in public only twice as the accompanist of his own songs for which, on his own admission, he had to practise a good deal.

Berg's other activities during this period were almost entirely devoted to

---

[30] Karl Weigl (1884-1949), an Austrian composer of largely chamber music and songs, and at one time *répétiteur* under Mahler at the Hofoper.

[31] Schoenberg had for some years been the conductor of several working-men's choirs in Vienna.

[32] The *Gurrelieder* was the first of Schoenberg's compositions to employ this device.

work for Schoenberg. In 1911 the latter asked him to compile an index for the first edition of his *Harmonielehre* over which he took, with his usual conscientiousness and thoroughness, immense trouble. He could not find words to express his admiration for this important treatise, saying in an undated letter that

> Reading your *Harmonielehre* again and discovering always other new and splendid things in it, I feel how more and more indebted I become to you and that I must thank you again and will thank you until the end of my life and – beyond it.

Berg made the vocal score of the *Gurrelieder* and wrote a touching letter to Schoenberg of 27 November 1912 asking him whether he could not keep

> a few pages of the manuscript score. This would not only be a pleasant memory of my work on it, of the time when I also learned so much from you about the arrangement of a vocal score ... but it would also be the fulfilment of a long-standing desire to possess a *manuscript* of yours. To ask you for the whole – this would be *too much*, but I am only asking for a part, perhaps the Prelude and the Interlude ...

Schoenberg granted him this wish.

Berg also made a vocal score of the *Litanei* and *Entrückung* in Schoenberg's F sharp minor Quartet, op. 10, and a piano arrangement for (possibly) four hands of the Chamber Symphony, the manuscript of which is lost. To the same period belong Berg's thematic guides to the *Gurrelieder*, the Chamber Symphony and the tone poem, *Pelleas und Melisande*, which show his exceptional gift for lucid analysis and presentation. It was the excellence of these guides which later prompted Schoenberg to suggest to Berg to take up the career of a *Musikschriftsteller* or writer on music.

In 1911 Hertzka commissioned Berg to make a vocal score of Schreker's opera, *Der ferne Klang*, which entailed a thorough study of the full score which, as we shall see, left its traces on the orchestral style of *Wozzeck*. This vocal score was the subject of a letter in which Berg, usually good-natured and conciliatory, expressed himself with some force. Both Schreker and Hertzka had criticised it for being too difficult to play, whereupon Berg wrote to Schoenberg on 5 September 1912:

> Hertzka reproaches me that my piano scores are unplayable because of their difficulty. He himself of course understands nothing and probably takes his cue from Schreker, who, because he plays and sightreads badly, naturally cannot play my scores. At the time I was working on the vocal score of *Der ferne Klang*, he assured me daily that 'the score is not meant for children' and was furious with Scholz who wanted to make 'Diabelli exercises' of his opera. He even wrote to me saying that Bruno Walter had

found my score excellent. After all this he starts grumbling, whenever we meet, about the difficulty of my score and, with him, of course Hertzka. The latter I have cured of his mad idea in a letter which was none too friendly. But I won't try this with Schreker, particularly now when his success (with *Der ferne Klang*) will cause him megalomania.[33]

There is some truth in Schreker's remark, as is also proved by the piano accompaniment of some of Berg's Seven Early Songs. Not only Schreker but also Schoenberg was of the opinion that the piano reduction of a vocal or orchestral work should be easy to play, whereas Berg maintained that it was not merely a substitute for the original version but should function in its own right, as in a song with piano accompaniment. Schoenberg also thought, and rightly, that the first version of a piano reduction was always more difficult than its subsequent one and that, I presume, was the reason why the present edition of Berg's vocal score of *Der ferne Klang* bears the additional name of one Ferdinand Rebay who was engaged to simplify Berg's piano style.

The period with which this chapter is concerned closes with a theatrical event which was to be of crucial importance for Berg's carrer. In May 1914 he saw several performances at the Wiener Kammerspiele of Büchner's *Woyzeck* (with the celebrated Albert Steinrück in the title-role) which stirred Berg so profoundly that he decided to base an opera on this play. He had already begun with the adaptation of the text and some musical sketches when war broke out, and for the time being put a stop to Berg's work.

[33] As proved by other letters to Schoenberg, Berg entertained an unflattering view of Schreker as composer, which seems to have been partly due to personal antipathy. (Schoenberg appears to have seen Schreker in a more favourable light.) It is not without significance that Berg's contribution to the *Anbruch* number of March/April 1928 (p. 86), issued on the occasion of Schreker's 50th anniversaty, is, compared with other articles in this issue, extremely short and in essence confines itself to saying that Berg was the first to have recognised in *Der ferne Klang* an assured success.

FOUR

INTERLUDE:
PRE-WAR VIENNA

Before continuing our account of Berg's life, it will be interesting to cast a glance at Vienna during the period from about 1890 to 1914, the period of Berg's formative years and early maturity, and also make closer acquaintance with three men who, next to Schoenberg, influenced, to varying degrees, the composer's spiritual development and his *Weltbild*.

There is a strange paradox in the fact that, while the Habsburg monarchy was slowly disintegrating, its capital represented the most important cultural centre in central Europe. It was as though the slow process of political dissolution of the empire produced a most potent ferment in Vienna's artistic and intellectual life. Music, literature, painting and architecture, not to mention psychology and philosophy, flourished to an extent only rivalled by Paris of the same period. Pre-war Vienna was the city of Mahler and Schoenberg, of Klimt and Kokoschka, of Schnitzer and Hofmannsthal, of Otto Wagner and Loos, of Freud, Mach and Wittgenstein. Never before had Vienna shown such an accumulation of diverse talents and such a close interchange of ideas, aims and aspirations. To an outsider it must all have appeared as a tightly knit, organic entity inspired by a new spirit of artistic adventure and intellectual exploration. At the same time, the Vienna of Francis Joseph I appeared to the world as the gay city *par excellence*. With its waltzes and operettas, with its balls, cafés and air of *joie de vivre*, it proclaimed a hedonistic attitude to life to be found in no other capital. But there was a dark, negative side to this bright picture, and this was the ramshackle, tottering foundation on which the Austrian monarchy rested. Ominous rumblings of the volcano beneath had been going on since the last decade of the nineteenth century, if not indeed earlier. But the Viennese refused to pay attention, and when this volcano finally erupted in August 1914, they at first took scarcely any notice.[1] There is perhaps no better and more sharply focused picture of what life was like in the Hapsburg monarchy and, notably, its capital in the pre-war days than that given by Robert Musil in his great fragmentary novel, *The Man without Qualities*. In this satirical novel Musil coined for the Austrian empire the word 'Kakania', derived from the initials

---

[1] See Berg's letter to Schoenberg quoted on p. 42.

K.K. – *Kaiserlich-Königlich* – the hallowed adjectives attached to the name of every public institution of the State. 'Kakania' also had a second, scatological connotation, from its use in the language of a children's nursery, denoting excrement or 'Shitland',[2] with which Musil obviously intended to suggest what he thought of his native country under the Emperor's reign.

Directly responsible for the total collapse of the Habsburg monarchy was of course its military defeat at the end of the 1914-18 war. But the rot had set in much earlier. Outward signs of it were the turbulent and often incredible scenes in the Austrian Parliament, where the representatives of the various races compounding the multi-national state behaved in a way which frequently forced the government to close the assembly and rule the country by special powers. The root cause of these and many other political troubles was the Emperor's unshakeable belief, tantamount to a religious dogma, in the apostolic *Hausmacht* of the Habsburgs, the oldest reigning dynasty in Europe, and his unwillingness to allow the constitution to be adjusted to the political, social and economic changes demanded by the twentieth century. Yet if the court, the aristocracy and the wealthy bourgeoisie ignored the need for urgent reforms of the body politic, and if a petrified bureaucracy continued to preserve the tradition and practices of the eighteenth century, there was a stratum of society which felt that there was something radically wrong with the Habsburg system of government, and that an insidious cancer was slowly eating away the foundations of the monarchy. This consisted of the young artists, writers and intellectuals – themselves the offspring of the conservative middle classes – who in their different ways gave vent in their creations to their feeling of a strong malaise, creations which in retrospect read like anxious warnings of the coming catastrophe. This was the time of Kokoschka's so-called 'black' period when, as the painter wrote, 'people lived in security, but they were all afraid. I felt it through their cultivated form of living … I painted them in their anxiety and pain.' If with these paintings Kokoschka implied also a critique of the Viennese bourgeoisie, of its smugness, conventionality and hypocrisy, there was Klimt who, socially less conscious than Kokoschka, protested against the ornate, decorative style practised by the Vienna Academy, a style best represented by Markart in his huge, antiquated historic canvases. In 1898 Klimt and a number of his pupils left the Academy and founded a rival institution in the *Sezession* (a significant name) the motto of which was, 'Der Zeit ihre Kunst, der Kunst ihre Freiheit' – 'To the Age its Art, to Art its Freedom'.

This movement[3] away from the old and towards a style in tune with the contemporary spirit also inspired Viennese literature of the *fin de siècle*, witness the young poets and writers around 1900, known as *Jung Wien*,

[2] Allan Janik and Stephen Toulmin, *Wittgenstein's Vienna*, London, 1973, p.13n.
[3] In its beginning it was much influenced by the French Impressionists.

whose main exponents were Hofmannsthal, Schnitzler, Altenberg, Beer-Hofmann and Zweig. It was the same in architecture, where men like Otto Wagner and Adolf Loos condemned the luxuriant, over-ornate style of building, and fought for a far more simple, more functional design. This was also the period when Schoenberg gradually moved away from the major-minor system, replacing it by a free atonal writing. All these novel and even revolutionary ideas developed under the eye of the emperor and his government and made Vienna, politically so sclerotic, a city outstanding in the richness, variety and advanced character of its cultural life. If there was a common denominator uniting these young artists and intellectuals, it was a quest for truthfulness, authenticity and sincerity in their creations. This was not merely an aesthetic but a moral demand; it concerned not only style and manner but also the ethos of a work. And this is where Karl Kraus – the most articulate journalistic mouthpiece of these lofty criteria – enters the scene.

Kraus (1974-1936), a baptised Jew[4] from Bohemia, was in the first place a polemical satirist who in 1899 founded a periodical with the significant title, *Die Fackel – The Torch* – of which from 1911 he was virtually his own and sole contributor. In this periodical Kraus waged a perpetual and relentless war against what he regarded the evil and corruption of Vienna's political and cultural life – its hypocrisy, its 'beautiful' lies, its sycophantic flattery of mediocrity, its venality and banality. This watchdog of politics, art and literature was a kind of Austrian Swift who had the Irishman's instinct for nosing out moral significance in even the most trivial things. When someone criticised this, Kraus's reply was: 'Gut, ich mache aus einer Mücke einen Elefanten. Ist das nicht Kunst?' ('Well, I make a mountain out of a molehill. Is this not art?'). Kraus's most deadly shafts were directed at the Viennese press, notably at Austria's most influential paper, *Die Neue Freie Presse*, which was his particular *bête noir*. In innumerable articles he castigated it for its crass commercialism, its servility to advertising interests, its obsessive preoccupation with fashion and gossip, and its addiction to the feuilleton, which in its Viennese variety represented to Kraus a mixture of mediocre literary essay and pure journalism dispensing cheap writing and literary chic. In the feuilleton, Kraus argued, objective facts were obscured by its author's highly subjective approach and excessive use of purely ornamental phrases which concealed only half-truths, if not indeed plain lies. A monomaniac in respect of the German language, he regarded the use of syntax, grammar, punctuation down to the placing of a comma and, above

---

[4] Baptism of Jews in the Austrian monarchy was very frequent in order to remove obstacles to their career, as was the case with Mahler and Schoenberg. Anti-Semitism was then not of the racial but of the religious kind, and could be silenced by a conversion to Roman Catholicism or Protestantism. Incidentally, the number of distinguished artists, writers and scientists of Jewish origin in pre-war Vienna was considerable. A vivid picture of this time is given in Schnitzler's famous novel, *Der Weg ins Freie*.

all, the relationship of words and their precise meaning as revealing a writer's ego. 'Language', he said, 'is the divining rod which discovers wells of truth ... it is the key to the recognition of good and evil ... the mother of thought.' This high moral view of language Kraus appears to have derived from the Old Testament – more particularly from God's revelation of the Ten Commandments to Moses – and it is not difficult to see the Krausian influence in Schoenberg's *Moses und Aron*. Kraus's insistence that great art can only be achieved on the basis of truthfulness, authenticity and sincerity is reflected in the 'integer' music of the Second Viennese School. Schoenberg, Berg and Webern considered mere aestheticism and decorative composing to be a sin against the spirit of music, and we recall in this context Schoenberg's injunction to his pupils to be at all times true to themselves and only listen to their inner voice. He said somewhere that what matters is the idea behind the work, its ethos, and not its style. What Schoenberg thought of Kraus, whom he knew personally, emerges from the dedication inscribed in a copy of the first edition of his *Harmonielehre* (1912), which he presented to the author of *Die Fackel:* 'I have perhaps learned more from you than one can learn if one is to remain independent.'

Kraus combined in his person the irony of the cultivated assimilated Viennese Jew with a typically Austrian trait, which is to see, in the first place, the negitive aspect of life and of its mundane institutions. He took an apocalyptic view of the world, and was the prophet of doom[5] calling the Austria of Francis Joseph I the 'research laboratory for the destruction of mankind', and predicting the collapse of the Habsburg monarchy.[6] True, Kraus expressed himself in terms of almost pathological aggressiveness, intransigence and intolerance, but he was right in many things on which he poured his vitriolic wit. The measure of Kraus's intellectual stature may be gauged from the fact that in the 1920s he was several times considered a candidate for the Nobel Prize. And the light in which he was seen by the younger Austrian poets and writers emerges from a verse by Georg Trackl, (1887-1914), a *poète maudit*, who committed suicide at the age of twenty-seven:

Weisser Hohepriester der Wahrheit,	White high-priest of truth,
Kristallne Stimme, in der Gottes	Crystalline voice in which dwells
eisiger Atem wohnt,	God's icy breath,
Zürnender Magier,	Irate magician,
Dem unter flammenden Mantel	Under whose flaming cloak clanks
der blaue Panzer des	the blue armour of the warrior.
Kriegers klirrt.	

[5] Stefan Zweig, in his memoir, *Die Welt von Gestern* (1947), called Kraus the 'Thersites of Viennese literature'.

[6] The characteristic title of his anti-war book-drama, which consists very largely of quotations

Kraus did not live to witness the incorporation of Austria into the Third Reich, but in his posthumous collection of essays, *Die dritte Walpurgisnacht* (publ. 1952), he foresaw the unspeakable evil and terror which Hitler was to unleash on Europe.

Kraus and all he stood for made a lasting impression on Berg, who had already in his youth become a voracious reader of *Die Fackel*, and there are many references to Kraus and his periodical in Berg's letters to his wife and Schoenberg. In literature Berg took his cue from Kraus, who was a declared enemy of such writers as Schnitzler and Hofmannsthal, and condemned the 'willowy', ornamental *Jugendstil* or *art nouveau* in the arts of the two decades before the First World War, a style of which at first the young Berg was a follower. To some extent, Berg's own *Weltbild*, his pessimistic view of life, was nurtured by Kraus's writing, just as the latter's literary style, with its mixture of matter-of-fact thinking, polemical attitude and irony coloured the composer's own mode of literary expression. Good examples of this are Berg's famous reply to Pfitzner in *The Musical Impotence of Hans Pfitzner's 'new Aesthetics'*, and his two essays on Schoenberg and the music critics.

Berg seems to have had his first, though indirect, contact with Kraus when the latter produced Wedekind's second Lulu play, *Die Büchse der Pandora*, at the small Trianon Theatre on 24 May 1905, giving an introductory talk of which Berg made copious notes. In the twenty-year-old composer a seed was sown which was to bear rich fruit in his second opera, which is coloured by Kraus's progressive views on prostitution and homosexuality,[7] defending them on moral and social grounds. Yet in marked contrast to Wedekind, Kraus saw feminine sexuality not in terms of a destructive power, but as an element fecundating and inspiring masculine reason. And, as we shall see in the chapter on *Lulu*, the motive of the 'hounded grace of woman eternally misunderstood' by the men who avenge themselves on her for their own guilt, was Kraus's interpretation of the tragedy and was taken over by Berg. It is absent from Wedekind's plays.

Berg made Kraus's personal acquaintance in 1909 through their mutual friend, Peter Altenberg, and subsequently attended his famous poetry readings (*Theatre of Poetry*), as well as his one-man productions of Offenbach operettas in which Kraus, who was not particularly musical, sang with a kind of *Sprechstimme* which Berg declared to show an instinctive feeling for musical rhythm. On Kraus's sixtieth birthday (24 April 1934), a *Festschrift* was published with contributions, among others, by Hamsun, Čapek and

---

from the Austrian Press given without comment, is *The Last Days of Mankind*. It recalls a more recent English play with a similar anti-war message, *Oh! What a Lovely War!*

[7] We notice the Krausian influence already in Berg's famous letter to his future father-in-law quoted on p. 17.

Brecht, while Berg's contribution took the form of a quotation of six bars from *Lulu* which was the setting of the wonderful line, 'Eine Seele, die sich im Jenseits den Schlaf aus den Augen reibt'. Kraus was acquainted with the leading musicians of his time, notably Schoenberg, and published the facsimilie of one of the latter's songs in a number of *Die Fackel*. The young Krenek belonged to Kraus's more intimate circle and wrote most perceptively on the analogy between Kraus's thoughts on language and Schoenberg's musical thinking.

Another personality who exerted, albeit to a lesser degree than Kraus, an influence on young Berg was Peter Altenberg (1859-1919). Altenberg, whose real name was Richard Engländer, was a kind of literary Erik Satie translated to the Vienna scene at the turn of the last century, though he called himself the 'Verlaine d'Autriche', on account of a certain facial resemblance to the French poet. He was an *enfant terrible* and the precursor of the modern hippy. He led the life of an arch-bohemian, living in cheap hotels and passing his time in coffee-houses – first the Café Griensteidl in the Michaeler Platz and, after its demolition in 1896, in the Café Central, which was the meeting-place of Vienna's literati and musicians. Kraus was the first to appreciate Altenberg's prose poems (he saw in him an artist after his own heart), and was instrumental in getting them published.

Altenberg's credo was: 'Artist, remain true to yourself! Listen to your inner voice and be not ashamed of yourself! Have the courage to confess to your nakedness!' (This might be Schoenberg speaking to his pupils.) This emphasis on absolute truth and fidelity in art and on the prerogative of the modern artist to allow his private personality to saturate his work was, as we intimated, the motto of all Viennese artists in the two decades before the First World War, and finally led to the expressionism of the 1920s. Altenberg referred to himself as the 'Reporter of the Soul', who in his miniature poems wished to give a glimpse of his inner self. 'Are my little verses poems?' he asked in his autobiographical sketch. 'No, they are extracts from life.'

It was Altenberg who introduced into Austrian poetry the so-called 'telegram style', his aim being 'to describe a person in a *single* sentence, the experience of the soul on a *single* page, and a landscape in a *single* word'. His was pointillist art aiming at the utmost concentration of thought, which found its musical equivalent in Webern's style. Many of his poems read like brief diary entries or short excerpts from letters, and deal almost exclusively with non-carnal, platonic love, with children and nature, in which Altenberg saw the symbol of pure life. His aphorisms and *aperçus* show a marked ambivalence, for behind their brilliant *jeux d'esprit* there lurk bitter despair and pessimism – features which may have attracted the similarly constituted Berg. Seen in the context of the Vienna literary scene of his time, Altenberg was an outsider who in his life and creations represented a tenuous link with the *morbidezza* of the *Jugendstil*. He was a highly sensitive poet who achieved a measure of originality in the juxtaposition of startlingly unexpected, disparate images welded into a unity by the underlying mood of the verse, as for instance in the poems set by Berg in his *Five Songs after Picture Post-Cards*. The curious title derives from the fact that Altenberg was in the habit of sending to his many friends picture post-cards with short verses written on them. Here are two examples to show his combination of heterogeneous images. In the first poem (Berg's no. 2) the unexpected juxtaposition occurs in the last line:

> Did you see the woods after the rainstorm?! ?!
> Everything is at peace and is more beautiful than before.
> Look, *woman*, you too need a *rainstorm*!

In the second verse (Berg's no. 5) the poet seeks peace for his lacerated soul in nature, far away from all human contact. The disparate images occur in the second and last lines:

> See, here is no-one, no human dwelling ...
> here is *peace*!
> Here the *snow drops gently into a pool of water* ...

Berg's own literary style, notably during his early years, shows the influence of Altenberg in his predilection for the simultaneous use of question and exclamation marks (as in the initial line of the first of the two poems), for meaningful dots and dashes after a word and for the underlining and bracketing of sentences.

The Bergs were on terms of warm friendship with Altenberg, who in three of his verses dedicated to Helene Berg refers to her ordeal before her marriage – *H.N.* (which is a love poem), *Bekanntschaft* (in which Berg himself appears) and *Besuch im einsamen Park*. They were published in a volume entitled *Neues Altes* (1911), which also contains the poems set by Berg. In 1913 the poet suffered from persecution mania and was for a time in Steinhof, a mental hospital near Vienna, where the composer visited him and described his life as 'an inferno' (Hugo Wolf was an inmate there).

The third personality whose theories and practical work greatly appealed to Berg and, indeed, to the whole of the Schoenberg circle, was the architect, Adolf Loos (1870-1933), who was an intimate friend of Karl Kraus, Altenberg and the painter Kokoschka. Following in the footsteps of another progressive Viennese architect, Otto Wagner, Loos utterly condemned the ornate, antiquated and pretentious style of the so-called *Gründerzeit* of the 1860s and 1870s, when new buildings in a pseudo-Gothic and pseudo-Renaissance manner were erected on Vienna's famous Ringstrasse, which replaced the old Bastei or fortification. Loos declared all ornamental by-work a crime against architecture, just as Kraus attacked the 'beautiful' phrases of the Viennese feuilleton as a crime against the German language. Instead,

Loos advocated a strictly functional style in the design of objects serving a practical use, a style completely unadorned, economic and purposeful. His aim was to achieve a *Neue Sachlichkeit* in buildings, practical examples of which he gave with his blocks of flats and offices, and private villas which, because of their plain, unadorned façades, were nicknamed 'Houses without eyebrows'. His most famous buildings were the Café Capua in the Inner City and the Haus am Michaeler Platz, a commercial building, which caused an uproar in conservative Viennese circles who considered its functional simplicity and total lack of decorative features an insult to the emperor, since it contrasted so strikingly with the highly ornate, domed entrance to the Hofburg opposite. Loos may be said to have been, together with Otto Wagner, the first of a line to which belong Walter Gropius, Le Corbusier and Frank Lloyd Wright.

For two years he was head of the Vienna Housing Department and published in 1919 a symposium, *Richtlinien für ein Kunstamt* ('Guiding Lines for an Arts Council') to which Schoenberg, with whom he was well acquainted, contributed an essay in which he elaborated his ideas for a reform of Vienna's musical life and institutions. On his sixtieth birthday (10 December 1930) a *Festschrift* came out which contained a generous appreciation of Loos's achievements; Berg contributed a double acrostic in which the initial letters of the nine lines spelled 'Adolf Loos' and 'Berg Alban'. Despite his impaired hearing, Loos was very musical and a man of wide culture whose company Berg greatly enjoyed.

FIVE

WAR YEARS
1914-18

In August 1914 the First World War broke out. Berg was at first filled with a most ardent patriotic feeling and desired nothing more intensely than the victory of his country, finding it 'very shameful to be merely an onlooker at these great events' and 'sometimes even downright wicked to be thinking of other things but the war ... the urge to take active part in it, the feeling of powerlessness and inability to serve the fatherland don't let me work'. (Letters to Schoenberg of 24 August and 8 September 1914.) He was called up at the end of September but was declared unfit for military service, which for the above reasons greatly depressed him. In November he was trying to engage new staff for the Berghof since the old steward had been conscripted, and he also busied himself with one or two inventions. Thus in December he thought he had invented a new firearm which (writing to his mentor on 15 December)'will give us such an ascendancy over our enemies that we should be able to beat any superior power'. He intended to send this invention to the War Ministry, but did not explain to Schoenberg its nature. A week later he informed him of another invention designed, however, for a peaceful purpose. This was a machine, apparently constructed like a Morse telegraph, on which a composer would be able to record, by means of keys and a revolving tape, every fluctuation of tempo, and thus provide an authentic guide for performers and conductors. Of neither invention do we hear anything further.

Berg, with his idealism and high moral purpose, found Vienna's gay life and total unconcern with the war revolting, and wrote a somewhat priggish letter to Schoenberg (1 January 1915):

> Life *outside* goes on just as usual. I tell you, dear Mr Schoenberg, to watch this is as nauseating as the war is terribly painful. As if nothing had happened, people in Vienna live completely without restraint, operettas and farces 'adapted to the times' are produced, and every theatre and cinema are filled to bursting point. If it were not for the rise in living costs, there would not be any reason to think of the war as other than a sensational event which stirs only the readers of newspapers ... If the war should do what it is supposed to do – to act as a cathartic element – it is far from achieving this. The dirt remains as before – only in different form.

Schoenberg, who with the outbreak of the war found himself again in precarious circumstances, came in April 1915 from Berlin to Vienna to conduct a benefit concert at the Grosse Musikvereinssaal, with Beethoven's Ninth Symphony in the programme but in Mahler's rescoring. Berg, who had helped with the preparations for this concert, wondered about these retouches in the Beethoven score and wrote to Schoenberg on 30 March: 'I am quite beside myself. I think that with many passages it needs great courage to make such radical alterations, and in a work by one of the greatest masters!' Incidentally, Schoenberg was to add retouches of his own to the score!

In June Berg was called up again and this time declared fit. Highly pleased about it, he dilated to Schoenberg on the significance of the number 23 in his life, seeing it operating also in his conscription, though he did not say in which way, and adduced scientific support for his belief by quoting from *Von Leben und Tod*, by Wilhelm Fliess. In it this German biologist and friend of Freud's propounded a theory according to which the life cycle of all animate things runs in periods which, with the males, are divisible by twenty-three and, with females, by twenty-eight.[1] In his letter (20 June 1915) Berg drew a table to convince Schoenberg that 23 was his number. He frequently arranged the completion of a composition to coincide with the 23rd day of the month and, as we shall see, 23 and its multiples play an important role in the Lyric Suite and the Violin Concerto.

Berg had to join the Deutschmeisterregimen 1, a Viennese regiment which suited him well, since he wished to remain in Vienna as long as possible to look after the affairs of his mother's property, Charly having meanwhile also been conscripted. At the beginning of October Berg, who was an Einjährig Freiwilliger[2], was transferred to the training camp at Bruck an der Leitha, near the Austro-Hungarian frontier, whence he sent on 4 October the following SOS to his wife:

There reigns hell here in the truest sense of the word. Please come on Wednesday when I shall tell you all about it. My experiences here are such that the latest ones blot out the previous ones ... Imagine! An hour standing in the rain *in front* of the military transport, then at 1.30 p.m. we squeezed, sopping wet, into the compartment. For the distance which a normal passenger train covers in an hour and a quarter, we needed more than seven hours. From 6.30 p.m. till 9 p.m. we sat in the dark train which mostly remained stationary. Then at the double to the camp which is

[1] Freud himself once asked Fliess whether his numerical computations enabled him to predict which of the two men, born in the same year, would die first – Freud's father or Bismarck. Ernest Jones, *Sigmund Freud: Life and Work*, London, 1956, vol. I, p.210.

[2] An officer cadet who on account of his academic schooling became an officer proper after only a year's training, instead of the normal three years.

about half-an-hour's distance away, where we were given black coffee, after having had our last meal in Vienna at 10.30 a.m. If you had not given me the two sandwiches, my kind, thoughtful one!!! Then freezing in bed, half-dressed. Our bags had not arrived yet. But these physical trials are as nothing compared with the moral ones today. Pferscherl, come, soon, I need you more than ever before! I am uprooted.

To Gottfried Kassowitz, a pupil of Berg's who visited him at the training camp, he spoke of the sleeping recruits and described this 'polyphonic breathing, gasping and groaning' as the strangest chorus he had ever heard. It was to him like a primeval sound or a sound of nature[3] which he later reproduced in the snoring chorus of the soldiers in Act II of *Wozzeck*.

Due to his frail constitution, the field exercises with full marching pack proved too much for him. He suffered from shortness of breath and acute attacks of asthma, and developed a bronchial catarrh, till at the beginning of November his health broke down completely. On 6 November he was transferred to the military hospital at Bruck, whence he sent his wife the medical report which declared him suitable only for orderly duties. Berg was sent back to Vienna, where at first he was made to do guard duty, though his rank as an officer cadet should have exempted him from it. As this also proved too strenuous, he applied as a matter of urgency for a change, but it was not until May 1916 that he became an official at the War Ministry, where he served the rest of his military career. Although his duties at the ministry were far less exacting, consisting as they did of paperwork, and allowed him time to work on *Wozzeck*, he yet found them an unbearable drudgery and soul-destroying. He summed up his war experiences in the letter to his wife (quoted on p. 19) in which he drew a parallel between himself and the hero of his opera.

There was yet another source of unhappiness for Berg, and this was the growing tension between him and his former master, resulting in a deterioration of their friendship, which reached its lowest point in the period from May to about December 1915. Ever since the spring of 1914, when Berg had accompanied Schoenberg to Amsterdam to attend a performance of *Pelleas und Melisande* under Mengelberg, he had felt that Schoenberg had become more and more irritated by him and had begun to cold-shoulder him. What were the reasons for this estrangement? We gather from a letter which Berg wrote to Schoenberg from the military hospital at Bruck an der Leitha (November 1915) that the latter had again criticised a number of things in his artistic and private life. (Berg's letter is the longest he ever penned to his former teacher, covering no less than thirteen large pages in the original, and gives some idea of the rather straitened circumstances in which

---

[3] W. Reich, *The Life and Work of Alban Berg*, p. 43. See also Kurt Bleikopf, 'Autobiographische Elemente in Alban Berg's "Wozzeck" ', *Österreichische Musikzeitung*, 9, 1954.

PLATE 5: Alban and Helene Berg on their Wedding Day (May 1911)

PLATE 6: Alban and Helene Berg

PLATE 7: Helene Berg standing next to their Ford Car (1932)

PLATE 8: Berg as Officer Cadet (1915)

the Bergs lived before the artistic as well as financial success of *Wozzeck*. I have reproduced it *in toto* in Appendix A.) As to Berg's creative work, we recall that already in June 1913, at the end of Berg's visit to him in Berlin, Schoenberg had found a certain tailing-off of creative strength, seen in the slightness of the Altenberg Songs and the Four Clarinet Pieces. Now it was the Three Orchestral Pieces with which Schoenberg was dissatisfied. As on all previous similar occasions Berg, while always remaining modest and reverential in manner, defended himself with tenacity and a firm conviction. Thus he writes about the orchestral pieces that

> they sprang from the most sincere intention to compose 'character' pieces in the form in which you desired them – of normal length, rich in thematic work, written without any recourse to new devices at all costs, in short, to give of my best in them. If I were not a slow worker and if the war had not broken out, which at first detroyed every desire in me to compose and which about doubled my work in connection with the administration of my mother's Vienna houses and the Berghof, I might perhaps done *more* ... but I have done what I could.

Schoenberg may have criticised Berg for the paucity of new works. He also found fault with Berg's piano arrangement of his Chamber Symphony, regarding it as too difficult, a point, we recall, Schreker also had made about his vocal score of *Der ferne Klang*. Berg countered this by referring to Webern and Steuermann,[4] who both attested that Berg had done 'something good, that is, something that is relatively easy to play and that sounds well'.

As to Berg's private life, it was in Schoenberg's view too dependent on Berg's own family and that of his wife, in which he saw one of the reasons why he neglected his creative work. Berg admits the essential truth of this when he says that there had been a certain financial dependence on his mother which forced him to devote to her affairs a large amount of time which, with better organisation, he could have spent on composing. Schoenberg also reproached him for the illegibility of his handwriting, the erratic and confused style of his letters and his sartorial negligence. To make matters worse, there had been a certain friction between the two families, the Schoenbergs feeling they had been slighted by the Bergs and the Bergs by the Schoenbergs. In short, a situation had arisen in which Schoenberg's touchiness and his tendency to take offence at imaginary slights to his person were fully matched by Berg's hypersensitivity and vulnerability. It should, however, be added that both men were in a state of nervous irritability and constant tension – Berg because of his experiences at the training camp at Bruck, and Schoenberg because he was due to start his military service about

---

[4] Eduard Steuermann (1892-1964), a pianist who belonged to the Schoenberg circle and had himself made piano arrangements of some of the composer's orchestral works.

the middle of December 1915, which was to last till October 1916 and again from September to October 1917. Yet by this last date the air had been completely cleared of mutual misunderstandings, and Schoenberg, as a sign of his affection for his former pupil, offered Berg the intimate *Du*.[5] This occurred on 23 (!) June 1917 to which Berg replied on the following day:

> I have to write to you today because yesterday when you offered me the 'Du', I was unable to find words for it. Nor have I found them today. But at least I may tell you that this was for me the most happy event in the last few years ... because after the long years of servitude during which I was deeply insulted, even humiliated to the point of self-contempt, a feeling of real life begins to grow in me for being received back into your dear home.

There were other signs of Schoenberg's friendship for Berg. Thus, in September 1918 he tried, through the intervention of some friends, to obtain his release from the War Ministry by claiming that his presence was required as assistant to the Swiss conductor, Volkmar Andreae, who was preparing a performance of the *Gurrelieder* in Zurich on 4 November. Another possibility which Schoenberg considered was that Hermann Bahr, a well-known Austrian writer and dramatist, should commission from Berg incidental music for one of his plays, and yet a third alternative was that Berg should apply for a post in the Army Press Office. None of these three possibilities materialised, but Berg did not have to wait long to be released from his 'servitude' – on 3 November 1918 the Armistice was signed between the Allies and Austria, and Berg left the War Ministry.

[5] With Webern, Schoenberg had been on these terms since 1913.

SIX

THE TIME OF *WOZZECK*
1918-25

The end of the war coincided with a musical event which for the following three years was to be of great practical importance for the whole Schoenberg circle. This was the foundation in November 1918 of the Verein für musikalische Privataufführungen or Society for Private Musical Performances under the presidency of Schoenberg, who with it realised a novel and original plan that had been simmering in his mind for some time. This plan sprang from Schoenberg's deeply felt need to create a closer, more intimate relationship between the contemporary composer and his public, a relationship which, as stated in the prospectus, written by Berg and published in February 1919, had in the past been bedevilled by the lack of 'real and accurate' knowledge of modern music on the part of the public. This was due to the unclear, vague impressions the public received from performances in the normal run of concerts which suffered from insufficient preparation. To change this and make the listener more familiar with the 'purpose, direction, intention, method of expression, value and nature' of the new music, three things were necessary:

1. Clear and well-prepared performances.
2. Frequent repetitions of the same works.
3. Exclusion of corrupting publicity from these concerts, such as competition, applause, expression of disapproval, and critics[1]

In order to exclude the spirit of competition, the choice of performers was in most cases made from young and lesser-known artists who were prepared to serve music and music alone, avoiding all self-seeking virtuosity and display of their personalities. Moreover, it was not the object of the Society to make propaganda for particular composers and their works – on the contrary, all modern music was to be performed, from Mahler and Strauss to the most recent composers who got no hearing at all or only an inadequate one. There was an almost unlimited number of rehearsals to ensure the highest degree of clarity of performance in order to realise the composer's intentions in full measure. If this could not be achieved with a given work, it

---

[1] This last condition was not always strictly adhered to as, for instance, in a concert of music by Ravel at which a number of critics were present.

was not performed. The programmes included in the first place songs, piano pieces, chamber music and works for small chorus and, since the Society's financial resources were inadequate for the performance of orchestral works, these were presented in an *ad hoc* piano arrangement for four to eight hands. This was, as the prospectus remarked, making a virtue of necessity, for these piano arrangements removed the factor of orchestral colour, the purely sensuous element. Stripped down to their essentials, these compositions would show the characteristics of all good music – melodic invention, harmonic wealth, polyphony, architecture and so on. The aims of the Society, comparatively brief as its existence was, represented a real breakthrough in Vienna's musical life, both in the choice of programmes and the method of preparation.

Schoenberg nominated five so-called *Vortragsmeister* or directors of performance, two of whom were Berg and Webern.[2] Attendance at concerts was restricted to members of the Society, which gave weekly concerts on Sunday mornings or Monday evenings. The inaugural concert took place on 29 December 1918 and the last concert on 5 December 1921 when, owing to the catastrophic depreciation of the Austrian currency, the Society was compelled to cease its activities. During its three years of existence it gave a total of 117 concerts, with no fewer than 154 contemporary works in the programmes. The most frequently performed composers were Reger (24 works), Debussy (16 works), Bartók and Schoenberg (12 works each).[3] It must be added, however, that it was not until the spring of 1920 that Schoenberg permitted the inclusion of his own works in these concerts. There were two 'propaganda' evenings, a concert of works by Ravel, who came specially from Paris for this occasion,[4] and several performances of *Pierrot Lunaire* which also figured in the programme of the very last concert. In May 1921 there was a matinée in which the whole text of Schoenberg's unfinished oratorio, *Die Jakobsleiter*,[5] was recited by the actor Wilhelm Klitsch. Of Berg's music the Four Clarinet Pieces, op. 5, were first performed on 17 October. Mention must also be made of an evening (27 May 1921) when four waltzes of Johann Strauss were played in a transcription for string quintet, piano and harmonium – *Rosen aus dem Süden* and the *Lagunenwalzer* arranged by Schoenberg, the 'Schatzwalzer' from *The Gypsy Baron* (arr. Webern), and *Wein, Weib und Gesang* (arr. Berg). Schoenberg played first violin together with Rudolf Kolisch, Karl Rankl second violin, Steinbauer the viola, Webern the cello, Steuermann the piano and Berg the harmonium. There had been

---

[2] The other three were Erwin Stein, Eduard Steuermann and the composer, Benno Sachs.

[3] See W. Reich, *Schoenberg: A Critical Biography*, London, 1971, p. 122.

[4] Puccini, who happened to be in Vienna at that time, expressed the wish to come to one of the Society's concerts to hear some of Schoenberg's orchestral works, but nothing came of it.

[5] A year before, Berg had discovered that a picture hanging above his bed at Trahütten was a reproduction of *Die Jakobsleiter* by Ferdinand Bol, one of Rembrandt's first pupils.

five rehearsals each lasting five hours! After the concert was over, the manuscripts of the various arrangements were put up for auction by Schoenberg to raise funds for a chamber orchestra.[6]

Berg devoted himself body and soul to the work for the Society, devising programmes, directing rehearsals, making piano arrangements and looking after the administration. At times he worked fourteen hours and more, so that he was amazed that with all the toil and labour involved his health did not break down. At the same time, he was plagued by the thought that he would never be able to finish *Wozzeck*, and in August 1921 he wrote to Schoenberg asking him to extend his leave of absence from the Society. He had hoped, he said, to complete the opera that summer, but now realised that this would be impossible. Indeed, he despaired whether he would ever be capable of summoning the last ounce of energy to finish the opera 'to which I have devoted so much labour, time and love (I would almost say: Faith, Love and Hope) which I fear might all be in vain'. His qualms, however, proved groundless, for by October 1921 the short score of *Wozzeck* was finished and Berg could begin the instrumentation.

In addition to his work for the Society, Berg was busy with commissions from Universal Edition,[7] the latest of which was a thematic analysis of Schoenberg's *Pelleas und Melisande*; there were lessons to give and there was the burdensome administration of his mother's property. The first half of 1920 he spent at the Berghof, where he had to deal with prospective buyers of the estate, among them profiteers and other shady characters, and where he was compelled to do even menial work. What made him detest his stay at the Berghof in particular was the fact that it had prevented him accepting Schoenberg's offer to write a monograph on him. Writing on 15 January 1920 he says:

> What adds to my depression here is that I *have* to decline your offer, which really honoured me. It has always been my greatest wish – and particularly now when I so much enjoyed doing the *Pelleas* analysis – to write something biographical about you, to take time for this, make every effort and be advised by you. I would like nothing better than – apart from

[6] An amusing incident occurred at a concert in which some of Satie's music was performed. The choice fell on some piano pieces taken from *Vieux sequins et vieilles cuirasses*, *Chapitres tournés en tout sens* and *Descriptions automatiques*, all bearing some facetious expression marks. For instance, in 'Le porteur des grosses pierres' of the first collection some phrases are to be played 'avec beaucoup de mal, péniblement et par à-coup' and 'en traînant les jambes'. The pieces were played by Eduard Steuermann, and Schoenberg, in perfectly good faith and out of respect for the French composer, had these remarks read aloud during the performance. Satie was furious. (Personal communication from the late Darius Milhaud.)

[7] Berg's close connexion with the music publishing firm began in September 1919, when it undertook the distribution of the orchestral parts of the Three Orchestral Pieces, op. 6. In April 1923 the Universal Edition drew up a formal agreement with Berg for *Wozzeck* and all future works up to 1932, and started paying him a monthly retainer.

composing – writing guides, analyses and articles about you and making piano scores of your compositions. And now that the opportunity *has come*, I cannot take it[8] ... my presence here – however much it torments me spiritually, mentally and also physically, and is bad for me – is absolutely necessary until we find a solution – to lease the Berghof or sell it.

At first the Berg family had thought of leasing the estate, but this was unlikely to bring in enough income for the mother and sister to live on, and so it was decided to sell it to an Italian. He turned it into a factory for shoe-trees, for which the whole surrounding forest was felled!

The years 1920 and 1921 saw Berg adding to his activities that of a writer on music to which, we recall, Schoenberg had encouraged him after his excellent Guides to the *Gurrelieder* and the Chamber Symphony. In reply to a polemical essay by Pfitzner against modernism in music, *Die neue Aesthetik der musikalischen Impotenz* (1919), Berg wrote his first and equally polemical essay, *Die musikalische Impotenz der 'neuen Aesthetik' Hans Pfitzners*, published in the June 1920 number of *Die Musikblätter des Anbruch*, the house journal of Universal Edition. This essay found such acclaim among progressive readers[9] that it prompted Hertzka to offer him the editorship of the paper. Berg accepted, yet not without serious qualms, as emerges from a letter to Webern of 14 August – he was to start his editorship on 1 September – in which he seriously questions his suitability for the job:[10]

Will I really be able to do what is needed ... just to get the articles together to fill such a number, and a fortnight later another one, and so twenty times a year! ... Believe me: I've spent so many sleepless nights wishing I had never laid a finger on the *Anbruch* ... Truly, if I did not *have* to do it, if I did not stand before the necessity of scraping some means of existence, I would write to Hertzka today and throw the whole thing over, come what may, and spend the winter here (Trahütten) and compose my opera and finish the instrumentation. But, as it is, I have to stake my

[8] In the event, the monograph was written by Egon Wellesz – *Arnold Schönberg*, Vienna, 1921.

[9] But one of the people who objected to it was Alma Maria Mahler who, as we know from her memoirs, was a great admirer of Pfitzner. As Berg informed Schoenberg on 12 July 1920, Frau Mahler had written to Helene Berg saying: 'All Pfitzner quotations prove that *he* is right. Music is inexplicable, above all melody which is not ABCD, XYZ. Does Alban really believe that anything can be explained in this way – anything at all?' Berg added: 'Well, this was only to be expected, namely that she would condemn the article in *general* and not be able to contradict a *single* one of my statements.'
The polemic revolved around Pfitzner's axiom that a musical *Einfall* or inspired idea cannot be analysed but only felt. Berg on the other hand declared that it *can* be analysed and proceeded to do this with Schumann's *Träumerei* which Pfitzner had adduced as an example of a pure *Einfall*. For a full discussion of this polemic and the problems involved, see Mosco Carner, 'Pfitzner versus Berg', *Major and Minor*, London, 1980, pp.253-7.

[10] Letter reproduced in Reich, *The Life and Work of Alban Berg*, pp. 52-3.

immediate future (or my whole future) on a 'career' (horrible word!) that means nothing to me but the bare possibility of existence. So from 1 September I throw myself into the arms of the public.

Berg, who was editor of the *Anbruch* for barely a year (until autumn 1921), wrote at the end of August 1920 a second essay for it, entitled '*Zwei Feuilletons – Ein Beitrag zum Kapitel "Schönberg und die Kritik"*', in which he pilloried certain critics for their hostility towards Schoenberg's music. It was in order not to offend the sensibilities of these critics that this essay was not published. Berg reworked it in January 1921 for publication in the German periodical, *Melos*, but this did not materialise, and he later gave it to Reich for his own paper, *23 – Eine Wiener Musikzeitung*. But it proved too long and is now reproduced in its entirety in Reich's *Life and Work of Alban Berg*, pp. 219-26.

A word on Reich's paper, in whose fortunes Berg took an active interest. Its aim was to do for Vienna's music what Karl Kraus was doing in *Die Fackel* for literature. Officially, the '23' of its title derived from the number of the paragraph in the Austrian press law which deals with the correction of false or untrue statements made in a published newspaper article. Unofficially, however, '23' referred to Berg's fateful number. Thirty-three numbers came out between 1932 and 1937; all were reprinted as recently as 1971.

To return to 1921. In the autumn of that year a Munich publisher approached Berg with the offer to write, as part of a series on modern composers, a volume on Schoenberg's music, an offer which he accepted with alacrity and for which, according to a letter to Schoenberg, he seems to have done a great deal of work. Writing to the latter on 26 October, Berg says that he is most anxious to correct 'that nonsense about *Atonality*, Impressionism and Expressionism – especially the useless term Atonality', instead of which he would use Polytonality, as suggested by Schoenberg ... or Pantonality. The manuscript of this book, if it ever existed, can no longer be traced.

To come back for a moment to Berg's letter to Webern on p. 50. One senses in it his concern that his activity as an editor might overshadow his true calling, and it was this which in the summer of 1920 decided him to have his compositions to date published at his own expense, so as to make them readily available and bring himself to the attention of a wider public. Moreover, performances, however few, meant an addition to his financial resources which, as he implied in the above letter, were slender enough at that time. Indeed, the material circumstances of Berg, Webern and Stein became, due to the devaluation of the Austrian currency, so precarious that in 1923 Schoenberg suggested the three as the most deserving candidates to be assisted by the American Relief Fund for German and Austrian musicians.

In defraying the cost of the publication of his compositions Berg, however, was anxious that neither Schoenberg nor Webern should interpret his decision as being dictated by mere ambition to make a 'career', a word which, as we saw, he detested; and he wrote to both of them in almost identical terms. I quote from his more detailed letter to Schoenberg, of 4 August 1920:

> Dear Friend,
>
> I always wanted to tell you something or, better, to confess to you. You know that since the end of the war I have thought of publishing some things of mine. The *general reason* for this I need not explain to you. But now a *special reason* has arisen: I am compelled, as you also know, to find, so to speak, a means of existence. Since my return from the Berghof I receive *nothing* from my family, and the interest accruing from my wife's money, which grows less and less, means practically nothing these days. You can imagine − also from *the point of view of my material existence*− how welcome to me is the combination of *Anbruch* and *Verein*.

Berg then assures Schoenberg that he would have liked nothing better than to live a secluded life dedicated to composition and to writing about his former teacher and his music, but the struggle for existence forces him now to appear before the public as a composer. And to achieve this, it is necessary that

> my music should be readily available. Thanks to *you*, there have been plenty of performances of it during the last two years. All that is needed now is easy access to my compositions for all those who are interested in them, want to know them and possibly perform them.

Berg continues by saying that outside the Schoenberg circle the possibility of a performance does not exist, and it was this which decided him to publish his music at his own expense in order to strengthen his public position. It was unlikely that Hertzka would publish anything of his − he had not done it for the last ten years although he (Berg) had offered to pay for the engraving of his Piano Sonata. Even if Hertzka did accept one or the other of his compositions, it would not appear before the next spring and a whole season would thus be lost. Moreover, his position as an editor of the house journal of the Universal Edition would not permit him to have any other association with the publishing firm, for otherwise he would appear in a false light, particularly with the public.

Berg sold some old pictures and antiques in order to obtain the money with which to pay for the reprint of his Piano Sonata and the Four Songs, op. 2, both of which had come out before the war and were now re-issued with numerous revisions made by the composer after their first performances. Berg also paid for the publication of his String Quartet, op. 3, and the Four Clarinet Pieces, op. 5, and all the four works were brought out by the firm of

Tobias Haslinger in the autumn of 1920, to be later taken over by Universal Edition.

The spring of 1923 saw further clouds gathering on Berg's relationship with his former teacher. There was, for instance, the matter of the Chamber Concerto, of which Berg had not yet put the first note on paper but which he must have mentioned to Schoenberg. On 29 March Berg writes to his wife:

> The Schoenbergs were in good spirits. Nevertheless, it was not too pleasant because Schoenberg pestered [*penzte*] me constantly about the Chamber Concerto. He is *against* the piano in this combination. But he does not know that this is a *concerto*, not an ordinary octet.[11] And yet he wants me to tell him already how the piece is shaping, what character it will have; and all these questions are mixed with advice, admonitions and warnings, in short, he is pouring cold water on me. I am rather in fear of Easter Sunday when I am invited to lunch and tea there.

Then there was the manner in which Schoenberg, using his name and influence, tried to promote Berg's music in Germany. Berg felt that he set about it in the wrong way, as he told Helene in the same letter:

> However pleased I am with all this and however much it might help me (although it is precisely this which I doubt, since the people he is approaching are mostly without influence), I feel that I am being patronised by him, even forced, which is more annoying than pleasing. And he has an air of doing something special for me, instead of using a straighforward and effective method. To make myself clear:
>
> He recommends, for instance, my work for wind instruments – which as yet does not exist – to a Copenhagen Ensemble and already demands a fee for me, instead of recommending my orchestral pieces finished long ago, to one of the leading conductors in Germany and Austria. His name would be sufficient to get a performance. Or he could recommend my quartet to one of the many German teams who perform his and Webern's quartets, or to one of the many big German publishers who are very keen to have Schoenberg's works. Nor is he particularly interested in my *Wozzeck* negotiations with Hertzka because *Wozzeck* is not his.[12]

As to *Wozzeck*, Schoenberg's views of it were at first not at all favourable. In his reminiscences of Berg (1949),[13] he wrote that he was greatly surprised when this

> soft-hearted, timid young man had the courage to engage in a venture which seemed to invite misfortune: to compose *Wozzeck*, a drama of such

---

[11] See pp. 54-5.

[12] Berg was simultaneously negotiating about the publication of the opera with Universal Edition and the music publishing firm of G. Schirmer, New York.

[13] Reproduced in Redlich, *Alban Berg*, p. 328.

extraordinary tragedy that seemed forbidding to music. And even more: it contained scenes of every-day life which were contrary to the concept of opera which still lives on stylised costumes and conventionalised characters. He succeeded. *Wozzeck* was one of the greatest successes of opera.[14]

But this was said long *post festum*.

Ever since Berg began work on *Wozzeck*, Schoenberg was making discouraging remarks about it so that at the end of 1916 or beginning of 1917 he dropped the whole idea of an opera based on that subject and searched for new subjects among the Strindberg plays, toying also with the idea of composing an opera after Goethe's *Faust I*. As late as 1923 Schoenberg still entertained serious doubts about the opera; this becomes clear from a letter Berg wrote to his wife on 8 April:

> Schoenberg was again intolerable. He criticised everything about me: that I am still working on *Wozzeck* – 'very Karl Krausian, this eternal correcting', that 'I shouldn't imagine *Wozzeck* will have any success, it's too difficult' and worst of all that I have still not started with the chamber music for wind.

This seems to have been the last occasion when Schoenberg and Berg did not see eye to eye in artistic matters. From now onwards their intimate friendship remained untroubled and happy until Berg's death.

Schoenberg's doubts about *Wozzeck* may be partly explained by the fact that the opera contained scenes of ordinary every-day life which was contrary to his concept of opera, and sprang (as did Beethoven's indignation at the subjects of Mozart's *Don Giovanni* and *Così fan tutte*) from a moral premise. His view of opera was of a noble, idealistic stage-work untainted by any realism, as may be seen from his own *Erwartung, Die glückliche Hand* and, notably, *Moses und Aron*. It was only after his move to Berlin, a city where, in strongest contrast to conservative Vienna, a provocative, anti-establishment wind began to blow through the arts in the 1920s (Hindemith, Weill, Krenek, Brecht, Kaiser, Toller etc.) that Schoenberg modified his view of opera to some extent, as witness his one-act comic opera, *Von Heute auf Morgen* (1929), on a subject drawn from trivial every-day life.

Before dealing with the genesis of *Wozzeck* it will be better first to clear the decks and mention the two compositions Berg wrote after the completion of the opera. The first was the Chamber Concerto for Piano and Violin with Thirteen Wind Instruments, which Berg began in the summer of 1923 and completed on 9 February 1925, the exact date of the composer's fortieth birthday, though the instrumentation was not finished until 23 July. The idea

---

[14] This text was written in Schoenberg's own English.

for it derived partly from the wind music intended for the Copenhagen Ensemble mentioned in Berg's letter to his wife of 29 March 1923, and partly from a piano concerto he had been planning for a long time. Originally Berg thought of employing eight and later ten wind instruments, until he settled on thirteen for the accompanying orchestra. The work is dedicated to Schoenberg on the occasion of his fiftieth birthday in 1924, and in an 'Open Letter[15] to him he described it as a 'small monument to our twenty-year-old friendship'.

The second composition was a setting of the Storm verse, 'Schliesse mir die Augen beide', which Berg had already set before, as early as 1907. The new setting was Berg's first attempt to employ Schoenberg's twelve-note method of composition.[16] In a note accompanying Reich's publication, Berg stated that the two settings illustrated the development of music from 1900 to 1925, a development which had been observed by one publisher only – Emil Hertzka of Universal Edition. The two songs were dedicated to Hertzka on the occasion of the twenty-fifth anniversary of the foundation of this progressive firm (1926). The *Anbruch* marked this occasion with a special number, *25 Jahre Neue Musik*, with articles by Schoenberg, Krenek, Wellesz, Weill, Malipiero and others. Berg contributed 'Verbindliche Antwort auf eine unverbindliche Rundfrage', in which he tried to show how unreliable public opinion is in distinguishing the music of great composers (Hugo Wolf, Bruckner, Mahler, Debussy and Schoenberg) from that of minor lights.

Although it was *Wozzeck* which, after its first production in 1925, established Berg as one of the outstanding figures of contemporary music, there were two previous occasions that brought his name to the attention of a wider musical public. On 5 June 1923, during an Austrian Musikfestwoche in Berlin, the *Praeludium* and *Reigen* of his op. 6 were first heard under the direction of Webern. Webern's original intention was to do the complete work, but insufficient rehearsal time decided him to omit the last piece, the *Marsch*. The reception was on the whole very favourable though, strangely, some critics pointed to Debussy's influence in the music. (The first complete performance of op. 6 took place at Oldenburg in 1930).

Shortly afterwards, Berg achieved the first great triumph of his career. This was at the Festival of the International Society for Contemporary Music at Salzburg in August 1923,[17] when his String Quartet, op. 3, had its first public performance given by the Havemann String Quartet. In a letter to his wife of 3 August, Berg reports that at the end

there was almost frenetic general applause .... Quite an important success

---

[15] First published in the periodical, *Pult und Takstock*, Vienna, February 1925, and reproduced in Reich, *The Life and Work of Alban Berg*, pp. 143-8.

[16] Both settings were published by Willi Reich in *Die Musik* of February 1930, and have been available, with a Preface by H. F. Redlich, from Universal Edition since 1954.

[17] The Society was founded a year before (1922).

for Salzburg and for such a small chamber music work. The rest of the programme, rather surprisingly, fell off in comparison. The general opinion was that I carried off the prize that evening ... Everybody was most astonished [*paff*] that the quartet is $13\frac{1}{2}$ years old.[18]

In the same letter Berg mentions Hermann Scherchen, a conductor most closely associated with modern music, who seems to have suggested that Berg should make a suite from *Wozzeck* so as to interest people in the opera. The *Drei Bruchstücke* or *Three Fragments from Wozzeck* were first heard under Scherchen in Frankfort on 15 June 1924, when indeed considerable interest was aroused in the whole work, which by then had already been accepted by Erich Kleiber for Berlin.

We recall that Berg saw a Vienna production of Büchner's drama in May 1914, but not, as we now know, in the Franzos version but that of Paul Landau (see pp. 173-4). Berg was deeply shaken by the hero's fate, a creature abused and tormented by his superiors, and carried away by the tremendous emotional impact of certain individual scenes. He decided there and then on an opera based on the play and almost at once began with the adaptation of the text and some musical sketches, the first of which was for the 'Street' scene of Act II. The war seriously interrupted work on it which Berg seems to have resumed again in the summer of 1917. But progress was slow and it was not until mid-October 1921 that he completed the opera in short score and its instrumentation by the end of April 1922. A fair copy of the full score was finished towards the end of August. Allowing for the interruptions caused by the war, Berg worked altogether eight years on *Wozzeck*. Yet, with his obsessional sense of perfection he continued, as we gather from a letter to his wife of April 1923, to make improvements well into that year. Under his supervision his pupil, F. H. Klein, had finished the vocal score in June 1922, and with the financial help of Alma Maria Mahler,[19] to whom the opera is dedicated, he published it at his own expense, selling it direct on a subscription basis.

In the previous December Berg, accompanied by his pianist friend Steuermann, travelled to Frankfort and Darmstadt where the latter played the opera to the theatre *Intendanten*, but nothing came of it. Berg shied away from playing the score himself, partly because he was a bad pianist, and partly because he found it 'embarrassing to play my *own* work', as he informed

---

[18] At this same Festival William Walton's unpublished String Quartet received its first performance. Berg was so enthusiastic about it that he hailed Walton as the leader of the English atonal school. The composer later withdrew the quartet as he considered it immature and full of 'undigested Bartók and Schoenberg'.

[19] At first it was an American friend of Berg's sister, May Keller, who was to have paid for the printing.

Schoenberg. After these two abortive attempts to interest a theatre in his opera, he sent copies of the vocal score to a number of important German opera houses, yet with the same negative result. Schoenberg seems to have been right when he declared the work too difficult. With certain periodicals, however, Berg was more successful. Stein published in the *Anbruch* of January 1923 the first article on the opera, and in April there appeared in *Die Musik* a very favourable review by Ernst Viebig, accompanied by a reproduction of Marie's Lullaby in the supplement. Berg was highly satisfied with this review. Writing to Helene on 11 April he says that the author

> stresses the *purely human element* (the people) and not the individual fate ... And *everything* is so *true* as if I had told it to him myself. I had not thought it possible that a writer could discover by *himself* all that I intended with *Wozzeck* – morally, musically, theatrically etc.

It is amusing to note that the same periodical published about a year later (February 1924) a most hostile article by Emil Petschnig, entitled 'Atonales Opernschaffen', together with Berg's reply, 'Die musikalischen Formen meiner Oper "Wozzeck"'. The first ray of hope appeared in August 1923, when Berg was told that Erich Kleiber, who in the autumn was to become Generalmusikdirektor of the Berlin Staatsoper, had seen the vocal score, had liked the music very much and was considering a production of the opera. At that time the composer knew Kleiber only by name. In January 1924 Kleiber came to Vienna, and through Hertzka sent Berg an invitation for an 'audition' at which Berg's pupil, the pianist Ernst Bachrich, played the opera. Already after the second scene of the first act Kleiber was so impressed that he decided then and there to accept the opera for performance: 'It's settled! I am going to do the opera in Berlin, even if it costs me my job!' Less than two years later, on 14 December 1925, *Wozzeck* had its Berlin première.

Nowadays, when the opera has become a modern classic and when the technical advances made by orchestral players enable them to tackle infinitely more exacting scores successfully and with far fewer rehearsals, it seems incredible that the first night of *Wozzeck* was preceded by thirty-four orchestral and fourteen ensemble rehearsals – a measure of the work's difficulties, which were then unheard-of. (Kleiber, however, stated later that on the basis of entries in the Rehearsal Book of the Berlin Staatsoper, there had been only fifteen orchestral rehearsals including those for strings and wind separately.)[20] Berg came to Berlin twice – once in the middle of November and then again at the beginning of December. While the opera was in preparation and even some time before, cabals and machinations were

---

[20] *Theaterwelt V*, 1930, 10, quoted in Ernst Hilmar, *Wozzeck von Alban Berg. Entstehung-Erste Erfolge*. Vienna, 1975, p. 50.

set in motion against Kleiber by Pfitzner (who evidently could not forget Berg's article against him) and the nationalist press, for whom the opera was anathema, and not only on aesthetic grounds. This put the conductor on his mettle to achieve his best, since his position depended on the success of this production. There had also been a protracted crisis at the Staatsoper, culminating in the resignation in November of its Intendant, Max von Schillings, which rendered Kleiber's position more precarious still. 'Kleiber stands or falls with the outcome of the première', Berg wrote to his wife. He had unbounded admiration for this conductor:

> I would never have dreamed I could find such understanding as a musician and dramatist as I am finding with Kleiber. And of course this is transferred to the singers who are almost all first-rate. The sets (at least on paper) are magnificent, the production (and what production!) is really Kleiber's, and Hörth's[21] role in it has been reduced to a minimum. Everybody concerned is enthusiastic to the highest degree. I can confidently leave *everything* to Kleiber.

Wozzeck was Leo Schützendorf and Marie, Sigrid Johanson; the stage designer was the Greek painter, Panos Aravantinos.

As was to be expected, there were violent disturbances during the performance – hissing, whistling and even fisticuffs between the followers of the two opposite camps; and the same division applied to the critics. There were those of a progressive, forward-looking cast of mind who wrote in favour of the opera, and those belonging to the reactionary, nationalist press who poured ridicule and scorn on it.[22] After the première and a banquet given in honour of Berg and the artists, the composer and his pupil Adorno walked the streets of Berlin late into the night, Adorno trying to console the composer for what was to remain the greatest success of his career. 'If the opera pleases people so much', Berg said, 'then there must be something wrong with it'.[23] The Berlin production had for Berg the practical outcome that almost overnight, due to the royalties, his material circumstances improved.

There were altogether ten performances of *Wozzeck* in Berlin in the season 1925-6. The Prague Czech National Theatre followed suit in November 1926, when under Otokar Ostrcil it was given with singers who were so good that Berg was moved to write to Schoenberg on 10 November:

> The best thing of all in this production is the fact that when there is

[21] Chief producer of the Berlin Staatsoper.

[22] In 1926 Universal Edition published a little book, *Alban Berg's 'Wozzeck' und die Musikkritik*, in which all the various press notices were collected. The unfavourable ones make highly amusing reading today.

[23] Theodor W. Adorno, 'Alban Berg', in *Klangfiguren*, Frankfort, 1959, p. 122.

something to sing, it is really sung and for the most part by splendid voices. The sadness I felt since Berlin, that in the vocal writing I had made *impossible* demands, has now completely disappeared.

And he goes on to praise the singers for singing in accurate pitch, which he attributed to the 'amazing musicality of the Czech'. But it came only to three performances due to violent political scandals instigated by the nationalist press – one paper called the composer 'Aaron Berg, the Jew from Berlin' – which forced the authorities to intervene and cancel all further performances.

Next came Leningrad, where *Wozzeck* was staged in June 1927 in the composer's presence. This was at the height of Soviet Russia's liberal period, the so-called NEP or New Economic Policy when creative artists were permitted a large measure of freedom under the enlightened Commissar for Culture, A. V. Lunatcharsky, and when Western 'formalistic' music was welcomed with open arms. In an interview[24] Berg later declared that he had come to Leningrad in

> rather an anxious frame of mind, and I asked myself over and over again how the conductor and the singers – none too familiar with the latest operatic music – would find their way about in my complicated score. I was in for a most pleasant surprise. Dranishnikov, the conductor, had done excellent work. They had been studying the opera for six months. There *Wozzeck* was sung with real *bel canto*. Yes, a modern opera needs just as nice singing as *Trovatore*!

Present-day singers of *Wozzeck* have fully vindicated Berg's demand.

It was not until the Oldenburg production of March 1929, under Johannes Schuler, that it was proved that the opera could be performed with far fewer rehearsals than in Berlin and without upsetting the normal repertory. Moreover, to enable smaller theatres such as that at Oldenburg to stage *Wozzeck*, Berg asked Erwin Stein to arrange the orchestral score for triple instead of the prescribed quadruple wind, which was first performed at Oldenburg. This is the so-called 'reduced version'. Stein made an arrangement also for chamber orchestra which was used at Aachen in 1930 but which was subsequently withdrawn by the Universal Edition. Apart from a large number of German theatres, *Wozzeck* was given, up to Berg's death, in Vienna (1930), Amsterdam (1930), Philadelphia and New York (1931), Brussels (1932) and London, in a BBC concert under Adrian Boult, at the Queen's Hall on 14 March 1934. In this context, it is worth mentioning also that Covent Garden, then under the direction of Thomas Beecham and Geoffrey Toye, accepted the opera for a production fixed for 30

[24] Reproduced in Reich, *The Life and Work of Alban Berg*, p. 69.

April 1935.[25] The BBC, having already done a concert version, was to have been responsible for the musical side, and Toye, in the hope of reducing the costs still further, approached some of the large German opera houses (Berlin, Frankfort and Vienna) to purchase from them the costumes and scenery of *Wozzeck*, as he had done in the case of Weinberger's *Schwanda, the Bagpiper*. He also got in touch with John Christie about sharing the producer, Carl Ebert, who was in charge of the 1935 season at Glyndebourne. Ebert had produced *Wozzeck* in Germany and, as Toye was given to understand by Berg, had pleased the composer very much. But nothing came of Toye's project since by 1935 – two years after the Nazis had come to power – all German theatres had destroyed their scenic material. The Berlin Intendant, in his reply to Toye, put it diplomatically by saying that the scenery had already been stowed away, while Clemens Krauss wired back to the effect that, apart from the fact that the sets were not transportable, they were needed for a production at the Vienna Staatsoper in that season. This was another diplomatic excuse, for in view of the prevalent political situation in Central Europe a production of *Wozzeck* in Vienna was no longer possible. (In the end Covent Garden did not stage the opera until 1952, with Kleiber conducting.)

In this context a fact little known outside Italy must be mentioned. This was the first Italian production of *Wozzeck* in the midst of the war when Mussolini was still in power. To the rest of the world who only knew of the total ban imposed in Hitler's Germany on what was called 'entartete Kunst' and 'Kulturbolschewismus' – and Berg's opera was in the eyes of the Nazis 'degenerate art' *par excellence* – this production must appear as one of the most extraordinary ventures undertaken in the name of art. But this was not quite so. For, in marked contrast to Germany, cultural and artistic life in fascist Italy was allowed considerable freedom, the argument of the authorities running along the lines that contemporary, advanced works such as plays and operas appealed only to a comparatively small minority of the population, the intellectual and artistic élite, and that it was much more preferable to please these circles than to prohibit the performance of works which, they felt, presented no risk or danger to the regime. (This did not, however, apply to the mass media like radio and films, and, in addition, with the signing of the Steel Pact between Hitler and Mussolini, works of Jewish authors, playwrights and composers were wholly banned.) This explains the fact that a number of music festivals were held under Mussolini (e.g. the *Maggio musicale* and the Venice Biennale) with modern works in the programme. Thus in October/November 1942 a short festival was given at the Teatro Reale dell'Opera of Rome in which operas by Busoni, Malipiero

---

[25] In a letter to Malipiero of 27 December 1934, Berg, with great joy, informs him of this London production as evidence of 'my success abroad'.

Respighi, Dallapiccola and Petrassi were staged, among them *Wozzeck* on 3 November. The title-role was sung by Tito Gobbi, Marie was Gabriella Gatti and the Doctor, Italo Tajo. The conductor was Tullio Serafin. The press and a select audience accorded the work a most enthusiastic reception. (I am indebted for this information to the Roman critic Fedele D'Amico.)

We return to the year 1926. Apropos of the first Vienna performance of the *Three Wozzeck Fragments*, it was during the rehearsals that Berg made some interesting observations on the question of instrumentation and dynamics of which he informed Schoenberg on 13 March. The gist of his letter is that there cannot be absolute certainty about the instrumentation in relation to the dynamics, which have to be adapted to the particular acoustics of the locality in which a work is played. In the Vienna rehearsals Berg found that the effect of the strings in relation to the wind was the opposite to that in Berlin. Moreover, a composer has to consider the seating arrangements and the position of the orchestra and whether it plays in a theatre or a concert hall. Berg closes by saying: 'I really do not know any longer how to handle the dynamics. For instance the alterations which I made especially for Prague, I had to cross out again for Vienna.'

It was at Oldenburg that Berg, in order to assist the audience in their appreciation of the music, gave his first lecture on *Wozzeck*, which he illustrated at the piano as well as with the singers and orchestra. This lecture, which he repeated at a number of German theatres in the following three years, was first reproduced in Redlich's book.[26] In 1930 Berg wrote his *Praktische Anweisungen zur Einstudierung des 'Wozzeck'*, which accompanied the performing material of the opera.[27] In the same year he brought out his *'Wozzeck'-Bemerkungen* which, except for a new introduction, is identical with the 'Pro Domo' section of his article, 'Das Opernproblem', in the *Neue Musikzeitung* of September 1928.

[26] *Alban Berg*, pp. 311-27.
[27] First published in Reich, *Alban Berg ...*, Vienna, 1937, pp. 166-72.

SEVEN

BERG AT THE HEIGHT OF HIS CAREER
1926-34

In the autumn of 1925, when *Wozzeck* was about to go into rehearsal in Berlin, Berg began the Lyric Suite for string quartet which he finished in the, for him, comparatively short time of a year. In the summer of 1926, when it was nearing completion, Berg wrote from Trahütten a highly interesting letter to Schoenberg (13 July) which throws some light on the way in which he assimilated the twelve-note method of composition and on his view of other, non-dodecaphonic, music. He begins by saying that they would have to leave Trahütten so as to make room for other members of the Nahowski family, and then continues:

> For this reason I work with great pressure, even nervousness and in a different manner from usual, namely, simultaneously at different movements (of the Lyric Suite), merely sketching out some portions in order to get down on paper as much as possible of the *whole*, leaving the completion for Vienna where actual composing is difficult for me. I think I have already told you that it will be a suite for string quartet in six movements of a lyrical character ... I certainly hope to finish it in the autumn.

> About the experiences I had while working on it (and also before) with the 'composition with 12 notes',[1] I permit myself to outline them on the enclosed sheet ... (see p. 125, 18n). Slowly I am finding my way into this mode of composition which is a great consolation for me. For it would have grieved me immensely if I had been denied the possibility to express myself in *such a manner*. For I know that, apart from personal ambition (and idealism) one will compose in *this style* after all the piping and whistling [*Gedudel*] of the ISCM have long disappeared into limbo. All one needs to do, if one does not think of the greatest: you, Mahler and the classics, is to hear, one after the other, the famous *Pacific* (Honegger) and *Till Eulenspiegel*, in order to see clearly in what state this *international* music finds itself.

Berg completed the Lyric Suite in October 1926 and dedicated it to

---

[1] The Storm Song, no. 2.

Zemlinsky, from whose Lyric Symphony he quoted a passage in the fourth movement.[2] Its first performance took place in Vienna on 8 January 1927, with the Kolisch String Quartet, an ensemble founded in 1921 under the name 'Neues Wiener Streichquartet', which was closely associated with the music of the Schoenberg school.[3] The work was received with great acclaim, the public applauding after every movement. In 1928, at Hertzka's suggestion, Berg made an arrangement for string orchestra of the three middle movements which was first played in Berlin on 31 January 1929; the conductor was Jascha Horenstein, much esteemed by Berg. At the time of the Lyric Suite Berg intended also to compose choral settings of poems by Pierre Ronsard to whom Franz Werfel, the husband of Alma Maria Mahler, had drawn his attention, but this did not materialise. Berg was to set verses by another great Fench poet, Charles Baudelaire, three years later in his concert aria, *Der Wein*, but secretly he had already resorted to Baudelaire in a suppressed setting in the finale of the Lyric Suite of 1926. And this brings us to an important event in Berg's private life which created such a sensation in musical circles when it was first brought to light in 1977 and which has a crucial bearing on the composition of the Lyric Suite as a work of an exclusively autobiographical character.

In May 1925 the Three Fragments from *Wozzeck* were performed, under Zemlinsky at the Prague Festival of the ISCM which Berg attended. On that occasion he stayed, possibly through the intervention of the Werfels, at the home of Herbert Fuchs-Robettin, a wealthy industrialist whose wife, Hanna, was the sister of Franz Werfel, Alma Maria Mahler's third husband. Berg, at the age of forty, fell passionately in love with Hanna – it appears to have been a case of elective affinities – an affair which lasted, at least on his part, until his death ten years later. How it all began and what consequences it was to have for Berg's creative life will be related anon. First, let us read a letter which berg wrote to Hanna as late as October 1931,[3a] that is six years after their relationship started. Apart from the unabated passionate ardour it expresses, it also sheds light on the psychological 'split' Berg suffered through this affair, and on his life with his wife. He writes:

[2] Alexander von Zemlinsky (1871-1942) was for a time Schoenberg's teacher and the brother of Schoenberg's first wife, Mathilde. He was a post-Mahlerian of little individuality but of great skill and technical refinement, and achieved passing fame with his seven stage-works, of which *kleider machen Leute* (Vienna, 1910) and *Der Kreidekreis* (Zurich, 1933) are perhaps his most successful. Berg, who intended in 1920 to write a book on Zemlinsky, considered his music to be of a 'chaste beauty and reserved'. On 9 July, announcing to Schoenberg his intention to write an article on Zemlinsky for the *Anbruch*, in preparation for his book, he declared: 'It *must* be said once and for all that here is one of the masters living hidden from the public, a composer to whom the officially accredited "masters" Pfitzner, Schreker and the whole crew of teutonic and nordic composers cannot hold a candle.'

[3] Its leader, Rudolf Kolisch, was the brother of Schoenberg's second wife, Gertrud.

[3a] Reprinted in Newsletter No. 6, June 1978, *International Alban Berg Society*. pp. 2-3.

Hanna,

I am using the opportunity of having transmitted to you a letter to write you once again after a long, long time. I have longed for this opportunity. More than ever! For in the last few months I have been seized, more an more, by a terrible fear: that you might believe that my love for you has cooled off, that during the years of 'resignation' the passion dominating my whole being might have turned into indifference.

That could never happen. For feelings like these which can only be measured in terms of eternity cannot have an end. This will never happen. You must believe me – and should months and years pass by without our seeing each other and without your hearing from me more than such pitiful letters as the one I'm just writing.

Not a day passes, not half a day, not a night when I do not think of you, not a week when I am not suddenly flooded by yearning, which submerges all my thoughts and feelings and wishes in an ardour which is not weaker by a breath than that of May 1925 – only still shadowed by a grief which since that time rules me more and more, and which, for a long time now, has made me into a double, or better said, a play-acting person. For you must know: everything that you may hear of me, and perhaps read about me, pertains, insofar as it is not completely false – as, for example, in a Zurich programme: 'A completely happy domesticity with which his wife has surrounded him, allows him to create without disturbance' – pertains to what is only peripheral.

Berg then elaborates on his 'double' life and continues:

But believe me, Hanna (and now I can finally address you properly: *one* and *only eternal love*), all this pertains only to the exterior person, the one I have been forced to present myself as to my fellow human beings and whom (thank God!) you have never known and who (only) in order to characterize him in *some* way might for a time be fulfilled with the joys of motoring, but could never compose *Lulu*. That I am, however, doing this may be proof to you that the other person (and now I can speak again in the first person), that *I* still exist! When I work and take hold of your pen [Hanna had made him a present of a golden fountain-pen], at that moment *I* am here, and am also with you, as I am with myself when I am with you in thought ...

This is one of the fourteen love letters Berg is said to have written to Hanna Fuchs in the ten years of their friendship, and which are now in the possession of her daughter Dorothea. The chief go-betweens in this secret affair were the Werfels, who apparently delivered Berg's letters to Hanna, on their occasional visits to Prague (Werfel was born in Prague), while her letters to the composer were sent to the address of one of his pupils (Fritz Mahler).

It is highly interesting to read what Berg wrote to his wife on the two occasions (May and November 1925) on which he stayed with the Fuchs-Robettins. On 11 May he tells her that he could not help enjoying the 'matter-of-course luxury' ('*selbstverständlichen Luxus*') of this life in which every step he makes, he makes by car – 'and what a car_'.

> My hosts spoil me; room with hot water, glorious view, Roger-Gallet soap, Venetian blinds so that you can sleep with the windows open at night ... At eight o'clock a knock on the door and in burst two children, who will not be satisfied unless they can see the 'famous' composer. A seven-year-old boy and a girl (Dorothea) of 3½. Very sweet. I found it most refreshing.

On 11 November he refers, in an ostensibly harmless manner, to Hanna or Mopinka saying that

> it goes really against my grain to have to 'reassure' you about me and Mopinka. Perhaps I will just say that faithfulness is one of my chief qualities (I am sure I must have been a dog in a previous incarnation and perhaps shall be in a later one, but in any case, to start from the beginning, may I die of distemper if I ever sinned against faithfulness!) Faithfulness towards you, and also towards myself, Music, Schoenberg (and *he* makes this really hard for me) ... So: being of such a conservative disposition, how could I help, my darling, be anything but faithful to you and remain faithful for ever? Believe me as I believe the same of you ...

Berg was unable to finish the letter during the day, so he waited till the evening and added the following in bed. He returns once again to the topic of his hosts and concludes:

> Once you meet these people, you'll like them just as much as I do. It is really friendliness and a warm heart [*Herzlichkeit*] without any reserve. That's why, that's the only reason why I am so fond of them. And you will feel the same.
> You know, my darling, why I am making so much of this. Not because it's so terrific here (my thoughts are already in Berlin) [for the preparation of the first production of *Wozzeck*], but to stop you worrying about Mopinka's charms!

Berg's repeated emphasis on his 'faithfulness', with which he concealed from his wife his true feeling for Hanna, tallies with the picture of a husband who has committed an infidelity already in *thought*. Although he persisted until the end of his life in the juvenile pet-names with which he addressed *her* and signed *himself*, something fundamental in his relationship to Helene changed after May 1925. It is not an uncommon phenomenon that husbands, after a number of years of married life, even happily married life, fall in love with women younger than their wives – Alban and Helene were of exactly the same age – and are often prompted to solve this triangular situation by separation or divorce. But Berg was not one of them. He was morally a highly responsible man and was bound to consider the effect such a step would have on Helene who, like him, was highly strung, sensitive and vulnerable. Besides, he needed her as his spiritual companion, remained strongly attached to her and wanted, like herself, to preserve before the world the fiction of an idyllic domestic life. Hence his total secretiveness about his love affair with Hanna of which not even his closest friends, except the Werfels and one or two other people, had the slightest knowledge.

But did this double life, this play-acting, really weigh so heavily on Berg as his letter to Hanna suggests? Doubt is thrown on this by another person who knew of the affair from its very inception, and who was partly, though indirectly, involved in it. This was Theodor W. Adorno, who was a pupil of Berg's at the time when the composer's relationship with Hanna, a relationship that presumably remained platonic, began. In October 1955 Adorno wrote his *Aufzeichnungen über Berg* which contained a long section about Berg's love-life, but he stipulated that it must not be published until after the death of all persons directly or indirectly involved in the affair. This section has now been published[3b] and reads as follows:

Berg said about himself that in his life he had really never known the full bliss of sexuality as he imagined it – this, despite his extraordinary handsomeness and despite the fact that women were greatly attracted to Berg, notably since he became famous. He derived a certain pleasure in setting other people erotically on one another. For this purpose he once invited me together with a very charming singer who was considerably older than I and made us drunk. He himself had many love affairs which ended, however, always unhappily, in a sense the unhappy end was 'composed' into them, and one had the feeling that from their inception these affairs formed a part of his creative apparatus, that they were, as in the Austrian joke, desperate but not serious.[3c] At the time when I was studying with him the affair with Hanna, Werfel's sister, was taking its course. He used me as his *postillon d'amour* for which my frequent Prague visits to my friend, Hermann Grab, had to be the pretext. I was a clumsy player of this role, never spoke to Hanna alone, yet the whole thing was so openly arranged that her husband became suspicious. From the very beginning it was a hopeless affair because it was, on the one hand, burdened with such intense emotion [*Pathos*], and on the other, Berg did

---

[3b] 'Statt eines Nachworts zur Kontroverse' by Heinz-Klaus Metzger and Rainer Riehn in 'Alban Berg/Kammermusik II', *Musik-Konzept* 9, July 1979, pp. 8-10.

[3c] The full joke runs: Question: What is the chief difference between the Germans and the Austrians? Answer: for the Germans a situation is serious but not desperate – for the Austrians it is desperate but not serious.

not want to leave his wife nor Hanna her husband and her two children. He treated the matter with an immensely mysterious secrecy [*Geheimniskrämerei*], ostensibly not to make his wife aware of it, but really, perhaps, because he greatly enjoyed secrecy. Within this system of secrecy he made me carry out all kinds of functions. On the very first day he told me of the whole affair. The dedication he inscribed in my copy of the score of the Three Fragments from *Wozzeck* reads: 'the fragments of your Alban Berg' which referred to the fact that forced to renunciation he considered himself as fragmented [*zerbrochen*].

Adorno then goes on to say that the Lyric Suite *was* programme music with a secret programme, whereas in all his published writings he had always deliberately denied it a programmatic character, except for calling it a 'latent opera'. He further remarks that the *ländler* theme in 3/8 time of the Andante amoroso symbolized Hanna's husband and the third theme the two children. In this, as Berg's annotated score for Hanna proves (see p. 128), he was wrong, just as he was wrong in calling the girl the elder of the children. Adorno confirms that Berg's cryptograms – the musical initials of the composer's name (*A*lban *B*erg and that of his *innamorata. H*anna *F*uchs) which appear for the first time in the Andante (bars 56-8) – related to his predilection for number mysticism and astrology. 'Since he knew', Adorno concludes, 'how I felt about these things he scarcely ever admitted them to me openly. If Helene today calls up his spirit in seances, Berg would have presumably given his consent to these doings'. Incidentally, it is well within the bounds of possibility that in his secret programme of the Lyric Suite Berg may have thought also of Helene whose name begins with the same letter as Hanna's, but thought of her, inevitably, in terms of an antagonist who could not be represented in the music. As for Hanna, Adorno, unfortunately, tells us nothing about her. We do not know what kind of woman she was and whether her feelings for Berg were as ardent and lasting as were his for her. Was it likely, and Adorno confirms our strong doubts, that she would be prepared to sacrifice her social position as the wife of a wealthy industrialist and mother of two young children, to what she may well have regarded as an uncertain future with Berg, in spite of his growing fame; to say nothing of the scandal such a step was bound to evoke in the bourgeois *milieu* to which both the Fuchs-Robettins and the Bergs belonged? Moreover, Adorno speaks of Berg's love affairs as being a 'part of his creative apparatus' and says that, according to the Austrian joke, they were 'desperate but not serious'. What with this and the further light thrown on the affair by Helene's correspondence with Alma Maria Mahler, excerpts from which we shall quote presently, it would seem that Berg needed this experience as a creative stimulus. Imaginary suffering, unhappiness, a 'submission to fate', were after all one of the mainsprings of his creative process.

Berg's affair would not have such paramount interest for us, were it not that it found its strong and immediate echo in two compositions of his – the *second* setting of the Storm poem, 'Schliesse mir die Augen beide', and the Lyric Suite. The song has a special musical significance since it represents the composer's first attempt at twelve-note composition and exactly coincides with the beginning of his love affair with Hanna. It dates from the summer of 1925, soon after Berg's first meeting with her and consists of 20 bars, *i.e.* 2 x 10 bars, 10 being Hanna's 'number' in Berg's numerological symbolism. Moreover, it is based on a note-series beginning with F(uchs) and ending on H(anna), which is the German nomenclature for the English B. There is irony in the fact that Berg's *first* setting of the Storm verses was written for Helene in the spring-time of their love (1907), and that his first letter to her is headed by this poem.

The Lyric Suite came into being solely through Berg's love for Hanna and represents a personal document of the first order. More than that: it is a psychograph of an overwhelming erotic experience, the key to which has now been discovered. For Berg presented Hanna with a copy of the printed score that is studded with annotations for the inner programme of the music. This copy bears the dedication:

> For my Hanna – for whom, despite the official dedication [to Alexander von Zemlinsky] every note of this work was written. May it be a small monument of a great love.

The work is, significantly, based on the same series as the second Storm song and its third movement contains a cell-motive of four notes representing the musical initials of the names of Alban Berg and Hanna Fuchs. Berg's annotated copy is now in the possession of Hanna's daughter who lives in the United States and permitted George Perle access to it. It will be discussed in detail in the chapter dealing with the Lyric Suite.

Let us now turn to Helene, the third actor in this triangular drama. Thanks to a collection of letters[3d] from the Bergs to Alma Mahler-Werfel, it is now possible to obtain glimpses of that complex, highly sensitive and withdrawn woman who was Berg's wife, and who speaks here about herself and her relationship with her husband with a frankness and directness that must come as a surprise after the marked reticence and reserve she preserved as a public figure. From a letter of 2 August 1930 it becomes clear that by that time Helene was already deeply interested in spiritualism and was

---

[3d] This forms part of a much larger collection of private papers of Frau Mahler, consisting of over 5,000 items including letters by numerous leading figures on the artistic and cultural scene in the first half of the twentieth century. This collection was donated by Frau Mahler's daughter, Anna, to the University of Pennsylvania Library, and the section containing the Berg letters was made accessible to George Perle, who published them under the title *Mein geliebtes Almschi*, in the Newsletter No. 7, Autumn 1978, *International Alban Berg Society*.

reading books about occultism. It seems that under the influence of the mystic poet, Hildegard Jone, an intimate friend of Webern's who set a number of her verses to music (songs and the two late Cantatas), Helene had turned to occult science. After Alban's death she communicated with his spirit. Thus she told Frau Mahler, 'her beloved Almschi', in a letter of June 1936, that Alban would come regularly to the *Waldhaus* (the Bergs' villa in Carinthia), and tap out his messages to her on a table. He comes regularly in the morning, at noon and in the evening. Nothing more can happen to her. She knows that life here is only an illusion and that a 'real' life will begin in the beyond with him. Her love for Almschi also belongs to 'reality', that is, eternity.

In a letter of April 1936 from Barcelona where she attended the first performance of Berg's Violin Concerto, Helene defends herself against Frau Mahler's reproaches that in her marriage she 'sinned against the Holy Ghost', by attaching so much importance to trivialities of the household – going shopping, calculating and haggling, and returning home heavily burdened after a trip to the market which irritated and saddened Alban. How could Almschi believe that the price of butter and potatoes could suddenly have been for her so important that she irritated Alban by her enthusiastic interest in such things? No one had such need of comfort as Alban, all these seemingly laughable trivialities for which she is now reproached, had a purpose: to create the environment that this great and valuable man and artist needed for his work. True, he worried about her health which was never robust, and it was because of this concern that he asked Almschi to influence her not to be so frugal. She tried, except during their good years, to save a penny in order to afford Alban many small pleasures – a visit to the cinema or the coffee-house.

Alban's ever more difficult life during the past two years, with relatives ever more boldly and oppressively trying to fleece him, his many doubts whether he would have to give up his car and the Waldhaus, his despair over artistic life when so many, who had once been loyal friends, now distanced themselves from him, the grinding work – in the last two years he had not *once* allowed himself to take time off for recreation; about all this she will remain silent. That is a chapter in itself and she must come to terms with it, in the realization that it was his unalterable destiny and that he endured it. The good Lord loved him and took him, so that he should no longer have such a difficult time of it.

From an excerpt from a letter of 28 February 1936 we learn that Helene knew of Alban's love affair with Hanna. She implies that the reality of it was far less than the fantasy and that as an artist he needed to create romantic illusions for himself – Adorno's 'creative apparatus'. But he kept his poetic passion within *those* boundaries which he himself wanted. Alban himself invented obstacles and thereby created the romanticism which he required.

Perhaps it was also subconscious caution: he didn't want too close an association with this woman (Helene avoids mentioning Hanna by name), as he imagined her in the unheard-of florescence of his artist's fantasy, for fear of disappointment. For he was spoilt both mentally and physically. He avoided her.

Helene then relates two incidents to prove how he evaded Hanna who with her children sometimes spent her holidays at Velden, a little Carinthian town in the neighbourhood of the Waldhaus. It all comes, Helene continues, to one thing – flight from reality. Only in this way could the Lyric Suite have come to be. She must therefore acknowledge the sense of all that has happened, and remain silent. And therefore she can also say that there is no trace of bitterness in her, only emotion and melancholy. Nothing at all can ever dim her love for him. Helene will some day stand with Hanna before God.

Are we to take this last letter at its face value or as an attempt to conceal a wife's jealousy of a rival for Alban's love, even from her dearest and most intimate friend Alma? Jealousy Helene must have felt, and this has been linked with her singularly strange behaviour over the manuscript of the Lyric Suite which we shall relate presently, her suppression of Act III of *Lulu* and her initial total aversion to the Wedekind dramas in which she may have seen an allegory of the love of Alban for Hanna in that of Alwa for Lulu in the opera. More will be said about the latter point in the chapter dealing with *Lulu*. Let us now turn to the Lyric Suite.

For some considerable time it was assumed that its manuscript was in the possession of Zemlinsky, the official dedicatee of the work, or his heirs. But this proved a false assumption. Berg had given it to Hanna! Helene knew of this, probably from Frau Mahler, and in the Barcelona letter (19 April 1936) to her she wrote that Hanna Fuchs can keep the autograph score and, with what seems like irony, added that she can place it on her piano where everyone can see it. But after Hanna's death it must go to the Alban Berg Stiftung[3e] to which the composer's books and manuscripts will also belong. This was Alban's wish. (Helene had evidently received a message from the beyond.) Frau Mahler later persuaded her sister-in-law to cede the manuscript to Helene which was done through the Catholic priest, Johannes Höllensteiner, a friend of Alma's. Helene's subsequent behaviour is nothing if not extraordinary and can only be understood as a jealous widow's efforts to prevent public knowledge that she had had a serious rival for her husband's affection to whom he had given the autograph. There is no need to go into the involved details of the story. Suffice it to say that at first Frau Berg pretended that the manuscript was in the hands of the Zemlinskys, yet when Frau Zemlinsky, in a letter to the Universal Edition of early 1962, firmly denied this, she simulated alarm about its having been lost, when in fact it

[3e] This was not founded by Helene until 1968.

had been in *her* possession for some time. She told the same story to the musicologist and author of a fine book on Berg, H. F. Redlich, and trying to cover up the truth, she asked him to locate the whereabouts of the manuscript. When Redlich questioned what he considered a fictional account, Helene repeated it but with a new twist, in order to explain how the autograph had come into her ownership. It is now deposited with the Music Section of the Österreichische National Bibliothek and known as 'Studienpartitur' (Frau Berg's name) since Berg used it at rehearsals of the Lyric Suite.

After the Lyric Suite Berg began to scan the literary horizon for another suitable subject for an opera. Thus in early 1927 he showed interest in *Rheinische Rebellen* by Arnold Bronnen and particularly in the anti-war drama, *Das Grabmal des unbekannten Soldaten* (1924), by the French playwright, Paul Raynal, which he considered to be not only one of the best war plays but 'real theatre and full of poetry. For some time it tempted me very much to make an opera of it. What do you think?' he asked Schoenberg on 10 January 1927. Another drama that greatly appealed to him was the famous Yiddish play, *The Dybbuk or Between Two Worlds*, by Salomon Ansky – a study in demonic possession of the living by the dead dealing with the Hassidic doctrine of pre-ordained relationship. But he gave this idea up, as he felt that this was a subject that could be treated successfully only by a Jewish composer acquainted with Hassidic legend and ritual.[4]

While none of these plans matured, there was, however, one which Berg had been seriously considering since January 1926, almost immediately after the Berlin production of *Wozzeck*, and on which he worked, including some musical sketches, up to about the middle of 1928. This was the dramatic fairy-tale, *Und Pippa tanzt* (1906), by Gerhart Hauptmann, whom Berg had much admired in his youth but for whom his enthusiasm later cooled off – possibly under the influence of Karl Kraus. Nevertheless this play, which is set among Silesian glass-blowers, and was frequently given at the Vienna Burgtheater, strongly attracted Berg, for reasons which we shall mention in a moment. Yet in the autumn of 1927 he was also toying with the idea for a *Lulu* after Wedekind's *Erdgeist* and *Die Büchse der Pandora*, and could not come to a clear-cut decision. In this undecided frame of mind he wrote to Adorno on 30 November asking for his advice:[5]

I have decided to start next spring with the composition of an opera. I have two projects *one* of which I shall *most certainly* carry out. But the question is, which of the two. For this reason I would like to have your

---

[4] Personal communication from Willi Reich. This play, however, was turned into an opera of the same name (Milan, 1934) by a non-Jewish Italian composer, Lodovico Rossi.

[5] Adorno, *Alban Berg*, p. 33. Incidentally, there are some Schoenberg sketches dating from about 1905 for an opera on Hauptmann's play.

advice: either *Und Pippa tanzt* or *Lulu* (by conflating *Erdgeist* and *Die Büchse der Pandora* into a three-act libretto of six or seven scenes; please use the utmost discretion about this). What do you think? As I shall certainly compose one of them (or both), I need a decision as to *which* of the two (or which first).

Berg's request to Adorno to preserve the utmost discretion about his plan to write an opera based on the two Wedekind plays may have been prompted by serious doubts entertained in the composer's circle of friends about the immorality (see p. 217) as well as the musicability of the text. Adorno strongly advised him to do the Wedekind opera, but also suggested *Der Turm* (1925) by Hofmannsthal; yet Berg, much biased against the Austrian poet and playwright by Kraus, would not hear of it. Until the spring of 1928 he felt more inclined towards the Hauptmann play, and was already thinking of how to adapt it for his purposes, intending, for instance, to telescope the third and fourth acts into a single act and thus remove what he considered the dramatic weakness of this part of the play. He even bought an ocarina, a primitive wind instrument played by one of Hauptmann's characters (Michel Hellriegel) in order to study its possibilities, just as he previously did with the accordion used in the 'Tavern' scene of Act III of *Wozzeck*. Berg also started some musical sketches for *Pippa*, evidence of which is his entry in May 1928 in the guest-book of Alfred Kalmus (a nephew of Hertzka and a director of Universal Edition) which I reproduce with the late Dr Kalmus's permission:

Example 1

The 'Pippa' motive at once recalls the 'Erdgeist' fourths in *Lulu*, which would suggest that Berg resorted for his opera to musical material already used in the abortive *Pippa*. Anxious as Berg seemed to be to set the Hauptmann play, in the event nothing came of it, for the playwright's publishers made such exorbitant financial conditions for the acquisition of the composing rights, that both Berg and Universal Edition found them unacceptable. As Berg wrote to Schoenberg (10 April 1928), they demanded fifty per cent of the royalties, twenty per cent of the sale of the libretto and five per cent of the sale of the vocal score.

It was perhaps no coincidence that, after having had to renounce *Pippa*, the composer turned to Wedekind's two Lulu tragedies. For there are striking parallels between the two subjects, parallels which, consciously or otherwise, Berg must have felt himself and which struck a deep chord in him. The heroine in both Hauptmann and Wedekind is a hunted, persecuted creature, and, as we know from *Wozzeck* and the Violin Concerto, this exerted a magnetic attraction on Berg, allowing him to identify with her to a most remarkable degree. Pippa is the incarnation of pure female beauty who is surrounded by five men, each of whom tried to assail her, to snatch at her – which is shown symbolically in the fact that she has to dance with each. Lulu is the incarnation of the pure sex instinct who, like Pippa, cannot help attracting men. Pippa is eventually crushed by an elemental instinctive force which is the sexual lust of the bestial old glass-blower Huhn, whose counterpart in Wedekind is the lust murderer, Jack the Ripper. Both plays illustrate a fight to death between the sexes. But in Hauptmann the violence is toned down, romanticised, as it were, and embedded in the atmosphere of a fairy-tale, in marked contrast to the stark realism of Wedekind's *Grand Guignol*. *Lulu* is certainly a masterpiece of its kind, but it is my conviction that the deep romantic colours of the Hauptmann play would have lent themselves more readily to musical treatment than the stark Lulu tragedy, not to mention the fact that in certain places of the drama Hauptmann demands dancing, singing and music. Moreover, being a fairy-tale, with all that this implies, *Pippa* is a timeless drama, whereas the Wedekind plays are too closely geared to their time and place – Germany in the late nineteenth century – and to sexual problems which in our age are no longer regarded as problems. Moreover, erotic demonism belongs to the literary climate of the *fin de siècle*, the period when Wedekind wrote the plays, and seems to us rather antiquated. Seen from the standpoint of the modern spectator, there hangs about the Wedekind text the air of the dated and *passé* which productions that move the time of the action forward to the 1920s or 1930s cannot conceal and which is only redeemed by Berg's inspired score. And yet I feel that with *Pippa* Berg would have achieved a lyricism warmer, more intense and more pervasive than is the case in *Lulu*.

In passing, the question may be asked why it was that in the autumn of 1926 Berg was so strongly attracted by dramas that have as their larger theme the theme of sexual attraction and sexual destruction in common. I offer the following suggestion. It seems that there is a link between Berg's choice of a sex drama and his love affair with Hanna Fuchs, begun two years before this choice. This love affair, whether platonic or otherwise, whether more a thing of fantasy than of reality – a 'romantic illusion' as Helene Berg called it – was, nevertheless, a deep and lasting experience for the composer: it made him ponder and reflect on the mystery of erotic love in both its positive (life-enhancing) and negative (life-destroying) aspects. And it was this, I believe, that aroused in Berg the idea of choosing for an operatic subject a drama that deals with those aspects of sexual relationships. This in no way ignores the profound impression which indeed may have sown the first seed, when Berg at the age of twenty saw *Pandora's Box* in Vienna in May 1905.

Wedekind having died in 1918, Berg entered into negotiations for the composing rights for the two Lulu dramas with the playwright's widow, whom he met in Berlin in October 1928, on the occasion of a revival of *Wozzeck*. Frau Wedekind made financial conditions far more acceptable than those demanded by Hauptmann's publisher for *Pippa*, yet even before coming to an agreement with her, Berg had already started work on the libretto. Its conflation of the two original plays may have been suggested to the composer by Wedekind's own single-play version in five acts of 1913. But progress was slow. As Berg explained to Schoenberg in a letter of 9 July 1928, nearly two years had gone by during which he had written nothing new, and this made it hard for him to get into his stride again. True, he was making an orchestral version of his Seven Early Songs which had their first performances on 6 November (soloist, Claire Born; conductor, Robert Heger), but this was undemanding creative work. In the same letter he complained that his asthma was again troubling him and slowing down *Lulu*, whereupon Schoenberg advised him to spend some time in the south. Berg replied that he was contemplating doing this in the autumn or winter, 'since something has to be absolutely done to make me stronger again, but at the moment Trahütten and (from 1 August) the Berghof must suffice, for financial reasons!'

Another factor which retarded his work on *Lulu* was basing the whole opera on a single row, but by September he found the solution to this problem by deriving other rows from the basic series (see p. 226ff.). Writing to Schoenberg on 1 September he informed him that 'although I have composed over 300 bars, this is merely the beginning of an opera which will have 3000 bars and more. And goodness knows what fate my plans will suffer in the course of the work, in spite of the strictest disposition'. It may well be that there was some psychological blockage in Berg that slowed down the progress of *Lulu*, namely, the temporary 'split' in his personality referred to so vividly in his letter to Hanna (p. 64). Possibly, Berg may also have had a vague premonition that he would not live long enough to complete the opera. Nearly two years later he was still toiling with the first act, his slowness being due to recurrent attacks of asthma and attendances and lectures in connection with productions of *Wozzeck* at a number of German theatres. 'I hope I still know how to compose,' he wrote to his mentor on 18 May 1930, 'these long interruptions are the cause of terrible doubts in me. How splendid *you* are! Again a new work!' Berg was referring to Schoenberg's *Musik zu einer Lichtspielszene*, op. 34, adding that he was convinced as firmly as a rock of the future of the sound-film 'also for our kind of music', a remark which has a close bearing on the filmed Interlude in *Lulu*. In this connexion it is worth noting that Berg considered his *Wozzeck* as eminently suited for the sound-film, because its quick sequence of short scenes seemed to him to correspond closely to screen technique; and because certain details such as, for instance, the Street Scene of Act II, could be realised in a film, through close-ups and long-shots, with far greater clarity than in the opera.

Berg's despairing 'I hope I still know how to compose' was a momentary outcry and is contradicted by the fact that a year earlier he had, within a few months, written a concert aria commissioned from him by a singer.

In the spring of 1929 Ružena Herlinger, a Viennese singer of Czech origin, who specialied in contemporary music and had met Berg through the ISCM,[6] approached the composer with the request to write an aria with orchestral accompaniment for her. This commission, which meant an interruption of his work on the opera, was very tempting, Frau Herlinger offering the composer a fee of five thousand Austrian schillings. The choice of Baudelaire's *Le Vin*, in a German translation by Stefan George, was Berg's own – he had been in the habit of reading verses by the founder of the French symbolist movement since the age of twenty-five.[7] Frau Herlinger sent Berg a volume of Mozart's concert arias to show him the kind of vocal music she had in mind, and visited him several times to sing to him songs and arias by Schubert, Reger, Mahler, Verdi and Puccini, so as to enable him to assess the character and range of her soprano voice. Berg started with the piece in late May, completing it on 23 July and the full orchestration a month later. To judge from the vocal writing, Frau Herlinger's soprano must have commanded a flexible top register, though Berg did not intend the aria exclusively for a soprano but also a tenor. *Der Wein* is to be regarded as a study for Lulu's *Lied* in Act II of the opera. In adapting the music to the French original, which in the vocal score is printed under the German translation, Berg was guilty of faulty accentuation, which he later corrected with the aid of Ernest Ansermet, whom he met in Winterthur in November 1931. The piece was first heard at the Königsberg Festival of the Deutsche Musikverein, on 4 June 1930, and since Frau Herlinger possessed the sole

---

[6] In March 1928 she sang at a private concert in Paris Berg's Four Songs, op. 2, and Marie's Cradle Song from *Wozzeck*, with the composer at the piano. At this same concert also the Lyric Suite was performed for the first time in the French capital, and with great success, which was in marked contrast to a performance of the Chamber Concerto earlier that year, when it was hissed and booed and the conductor, Walter Straram, who tried to address the audience, shouted down. See Douglas Jarman, 'Two Unpublished Letters from Berg', in the *Musical Times*, April 1972.

[7] Personal communication from the late Helene Berg.

performing rights for two years she also sang it at the Vienna Festival of ISCM on 21 June 1932, with Webern conducting.

After the completion of the concert aria, Berg was most anxious to resume work on *Lulu*, but what slowed down progress on it was the adaptation of the libretto. He had cut four-fifths of Wedekind's text and altered the rest hand in hand with the composition, yet, as he wrote to Schoenberg on 8 August 1930, he had the whole libretto clearly in his mind, and sketched for him the scenario showing the relation between Wedekind's two dramas and the opera. We shall come back to his interesting letter in the chapter on *Lulu*. A year later, on 6 August 1931, he sent his mentor another report on work in progress pointing out, among other things, the difficulty he had in making the dramatic and textual development coincide with the musical development of Dr Schön's Sonata. He writes:

> But I think I have succeeded, which consoles me for the fact that I make such slow progress. After all, I cannot treat the whole thing as if it were a mail-order for Philadelphia which Universal Edition and Stokowski would like me to do.[8] For the time being I have put off both Philadelphia and Universal Edition to the 1932/33 season as the date of the projected world première. And I will try to *keep this date* which is the reason why I shall spend autumn and winter away from Vienna where there is really nothing to hold me.

This letter was written from the Grossglockner, to which the Bergs had driven in their recently acquired motor-car.

Due largely to the royalties from *Wozzeck*, Berg's financial circumstances had greatly improved, and enabled him to buy in September 1930 an English Ford in which he and his wife drove in the afternoons to parts of Carinthia otherwise not easily accessible. Berg treasured the car for the physical independence it afforded him but, as he wrote to Schoenberg, what troubled him was the fact that before he possessed a car he used to compose in his head while on walks and longer excursions by foot; whereas now he was forced to think of nothing else but the road. 'Yet in time I hope to drive ahead not only with the Ford but also with *Lulu*.' After Helene passed her driving test in 1931, she would often take over the wheel from Berg, thus allowing him freedom to think and 'drive ahead also with *Lulu*'.

At the end of 1931 the Bergs had the intention of travelling by car to Barcelona to join the Schoenbergs there and remain in the south of Spain until the summer, but nothing came of his plan. Incidentally Berg, like Puccini, had a foible for mechanical gadgets and devices – we recall his two

---

[8] The first production of *Lulu* was originally fixed to take place in Philadelphia under Leopold Stokowski, who in 1931 had conducted there the first American production of *Wozzeck*. Berg, however, had promised the première of the new opera to Kleiber in Berlin.

PLATE 9: The Villa Na-
howski at Trahütten

PLATE 10: Berg in the
Vienna Studio of the Swiss
Painter, Franz Rederer
(1935)

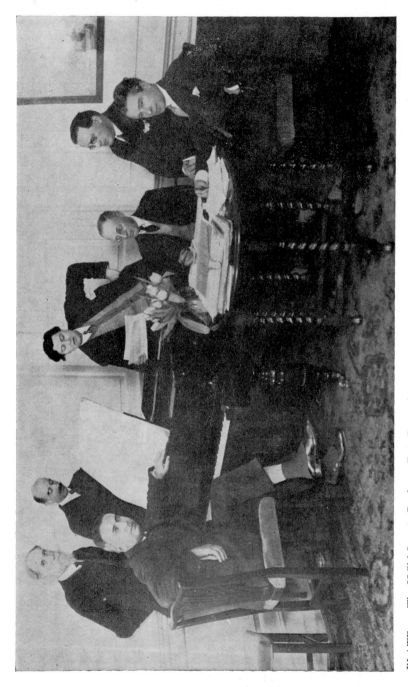

PLATE 11: The ISCM Jury in Professor E. J. Dent's home at Cambridge, January 1931. From Left to Right: Casella (at the piano), Koechlin, Boult, Berg (holding the score of Webern's Symphony, Op. 21), Dent, Fitelberg and Defauw

inventions at the beginning of the war; now he had a car and also derived great pleasure from a five-valve radio set placed at his disposal by the German firm of Siemens & Halske, with which he was able to tune in to most European stations.

In August 1932 Helene sold her parents' estate at Trahütten and from this money the Bergs acquired a new house, near Velden on the Wörthersee, not far from where Brahms had stayed and composed his Second Symphony and the Violin Concerto. Berg's time was much taken up with the negotiations, so that *Lulu* had to be neglected. Finally, in December the deal was completed, and in a short time Helene was able to convert what was an almost uninhabitable place into a comfortable villa in which they could also spend the winter. The Waldhaus, as they baptised it, stood in grounds large enough to isolate it from neighbours, and thus secured for Berg the seclusion and tranquillity he needed for his creative work. In an amusing letter to Schoenberg, written on 9 December 1933, by which time his former master had emigrated to the safe haven of America, Berg describes his life at the Waldhaus:

> So we are really still here in this wilderness, surrounded by snow and ice for the last two months. Besides my work on *Lulu*, we are encumbered with all the small and petty worries of such a life, as for instance (to confine myself to a few things which may illustrate the contrast between your life and ours): which farmer sells the dryest wood, or whether or not the pipes are going to freeze tonight, or whether we shall risk a little trip to Klagenfurt or Velden for the pleasure of a warm bath, and so on. Having given you an idea of all this, yet repeating once again that I would rather be here than in Vienna, for only in this way can I find the concentration for composition, you will not be surprised that we describe our self-inflicted exile as a 'concentration camp'...

By this time Berg's material resources had much deteriorated, owing to the ban imposed on his music in Nazi Germany, and he therefore asked Schoenberg whether he could not assist him in selling the three-volume manuscript of the full score of *Wozzeck*. It was Carl Engel, the then director of the Music Division of the Library of Congress, Washington, and an ardent admirer of Schoenberg and his school who, through Schoenberg's intervention, bought the score for the Library in 1934.

As for the completion of *Lulu*, Berg was unable to keep to the date he had set himself (1932-33), but was hoping to have the opera ready for a Berlin production under Kleiber in the 1934-5 season, and therefore spent the whole of the preceding winter in the Waldhaus. By the beginning of May 1934 he had all but completed the score, but writing to Webern on 6 May he says:[9]

---

[9] Quoted in Reich, *The Life and Work of Alban Berg*, pp. 92-3.

Writing *finis* at the end of the composition of *Lulu* has not made my
happiness as complete as one might have imagined. Just in the
penultimate part [Act III, Scene 1] I have only fleetingly sketched some
things and postponed the execution of them until later. And besides, I
now have to 'overhaul' (as one says of a car) the whole composition from
the beginning! A work that stretches over the years and a musical
development that cannot be *quite* completely surveyed right from the start
forces one to look back over it, and there will be things that will have to be
touched up. This will take another two or three weeks, so that I can only
start on the instrumentation in June ... and the time available (till the
autumn!) gets shorter and shorter and with it my nervousness longer and
longer.

Berg began his first sketch for *Lulu* on 23 June 1928. The particella of Act I
was complete in summer 1931, of Act II in September 1932, and of Act III by
April 1934. He then turned to the scoring of the Suite, now known as
Symphonic Pieces, and after completing it, went back to the beginning of the
opera orchestrating the rest of the music in its correct order of sequence.

Meanwhile the political and, with it, the artistic situation in Germany had
changed out of all recognition. With the drive of the Nazi authorities against
'decadent modern art' and 'cultural bolshevism', a German production of
Lulu became more and more dubious. On Kleiber's advice Berg wrote to the
Intendant of the Staatsoper, Heinz Tietjen, and also to Furtwängler, who
had become a *Staatsrat* and, as such, had much influence in musical matters.
But Furtwängler's reply was negative, although as Berg wrote to Kleiber on
29 May, 'he knows (and "they" know) that I am a German composer and an
Aryan and also that Wedekind is German and an Aryan'. In this same letter
Berg tells Kleiber[10]

I am now making a suite out of *Lulu* which will last approximately 25
minutes. Universal Edition wants to publish it as soon as possible so that
in the autumn all the orchestral societies (of the world!) can play it.
Naturally they are thinking primarily of you. Do you have the desire and
the opportunity and the courage to do the first performance?

Berg completed the suite in July and it was first heard, despite immense
political difficulties, in Berlin on 30 November 1934, with Kleiber
conducting. (A few days later Kleiber resigned his post and left Germany
early in 1935.) In Vienna the suite was given on 11 December 1935, by the
Vienna Symphony Orchestra under Oswald Kabasta. It was the last time
that Berg, by then already very ill, heard any music.

Berg dedicated *Lulu* to Schoenberg on his sixtieth birthday,[11] and in his

---

[10] Quoted in Reich, *The Life and Work of Alban Berg*, p. 93.
[11] Lulu's *Lied* in Act II is inscribed to Webern on his fiftieth anniversary.

letter of dedication of 29 August 1934 he described the opera as being

> not only the product of years of work consecrated to you but also a documentation: the whole world and also the German people shall recognise in the dedication of this German opera that it and my entire work are firmly rooted in that realm of the most German of music which will for all time bear your name.

Moreover, to a *Festschrift* published by Universal Edition for Schoenberg's sixtieth birthday and edited by Webern, Berg contributed an acrostic in which the initial letters of the twenty lines spelt out the three cardinal Christian virtues, – *Glaube, Hoffnung und Liebe* – Faith, Hope and Charity, and which included the prophecy (which has come true) that Schoenberg would be fully recognised in Germany and Austria on his centenary in 1974.

We have to retrace our steps in order to pass in review Berg's other activities between 1926 and 1934. As already mentioned, in the early 1930s much of his time was taken up with attending and lecturing at productions of *Wozzeck* at many German theatres. Inevitably, the composer of this famous opera was now invited to serve on various selection juries. The first jury in which he seems to have taken part was that of the ISCM in Zurich in March 1928, about which he wrote to his wife a slightly ironical letter: 'The first session was in French spoken by Casella with an Italian accent, by Volkmar Andreae with a Swiss, by Dent with an English and by Jirak with a Czech accent.' But he was far more ironic in what he wrote to Schoenberg on 30 March which shows that, like most creative artists, Berg had little or no understanding of the music of composers outside his own circle:

> As this year there will be only three chamber-music concerts[12] it was not easy to distribute fairly the works to be chosen among the many nations which fancy themselves to be creatively productive. All the same, I have succeeded in causing Austria to be represented with dignity by Webern's Trio [Op. 20] and the latest quartet by Zemlinsky. The members of the Jury were perhaps not all aware that Zemlinsky can write a quartet movement not much worse than that by [Frank] Bridge,[13] that his inventive power is perhaps not less than that of Bloch, and that he is scarcely less up-to-date than Alfano, who mostly belong to those composers of whom two can be had for a penny.

In the autumn of the same year Berg sat on the selection committee of the Deutsche Musikverein at Duisburg, for which he had to adjudicate on no fewer than fifty operas. 'Never again!' he wrote to Schoenberg on 6 November 1928.

[12] The Festival was to be held in Siena in the summer.
[13] One of the twelve composers to be represented at the Siena Festival.

In the course of September and October I had to go through 300
kilogrammes of operas – full score, vocal score and libretto. It was like
cleansing a sewer! The sad thing about this was that slowly but surely I
was dragged away from my own work on *Lulu* so that I didn't progress as I
was entitled to hope after a four-month summer.

January 1931 saw him a member of the ISCM Jury at Cambridge, under the
chairmanship of Professor Dent,[14] who was like 'a good nanny' to him.
Cambridge made a profound impression on Berg, notably Trinity College ('a
highly interesting building in the perpendicular style'), and his attendance
one evening at High Table among dons and undergraduates was 'really an
unforgettable experience'. (Letter to his wife of 15 January.)

Berg's last participation in a jury seems to have been in Munich at the end
of February 1933, for the Deutsche Musikverein, when he felt ill at ease since,
owing to the new art policy of the Nazis, works by avant-gardists and Jewish
composers could no longer be submitted. In April, Berg was guest of honour
at the Music Congress held in Florence in conjunction with the first Maggio
Musicale.[15] The great welcome with which he was received did much to
cheer up his spirits, greatly depressed on account of the political events
which had taken place in Germany. Over-conscientious as he was, Berg
attended every meeting of the Congress, and sometimes amused himself with
drawing caricatures of the speaker. With his abiding interest in matters
culinary – his letters to Helene are studded with minute decriptions of meals
he had at a friend's house or a restaurant – he insisted on trying out unknown
Italian dishes on the menu, and refused to be discouraged when they utterly
failed to come up to his expectation. During this Florentine visit, he delivered
a judgment on Italian folk music which, like the views he expressed on other
composers, showed a total lack of insight and sympathy. Berg was also taken
to visit Lucca, where he saw Puccini's birthplace and also the Puccini villa at
Torre del Lago which had been turned into a museum-cum-mausoleum.
Berg was much touched to see that everything was exactly as it was left when
Puccini undertook his fateful journey to Brussels in November 1924. Little
did Berg then suspect that his Vienna home would also be preserved in the
exact condition in which he had spent most of his composing life when he left
it to die at the premature age of fifty.

In the autumn of 1934 Berg was again in Italy, this time to attend, during
the Venice Biennale, the first Italian performance of *Der Wein*. There was an
involved and, for Berg, highly unpleasant prelude to this event, the gist of
which is as follows:

---

[14] On the journey Berg was involved in an amusing incident on the train when he pulled the
communication cord. See letter to his wife of 10 January 1931.

[15] Other composers present on this occasion were Strauss, Milhaud, Malipiero, Bartók,
Roussel and the young Krenek.

Among the works down for performance at this Festival was the Lyric Suite, which had been announced in advance publicity since the previous autumn. Suddenly the work and, with it, Berg's name were removed from the programme. The composer at once suspected – quite wrongly, as it turned out – that political intrigues behind the scene instigated by certain hostile quarters in Nazi Germany were responsible for what he considered an intolerable affront to him. On the face of it, he seemed right in this suspicion. First, there was the general political climate in Central Europe created by Hitler's advent to power in January 1933 and now also affecting Italy. Secondly, there was the foundation under German patronage of a rival organisation to the ISCM which was to give its inaugural concert at Venice during the Biennale. And thirdly, there was the personality of the chairman of the executive committee of the Festival's music section, Adriano Lualdi, who was known as an intransigent Fascist[16] and an ardent admirer of Nazi ideology and, hence, wholly antagonistic to modern music, especially that of Schoenberg and his circle. On hearing of the removal of the Lyric Suite from the Festival's programme, Berg wrote on the 17 July to Malipiero who, together with Casella, was one of the five members of the executive committee, saying among other things that

> the damage done to me is all the greater because, being officially invited to this international Festival, a Festival also exceptional for Italy, would have been compensation for all the many other wrongs I have been and am suffering in these disturbed times. Imagine! Since the Berlin Reichstag fire [spring 1933] not a single note of mine has been heard in Germany – although I am not a Jew. And in my own country things are not much different. For with the present tendency in Austria to glorify the Jews as martyrs, *I am hardly ever performed*. Therefore, the removal of my name from the Venice Festival will be regarded as almost a confirmation of the measures taken against me.[17]

It was either Malipiero or Casella or Lualdi who informed Berg of the true reason for the removal of the Lyric Suite, which was not political at all, but lay in the statutes then in force at the Venice Festival. These stipulated that the only works which could be included in the programmes were those which had not been performed anywhere else and would thus receive their world première at Venice, or works not heard before in Italy. The Lyric Suite had been played in Italy by the Kolisch Quartet and was therefore not eligible, and the same was true of the *Wozzeck Fragments*, which had been performed in Rome and which Berg had suggested as an alternative to the Lyric Suite

---

[16] Lualdi represented the Sindicato dei Musicisti in Mussolini's so-called 'Parliament'.
[17] I am indebted to the late Maestro Malipiero for kindly sending me, through the good offices of my friend, the Roman music critic, Fedele D'Amico, a photostat of this letter.

Malipiero, in several letters to Berg,[18] expressed his disgust at the whole affair, and now he and Casella[19] began to move heaven and earth to get Berg's name back on the programme. But this could only be done if Berg selected one of his works not yet heard in Italy. It was Berg who suggested *Der Wein*, to be conducted by Stein or Scherchen, the latter having been in charge of the first performance in Königsberg in 1930 and being also due to direct some one-act operas at Venice. As singers, the composer proposed Hanna Schwarz or Ružena Herlinger, but reading between the lines of his letter to Malipiero, he considered neither first-rate, though Malipiero thought that Schwarz's soprano would please the Italian public. Anyway, the shortage of time available made the choice of one or the other singer most urgent. Berg's proposal for the concert aria to be sung by Schwarz was accepted, except that Lualdi wanted Berg himself to conduct, and therefore inserted the piece in a programme of works to be directed by their own composers. Berg refused and, in a letter to Lualdi, said that he had never conducted in his life,[20] and that what would be the easiest thing in the world for a professional conductor would turn into a catastrophe if he stood on the rostrum. So *Der Wein* was put back again in the proper programme and Scherchen was called in, it seems, at the last moment.[21] The work was given at the Teatro la Fenice on 11 September, with Berg and his wife present. (An indication of the precarious financial circumstances in which the Bergs lived is to be found in a latter to Malipiero, in which Berg asks whether there were special price reductions on trains and hotels for those invited to the Festival.) Although there was insufficient time for rehearsal – for which the late inclusion of *Der Wein* in the Festival had been the reason – it was received with general acclaim, except by a few Nazi critics and by Malipiero himself, who gave it as his opinion that he failed to discover Berg's true voice in the new composition and that it did not help to understand *Wozzeck*. There is a grain of truth in this.

As we saw from Berg's letter to Malipiero (quoted on p. 81) he and the whole Schoenberg circle were now completely ignored even in their native Austria. True, in 1930 Berg had received the 'Kunstpreis der Stadt Wien' for his *Wozzeck*, but this was little solace for a composer who, with all his modesty, well knew his worth, and whose reputation stood so high in other countries. Writing to Webern on 10 February to thank him for his

---

[18] The late Helene Berg was kind enough to send me copies of these letters.

[19] It was Casella who had suggested the first Italian performance of the Lyric Suite in Florence and he should have remembered this when the work was put on again at the Venice Biennale.

[20] This was not quite correct, since we recall that in 1913 he had directed the chorus in rehearsals for the first performance of Schoenberg's *Gurrelieder*, which was admittedly his only conducting experience.

[21] Scherchen was to play again the role of *deus ex machina* at the first performance of Berg's Violin Concerto in Barcelona two years later.

congratulations on receiving this Prize, he adds with irony:[22]

> An academic post is not linked with it. Nevertheless, it gave me great joy especially because of Vienna, that is, Austria, which for years has overwhelmed us with honours and official positions.

The extent to which Vienna, after 1933, began to cold-shoulder Berg may be seen from a letter to Malipiero of 27 December 1934:

> Although I have been living in Vienna for fifty years and although I have always declined an official teaching post *abroad*, I am considered here, *more than ever*, as not 'indigenous' [*bodenständig*] and am treated as I would be treated if I were, for example, a *Jew* and living in Germany. While here composers are becoming important of whom one had never heard, and small talents like Marx and Rinaldini receive the highest musical honour [*Staatsräte!*], the like of us are being suppressed in *every* respect. Indeed, I have it from the highest official quarter that the production some years ago of my *Wozzeck* was being regarded as a 'desecration' of the Vienna Staatsoper. This is only one example to show how one is treated ... I could give you a few dozen more.

Berg was most profoundly hurt by a speech made by the Austrian Minister of Education in early 1935 in which, announcing the programme for the coming Vienna Festwochen, he said that they would perform works only of truly native composers and thus demonstrate to the world that they were very different from those two or three names whose owners made themselves widely known abroad, but had never been genuine Austrians. Even the musical celebration and appreciations on the occasion of his fiftieth birthday (9 February) were unable to dispel his mood of despair. A little later he sent out to his various friends a picture post-card which in the centre showed an old engraving of the house at Tuchlauben 8, under which he wrote with suppressed bitterness:

> I, who was born in this house on 9 February 1885, had to learn that, after fifty years which I spent in my native city without interruption, am not a native composer.

In 1942, in the midst of the War, Helene Berg was approached by one of her relatives with the suggestion that, since Berg was of pure Aryan blood, she should approach Baldur von Schirach, Hitler's *Gauleiter* in Vienna, with the request to permit performances of her late husband's works. Frau Berg firmly declined to contemplate any such thing, saying that it would seem to her only a profanation that people who were completely alien to Berg's music and must remain so, should now promote it. To her this would have been a sin against the Holy Ghost.[23]

---

[22] The letter is reproduced in Redlich, *Alban Berg*, pp. 305-6.
[23] Helene Berg, *Alban Berg*, p. 655.

We close this chapter with a brief account of the opportunities offered to Berg to accept an official teaching post in Germany. Just as with Schoenberg, it was pre-Nazi Germany which first showed a recognition of his achievements and in 1930 nominated him a member of the Prussian Academy of Arts. Berg was three times offered a professorship at the Berlin Hochschule für Musik, but it seems that his curious love-hate relationship with Vienna prevented him from accepting it. In December 1925, on the occasion of Berg's stay in Berlin for the first production of *Wozzeck*, he had a talk with Schreker, the director of the Hochschule, about an appointment there, but, ostensibly dissatisfied with the salary, did not accept. In the spring of 1930 when Schoenberg encouraged him to consider a second offer by Schreker, he refused on the grounds that a professorship would seriously interfere with his work on *Lulu*. Berg could afford to decline on account of the royalties accruing to him from *Wozzeck* and other works. But when in May 1933 Hindemith, who had succeeded Schreker as director of the Hochschule, again offered him a teaching post, Berg, to judge from a letter to his wife (15 May), seems to have been more favourably inclined – probably because of his dwindling financial resources – yet in the event nothing came of it. It is indeed very doubtful whether Berg, without making a *sacrificium intellectus* of which he was wholly incapable, would have been found acceptable to the Nazi authorities.

EIGHT

THE LAST YEAR

It was largely the deterioration of his material circumstances since 1933 that induced Berg in the early spring of 1935 to interrupt his work on *Lulu*, which in any case could no longer be produced in Germany as he had intended, and to accept a lucrative commission from the American violinist, Louis Krasner, to write a violin concerto for him.[1] Already as a student Krasner had shown great interest in contemporary music, playing works by Cowell and Ives during his days at the Boston Conservatory. In the early 1930s he became much attracted to twelve-note music, which he considered to be the only path leading to the future, and this was the main reason why he began toying with the idea of commissioning a concerto from a dodecaphonic composer, and not from such tonal masters as Bartók, Hindemith and Stravinsky. On the other hand, Krasner was not quite sure how the serial method of composition would respond to the melodic-lyrical needs of the violin. That his choice ultimately fell on Berg was due to Kresner's conviction that, of the three leading twelve-note musicians, Berg was the one to show a markedly lyrical vein in his music, as in the Piano Sonata, Marie's part in *Wozzeck*, and the Lyric Suite, and was therefore most likely to meet the demands of a fiddle concerto.[2]

Krasner met Berg in Vienna early in 1935, through the intervention of a mutual friend, Dr Rita Kurzmann, a musicologist and pianist (she was also Krasner's accompanist), who stood very close to the Schoenberg circle and later made the piano score of Berg's Violin Concerto. Dr Kurzmann had been playing the composer's Piano Sonata a great deal and Krasner was much impressed by it – notably by its lyrical quality. It was this work which prompted him to commission Berg, though his Viennese friends tried to dissuade him from this idea on the ground that Berg was not likely to accept a commission, which seems strange since he had written *Der Wein* on order. During his stay in Vienna in early 1935, Krasner had the opportunity to hear a private performance of the Lyric Suite given by the Galimir String Quartet, a team consisting of a brother and three sisters,[3] the only other team apart

[1] Mr Krasner was kind enough to answer a number of questions which I put to him about the genesis of the Violin Concerto and other related matters.

[2] Krasner was instrumental in getting Kussevitzky, who later conducted the first American performance of the *Lulu* Suite in Boston, interested in Berg's music. It was planned to invite Berg to be present at this concert, but for financial reasons the project came to nothing.

[3] Its second violinist became Krasner's wife. The Galimir Quartet were intimate friends of mine in my Vienna days.

from the Kolisch Quartet to play this work. Krasner subsequently carefully studied the string writing of the Suite and, though a violin concerto calls for a more virtuoso treatment, it confirmed him in the view that in Berg he had chosen the right composer. As Krasner was not known to the Schoenberg circle, Berg, who had heard of his intention, first made discreet enquiries about the violinist and his musical background before agreeing to meet him. At first Berg was not at all taken with the idea of a violin concerto, objecting that a virtuoso work was not his line of country and that he was not able to write a concerto à la Vieuxtemps and Wieniawski. To which Krasner retorted that, after all, Beethoven and Brahms had written a violin concerto.

What seems to have tipped the scale and represented a challenge to Berg was Krasner's observation that, so far, twelve-note music had always been declared to be cerebral, intellectual and almost mathematical stuff: perhaps Berg could prove that it was possible to write in this style a work just as lyrical and expressive as a tonal work. (Krasner, using the same argument, later suggested to Webern that he should compose a solo sonata for him, but nothing came of it.) Berg relented and promised Krasner to consider his idea very seriously. After the violinist left for America, his Vienna friends informed him that Berg was now seen at violin recitals, which was a most encouraging sign, as he was not in the habit of going to solo recitals. Berg decided to accept Krasner's commission, but at first planned to write an 'absolute' concerto, though he was uncertain as to the character and form it should take. The solution came unexpectedly and in a tragic way. Manon Gropius, the eighteen-year-old daughter of Alma Maria Mahler by her second marriage, died on 22 April 1935 of paralysis of the spine, which was the result of poliomyelitis contracted a year before. The Bergs, we recall, were on terms of intimate friendship with Frau Mahler and her family – 'Mutzi', the pet-name for Manon, occurs several times in the composer's letters to his wife. Berg was most profoundly shaken by her sudden death, and it was this impact which suggested to him the idea of giving the concerto the character of a Requiem inscribed 'To the Memory of an Angel'. He little suspected that he was also writing his own Requiem.

Berg discussed with Krasner the violin part, yet at first refused to show him what he had written. During several visits to Berg's Vienna home he asked him to improvise for hours on end – 'Präludieren Sie nur!', and not play any concerto. Berg would busy himself about the house and would come into the room from time to time urging the violinist to continue with his improvisations. It was an ingenious way of finding out which kind of technical devices – passage-work, arpeggios, double and triple stops, harmonics and so on – came naturally and most readily to Krasner, who later realised that most of these devices were used in the concerto. In a sense it was a 'bespoke' concerto. There were, however, a number of solo passages which seemed to Krasner not very idiomatic and Berg agreed to alter them, but when he was about to erase with a large rubber what he had written, Krasner, seized by panic, asked the composer to wait for a while before making changes. In the event none were made!

Back in America, Krasner received from Berg a letter, dated 16 July, in which he said:

> Yesterday I finished the composition of our Violin Concerto. I am more surprised at this than you will be perhaps. To be sure, I was keen on it as I have never been before in my life and must add that the work gave me more and more joy. I hope, no, I have even the confident belief, I have succeeded.

He went on to say that he would then start with the instrumentation of the second part of the concerto, expecting to complete it by the beginning of August. Indeed, the instrumentation was finished on 11 August. Altogether Berg had take a little over four months – April to August – to write the concerto, which, for him, who was as a rule a slow worker, was an astonishingly short time.

It was first heard at the ISCM Festival in Barcelona on 19 March 1936, with Krasner, to whom the work is dedicated, as soloist. Webern was to have conducted, but the impact of Berg's death some three months before had been too shattering for him. Of the three rehearsals at his disposal, he used the first two for the first movement only and, in addition, he had great language difficulties with the Spanish orchestra. Webern withdrew and Scherchen stepped in to save the performance with a single rehearsal. Two years later (1 January 1938) Webern wrote to Scherchen about those unhappy days in Barcelona saying:

> To think that absolutely no one understood me! No one understood how I felt so soon after Berg's death and that I was simply not up to the task of conducting the first performance of his last work – so soon after the event! Right up to the last moment I hoped to be able to do it. But it did not work out like this.[4]

Yet Webern soon recovered and was able to conduct the English performance in a BBC concert in May 1936 at which I was present.

Soon after the completion of the Violin Concerto, Berg developed an abscess on the lower part of his back which he attributed to an insect sting. (In August 1932 he had been attacked at Trahütten by a swarm of wasps and was ill in bed for a week.) Yet, as he had at the same time a carbuncle on his left foot, it seems probable that he had a staphylococcal infection which he had had several times before. The abscess was surgically treated and appeared to heal. None the less, he was not well enough to attend, as the

[4] The entire letter is reproduced in *Die Reihe*, Vienna, 1955, vol. 2, p. 19.

delegate of the Austrian section, the ISCM Festival in Prague in early September when his *Lulu* Symphony was played. On 12 November he returned from the Waldhaus ill and with his energies drained by intermittent fever. On 30 November he wrote what was his last letter to Schoenberg, mentioning his gratification at the many performances of the *Lulu* Symphony and then continued:

> But in spite of all that, things are not going well for me. Badly in a *pecuniary* respect because I cannot maintain my previous standard of life, including the Waldhaus – yet I cannot make up my mind to sell the place where in two years I did *more* work than in the preceding ten. Badly as concerns my *health* because for months I have been having boils (I still have them which explains my horizontal position!). They began, shortly after I had finished the concerto, with an atrocious carbuncle resulting from an insect sting. This disposed of all chance to recuperate in the autumn – which I rather needed after the summer's hard work and the preceding *Lulu* years. Finally, things are bad *morally* – this will not astonish you coming from someone who suddenly discovers that he is not 'indigenous' in his fatherland and therefore completely homeless. All this is heightened by the fact that such things do not proceed without friction and deep human disappointments – these persist. But it is not for me to tell *you* such things, since you have been through it all on a colossal scale in comparison with which my experiences are pocket-sized. After all, I still live in my native country and can speak my mother tongue ...

Berg managed to attend the rehearsals for the *Lulu* Symphony in Vienna, which was heard on 11 December,[5] and had the strength to go with Dr Kurzmann through the piano score she had made of the Violin Concerto.

On 16 December his pains suddenly ceased, which seemed to be a sign that the abscess had broken into the blood stream. The next day he was taken to the Erzherzog Rudolf Hospital and, while he was being transported, his black humour expressed itself in the remark that he was already half-way to the Zentralfriedhof, Vienna's principal cemetery. He was at once operated on, but the source of the blood infection could not be established either then or at a second operation or in the *post mortem*. On 19 December Berg was given a blood transfusion, which resulted in a temporary improvement. He asked to see the donor, an ordinary young Viennese, in order to thank him, and then said to Reich: 'So long as I don't turn into a composer of operettas now!'. The next few days he passed in comparative comfort, but on 22 December he suddenly collapsed. His heart, which had been strengthened by drugs during the previous days, gave out and the death struggle began. On

---

[5] Ernst Roth, who met Berg at the performance, wrote that he looked pale and complained about pains in the legs – 'toothache in the wrong place!' Ernst Roth, *The Business of Music: Reflections of a Music Publisher*, London, 1969, p. 150.

23 December Berg became conscious again and calmly remarked: 'Today is the 23rd. It will be a decisive day!' In his subsequent delirium he thought of *Lulu* and made conducting movements, calling out several times, 'Ein Auftakt! Ein Auftakt!' (An upbeat!').

Berg died on 24 December at quarter past one in the morning, aged fifty years and eleven months. If antibiotics had been discovered at that time, the odds are that his life could have been saved. The death mask was taken by Alma Maria Mahler's daughter, Anna. Berg was buried in the Hietzing cemetery in a grave of honour provided by the Vienna Municipality.

Through Berg's premature death not only the last act of *Lulu* remained incomplete, but the world of music was also deprived of a number of works he intended to write after the opera – a string quartet commissioned by the Coolidge Foundation, a chamber music piece with piano, a symphony, and a composition for the sound film in which, we recall, he was keenly interested.

By way of an epitaph I quote from a letter which Schoenberg wrote to Webern (Hollywood, 15 January 1936) on Berg's death:

> It is too terrible. One is gone from us who in any case were only three, and now we two alone have to bear this artistic isolation. And the saddest thing: the one of us who has had success, could have at least enjoyed it. Had he lived longer he would not have felt this bitterness to the same extent, as we do, of seeing himself robbed of the joy in the performances of his works and in his (creative) activity! Certainly, he too had had to suffer from the general ostracism of us three, from the hate with which we are persecuted. Yet, thanks to some amiable features of his nature (*Anlagen*), people believed in him, and he could have enjoyed it.[6]

---

[6] *Arnold Schönberg. Gedenkausstellung 1974*, ed. E. Hilmar, Vienna 1974, p. 61.

THE WORK

'Denn der innere Gehalt des Gegenstandes ist
der Anfang und das Ende der Kunst – For the
inner content of the subject is the alpha and
omega of art'. – Goethe, *Aus meinem Leben.
Dichtung und Wahrheit.*

NINE

VOCAL COMPOSITIONS

UNPUBLISHED SONGS

Berg began his composing life with songs. Although he gave up song-writing with the *Altenberg Lieder* of 1912, returning to this miniature form only once more in 1925 (Storm Song no. 2), it was a significant beginning. For an intense lyricism, though Berg himself denied having a marked lyrical gift,[1] combined with a dynamic dramatic vein, formed the most characteristic general feature of his mature style, and both these traits are already present in his early songs. There are seventy-three unpublished songs in the Österreichische Nationalbibliothek in Vienna, and twelve holographs of them are deposited in the Library of Congress, Washington. Some thirty songs date from 1900 to ca. 1904, while the rest were composed during the period of Berg's studies with Schoenberg. What is notable about these unpublished pieces is the choice of verses by poets many of whom are eminent in German literature – a testimony to the young composer's literary taste, perhaps not surprising in one who first wanted to be a poet himself and later wielded the pen with such distinction. Berg set verses by Goethe, Mörike, Heine, Rückert, Eichendorff and Geibel, but he also chose poems by writers who at the turn of the century enjoyed a certain reputation but are now forgotten, such as Busse, Hamerling, Dörmann and Hohenberg. Equally noteworthy is Berg's avoidance of poets who were favourites with Strauss, Reger and Schoenberg (Dehmel, Holz and Stefan George), and his selection of writers who at the time were perhaps not widely known but already displayed a distinct originality like Altenberg, Mombert, Hofmannsthal, Schlaf, Rilke and Mell. There are altogether fifty-seven different poets whose verses Berg set between 1900 and 1912.

What are the unpublished songs like? We recall that Berg regarded the majority of them as derivative and immature and therefore wanted them to be destroyed, and we also remember that when Schoenberg first saw them he found them to be 'in a style between Hugo Wolf and Brahms'. Nicholas Chadwick, who has carefully examined them,[2] distinguishes four stylistic periods and suggests that certainly the first- and, most likely, the second-

---

[1] Adorno, *Alban Berg*, p. 30.
[2] 'Berg's Unpublished Songs', pp. 123-40.

period songs were composed before Berg began to study with Schoenberg. These songs show, to a varying degree, the influence of Schubert, Schumann, Wagner, Wolf, Mahler (especially), and some even of Debussy. With the third period Berg entered, according to Chadwick, a marked Brahmsian phase, seen in the greater richness of texture, skilful contrapuntal manipulation of the piano part, greater independence of the voice part, and the use of accentuated suspension and appoggiatura in the harmony. Chadwick believes that these 'Brahmsian' songs were already composed under Schoenberg and that, in their evident technical skill which outweighs their imaginative content, they indicate the rigorous discipline which the teacher demanded of his pupil in order to achieve a solid craftsmanship. In the fourth period Berg's own song style emerges quite clearly, while the fruit of Schoenberg's teaching is manifest in the pre-occupation with thematic integration or thematicism and/or a higher degree of contapuntal resourcefulness. Chadwick considers as the best of Berg's unpublished songs 'Das stille Königreich' (Busse, 1908) which he reproduces in its entirety in his thesis.[3] A study of this song not only confirms this view, but makes one wonder why Berg did not find it worthy of inclusion in his Seven Early Songs, instead of the rather undistinguished 'Schilflied'.

PUBLISHED SONGS

That Berg considered a number of his early songs to be of a satisfactory aesthetic quality and characteristic of his style at a certain point of its evolution, we see from the fact that twenty years later, in 1928, by which date he had already adopted the twelve-note method of composition, he published seven in their original version with piano accompaniment and made also a version for full orchestra. It was as if Berg, conscious of his romantic past, wanted to show whence he really came. His own printed date, 1907, for the Seven Early Songs, is incorrect and should be amended to '1905–8', which is the period in which they were composed. Nor is the order in which they were composed identical with the order of their publication which was, most likely, dictated by aesthetic considerations such as musical weight, character and emotional contrast. The following table gives their chronological order and dates and the order in which they are published:

Chronological Order	*Order of Publication*
No. 1, 'Im Zimmer' (Schlaf). Summer 1905	No. 5
No. 2, 'Die Nachtigall' (Storm). 1905(–6)	No. 3
No. 3, 'Liebesode' (Hartleben). Autumn 1906	No. 6
No. 4, 'Traumgekrönt' (Rilke). Summer 1907	No. 4
No. 5, 'Nacht' (Hauptmann). Spring 1908	No. 1
No. 6, 'Schilflied' (Lenau). Spring 1908	No. 2
No. 7, 'Sommertage' (Hohenberg). Summer 1908	No. 7

[3] 'A Survey of the Early Songs of Alban Berg'.

'Im zimmer' and 'Die Nachtigall' are in Brahmsian vein, notably the latter with its undulating voice part, the syncopated piano accompaniment in the middle section in F sharp minor, and the 'Schwungvoll' of the postlude which is somewhat reminiscent of the accompaniment of Brahams's 'Meine Liebe ist grün'. Schoenberg's hand can be seen in the contrapuntal intertwining of voice and piano and the imitative writing in the last five bars. 'Im Zimmer' is a delicate little piece, lightly handled and of remarkable transparency. Berg avoids the tonic chord in root position until the very last bar, when the B flat major triad enters with the effect of an almost fresh chord. Another exquisite song in a very slow tempo is 'Liebesode' in which voice and piano are completely independent, the instrumental accompaniment being formed of sequence-like repetitions of a melodic appoggiatura motive which, in bar fourteen, is inverted to return to its original shape in the last three bars. This ostinato treatment of the piano parts points to Wolf,[4] while the vocal line and the harmony breathe a Wagnerian air. Notable, too, is the predominantly four-bar structure of this stanzaic setting. 'Traumgekrönt' is to my mind the outstanding song of the set, transmuting the quiet rapture of Rilke's love poem in music of remarkable lyrical imagination. The form is binary, but is so treated as to suggest sonata form without the development section. There are three themes, the first two of which – one instrumental (A), the other vocal (B) – are combined at the opening:

Example 2

At the recapitulation (bar 16) these two themes exchange their position in invertible counterpoint. When the third theme, quasi second subject, enters on the voice at 'Und dann, dann kamst Du ...', it is accompanied by theme B. In other words, the song shows strict thematicism and skilful use of counterpoint which are clearly the result of Berg's studies with Schoenberg,

---

[4] See, for instance, Wolf's 'Geistliche Gesänge' in the *Spanisches Liederbuch*.

just as is the vocal line with its wide span. 'Nacht', which together with 'Sommertage', is the longest of these songs, is the first of Berg's published settings to resort to the whole-tone scale both horizontally and vertically. This scale established itself in Western music through the Russian nationalists and Debussy; Schoenberg used it in the form of parallel shifts of augmented triads in his symphonic poem, *Pelleas und Melisande*. Like his master, Berg deploys it, not as unrelated to the major-minor tonality, as an alien enclave in tonal territory as in Debussy, but embedded in functional harmony. This 'functionalisation' of the whole-tone scale conforms to Schoenberg's own practice which he discussed in his *Harmonielehre*,[5] quoting (p. 475) a whole-tone chord on E (dominant) with its resolution to A major (tonic), as it occurs in bars 8-9 of 'Nacht'. Here is the opening of the song which shows the simultaneous melodic and harmonic use of the whole-tone scale:

Example 3

The vocal line displays amplitude and sweep, its compass extending from middle C to G sharp above the stave, and something of Brangäne's call in Act

[5] 3rd ed., Vienna, 1921, pp. 467 ff.

II of *Tristan* seems to echo in the tender phrase, 'O gib acht!'. The melancholy 'Schilflied' is marked by intense Wagnerian chromaticism and seems to have been influenced by Schoenberg's Eight Songs, op. 6. Finally, 'Sommertage' is, like 'Traumgekrönt', a contrapuntal song, but its mood is one of rousing ecstasy manifest especially in the voice part, which is almost Straussian in its soaring tendency.

It is a measure of Berg's sense of style that the orchestration of the Seven Early Songs not only preserves but reinforces their late romantic character. By the time he scored them, he had *Wozzeck* behind him, yet there is very little in the orchestral language of the settings to remind us of the opera. Berg's instrumental palette here ranges from warm, rich, bright colours to delicate, subdued tints. This is not a mere transcription for orchestra, not a mere clothing of the music from outside, but a realisation of the immanent symphonic nature of these songs. The extraordinary thing is that when he wrote them he had, on his admission, little idea of the mechanics of the orchestra and yet the piano writing gives the impression of being a substitute for an imaginary orchestra. To speak from my own experience, these songs come fully to life only in the orchestral version, in which the rather complex and intricate piano texture is greatly loosened up and made more plastic and clearer by a different lay-out. Except for a few counter-motives, doublings of the voice part and pointillistic additions, the orchestral version is identical with the piano version. Berg's general principle in scoring these songs was to aim at an almost continual change in the mixture of timbres,[6] but in the contrapuntal pieces ('Liebesode', 'Traumgekrönt' and 'Sommertage') the phrases are scored 'through' for one instrument or a group of instruments, in order to preserve the clarity of the polyphonic lines. Moreover, Berg chooses a different combination for each song, his choice being evidently dictated by the character of the music and also by the desire to create a measure of symmetrical instrumental design. Thus, 'Nacht' and 'Sommertage' are scored for large orchestra which, as in Mahler, is however rarely used as a tutti but for the purpose of achieving multi-coloured chamber effects. At the opening of 'Nacht', the orchestration of the oscillating whole-tone chord for woodwind and upper strings possibly owes something to Debussy's 'Nuages'. The inner five songs utilize smaller forces of different combinations. Thus, in 'Schilflied' Berg resorts to fifteen solo instruments, while 'Die Nachtigall' is scored for strings only, one half playing with mutes. Again, 'Im Zimmer' employs wind only, with the woodwind much in prominence, plus harp and cymbal.[7] Noteworthy, too, is the important role Berg allots to the harp to lend a light, shimmering colour to the music. Indeed this instrument, so

---

[6] See Theodor W. Adorno, 'Die Instrumentation von Bergs frühen Liedern' in *Klangfiguren*, Frankfort, 1959, pp. 138-56.

[7] Note the delicate impressionist touch of the cymbal roll at the words, 'Ein Feuerlein rot knistert im Ofenloch'.

integral to the romantic orchestra, is employed in all but one song.

It is interesting to read what Berg replied to Schoenberg's congratulatory telegram after hearing the Seven Early Songs in Berlin in the spring of 1929:

> The fact that these songs are so intimately connected with the time of my studies with you, makes them for me more valuable than they actually are. And that I succeeded in scoring these piano songs in such a way that *you* found they sounded well, has brought this past still nearer to me.

A propos of Berg's 'fateful' number, when he published the Seven Early Songs in 1928 he altered the original metronome markings of 'Im Zimmer' and 'Liebesode' into multiples of 23.

With the Four Songs, op. 2 (early 1909 – spring 1910), Berg went through a crisis in his style which is seen in the simultaneous pull exercised on him by the major-minor tonality, however widely expanded, and pure atonality as illustrated in, for instance, Schoenberg's *Das Buch der hängenden Gärten*, op. 15. The Hebbel song and the first two of the three Mombert settings are still anchored in a key and have the appropriate key signatures, whereas the last Mombert song has no tonal centre and is without a key-signature. Moreover, influenced by Schoenberg's and Webern's aphoristic style at that time, the first two Mombert settings are very short – the one extending to eighteen bars and the other to twelve, thus preparing us for the miniatures of the *Altenberg Lieder* and the Four Clarinet Pieces. That this brevity was with Berg (in marked contrast to Webern) only a passing phase is shown by his extensive Three Orchestral Pieces, op. 6.

'Schlafen, schlafen' from Hebbel's *Dem Schmerz sein Recht* expresses romantic world-weariness: the poet seeks escape from painful reality in sleep. It is this pain which dictates the whole character of the song and, notably, its harmonic aspect, which may be described as a study in the emotional effect of downward appoggiaturas as the musical symbol for a sigh. No less suggestive is the drooping tendency of the voice part. Virtually every chord in this setting, which looks backwards via Wolf to *Tristan*, can be interpreted as a suspension in the form of chromatically 'altered' dominant sevenths and ninths containing the major and minor third (as in Ravel), as well as the perfect and agumented fourth which recalls Scriabin's chord structure. While the intense application of chromatic appoggiaturas much obscures the tonality, functional relationship is maintained and the song begins and ends in a clear D minor, with the tonic root forming a ten-bar bass pedal in the opening. The accompaniment at the phrase 'Jener Wehen, die mich trafen' foreshadows Wozzeck's 'Der Mensch ist ein Abgrund' in Act II, Scene 3 of the opera. At the climax, 'Wenn des Lebens Fülle nieder klingt', Berg conveys the 'richness of life' by luxuriating seven-note suspensions: (Ex. 4).

The next three songs of op. 2 are settings from *Der Glühende* by Alfred Mombert, a poet and dramatist who in his exclusive ego-related style and the

Example 4

esoteric, ecstatic nature of his vision was one of the early German expressionists. His three poems are essentially interior monologues with all the apparent unrelatedness or, at any rate, ellipsis of the thought processes. Berg's choice of Mombert is a clear indication of the new aesthetic direction in which his music was moving. His response to this novel kind of verse is a predominantly muted lyricism with which he seeks to project the rarified air of the text. The first two songs are in E flat minor and C flat major, respectively, the second showing 'progressive tonality' by ending on the upper mediant, E flat major.

'Schlafend trägt man mich ...' is, like 'Traumgekrönt' in the Seven Early Songs, a polyphonic setting in which the processional opening phrase consists of a closely interlocked instrumental and vocal theme:

Example 5

which, as in that earlier song, change their places in bars 8-10. The succession of perfect fourths in the bass line clearly points to the opening of Schoenberg's Chamber Symphony, op. 9. In the second Mombert song, 'Nun ich der Riesen Stärksten überwand', a powerful fourth motive is prominent on the piano, symbolising, it appears, the struggle to 'overcome the strongest of the giants', while the voice part represents partly a development of its opening phrase. The third Mombert setting is Berg's first essay in atonality in which all feeling for a basic key is liquidated. The verses show disparate images (similar to the Altenberg poems in Berg's op. 4), and abandon the rhyme and regular metre of traditional poetry in favour of poetic prose. Hence the athematic structure of the song in which, as in Schoenberg's *Erwartung*, no motive is repeated or elaborated; once it has appeared, it makes room for another motive. Although tonality is relinquished, there are, however, tonal associations as, for instance, the bass pedal C-G in the opening and the drones in bars 9-12; while the ending suggests a much obscured key of B. This ending shows a most interesting and, for its time, daring harmonic progression. As in the opening of the first Mombert song (Ex. 5), the bass rises in perfect fourths from B flat to B while the upper harmonies are a chromatic side-slipping of telescoped perfect and augmented fourths, as indeed fourth formations are a common feature of all the four songs of op. 2:

Example 6

Schoenberg found the chords *x* and *y* remarkable enough to quote them in his *Harmonielehre*,[8] but felt unable to say why this was a perfectly acceptable progression, and suggested that, with the exception of E flat and B, the second chord is complementary to the first in that *y* introduces the chromatic notes adjacent to those of *x*. The song ends on chord *x* which consists of a minor seventh and a major and minor third, that is a chromatically altered dominant seventh on B. This Mombert setting shows some affinity with no. 4 of Schoenberg's *Buch der hängenden Gärten* in its opening and at the climax, 'Er kommt noch nicht. Er lässt mich warten'. The sudden glissando, on the 'white key' notes in the left hand and the 'black key' notes in the right,[9] and the following collapse in a descending movement down to the *martellato* note B flat, bursts the framework of a song and has the air of a dramatic gesture in opera. Worth mentioning also are the illustrative touches in this song, such as the flute-like piano passage at 'Horch, es flötet die Nachtigall', the coloratura phrase at 'Ich will singen', and the sharp 'icy' staccato chords on the high treble at 'es schmiltz and glitzert kalter Schnee'. It was this song which, together with Schoenberg's *Herzgewächse* and one of Webern's Trackl songs,

---

[8] p. 504. (3rd edition).

[9] This division was a favourite device of Berg's which we shall find again in *Wozzeck*, the Lyric Suite, and *Lulu*.

was published in the expressionist manifesto, *Der blaue Reiter*. It should be added that René Leibowitz, evidently following Berg's precedent of scoring his Seven Early Songs, made an orchestral version of op. 2 which was at one time available on a gramophone disc (Esquire, TW. 4-001).

With the *Five Orchestral Songs after Picture Post Cards of Peter Altenberg*, op. 4 (1912), written at Schoenberg's suggestion, Berg continued on the path on which he had first started out in the third Mombert song of op. 2 and the String Quartet, op. 3, that is atonal expressionism. His choice of five of Altenberg's prose poems is already significant. Like the Mombert verses, they are intensely ego-related and aphoristic pieces and marked by a similar ellipsis of thought processes and juxtaposition of disparate verbal images. Berg's settings are very short – no. 2 for instance extends to only eleven bars – a fact which he specially mentioned in a letter to Schoenberg of 9 January 1913. The Altenberg Songs were his first composition for orchestra, yet no praise can be too high for the consummate command of instrumental technique and sound imagination the young composer displays in them. In this respect his particular models were Schoenberg's Five Orchestral Pieces, op. 16, and Webern's Six Orchestral Pieces, op. 6, in which there is also the same deliberate discrepancy between the brevity of the music and the mammoth forces employed.[10] Yet for all three composers the original model was Mahler. And, like Mahler, they resorted to such extravagant means in order to achieve for the most part intimate and subtle chamber effects, the immense variety of which was only possible with the use of a huge orchestra. Berg aims at delicate colour schemes particularly in the three middle songs, and it is only in the opening and closing pieces that he has recourse, and this only very occasionally, to massive tuttis.

The score of op. 4 is perhaps the most daring Berg ever wrote, and one in which he seeks to obtain all kinds of novel sounds. That he felt some qualms about this, we recall from his letter to Schoenberg of 17 January 1913, in which he compares himself with a child who uses foreign words, but foreign words the meaning of which he understands (see p. 26). Berg's 'foreign words' – some are indeed neologisms – include various sorts of glissandi, among them trombone glissandi (no. 5), which may have been suggested to him by the first piece of Schoenberg's op. 16, glissando harmonics for the violins on the E string followed by toneless bowing on the lower strings 'on the holes of the saddle' (end of no. 1), and glissandi on the drum produced by tuning it down during a drum roll (no. 4). There is also frequent use of *Flatterzunge*, not only on the woodwind, but trumpets and trombones (no. 5). And, finally, Berg demands a *scordatura* for the first violins, which have to

---

[10] The orchestra in the Altenberg Songs comprises triple woodwind (4 clarinets), 4 horns, 3 trumpets, 4 trombones and bass tuba, timpani and an array of percussion, plus glockenspiel, xylophone, harp, celesta, piano, harmonium, and strings.

tune the D string down to D flat (no. 2).

The vocal style appears to have been modelled on that of Schoenberg's opp. 15 and 17, in that narrow and mostly chromatic steps are balance by wide leaps, with the compass of the voice part extending from A flat below the stave in no. 4 to top C in no. 3. In Berg's view, the easiest songs for the singer are nos. 2 and 5. No. 3 is of medium difficulty, while the most exacting ones are nos. 1 and 4. As a rule, voice and orchestra have independent material, but there are exceptions, as when the composer doubles the vocal line on an instrument or treats voice and instruments in imitation.

The songs were not composed in the order in which they appear in print, though Berg conceived them as a cycle, but thought they could be performed separately, as was done at the Vienna concert on 31 March 1913, when Schoenberg selected nos. 2 and 3 from them. Berg's sure sense of form is seen in the fact that the two longest songs, nos. 1 and 5, enclose the shorter middle songs, nos. 2, 3 and 4. Moreover, there are quotations of motives from one song in another, such as for instance the phrase 'Siehe, Frau' of no. 2 which recurs in permutation in 'Siehe, hier sind keine Menschen!' of no. 5; or the ascending fourths – a highly characteristic fingerprint in Berg – in bar 9 of no. 1 (celesta), bar 6 of no. 2 (solo cello), bars 20-1 of no. 4 (descending fourths on solo cello) and bars 7 ff.[11] Similarly, the flute theme of no. 5 (Ex. 9b) is anticipated by the viola in bars 9 ff. of no. 1. These belong to the most important cross-references of op. 4, all introduced to lend the five songs a measure of motivic cohesion. We now turn to a brief discussion of the individual songs.

In the poem of no. 1 Altenberg's apostrophises the soul, saying that, like Nature, it has its snowstorms which give it depth and beauty. Berg seizes first on the image of the soul's snowstorm which he depicts in the 19-bar long orchestral introduction. This is an 'exotic' storm in which he resorts to a pentatonic main-motive, as well as a kind of polyrhythmic heterophony, both features of Asiatic music, notable the Javanese *gamelan* (Exx. 7a and b).[12]

Note in 7b the rhythmic displacement of the pentatonic motive which is brought about by harnessing its 5/8 metre to the song's basic 4/8 metre, and the canon between glockenspiel and xylophone. The climax of the introduction is reached in bar 15 where Berg introduced another of his favourite devices, which is the combination of whole-tone with chromatic runs.[13] The sudden reduction of the orchestral forces in bars 18-19 prepares for the entry of the voice, which opens wordless and 'like a breath', on a soft

---

[11] Undoubtedly influenced by the famous opening of Schoenberg's Chamber Symphony, op. 9; they first occur in Berg's published works in the Piano Sonata, nos. 1 and 3 of the Mombert settings, and as late as *Und Pippa tanzt* (Ex. 1, p. 72), and the *Erdgeist* fourths of *Lulu*.

[12] Ex. 7a is quoted from Willi Apel, *Harvard Dictionary of Music*, London, 1951, p. 373.

[13] In Schoenberg's *Erwartung* (1909), the last bar combines a chromatic scale in the treble with a whole-tone scale in the bass in contrary motion.

Example 7a

note to be sung, first, with 'lightly closed lips' and then with 'open mouth'. It is as if Berg meant to show the growth from near-imperceptibility to audible sound. One discerns in this song something like a ternary form, A-B-C, in which the last section shows a complete fragmentation and dissociation of the texture. The second climax (29) introduces fourth chords (trumpets and trombones) in parallel chromatic shifts which we first came across in the third Mombert song of op. 2. There is an almost surrealistic touch about bars 31-3 which in turn are to be played 'roh' (coarsely), 'grell' (shrilly), 'ordinär' (vulgarly), and 'klagend' (lamentingly), and which at once recalls Mahler.

The poem of the second song continues the idea of a storm purifying the soul, yet with an erotic overtone. Altenberg here addresses a woman, saying

Example 7b

that the forest looks brighter and glistens after a rainstorm – 'Siehe, Fraue, auch du brauchst Gewitterregen!' In this, the shortest of the five songs, the orchestra is greatly reduced, with the strings divided into soli and tutti. There are two noteworthy features about this setting. One is the appearance in the voice part of two descending fourths (bar 2) which are prophetic of the 'Erdgeist' fourths in *Lulu*. The second is the sudden interruption of the declamatory voice part by a coloratura on the word 'schöner' (bar 5). A tenuous link with tonality is preserved in the bass note F which occurs in bars 2, 6-7 and 11.

The verses of the third song express a somewhat abstract philosophical thought which I interpret as meaning that a mind used to musing on eternity is impervious to the disillusionments and frustrations of life on this earth. Berg symbolises the opening line, 'Über die Grenzen des All blicktest du sinnend hinaus', by wind chord which contains *all* the twelve notes of the chromatic scale, that is, the 'universe' of the text is reflected in the *totality* of notes used in the Western system. The chord foreshadows the *Todesschrei* in *Lulu*, Act III, Scene 2, though in the opera it is arrived at in a different way. The twelve-note chord in the song is sustained for seven bars but in a constantly changing orchestration, with its individual notes passing from one instrument to the other. The evident model for this was the *Klangfarben-Akkord* in no. 3 of Schoenberg's Five Orchestral Pieces, op. 16. Berg's chord is scored for solo wind only and its constituent notes are so laid out as to tone down its acutely dissonant character, just as Schoenberg did in op. 16 and also in the eleven-note chord (in an orchestration similar to Berg's), in the monodrama *Erwartung*, quoted as Ex. 340 in his *Harmonielehre*.[14] Moreover, the vocal line embedded in this chord unrolls eleven of the twelve chromatic notes. The song, in strict tripartite form, closes with the opening passage but the initial twelve-note chord is now gradually assembled on the strings *horizontally* Berg thus anticipates Schoenberg's later theory of the identity of the tonal space in serial music. Another notable feature is the exquisitely shaped coloratura on the word 'sinnend' (7-8), which at the end is repeated in diminution. There is, moreover, an eerie dramatic effect about the whispered phrase, 'plötzlich is alles aus' (16-17), on the A below the stave.[15] The song is twelve-note, but not serial.

The words of the fourth song express the sadness and despair of a woman[16] who has waited in vain for the longing of her soul to be stilled, and in this expectation has grown old. As an example of Berg's method of lengthening a tiny semitonal motive (G-A flat) I quote bars 10-13:

---

[14] p. 502.
[15] See also the toneless 'Stirb' on the same note at the end of no. 4 of op. 2.
[16] In a letter to Schoenberg, Berg described this song as a 'woman's song'.

Example 8

The passage is also noteworthy for the doubling of an expressive vocal phrase on the dry, soulless xylophone. Nothing, I think, could better convey the basic mood of this song than its opening, with a solitary high flute and cor anglais accompanying the voice. Further on, the 'fluttering hair' is caught in quick runs on the upper woodwind; and how poignant is the ending in which the voice slides down to the A flat below the stave on the words, 'um mein bleiches Antlitz', accompanied (as in the beginning) by a high flute and a chromatic glissando on the drum.[17]

In the poem of the last song Altenberg seeks peace for his lacerated soul in the solitude of snow-bound nature, far away from humans and their dwellings. This is highly organised setting in the form of a passacaglia, and is a good example of how Berg channels and controls his intense lyrical outpourings by means of a strict formal design. It is an unusual kind of passacaglia, for, besides the theme of the ground bass (Ex. 9*a*), it has two more ideas. One is the theme (Ex. 9*b*) which unfolds all the twelve notes of the chromatic scale and on its several repititions[18] adheres to the original order of sequence of the notes, thus anticipating Schoenberg's serial method by some eleven years. The other idea is a figure consisting of four rising fourths (Ex. 9*c*), which relates to the fourth motive of Song no. 2:

Example 9a

Example 9b

Example 9c

---

[17] The autograph sketches of nos. 4 and 5, which show divergencies from the published versions, were deposited at the Bodleian Library, Oxford, by Frau Berg.
[18] Bars 10-15, 29-35 and 39-45.

A striking feature of this setting is the immense flexibility with which these three ideas (sometimes slightly varied) intermingle, merge and dissociate in the course of the music until in bar 46 a variant of the passacaglia theme regains the hegemony. In general style this song differs from the preceding settings, in that its texture is on the whole less fragmented, with the thematic lines unfolding in longer, more coherent shapes. Also tonal associations are here more frequent, for example, the prolonged pedal on G (bars 45-51) and the marked use of thirds, sixths and octaves which, in analogy with the final movement of the Violin Concerto, Berg seems to have associated with the ultimate peace the poet is seeking. Of the illustrative touches in this song, the one at the words 'Hier tropf Schnee leise in Wasserlachen' is to be mentioned especially, with the piano depicting the gentle drops of snow, *sempre ppp*.

The two settings of Storm's 'Schliesse mir die Augen beide' (1907 and 1925) were first published, with Berg's authorisation, by Willi Reich in an article on the composer in 1930[19] but did not come out in print until 1953. Berg wrote the second song to commemorate the twenty-fifth anniversary of the foundation of Universal Edition (1901) and in Reich's publication prefaced the two songs with the following dedication:

Twenty-Five Years of Universal Edition[20]

are equivalent to the enormous distance which music has travelled from tonal composition to compositions with '12 notes only related to one another', from the C major triad to the 'mother chord'.[21] It is the everlasting merit of Emil Hertzka to have been the only publisher to have taken care of this distance from the very beginning. To Hertzka are dedicated the two settings of the same text by Theodor Storm which are intended to illustrate this development and are here published for the first time. They were composed – the one at the beginning, the other at the end of this quarter-century (1900[22] and 1925) by

Alban Berg.

[19] *Die Musik*, February 1930.

[20] Fünfundzwanzig Jahre Universal Edition

gleichbedeutend mit dem ungeheuren Weg, den die Musik von der tonalen Komposition zu der 'mit 12 nur aufeinander bezogenen Tönen', vom C-Dur Dreiklang zum Mutterakkord (der von Fritz Heinrich Klein entdeckte 12-Ton-Akkord, der auch alle zwölf Intervalle enthält) zurückgelegt hat, und den, als einziger Verleger, von Anfang an gegangen zu sein, das unvergängliche Verdienst E m i l H e r t z k a s ist. Ihm sind die umstehenden Zwei Lieder von Theodor Storm, die diesen Weg veranschaulichen sollen und hier ihre erste Veröffentlichung erfahren zugeeignet. Sie sind – das eine zu Anfang, das andere zu Ende des Jahrhundertviertels (1900-1925) – komponiert von

Alban Berg

[21] This was the twelve-note chord built from the so-called 'all-interval' series invented by Berg's pupil, F.H. Klein. More will be said about this chord and its series in connection with the Lyric Suite.

[22] Berg's memory played him false. The correct date of the first Storm song is 1907. See Reich, *The Life and Work of Alban Berg*, p. 109, and Chadwick, 'Berg's Unpublished Songs', p. 125.

Storm's poem is a lover's lullaby which is well caught in the music of the two songs, the first of which is for low and the second for high voice. The earlier setting belongs to Berg's Brahmsian phase, seen in his exploitation for expressive ends of appoggiaturas and the doubling of the voice in the piano. The form of this C major song is stanzaic, with a half close on A minor, while a Bergian touch is the masking of the basic 4/4 phrasing by a 5/4 metre. It is an attractive but uncharacteristic song.

The second song was completed in the summer of 1925 at Trahütten, whence Berg wrote to Webern saying that it was his first attempt at strict twelve-note composition in which 'unfortunately I am not yet so far advanced as you are'.[23] Berg's handling of the series has nothing tentative about it, though the voice-part is markedly simple and straightforward, with no inversions, retrogrades or transpositions of the row and it unfolds five times, always starting on F. The vocal part shows a remarkable sense of shape and balance, with a nicely calculated distribution of high and low notes. The irregularity lies in the piano part which begins with the last six notes of the series followed by its first six notes. There is also a canon at the unison between voice and piano in bars 5-12. The song closes on the 'mother chord' which, similar to the ending of no. 3 of the Altenberg songs, is assembled horizontally and finally comes to rest on the bass F, the implied tonality of the setting.

Berg's first acquaintaince with Baudelaire's poetry dates back to 1910. In a letter to his future wife of August of that year, he speaks with the greatest enthusiasm of the French writer whose *Petits Poèmes en prose* he had just read in a German translation and whose notion of man's ambivalent relationship to beauty in nature describes, Berg says, his own attitude very accurately. On and off, Berg continued to read Baudelaire for the rest of his life including, of course, his single major work, *Les Fleurs du mal* (1857), on which the poet's fame largely rests and which displays at its most imaginative his satanism and fascination by the beauty of evil, of morbid and corrupted things. Baudelaire-Berg! Does this conjunction not raise some interesting question of affinities? Was there something in Berg's *Weltbild* that closely linked him to the Baudelaire who wrote: '*Je ne conçois guère un type de beauté où il n'y ait du Malheur*'? It is certainly not without significance that Berg chose for his suppressed setting in the finale of the Lyric Suite verses by the French poet (see pp. 136ff.). Or was it the strong sensuality of Baudelaire's poetry that cast its spell over Berg (see pp. 7-8)? And finally, did Berg feel a measure of spiritual kinship with this rebellious poet? For the Viennese composer was also against the moral taboos and moral conventions of his society – both *Wozzeck* and *Lulu* are, truly, defiantly anti-establishment, the first against the

---

[23] Webern's first serial works (opp. 17 and 18) date from 1924 and 1925, respectively.

mindless authority of the state and its organs, and the second against the sexual hypocrisy of the bourgeois.

We recall that it was Berg who in 1929 suggested to Ružena Herlinger, as text for her concert aria, Baudelaire's cycle *Le Vin* contained as nos. 104-8 in *Les Fleurs du mal*. Berg used a German rendering by Stefan George – himself a representative of symbolism in Central Europe – which is, admittedly, rather free, yet remains faithful to the spirit of the French original and preserves the music of words so characteristic of Baudelaire's poetry. To regret that Berg did not set the French original seems to me sheer pedantry, but the vocal score contains both the German and French texts, the latter with alterations in the vocal line necessitated by Baudelaire's prosody.

Le Vin is an apostrophe to the juice of grape, to its intoxicating ambrosial power, to the happiness it brings to the drinker of wine. The cycle consists of five poems in the first of which, *L'Ame du Vin*, wine itself speaks, describing its mission as the bringer of joy and liberator of 'Homme, O cher déshérité' and ends by proclaiming its divine origin as the 'grain précieux jeté par l'eternel Semeur'. In the following four poems Baudelaire chooses four different types of drinkers on whom the wine confers the utmost bliss. In *Le Vin des chiffoniers* it is the wretched rag-pickers in the street of Paris; in *Le Vin de l'assassin* it is a man who has murdered his wife; in *Le Vin du solitaire* it is the solitary (Baudelaire himself?) who speaks of the solace the liquid brings him, giving him 'l'éspoir, la jeunesse et la vie'; and finally *Le Vin des amants* conjures the ecstasy of young lovers for whom wine is the wings on which they are transported into a land of dreams. Of these five poems Berg selected the first (*Die Seele des Weines*), the fourth (*Der Wein des Einsamen*) and the fifth (*Der Wein der Liebenden*). This selection is significant in that the three poems chosen stress the more idealistic, more 'innocent' aspect of Baudelaire's verses. The two poems omitted by Berg show, like the major part of *Les Fleurs du mal,* his preoccupation with the ugly and the evil.[24]

Berg reversed the original order of the last two poems obtaining in this way a ternary form of the text which he treated musically as a sonata movement in which the development section is replaced by a waltz-like scherzo, to be followed by a recapitulation of the first part. This procedure, whereby the text is so transposed and/or altered as to suggest a musical form such as sonata, rondo, scherzo and so on, is highly characteristic of Berg's musico-dramatic method in *Wozzeck* and, notably, *Lulu*. That he set the third poem as a free and much shortened recapitulation of the music to the first poem was due to the fact that its text represents a return to the essential mood of the opening.

[24] When in 1857 Baudelaire was prosecuted by the State for obscenity, indecency and offence against public morals, *Le Vin de l'assassin* was singled out as an example of his depravity. Yet, surprisingly, this was not one of the six poems which he had to omit from the second edition of *Les Fleurs du mal* in 1861.

After the second Storm song, *Der Wein* was Berg's next composition to be based entirely (in contrast to the intervening Lyric Suite) on the strict twelve-note method. The composer himself indicated that the basic row of the piece was Ex. 10a, yet his use of it in such strategically placed sections as the orchestral prelude and postlude and the first entry of the voice suggests that the series also takes the form shown in Ex. 10b:

Example 10a

Example 10b

The peculiarity of Ex. 10a is that it contains three triads (major, minor and minor-major) and several tritones, all of which are being utilised in the concert aria.[25] Moreover, the first seven notes of Ex. 10b form the harmonic D minor scale, and D is indeed the implied tonality of the music, as may be seen from its last bar, just as F is the implied tonic of the Lyric Suite and B flat of the Violin Concerto. This diatonic scale segment facilitates cantabile writing for the voice, as stepwise progressions are the means of best achieving a singable vocal style.[26]

After the Lyric Suite (see pp. 121ff.) Berg's handling of the row in *Der Wein* appears comparatively simple. Yet there are exceptions, one of which is the retrograde in the orchestral recapitulation of the vocal waltz of this Scherzo (142-70), the palindrome being Berg's favourite device for the repeat of a previous section. (Indeed, Berg's retrograde has been called 'a view of life'. To what extreme views a symbolic interpretation of this device in Berg may lead can be seen in a quotation from another writer (p. 153). Here and there he juxtaposes original and inversion to denote the antecedent and consequent of a theme (bars 15-20, O on D, I on E flat; bars 77-83, O on G sharp, I on C sharp). The wide leaps and the compass, which extends over nearly two octaves (middle C to B flat)[27] combine to make it an exacting piece, although it is not a typical coloratura aria as is Lulu's *Lied* in the opera for which it was a study; *Der Wein* can be sung by a lyric soprano or a

---

[25] For instance, E flat major and B flat minor in bitonal combination, bars 73 and 196; E minor, bar 60; B flat minor-major plus a major seventh, bar 59. Tritones are very frequent, notably in the Tango section.

[26] For instance, in bars 15-20, 56-58 and 92-96.

[27] The setting of the French text goes up to top C sharp (bar 208).

tenor. Realistic touches are not missing as, for instance, the suggestion of an inebriated state by means of downward portamenti or 'slides';[28] it is possible that 'Der Trunkene im Frühling' of Mahler's *Lied von der Erde* may have served Berg as a model, though in the symphonic movement there are no actual slides but portamento-like turns in the voice part. But Mahler's falling sixths seem to echo in the Tango, as, for example in bars 43-48. There is, significantly, no realism in the ecstatic Scherzo, (which to my mind represents the most imaginative section of *Der Wein*), except for the closing portamento a tenth down symbolising the lover's final escape into a land of dreams (bars 138-9). It would seem that Berg did not have complete confidence in the first singer of the aria, for there are a number of *ossia* for high-lying phrases and in some places the voice is doubled by an instrument, in order to ensure accurate intonation.

The orchestral forces employed are fairly large,[29] yet, as in the Altenberg songs of seventeen years before, they are rarely used for a full tutti but mostly in a chamber manner. The very translucency of the orchestral texture is a measure of Berg's concern for the voice and the balance between it and the instruments is well-nigh perfect. Though the composer mixes the colours of the various departments, each of them – woodwind, brass and strings – have as a rule their own melodic and rhythmic material. The textural hierarchy, which is so characteristic a feature of twelve-note music, is always carefully maintained in the division between leading, subsidiary and purely accompanying parts. Here and there we come across impressionist touches,[30] notably in the way in which Berg uses harp, piano, glockenspiel and some percussion. Yet, unlike Adorno, I find these touches of very secondary importance, for Berg's employment of the orchestra was not to create oscillating iridescent sound effects *per se*, but to achieve a multi-layered linear texture in which the voice, while standing out by its particular timbre, is treated in the manner of an obbligato. In other words, *Der Wein* is, like all genuine twelve-note music, conceived in primarily contrapuntal terms.

The concert aria is the first of Berg's compositions – the other is *Lulu* – into which he introduced jazz, to which, according to Adorno,[31] he was a late-comer, not becoming acquainted with it till the mid-1920s, by which time a number of composers had already made use of this exotic importation from North America.[32] At first his attitude towards jazz was guarded, and it may

[28] Bars 32, 63, 186 and 190.

[29] They include an alto saxophone, 3 clarinets, 3 bassoons, 4 horns, 2 trumpets, 2 trombones and tuba, harp, piano, glockenspiel and no less than 9 percussion instruments.

[30] Adorno goes even so far as to say (*Alban Berg*, p. 124) that nowhere did Berg so closely assimilate features of French impressionism to his own style as in *Der Wein*.

[31] ibid., p. 120.

[32] Stravinsky in *L'Histoire du soldat* (1918), Hindemith in the Kammermusik no. 1 (1921), Milhaud in *La Création du monde* (1923), Krenek in *Der Sprung über den Schatten* (1924), and Schoenberg in his opera, *Von Heute auf Morgen* (1926).

well be that Krenek's *Jonny spielt auf* (1927) decided him to resort to jazz in
Der Wein.[33] Though we know that he liked to listen to good jazz bands on the
radio, yet, to judge from *Lulu* where it is used to characterise the sham,
meretricious atmosphere of the theatre, Berg seems to have associated it with
something socially inferior and common. This is also the case with the Tango
in *Der Wein* where in the first song it serves to illustrate a plebeian Sunday
crowd and the banal informality of a domestic scene, while in the third song,
it accompanies the lines in which Baudelaire refers to gambling, flirtation,
and enervating music comparable to a distant cry of human agony. In fact,
Adorno, in speaking of Berg's jazz, interprets it as a banal merchandise and
links this with wider socio-philosophical notions[34] which seem too complex
and far-fetched to be applicable to the Tango of *Der Wein*. Berg's scoring of
the Tango sections employs the typical instruments of a jazz band including
a saxophone though this plays also in other non-jazz portions (such as the
Der Wein der Liebenden), a trumpet and two trombones with jazz mutes, a side-
drum, piano and strings which are plucked in the manner of a banjo.
Augmented and perfect fourths in the piano are here as characteristic as they
are in the English Waltz of *Lulu*:

Example 11

I do not consider *Der Wein* one of Berg's outstanding compositions, a view
first put forward by Malipiero (see p. 82). It is not without significance for
Berg's own feelings about it that at the mention of *Der Wein* an apologetic
expression would always appear on his face.[35]

---

[33] Webern did not yield to its lure until 1930 – in his Quartet, op. 22.

    It is interesting to observe that both Berg and Schoenberg recognised the genius in the music
of George Gershwin – Berg in 1928 when he gave Gershwin an inscribed copy of the Lyric Suite,
and Schoenberg after having settled in America in 1933 when he became personally acquainted
with the composer of *Porgy and Bess*.

[34] ibid., p. 122.

[35] *Alban Berg. Leben und Werk in Daten und Bilden*, edited by Erich Alban Berg, Frankfurt, 1976,
p. 34

TEN

CHAMBER MUSIC

As with the Vienna classics, for the Second Viennese School sonata form remained the principle formal norm – the form *par excellence*. Whether in their tonal, atonal or twelve-note periods, it was a constant presence in the minds of Schoenberg, Berg and Webern, and this despite the fact that with the abolition in atonal music of key and, with it, of functional harmony and the consequent loss of tension between harmonic zones, one chief characteristic of the classical form went overboard. (In the discussion of Berg's String Quartet we shall mention the means by which this and other losses were replaced). The reason why this form retained its cardinal position in their works was, I believe, because it was the only mould capacious enough to accommodate a weighty musical content and to allow a many-layered large-scale structure to be built on the basis of Schoenberg's overriding principle of continuous developing variation. In Berg's compositions sonata form, whether in its one-movement or cyclical design, is to be found no less than seven times – the Piano Sonata, op. I, the String Quartet, op. 3, the Four Clarinet Pieces, op. 5, the Lyric Suite, the concert aria, and certain scenes of *Wozzeck* and *Lulu*, which is ample proof of the hold this form had on his creative thinking.

PIANO SONATA, OP. I

The Piano Sonata (1907-8) was, we recall, not written as part of Berg's studies with Schoenberg, but started life independently, though the master kept an eye on its further progress. Although it is in one movement only, it stands on its own legs and is aesthetically sufficient unto itself. Yet Berg at one time did think of adding at least two more movements to it, but no suitable ideas for them would come, whereupon Schoenberg, according to the composer, remarked that this showed that he had said all there was to say;[1] which decided Berg to publish it as it stood. The work closely adheres to the three main divisions of the classical sonata, with even a formal repeat of the exposition. But what is striking is its emotional expression – a post-*Tristan*esque sadness punctuated by climactic outbursts of a highly dramatic character (not dissimilar to the last song of op. 2), which seems to point to the later opera composer. Like the majority of Berg's compositions, it is a

---

[1] Redlich, *Alban Berg*, p. 355, no. 47.

tragic work which comes out with particular poignancy in the opening and
the funereal closing sections:

Example 12a

What is particularly noteworthy about the Sonata is its thematic economy.
The first subject (which bears a strong family likeness to the second subject
in Schoenberg's Chamber Symphony in that both begin with a rising perfect
and augmented fourth), may be said to have spawned the second theme
through figure *x* of Ex. 12*a*, which figure also occurs in the codetta (Ex. 12*b*),
though the theme of the latter represents the augmentation of a motive in the
veloce transition (bar 38). Each of the three ideas has its own tempo – Allegro
moderato (tempo I), Più lento (tempo II) and Molto più lento (tempo III),
which is a peculiarity of Berg's method of distinguishing the various sections
of a movement. The labile nature of the tempo is further increased by
accelerandi and ritardandi which (as in Puccini) give the music a pervasive
rubato character[2] – possibly a reflection of the composer's nervous
sensibility. These perpetual tempo fluctuations are matched by the extreme
fluidity of the harmonic language in which the semitone is Berg's chief means
whereby to link chord progressions (see the bass of Exx. 12*a* and *b*). This
chromatic sliding of the bass line contrasts with the root positions of chords
as we find, for example, in Schoenberg's Chamber Symphony, and may be

[2] Almost constant tempo changes also characterise Schoenberg's String Quartets, opp. 7 and
10.

regarded as a musical expression of the temperamental difference between the two composers. Moreover, Berg's chromatic appoggiaturas, of which I spoke in connection with the first song of op. 2, combine with passing-notes to make the establishment of a key for any given passage rather difficult, except for the first subject (Ex. 12a) and the last five bars of the Sonata, both of which represent an extended cadence in B minor. From the harmonic point of view the work may be described as a study in the use of chromatically 'altered' suspensions and passing-note chords.

Another noteworthy feature of the Sonata is Berg's simplification of the development section in relation to the exposition. To have treated the former as a 'working out' would have been tautological, since the exposition shows already an intense development[3] – hence Berg's relaxation of the dense polyphonic texture in the proper development section in favour of a more homophonic writing, in which sequential treatment abounds. It is these sequences, together with the harmonic style, which are largely responsible for the *Tristan*esque character of the music. The end of the development which deals exclusively with the second subject, is followed by a short transition which is Berg's first attempt to achieve an almost imperceptible, seamless *Übergang* to the recapitulation (bars 118-120). This last section preserves the original order of the themes,[4] but it is extended and much varied in detail, and shows that Berg had well digested Schoenberg's injunction to his pupils: 'Never do what a copyist can do!' This is on a par with Berg's own words to a pupil who, in the recapitulation, repeated literally a theme from the exposition: 'How can you do this? Think of what your themes and motives have meanwhile "experienced"!'[5]

STRING QUARTET, OP. 3

Berg told Adorno that he wrote the String Quartet, op. 3, in a mood of defiance after a publisher had rejected his Piano Sonata.[6] Combativeness is certainly the characteristic attitude of the second movement, and a challenging gesture can be read into the gruff opening of the first movement. Whatever the reasons, the feelings the composer seems to project in this work are of an uncompromising nature and presented with a forceful directness which comes as a surprise after the *Jugendstil* softness of the Piano Sonata and some of the Seven Early Songs. In the treatment of form and other technical aspects it shows Berg standing on the threshold of his maturity and fully

[3] See for instance the spinning out of the first subject by means of developmental variation (bars 4-11).

[4] The chord of the dominant ninth on which the second subject first enters recurs at each of its subsequent appearances in development and recapitulation, on A, E and B, respectively.

[5] H. Schmidt-Garre, 'Berg als Lehrer', in *Melos* 20, 1955, p. 40.

[6] Adorno, *Alban Berg*, p. 63.

bears out Schoenberg's remarks (quoted on p. 15), notably in respect of 'the strength and sureness of its presentation' and 'its careful working'. Nominally it was his last 'prentice work, but actually it is his first minor masterpiece. If in the last of the Four Songs, op. 2, he made his first step in the direction of free atonality, in the Quartet he shows himself in total command of this style of writing. Moreover, while at the same time Schoenberg and Webern cultivated short, aphoristic pieces in the atonal manner, not daring to tackle large-scale instrumental works on account of its non-functional harmony and the resulting difficulty in erecting large architectures, the young Berg had the courage to pen a quartet with a firm and coherent structure, of which more anon. That it has only two movements is indeed rare in the quartet genre, but there are precedents in Beethoven's piano sonatas.[7] Two reasons suggest themselves. One is that the coda of the first movement has a pronounced Adagio character and thus may be taken to stand for the slow movement. The other and perhaps more valid one is that the two movements – the first a sonata movement and the second a rondo – are thematically related to one another and complementary in mood so as to form an artistically satisfying whole. No sympathetic listener feels that this quartet of about twenty minutes' duration is a torso needing one or two more movements for its completion.

Coming back to its structure, we find that Berg's chief means of articulating the music are: a marked contrast between the main themes and their different tempi, restatement of themes in their original or transposed pitch to replace the keys of tonal music, alteration in the density of texture, and, lastly, caesurae to mark off the individual sections. All this is brought into action to supplant the form-generating property of tonal harmony. There are, of course, tonal associations – they are not missing even in Berg's serial works – such as pedals and occasional quasi-cadences, to say nothing of elliptical chords whose resolution into a tonal harmony is suppressed. But all this is too vague and isolated to be made to serve as a framework of tonal references. Besides, most of what happens vertically in this quartet is the result of linear counterpoint, and thematic work swamps (as already in the tonal Piano Sonata) the section which in the classical form is reserved for a coherent and clear-cut exposition of the main material. As in the Piano Sonata but to a much higher degree of subtleness, developmental variation begins almost with the first bar and continues to the last.

In the Piano Sonata we had clearly defined, static themes of the traditional kind; in the Quartet these are replaced by dynamic, open-ended motives of diminutive shape, which flow into one another, as in the opening movement's first subject (Ex. 13a and b), or are contrapuntally combined, as in the second subject (Ex. 13c).

[7] Opp. 54, 78, 90 and 111.

This atomisation of themes into tiny particles is one of the novel features of op. 3 and allows Berg to achieve a strictly thematic texture, with each of the four parts presenting one or the other motives in its original version or in variants. About Ex. 13a three things are to be noted. First, its non-serial twelve-note structure; secondly, the whole-tone build of the opening figure (F –E flat – D flat – B, the last note preceded by its lower and upper changing notes), which on all its recurrences in the first and second movements preserves this shape; thirdly, the wedge-wise expansion or *Ausweitung* of the semitone to a perfect fourth, the whole passage conjuring up the image of a stone being thrown into water and causing ever-widening ripples. Ex. 13b clearly shows Berg's concern to invent a consequent which, by contrast with the antecedent, has wider intervals and is of a wider compass. A third motive[8] concludes the twelvebar-long first subject. The second subject (Ex. 13c) is marked by a cantabile on the first violin which dominates the codetta, imparting to it a pronounced lyrical character.

Example 13a

Example 13b

Example 13c

As to the development section, it has two noteworthy features. One is its brevity in relation to the length of the exposition – twenty-four bars as against eighty. We recall that in the Piano Sonata Berg simplified the development section; here he shortens it, thus suggesting an equation in his thinking of simplification with brevity. (In the opening movement of the

[8] Its first two bars are identical with the opening bar in the Prelude to Act V of Debussy's *Pelléas et Mélisande*. Its expansion is seen in Ex. 14.

Lyric Suite Berg omits the development section altogether.) Hand in hand
with this brevity goes a firm sense of direction and succinct utterance. The
second feature of this development is the absence from it of the first subject,
the evident reason for this being that its 'working-out' is taken up in the
much altered recapitulation of which the first thirty bars or so are devoted to
it. The main climax of the movement occurs in bar 101, towards the end of
the development, though both the remaining sections have their own
climaxes.[9] As already said, the reprise is greatly modified, introducing a
march-like episode in bars 108-119, and in the following eight bars Berg
expands the third motive of the opening subject into a soaring viola phrase
which is one of the most exquisite lyrical inventions of the young composer:

Example 14

The long coda, beginning with a variant of the march episode (bar 153), has
the character of a farewell (this is the section which may be regarded as
taking the place of an Adagio) which is manifest in the downward tendency
of the various motives. The movement ends with a literal restatement of the
first three bars of Ex. 13*a*.

If the first movement is for its greater part inward-looking and of a lyrical
character, the second is fierce, aggressive and suggestive of an intense
agitation. With the opening theme (Ex. 15*a*), marked significantly '*f*, sehr
heftig', Berg seems to throw down the gauntlet to imaginary enemies. Being
a rondo with sonata elements, its structure is perhaps less close-knit than
that of the first movement. On a first hearing, the listener may well feel
bewildered by what seems to him a casual, random succession of ideas – an
impression due to the radical transformation to which the composer subjects
his thematic material melodically and rhythmically.

The rondo ritornello has evidently grown on the same tree which produced
the opening of the first movement's main subject (Ex. 13*a*). And, like it, it
shows a non-serial twelve-note configuration and the same wedge-wise
expansion of an interval in its tail:

Example 15a

___

[9] Exposition, bar 32; recapitulation, bar 145.

Example 15b

The base of Ex. 15*b*, whose stentato on D^{10} will be an important signpost in the further course of the music, is a striking variant of Ex. 15*a* and shows a strong family likeness to the opening theme of the first movement of Mahler's Second Symphony. Four episodes can be discerned in this rondo which are separated from one another by variants of the ritornello. Episode 1 (bars 34-46) opens in the bass with the movement's leitharmony and includes a *grazioso* figure in bars 39-40. Episode 2 (bars 50-60) is based on an expressive chromatic motive. Episode 3, 'sehr bewegt' (72-85), refers back to the stentato of Ex.15*b* and introduces a motive closely similar to the second subject of the first movement (Ex. 13*c*). Finally, Episode 4, 'Sehr ruhig und mässig' (bars 119-50), unfolds on a step-wise rising theme which is clinched by a downward portamento over nearly an octave. Bar 151 marks the beginning of a free recapitulation in which the ritornello is viewed from yet another angle. In bar 168 Berg combines the stentato with the gruff figure from the opening movement (Ex. 13*a*), when also the march of that movement makes its reappearance (second violin, bars 179-85). In other words, the affinity between the two movements hitherto so well concealed now becomes overt. In the coda (*Pesante*, 217) Berg juxtaposes the rondo ritornello with the gruff figure to make their relationship fully audible and, after the stentato and a flourish for all four instruments, the movement ends on a chord cluster of four adjacent notes. It is of course possible to see in the rondo, as Redlich does,[11] a kind of second development of the first movement's expository material. But I am rather inclined to assume with Adorno[12] that Berg's aim was to invent variants of this material which only towards the end reveals its connection with the preceding movement.

A word on the technical style of the Quartet. Berg apparently would not attempt a string quartet until he had thoroughly familiarised himself with the essential requirements of this medium, which he probably did through a close study of Schoenberg's D minor and F sharp minor Quartets from which he could learn to perfection the art of a preponderantly linear counterpoint in four parts. Moreover, his treatment of the strings is highly idiomatic, which

---

[10] Cf. passage 65-71 in the finale of Schoenberg's String Quarter, op. 7.
[11] *Alban Berg*, p. 63.
[12] *ibid.*

could not be said of his piano writing in the Sonata; this is all the more remarkable since he was not a string player as his teacher was. It is, admittedly, a difficult work to perform – difficult if the distinction between leading and subsidiary parts, the subtle dynamic shades, and the almost constant tempo changes or rubati are to be accurately observed.

To sum up. In its rethinking of the classical sonata and rondo form, in thematic invention, contrapuntal treatment and the manipulation of Schoenberg's developing variation technique it is a masterly work and was recognised as such at the Salzburg Festival of 1923. That it is overshadowed by the Lyric Suite of some sixteen years later is to be regretted. Not only is Berg's op. 3 free of all the tentativeness which one might have expected in a composer of twenty-five, but it is also free, with the exception of the long coda of the first movement, of all tragic feeling, and has a youthful *élan*, freshness and directness of emotional projection which inevitably are missing in the more mellow music of his later string quartet.

FOUR PIECES FOR CLARINET AND PIANO, OP. 5

The instrumental miniature was a typical product of the romantic era. Short, concise pieces to express a single mood or single character trait were found to be most suitable for the projection of a marked subjectivism in the nineteenth century. Beethoven, Schubert, Chopin, Schumann and Brahms cultivated the miniature, and this was continued in the twentieth century by Debussy, Ravel and Bartók. There was therefore nothing exceptional in the fact that between 1908 and 1913 Schoenberg and his two disciples wrote a spate of miniatures which all carry, significantly, the words 'Pieces' or 'Bagatelles' in the title. There was, however, an additional reason for this, which was the mistaken belief that, because of the absence of functional harmony, atonal music had to exclude music of large-scale structure. Berg disproved this in his String Quartet, op. 3 and, even more strikingly, in his opera *Wozzeck*, though he himself still subscribed to the view that only short pieces could be written in the atonal style.[13]

With the examples of Schoenberg's op. 11 (1908) and op. 19 (1911), as well as Webern's op. 6 (1910) before him, Berg wrote in the spring of 1913 his Four Pieces for Clarinet and Piano, op. 5 – aphorisms of an expressionist order and the instrumental counterpart to the first and second of the Mombert songs of op. 2 and to some of the Altenberg Songs. At the same time there is evidence that the composer modelled them on Schoenberg's Six Little Pieces for Piano, op. 19. Thus his second piece is identical in length with Schoenberg's no. 2 and shows the same preoccupation with the major third as the harmonic basis, while Berg's third piece, in its light, fleeting

[13] See his Lecture on *Wozzeck* in Redlich, *Alban Berg,* p. 311.

character and the 6/8 metre, is closely linked to his master's no. 1. Similarly, the silent depression of a chord (quasi harmonics) at the end of Berg's fourth piece is anticipated by Schoenberg in no. 1 of his op. 11. The expressionist character of the Berg pieces lies not only in their brevity but also in the tension set up by the interplay of clarinet and piano which in nos. 1 and 4 explodes into a sudden outburst of the most violent kind.

Berg, we recall, first intended a series of six pieces, analogous to Schoenberg's op. 19, but in the event confined himself to only four. The reason for this may well have been his wish to suggest the four movements of a miniature sonata which, in view of the role this form played in the thinking of the Second Viennese School, would seem likely. Thus no. 1 corresponds to an Allegro, no. 2 to an Adagio, no. 3 is a Scherzo and Trio, and no. 4 takes the form of a rondo finale. There are, however, no thematic relationships between the pieces, as there are in the String Quartet, but what they have in common is a tendency to harmonic stasis, that is, the bass with its chordal superstructure remains unchanged for several bars. And, as in op. 3, there are no themes in the established sense, but mostly infusoria-like motives treated in developmental variation. Of tonal suggestions there are very few – D major at the opening of no. 2 which in the two closing bars turns into an augmented triad on B flat, C major at the opening and ending of no. 4, while no. 1 concludes on a Scriabin-like chord (telescoped perfect and augmented fourths) resting on a B in the bass. With the exception of no. 3, which has an expressionist *Ländler* as trio, the other pieces convey a mood of sadness, particularly the desolate no. 2.

Berg exploits the clarinet as to the manner born. All four pieces show warmly expressive writing; there are wide skips from the very high range to the *chalumeau* register, deep-toned gurgles and trills, *flatterzunge*, echo tones, and legato and staccato phrases. In short, op. 5 represents a brilliant contribution to the restricted literature of clarinet and piano. It was the first of the composer's works to bear a dedication to Schoenberg and to the Society for Private Musical Performances, where it was baptised on 17 October 1919.

LYRIC SUITE (STRING QUARTET NO. 2)

Nearly seventeen years separate the Lyric Suite from the first string quartet, years during which Berg had attained full maturity, eloquent testimony to which are *Wozzeck* and the Chamber Concerto. It is a sovereign master who wrote the Lyric Suite, transforming his early vocal lyricism into a mellow instrumental utterance of compelling effect, both in its emotional aspect and its formal-technical projection. The basic mood of the work is one of hopelessness and despair and, in the finale, of existential sadness. One is almost tempted to call it Berg's *Lied von der Erde*, with the same motto as in the Mahler piece – 'Dunkel ist das Leben, ist der Tod'. Whether Berg had this work at the back of his mind when writing the Suite, we do not know, but it is not without significance that it also consists of six movements different in character and tone, with a kind of farewell to life so poignantly suggested in the last movement in the gradual dying away of the music on the solitary viola which is, however, entirely different in effect from the sense of transfiguration we experience at the end of the Mahler finale. But here the similarity ends, for the Suite shows, apart from the fact that it belongs to an entirely different genre, a completely different formal design – a design which recalls the suite-like sequence of movements in Beethoven's late string quartets. Its point of departure is an Allegretto gioviale followed by five movements that grow in emotional intensity and in the process become alternately slower and faster.

Allegretto   Andante   Allegro   Adagio   Presto   Largo
gioviale   amoroso   misterioso   appassionato   delirando   desolato

It is the dynamic character of this *Stimmungssteigerung* (Berg) or emotional intensification which was responsible for the Suite being called a 'latent opera',[14] with the catastrophe in the Presto delirando and an epilogue in the Largo desolato. In other words, the Lyric Suite represents a composed accelerando and ritardando not dissimilar from the Monoritmica in *Lulu*.

The Suite is the most subjective, most ego-bound work of Berg's maturity, and I feel convinced that in it the composer projected an inner drama too intimate, too personal to be divulged in words. All he would say about it was that its emotional progress and intensification was a 'Schicksal erleidend', 'a submitting to fate'.[15] There are, in addition, two pointers to the underlying inner programme: first the literal quotations, in the Adagio, of a passage from Zemlinsky's Lyric Symphony (which may have suggested to Berg the title of his own work) and of the *Tristan* chord in the Largo. Both are quotations from vocal works which express a most poignant desire for mystic union with the beloved beyond this life. The other pointer to the close ego-related nature of the music is the presence in it of Berg's number 23 manifest in the bar length of movements and sections, and in the metronome marks.

The above was written some six years before the story of Berg's secret

[14] Adorno, *Alban Berg*, p. 110.

[15] W. Reich, ed., *Alban Berg. Bildnis im Wort*, Zurich, 1959, pp. 45-54. Also U. von Rauchhaupt, ed., *Schoenberg, Berg, Webern. Die Streichquartette. Eine Dokumentation*, Hamburg, 1971, pp. 92-5.

programme of the Lyric Suite came to light (1977). The story not only confirmed what Berg students had felt all along about the highly personal autobiographical character of the work, but it now makes it a psychological document of the first order. Together with the Violin Concerto, the Lyric Suite is the clearest evidence to show how very intimately life and art were interwoven in Berg's music.

In the following pages I shall draw on the annotated score of the Suite that Berg gave to Hanna and that George Perle fully described in his article.[16]

First, Berg's numerological symbolism: 23 was his own 'fateful' number, but we now know that Hanna's number was 10, and both these numbers and their multiples are brought into the closest interrelationship in the Lyric Suite in the following manner:

	Bar Lengths	*Metronome Marks*
Allegro gioviale	138 (6 x 23)	♩ = 100 (10 x 10)
Second subject	entry, bar 23	
Andante amoroso	150 (10 x 15)	Tempo I: ♪ = 100 (10 x 10)
		Tempo II: ♩. = 50 (10 x 5)
		Tempo III: ♪ = 69 (3 x 23)
Allegro misterioso	138 (6 x 23)	♩ = 150 (10 x 15)
Trio estatico	23, entry, bar 69	♩ = 150 (10 x 15)
Adagio appassionato	69 (3 x 23)	♩ = 69 (3 x 23)
Presto delirando	460 (2 x 23 x 10)	♩. = 115 (5 x 23)
Largo desolato	46 (2 x 23)	Tempo I: ♩ = 69 (3 x 23)
		Tempo II: ♩ = 46 (2 x 23)

The interrelationship between Berg's and Hanna's numbers is particularly close in the Allegro misterioso and the Presto delirando.

The series on which the Lyric Suite is based (Ex. 16) begins with F and ends on H (B), the initials of Berg's beloved. Moreover, Berg manipulates the series and its derivatives in such a way that the initials of both his and Hanna's names appear as the motives (A-B-H-F and its permutations), notably in the Allegro misterioso and the Largo desolato. The printed score has a Preface by Erwin Stein which concludes with the sentence, 'the seemingly limiting system of twelve-note composition has allowed the composer the freedom to quote the opening bars of *Tristan*'. Berg, in his

---

[16] 'The Secret Programme of the Lyric Suite', *Musical Times*, September 1977, pp. 709-13.

annotated score, underlines 'die Freiheit gelassen' and adds:

> Sie hat mir, meine Hanna, auch noch andere Freiheiten gelassen! Z. Bsp.
> die, in dieser Musik immer wieder unsere Buchstaben H.F. und A.B.
> hineinzugeheimnissen; jeden Satz und Satzteil in Beziehung zu unseren
> Zahlen 10 und 23 zu bringen. (It has also, my Hanna, allowed me other
> freedoms! For example, that of secretly inserting into this music our letters
> H.F. and A.B; and bringing into relationship our numbers 10 and 23 in
> every movement and section of a movement.)

The Lyric Suite was Berg's first major work to adopt Schoenberg's twelve-note method of composition; but it is characteristic of the composer's initially cautious approach that movements and/or sections in serial technique alternate with others in the free atonal style of *Wozzeck* and the Chamber Concerto, to say nothing of tonal enclaves. The basic note-row which underlies the first movement of the Suite is the same that Berg used in the second Storm song of 1925. Yet, while there its management, notably in the voice-part, is simple, in the later work Berg shows himself a consummate master in a more complex application of it. Generally speaking, he adheres to Schoenberg's dictum: 'Man folgt der Reihe, komponiert aber im übrigen wie vorher – One follows the row but for the rest composes as before'. But his treatment of the series is peculiar only to him and differs greatly from that of Webern. The 'expansive' Berg sought to enlarge the thematic possibilities of a row by transposing some of its notes and thus deriving new rows, as he does in the Suite and *Lulu*. The 'thrifty' Webern, on the other hand, kept strictly to the same row throughout all the movements of a work and reduced even its yield as a thematic reservoir by structuring it in such a way that it falls into several segments which represent inversions, retrogrades or transpositions of an initial 6-, 4- or 3-note motive.[17] In marked contrast to Berg, Webern never invents rows possessing tonal implications.

Berg used the original form of the basic row only in the first movement of the Lyric Suite:

Example 16

[17] See the series in the Symphony, op. 21; the Concerto for nine instruments, op. 24; the Piano Variations, op. 27, and the String Quarter, op. 29.

It is a so-called 'all-interval' series containing all the eleven different intervals possible in the chromatic system and was, as mentioned, invented by Berg's pupil, F.H. Klein. Berg thought it to be the only row of this kind and therefore found it a 'theoretically interesting case'. Yet his view of the uniqueness of this row has been shown to have been incorrect by such musicians as Krenek, Jelinek and Eimert, and more recent computer calculations have proved that there are no fewer than 1928 such rows possible.[18] Berg, however, was not so much concerned with the interval properties of Ex. 16, as with its symmetrical design. It will be seen that its first half consists of the 'white key' notes and the second of the 'black key' notes, the two halves standing in the relation of a tritone to each other, an interval which plays an important part in this movement. Moreover, a succession of fourths and fifths can be derived from its division into an upper and lower strand, of which Berg will make characteristic use in the course of the music, and by permutations we arrive at two hexachords, with their appropriate scale segments:

Example 17

Yet this row possesses one great disadvantage, which is that it has no independent retrograde, for the second half of Ex. 16, is, if transposed an augmented fourth down, identical with the crab of the first half, which inevitably reduces its scope as a thematic reservoir. Berg called it a 'somewhat mathematical' row and, as said, used it only in the first movement. For the other serial movements he changed the position of certain notes which, as he wrote in his annotation for Reich,[19] was 'not important for the line but important for the (musical) characters'.

With a composer so much given to thematic relationships and correspondences, as we have already seen in the String Quartet and will encounter again in the *jeu d'esprit* of the finale in the Chamber Concerto, it is not to be wondered at that they also occur in the Lyric Suite. Apart from the connection provided by the basic row and its variants in the serial movements of the work, there are melodic-rhythmic phrases to link certain movements. Thus, the second subject of I, bars 23-5, returns in changed

---

[18] See *Newsletter* no. 2, January 1971, publ. International Alban Berg Society, New York, p. 6.
 In his letter to Schoenberg of 13 July 1926, which appeared in an English translation in this *Newsletter*, Berg gives an explanation of how he used Klein's 'mother chord' horizontally and manipulated the row, and its derivatives.
[19] Reich (ed.), *Alban Berg. Bildnis im Wort*, p. 46.

rhythmic shape and transposed from D flat to E, in II, bars 16-23. This same episode introduces as if by stealth the first variant of the series (viola, 24-8) on which the Scherzo of the third movement is based (V_1, Ex. 21), just as the second variant (V_2, Ex. 25) on which the finale is built, is already anticipated in the fifth movement. Similarly, the Trio estatico of the third movement exposes the main material of the fourth movement, and the finale comes full circle with its references in bars 10 and 37-9 to I, bars 5-6 and 38-9. This procedure has aptly been compared to a play in which the same actors appear in different masks in the various acts.

Allegretto gioviale. In his programme annotations Berg described this opening movement as being of an 'introductory nature, a quasi *Intrada*' and a 'more objective piece',[20] though the up and down of the first subject and the loose-limbed rhythm of the whole would seem to stress the 'jovial' of the title. It is the only movement to be cast in sonata form yet without a development section. The process of the liquidation of this classical form had begun with Berg in the development section of the Piano Sonata, in which we found a considerable thinning out of the texture as compared with the other sections, and in the first movement of String Quartet, in which the development is of remarkable brevity. In the Allegretto of the Lyric Suite this section is completely omitted, reminding us of the binary form of the early (Scarlattian) sonata.[21] The exposition is orthodox, with first subject (2-12), transition (12-22), second subject (23-32) and closing motive (33-5). In the recapitulation the contrapuntal texture is altered, the transition much shortened, but the brief closing motive is extended to a coda of eight bars. Several details seem to me worthy of special mention. The tritone relationship of the two halves of the basic row (D – A flat) is accurately reflected in the antecedent and consequent of the first subject:

Example 18

Then the *Tristan* quotation from the Finale is hinted at in the chromatic motive of bars 5 (first violin) and 38-9 (original: cello; inversion: viola), as though the despairing mood of the last movement cast its shadow ahead. Furthermore, there are the scale segments derived from Ex. 17 which, like punctuation marks, indicate the end of the exposition and recapitulation, and recur in some of the later movements of the Suite. These scale segments

---

[20] ibid., p. 47. Its original marking was 'Allegretto giojoso'.
[21] Berg himself pointed to the binary form of this movement but added a question mark in brackets after it (ibid., p. 47).

bring us to the tonal implication of the basic row in the Allegretto. Apart from its 'white' and 'black' key structure, it is its fourths and fifths which readily lend themselves to the creation of tonal 'isles'. Thus the bass in bars 34-6 proceeds in a series of rising fifths and descending fourths. In other words, it describes a circle of fifths from F to A sharp (B flat),[22] which is repeated in bars 61-6, to say nothing of the drones (perfect fifths) in the transition (bars 12 and 48).

Lastly, the very first bar is like an 'Attention, please!', reminiscent of the fanfare in the ancient opera overtures, and represents nothing else than the verticalisation of the fourths and fifths of the basic row in a special order.

Andante amoroso. In Hanna's score Berg prefaced the movement with the dedication:

Dir und Deinen Kindern ist dieses 'Rondo' gewidmet: eine musikalische Form, in der die Themen (namentlich Deines) – den lieblichen Kreis schliessend – immer wiederkehren. (To you and your children I have dedicated this 'rondo': a musical form in which the themes (notably yours) – closing the charming circle – continually recur.)

This is the most heavily annotated movement of the Lyric Suite and I will mention only Berg's most important remarks. In order to indicate clearly the themes associated with Hanna and the two children, he used pencils of three different colours:

Red! for the mother: rondo ritornello, Tempo I (Ex. 19).

Blue for the boy of seven, named 'Munzo', second rondo episode, Tempo II (Ex. 20*a*). Berg inserted the comment, 'nicht ohne Absicht: mit einem leisen czechischen Einschlag' (not without intention: with a slight Czech touch). Miss Robetin explained to Perle that her brother was going to a Czech elementary school at the time and consequently spoke Czech more fluently than German.

Green for Dorothea, third rondo episode, Tempo III (Ex. 20*b*). Her nickname was 'Dodo' which Berg spells out in the repeated viola figure 'do-do', this being the Italian solmization name for the note C. When this figure subsequently reappears in octaves (73-9), it is marked with 'drohend' (menacing)[23] to which Berg added the remark, 'aber es ist nicht ernst zu nehmem – *poco f* – *dimin.* im Gegenteil *dolciss.*' (but it is not to be taken seriously – on the contrary *dolciss.*). The A-H-B-F motive appears for the first time as counterpoint to the 'do-do' figure in bars 56-8.

Lastly, in the right margin of p. 23 of the score Berg entered, 'Aus Spiel

[22] In *Wozzeck*, I, 1 (33-4) the descending circle of fourths suggest the 'eternity' of which the Captain speaks.

[23] At a rehearsal for the first performance of the Lyric Suite, Berg is said to have remarked that this passage was to be played as though one were 'menacing children'.

wird Ernst' (the play becomes serious) and at bar 131 ff., at the statement of the rondo ritornello (in augmentation) Berg says, 'da tritts Du dazwischen' (now you step between). It all seems like a sketch for a nursery scene.

As already intimated, the movement is a rondo with two episodes (A-B-A-C-A-coda) in which the last A represents a kind of development of all the three sections. The 'amoroso' mood is reserved for the three A's (6-8 Tempo I) which alternate with a gaily bouncing Mahlerian Ländler (3-8, Tempo II) and the music of the second episode C (2-8, Tempo III). Before considering this movement in greater detail, something has to be said about its harmonic aspect. It is essentially in free atonal style punctuated, however, by tonal configurations such as the diatonic and whole-tone scale segments. Yet the theme of the opening ritornello is of twelve-note build, similar to the themes of the Adagio in the Chamber Concerto; while the Ländler, as mentioned before, represents a rhythmic variant of the second subject in the serial Allegretto. It is this immense fluidity in the harmonic style, this unforced interplay and merging of elements from different tonal spheres, that gives this Andante, and indeed the whole of the Lyric Suite, its cachet.

The rondo ritornello unfolds in a leisurely, almost pastoral fashion; it has a tender gracefulness about it and is most exquisitely shaped in both its antecedent and consequent:

Example 19

Its opening figure (a semi-tone plus fourth) will be integrated into the principal theme of the Adagio appassionato, thus linking the two movements. The first episode B in 3-8 time is marked by yodelling figures (22-6) whose exhilaration is complementary to the serene mood of the rondo theme which returns in a slightly altered version. The strangeness of episode C – the quasi-'menacing' music – is heightened by *sul tasto* and *flautando* effects. It is punctuated by a syncopated rhythmic figure: (Ex. 20b).

Example 20a

Example 20b

Structurally and also emotionally, the most important part of this movement begins with the last return of the rondo ritornello (81) which marks the development-cum-recapitulation of all the three sections. The main theme appears both shortened and varied, and between bars 101-30 there is a duet-like alternation between first and second episodes. A gradual quickening of the tempo leads to a three-bar structure (bars 131-42) when the rondo theme, more precisely its consequent in augmentation, begins to reassert itself against fragments from both B and C, finally to emerge victorious in bar 143. The movement closes on a chord with C in the bass which can be interpreted as a chromatically altered dominant of the 'home key' of the Suite. The Andante is testimony to Berg's sense of drama, which is seen in the way in which he first juxtaposes the rondo theme and its two episodes, and then brings them into conflict with one another, a conflict finally resolved in favour of the rondo ritornello symbolizing Hanna.

Allegro misterioso. In his annotation Berg prefaces this movement with the date '20.5.25' doubly underlining it in red. (This was probably the day on which Berg and Hanna declared their love for each other, in the Trio ecstatico.) To the 'misterioso' of the title Berg added the remark, 'denn noch war alles Geheimnis – uns *selbst* Geheimnis' (for everything was still a mystery – a mystery to *us*). The first four notes of the underlying series form the cryptogram of the initials of Berg's and Hanna's names (Ex. 21, GR); it is a cell-motive which will be used in its original shape or in permutations, independently from the series, throughout the Scherzo section and also in the Trio ecstatico (69-70 and 84). At the beginning of the Scherzo repeat as a palindrome Berg wrote, 'Vergessen Sie es –!' (forget it – !). The change from the previous intimate 'Du' to the more formal 'Sie' is significant. Incidentally, in bar 89 the first violin plays a phrase which, except for its last note (G), is identical with the closing phrase of Marie's Lullaby in *Wozzeck*, I, 'Lauter kühle Wein muss es sein', which text Berg inserted above that phrase in the movement. This was certainly a veiled reference and the only one in the Lyric Suite to Hanna's husband, Herbert, who, according to his daughter, possessed one of the finest wine cellars in Prague, a fact highly appreciated by the gastronomically minded Berg during his stay at the Fuchs-Robettins.

The third movement is, as already mentioned, a Scherzo with a strongly contrasted Trio. The scherzo section is unique in Berg's output, and in character only comparable to the orchestral Interlude in *Lulu*, with which it also shares the repeat in the retrograde. It is really a *perpetuum mobile* unfolding in an all but ceaseless rushing, scurrying, and eddying of semiquaver figures, from which from time to time brief melodic fragments rise up like ghosts from a mysterious depth. And what with the four strings playing throughout with mutes, with the dynamic level never rising above *pp*, with special effects such as *pizz.*, *flautando*, *col legno*, and *sul tasto*, this music is indeed 'Luft von anderem Planeten'. When the Trio estatico comes, it is with the force of a volcanic eruption, the rumblings of which are heard already in bar 46 of the scherzo.

The scherzo is based on a variant of the original row whose fourth and tenth notes have changed places which, as alredy stated, Berg did in order to obtain a series with an independent crab to be used in the repeat of this movement. Through Berg's transportation of the original series from F to B flat, the Scherzo is, as it were, in the subdominant of the work's 'home-key'. Here is the altered version and its three transpositions:

Example 21a

Example 21b

Example 21c

Example 21d

(Inversion)

In altering the original series and transposing it to B flat, Berg arrived at a new series which in its first four notes formed for him an all-important cell-motive, namely the cryptogram symbolically uniting him with his beloved, and employed it as a sort of ostinato. In order to use the original motive and its three permutations, Berg experimented with the new series and found that the four-note group is contained in only three transpositions (Ex. 21*b, c,* *d*) (the third of which is the inversion on E flat); moreover, by severing[24] GR from the row, the remaining eight-note figure could be used independently. The original and two permutations of GR are introduced successively by themselves in bar 1 (first violin, second violin, viola) and recur again in augmentation on the cello, bars 6-9. Again, in bars 22-5, the first violin opens with GR, i.e. the notes 9-12 of the inverted row on E flat and then plays its remaining eight notes (1-8) while the cello answers in canon with the inverted row in identical transposition but in the correct sequence of its notes.

Berg found yet another ingenious way of exploiting V_1, by dividing it into two parts, an upper one of seven, a lower one of five notes, which yields a chromatic motive (*x*) and two complementary rhythms:[25]

Example 22a

Example 22b

This two-part rhythmic configuration and its inversion provide the model for some twenty stretti or close canons which begin in bar 10:

Example 23

---

[24] Berg's term is 'Abschnürung'.

[25] Berg applies the same procedure in arriving at the 'Schigolch' theme in *Lulu* (see Ex. 74 on p. 232).

With bar 46 (2 × 23!) starts the second half of the scherzo, in which all the four variants and their inversions of V_1 chase one another in continuous stretti and finally lead, in a chromatic ascent, to the Trio. The repeat of the scherzo after the Trio is in the form of a crab, but is shortened by some twenty bars[26] and ends with the retrograde of the original GR motive with which it began. The retrograde shows alterations to the *recto* made by Berg in order to avoid unisons or octaves between two instruments; in the infancy of twelve-note music this was considered taboo. Nevertheless, there is an octave on E flat formed by first violin and cello on the third beat of bar 11 and the corresponding place in bar 127.

The Scherzo is the first of the three movements, the other two being the Presto and the Largo, to show Berg's highly individual treatment of the Schoenbergian twelve-note series, a treatment in which the segmentation of the row into four plus eight-note groups and the division into a two-part configuration lead to a remarkable enrichment of its thematic possibilities.

The *Trio estatico* (in duple time) provides an excellent example of the composer's sense of dramatic contrast. In every respect – formal, dynamic, phraseological, textural and emotional – it is the exact antithesis of the Scherzo. The white-heat of its lyricism is almost unbearable – it is to be played *sempre f possible* – and its opening theme has a most remarkable sweep of line, with leaps (first violin) over an eleventh and thirteenth. The expressive force of this theme is greatly enhanced by the downward appoggiaturas, which foreshadow the *Tristan* motif of the finale. Though the Trio is as a whole free atonal style, its theme is, like the rondo ritornello of the Andante, of a twelve-note structure. It extends to nine bars, with the antecedent and consequent separated by a *stentato* rolling figure:

Example 24a

Example 24b

closing with the scale-passage of the opening movement, which is now turned into a rising and falling whole-tone phrase. The remaining section is taken up with a free development of this theme.

---

[26] Omitted from the original are bars 30-8, 40-2, and 46-57. Incidentally, there is a misprint in the Philharmonia Pocket score (U.E. 1927): bar 30, the second and fourth note on the cellos should read G natural and G flat respectively.

Adagio appassionato. In Hanna's score the movement is headed by Berg's remark, 'Tags darauf' (Next day) and the 'appassionato' of the title underlined. The free canon between viola and first violin (24 ff.) represents 'Ich und Du'. The first Zemlinsky quotation (32-3)[27] is accompanied by the original words in Zemlinsky's Lyric Symphony, but the speaker is now Berg himself: 'Ich: – "Du bist mein Eigen, mein Eigen" ', while at the second quotation the annotation reads: 'Nun sagst es auch Du: "Du bist mein Eigen, mein Eigen" '. Attention may be drawn to the fact that the cryptogram from the previous movement appears in bars 44, 54-7 and 62-3. This movement is the climax of the suite, in which Berg seems to elaborate on the things said in concentrated form in the Trio estatico. Significantly, with its sixty-nine bars it is three times the length of the Trio. At the first glance it appears to be a continuous developing variation of the material exposed in the Trio, and Berg himself was not certain as to its formal design. Without wishing to press the point, I venture to suggest that this movement comes near to the varied strophic form, consisting of three 'strophes', each beginning with the rolling figure (Ex. 24*b*) and each leading to an impassioned outburst of immense power: A_1 (bars 1-24), A_2 (25-50), A_3 (51-8) and coda (59-69). Opening with a four-part stretto, A_1 reverses the order of the Trio theme, beginning with its consequent and ending with its antecedent. The tortuous motif (bar 5, first violin) will be of much importance in the further course of the movement, and is partly an allusion to the opening of the 'Hanna' theme in the Andante, an allusion which becomes explicit in bars 30-1 where two bars of the Andante (9 and 10) are cited literally. The most important 'strophe' is A_2. It has the most extended climax (32-43) whose highest point is reached in bars 34-7, ushered in by the first quotation of the phrase, 'Du bist mein Eigen, mein Eigen', from the third section of Zemlinsky's Lyrical Symphony. In bar 40 enters the closing theme, *molto f e patetico* (cello), Berg calling this whole last section (40-50) 'quasi cadenza'. A_3 is very short, bringing the developing variation of the main theme to an overpowering climax (*molto pesante e ritenuto*), which is punctuated by ferocious chords of eight, seven and six notes, respectively, and something of the previous violence still echoes in the arpeggio chords of bars 58-9; all four strings now play with mutes to heighten the effect of a nocturnal stillness stealing on the 'scene'. Over bars 57 ff. Berg writes in the score, '*pesante e riten.* und verebbend ins ... ganz Vergeistigte, Seelenvolle, Überirdische' (and fading into ... the wholly spiritual, immaterial, transcendental). The whole movement, remarkable for its close-knit contrapuntal texture, ends on a seven-note chord anchored in the 'home key' note F.

Presto delirando. This movement represents the peripeteia in the psychological drama of the Lyric Suite. Berg inserts a continuous text in

---

[27] It will be noted that this quotation enters in bar 32 which is the retrograde of Berg's number 23, while the second Zemlinsky quotation (46-50) enters in bar 46 = 2 × 23.

Hanna's score, and begins by saying that 'dieses Presto delirando kann nur der verstehen, wer eine Ahnung hat von den Schrecken und Qualen, die nun folgten' (This Presto delirando can only be understood by one who has a foreboding of the terrors and torment which now followed). Perle says that the physical lay-out of Berg's text is *itself* part of that text thus lending it another, visual, dimension that can be fully shown only in a facsimile reproduction of the annotated score. I shall therefore give only a summary of Berg's further comments.

The delirando sections conjure up the days with their racing pulses, while the Tenebroso sections (the Trio of the Scherzo) express the torments of the nights, 'mit ihrem kaum Schlaf zu nennenden Dahindämmern' (with their drift into what can scarcely be called sleep). There are moments when 'sich der süsse Trost eines wirklichen, alles vergessenden Schlummers über einen senkte' (as though the sweet consolation of true, all-forgetful slumber sank over one); this is written over bars 274-306 of the *di nuovo tenebroso*. But day comes again and so it goes on, 'ohne Stillstand, dieses Delirium ohne Ende' (without cease, this delirium without end).

The movement is cast in the form of scherzo and trio, both of which are repeated (the composer here follows the Beethoven of the Fourth, Seventh and Ninth Symphonies), the former being most turbulent music, bearing out the 'delirando' of the title, while the trio, marked 'Tenebroso', belongs to the sphere of spectral, nightmarish things. Moreover, the scherzo is polyphonic in texture and a dynamic movement, whereas the trio is markedly homophonic for most of the time and completely static. Perhaps the strongest contrast concerns the style of writing – the scherzo is in free atonality, and the trio strictly twelve-note, while yet another interesting feature to do with Berg's number symbolism is the fact that the individual sections show a regular lengthening by 20 bars: Scherzo$_1$ 50 bars; Trio$_1$ 70 bars; Scherzo$_2$ 90 bars; Trio$_2$ 110 bars; the exception is Scherzo$_3$ with 140 bars – all multiples of Hanna's number 10.

Three sections can be discerned in the scherzo. The first (bars 1-14) is the main theme, dodecaphonic in the sequence of its notes in the first four bars which are grouped together into $3 \times 4 = 12$ notes. It shoots up rocket-like, to descend again as rapidly. The second section (bars 15-35) has no proper theme but only two motifs: the first is the 'menacing' figure from the Adante, whose duplets form a cross rhythm with the 3/8 metre of the scherzo, and the second is an upwards and downwards swaying seventh. The third section (bars 36-50) is a four-part stretto of this last motif now extended to a tenth and eleventh, with the close imitation generating a cumulative tension. Most of the last two sections in the scherzo show a five-bar structure thus anticipating a characteristic feature of the Trio. Scherzo$_2$ (bars 121-210) combines the principal motives, with Berg making pointed use of *col legno, glissando* and 'at the heel' playing, and Scherzo$_3$ (bars 321-460) reverses the

original order of the material at the beginning (321-42). The coda (441)
shows an interesting polyrhythmic structure, in that the three upper strings
play an ostinato (opening figure of main theme), the phrase length of which is
different in each instrument – three notes on the second violin, four notes on
the viola, and five notes on the first violin; to this the cello adds its 'menacing'
duplets. In others words, there is a simultaneity of different metres ranging
from 2/8 to 5/8, of which only the 3/8 of the second violin coincides with the
basic metre of the movement. Incidentally, the drones on the cello (446-60)
represent a tonal cadence in C (C: I-V-II-V-I). The Coda is 4 × 5 = 20 bars
long.

As already said, the Trios are in strictly serial writing, based on V_2, which
is the second variant of the basic row arrived at by changing the position of
five of the original notes:

Example 25

For the greater part of the Trios the row is verticalised or telescoped into
chords, the exception being some canonical passages in Trio II beginning in
bar 261. Berg makes use only of the original and its inversion. Thus Trio I
opens with the inversion of V_2 on E, while the original appears for the first
time on D flat in bar eighty-six. Again, Trio II opens with the original on G
flat and continues with it, transposed to E flat. Especially noteworthy is the
phrase structure of the Trios. We have already referred to the regular five-bar
build of the Scherzo; in the Trio Berg alters this in the following manner: he
reduces the five-bar phrase successively to four, three, two and one bars and
then increases it in the same progressive manner. Whether the equation
5+4+3+2+1 = 15 had for the composer an extramusical, symbolical
significance, similar to the number 3 in the Chamber Concerto and 10 and 23
in the present work, is not known; but that he considered it important
enough, may be seen from the fact that he specially mentions it in his
annotations. This gradual waning and waxing of the phrase length is
matched by the exquisite sonorities achieved in the Trios, as for instance in
the opening of Trio I, where chords of different duration overlap with one
another, the succeeding chord to enter imperceptibly and to be heard only
when the preceding chord has ceased to sound. The whole passage (51-74) is
of magical effect and may owe something to the 'Changing Chord' movement
of Schoenberg's Five Orchestral Pieces, op. 16.

Largo desolato. The affinity of this finale with the 'Abschied' in Mahler's
Lied von der Erde has already been remarked: in both there is an ebbing away
of the life force. Yet, while the close of the Mahler movement conjures up the

image of a transfiguration, Berg's piece ends in a mood of utter sadness and
desolation. Not for nothing does he cite the *Tristan* motive and, at the end,
turns Haydn's practical joke in the finale of his *Abschiedssymphonie* no. 45 into
a desperate gesture. The movement does not come to a firm halt but
gradually ceases. This *morendo* forcibly recalls to me a letter Berg wrote aged
eighteen to the mentor of his youth, Hermann Watznauer, which contains
this closing paragraph:

> Wir gingen zu Bett – Da lag ich nun mit schwerem Herzen darnieder –
> Ich hatte jenes Gefühl wo man beklommen ans Herz greift und immer nur
> bitten möchte, 'O! lass es langsamer gehn – ganz ruhig und sacht – lass es
> stille stehn!' Und ich schlief dann ein, mit dem seligen Glauben, für
> immer[28] –

> (We went to bed – I lay down with a heavy heart – I had the feeling when
> one anxiously touches the heart and would only like to pray, 'Oh! let it
> beat slower – quite gently and quietly – let it stand still!' – I then fell
> asleep, in the blissful belief, for ever.)

The death-wish expressed by the youthful Berg *verbally* seems to be the same
death-wish expressed *musically* at the close of the Largo.

Thanks to the investigation of Douglas M. Green[29] at the Österreichische
Nationalbibliothek, it has now been established that the Largo of the Lyric
Suite is a setting of Baudelaire's poem, *De Profundis Clamavi*, from his *Fleurs du
Mal*, in a German translation by Stefan George, the words of which Berg
suppressed. Inspecting a number of sketches for the Lyric Suite Green came
across the so-called *Studienpartitur*, the actual manuscript score which Berg
used at rehearsal for the work with the Kolisch Quartet. It was in this score
that Berg had pencilled in certain words of the Baudelaire text beneath some
staves while other words he omitted and replaced by dotted lines or
indicated them only with their initials. What made Green's detective work in
identifying this incomplete text and its author still more difficult was the fact
that in contrast to the almost calligraphic neatness of his musical scores,
Berg's handwriting often poses the greatest problem in deciphering it. (We
recall Schoenberg's frequent complaints about this). After several days of
study during which Green was led up blind alleys and followed
disappointing hunches, he was finally able to establish that the words were
those of a sonnet by Baudelaire in a German rendering. Here is the original
and George's translation:

---

[28] This letter is reproduced in *Alban Berg: Lieben und Werk in Daten* etc., op. cit., p. 79.
[29] 'Berg's *De Profundis*: the Finale of the Lyric Suite', Newsletter No. 5, June 1977, *International Alban Berg Society*, pp. 13-23.

DE PROFUNDIS CLAMAVI

J'implore ta pitié, Toi, l'unique que j'aime,
Du fond du gouffre obscur où mon coeur est tombé.
C'est un univers morne à l'horizon plombé,
Où nagent dans la nuit l'horreur et le blasphème;

Un soleil sans chaleur plane au-dessus six mois,
Et les six autres mois la nuit couvre la terre;
C'est un pays plus nu que la terre polaire:
Ni bêtes, ni ruisseaux, ni verdure, ni bois!

Or, il n'est pas d'horreur au monde qui surpasse
La froide cruauté de ce soleil de glace
Et cette immense nuit semblable au vieux Chaos:

Je jalouse le sort des plus vile animaux
Qui peuvent se plonger dans un sommeil stupide,
Tant l'écheveau de temps lentement se dévide.

Zu dir, du einzig Teure, dringt mein Schrei
Aus tiefster Schlucht darin mein Herz gefallen.
Dort ist die Gegend tot, die Luft wie Blei
Und in dem Finstern Fluch und Schrecken wallen.

Sechs Monde steht die Sonne ohne Warm,
In sechsen lagert Dunkel auf der Erde.
Sogar nicht das Polarland ist so arm,
Nicht einmal Bach und Baum noch Feld noch Herde.

Erreicht doch keine Schreckgeburt des Hirnes
Das kalte Grausen dieses Eisgestirnes
Und dieser Nacht! Ein Chaos riesengross.

Ich neide des gemeinen Tieres Los,
Das tauchen kann in stumpfen Schlafes Schwindel.
So langsam rollt sich ab der Zeitenspindel!
                    (Reprinted by kind permission of G. Bondi, Berlin).

I implore your pity, you, the unique one I love
From the depths of the dark gulf where my heart has fallen.
It is a dismal world with leaden horizon
Where horror and blasphemy swim in night;

A sun without warmth hovers above for six months,
And for the other six months, night covers the earth.
It is a country more naked than the polar land,

Neither beasts nor brooks nor foliage nor woods!

But there is no horror on earth that surpasses
The cold cruelty of this sun of ice
And this vast night like the ancient Chaos;

I envy the lot of the lowest brutes
Who can plunge themselves into a stupid sleep,
So slowly does the skein of time unwind!

Baudelaire wrote his sonnet in 1851, as part of a cycle of poems for Jeanne Duval, his cigar-smoking mulatto mistress. Berg selected it because of its mood of utter desolation and despair which coincided with his own feeling that his love for Hanna was destined to remain unfulfilled. Significantly, at the end of the finale he wrote in her score, after the *morendo* of the last bar:

ersterbend in Liebe, Sehnsucht und Trauer –
(dying away in love, yearning and grief –)

Hence the quotation of the *Tristan* motive which has been regarded as the most poignant expression of love unfulfilled in life, of yearning for union of the lovers in death.

Among the sketches of the finale examined by Douglas Green at the Nationalbibliothek none was found for a vocal part. Berg, however, indicated it in the *Studienpartitur* by carefully redrawing in red ink the stem, flag and beam of the notes in one or the other of the leading instruments. For the completely unvocal bars (19-20 and 31-2) of the quartet movement Berg wrote out a feasible singable part, even sketching in two vocal alternatives for the first passage, and adding the voice-part for the second under the cello line. This raises the question whether Berg seriously contemplated a vocal performance of the finale; the precedent for this would have been Schoenberg's F sharp minor Quarter, with its addition of a voice-part in the last two movements, for which, indeed, Berg made a vocal score in 1912.

On the available evidence it is not possible to come to a definite conclusion. It may be that, as Green suggests, the composer started the finale without a singer in mind, but subsequently came to toy with the idea of a vocal performance and, therefore, made the unvocal parts of the movement practicable. Yet such a performance would have led to the eventual disclosure of the inner programme of the finale and the Lyric Suite as a whole, and this Berg could have never contemplated in Helene's life-time. Now that with her death the chief obstacle to it has been removed, one would have thought that a vocal performance would greatly heighten the poignancy of the movement. But a transmission of the Lyric Suite by the BBC in December 1979, first with the instrumental finale and then with its vocal version proved to me a great disappointment. For one thing, the singing voice distracted from the string music to a disconcerting degree and, for another, the almost constant doubling of the voice-part on one or the other instrument (Ex. 28) destroyed the infinitely subtle delicately balanced texture of the four-part writing. Admittedly, Berg in *Lulu* doubled Alwa's part in the Hymn of Act II, throughout, yet this is not chamber music but the more coarse-grained texture of an operatic score in which the singing voice is the dominating element. The listener must, of course, know the content of the Baudelaire sonnet but he should not be expected to hear what is merely a *putative* vocal version of the finale.

In the *Studienpartitur* the movement is headed by the poem's title, *De Profundis Clamavi*, the name of its author and of the translator. The text is always written above or underneath one of the instrumental parts, except for those unvocal passages referred to above.

The Largo is in strict twelve-note technique and is based on V_2 of the preceding Presto. In the first and third movements we have seen how Berg, by dividing the basic row into two parts, increases its potential as a thematic reservoir. In the finale this division goes further and represents the crowning example of his structural ingenuity. V_2 is split into two halves, each of six notes, which form an upper and lower layer called by Berg 'half-series' or HS. Add to them their inversions and you have four different forms of V_2. Thus the basic row itself of the Lyric Suite is made to 'submit to fate'. I quote the first two forms, that is the original of V_2 and its half-series (Ex. 26):

Example 26

As though Berg intended to give a complete inventory (not dissimilar to Beethoven in the Overture to his Grosse Fuge, op. 133), from which all the thematic material, including the *Tristan* motive and other tonal configurations are derived, he assembles the four forms of V_2 in the six-bar introduction: I of V_2 (cello),[30] I of HS (viola); O of HS (first violin) and O of

---

[30] The C-string of the cello in this movement is to be tuned down a semi-tone to B (H) – Hanna's initial.

V_2 (second violin). Here are a few examples to show how these four forms are used in the course of the movement. For instance, the first allusion to the main theme is based on I of HS on A(7-8), while the main theme itself (13-15) derives from I of HS on E flat and I of V_2 on G. Again, the two layers of V_2 (Ex. 26) are combined to produce this two-part pattern (30):

Example 27

which recalls the canonical model in the Allegro misterioso. The Tristan motive (26-7) is quoted in exactly the rhythmic shape and pitch in which it appears in the opening of the opera's Prelude, and Baudelaire's words for its two bars call up the utter desolation, redolent of the beginning of Act III of *Tristan*, of the chilling landscape of the mind: 'Not even brook or tree, nor field nor flock'. Incidentally, Berg quotes the *Tristan* motive again in another, later, work – *Lulu*, at the point at which Alwa declares his love for Lulu in a passage that is preceded by the four melodic notes of that motive (solo violin II, i, 333). Encapsulated in the *Tristan* motive is the cell-motive (Ex. 21, GR) in a permutated version, which is sounded for the last time on the first violin in bars 34-5, *pp*, *flautando*. The movement ends as it began, with all the four versions of V_2 reappearing, but they are now brought together in *ten* (Hanna's number) overlapping statements, with one instrument after another falling silent.[31] The Viola has the last say and closes on the major third D flat – F. Berg demands that this interval be repeated after the 'official' ending of the finale to die away into nothingness and that the last note be F, thus hinting at Hanna's surname and suggesting the implied 'tonality' of the whole work. It is here that the composer wrote his words of farewell to his love quoted above.

In his notes for Reich the composer first described this Largo as 'liedförmig' or 'song-like', thus suggesting a ternary form, but then crossed this out and wrote instead 'cantabile throughout' to stress its lyrical character. In his preface to the pocket score[32] Erwin Stein calls it 'entirely free, almost rhapsodic'. At a first hearing the movement certainly makes this impression, which is heightened by the constant rubato style and the alternation of tranquil passages with others of intense passion and ardour. If it approximates to any of the established forms, it is that of a rondo, with an

---

[31] The descending melody of the second violin (40) is most suggestive of the image conjured up by the last line of the text which Berg wrote underneath it, 'So langsam rollt sich ab der Zeiten Spindel' (So slowly does the skein of time unwind).

[32] Philharmonic Verlag (U.E. 1927).

introduction. The pizzicato of the four strings in the introduction seems to conjure up a spectral atmosphere out of which rises impressively what is an allusion to the main or rondo theme (13-15), to sink back again into a mysterious tremolando. The opening of the following cello melody (10) recalls the second violin phrase of bar 6 of the first movement, after which enters the main theme which is one of Berg's most inspired inventions, instinct with an ardent lyricism and wide-ranging in its line:

Example 28

The wide leaps and its expressive character link it with the Trio patetico of the third movement. On its last return (31-2) merely the rhythm of its opening bar is indicated, in the accentuated notes of this turbulent passage whose collapse in the second half of bar 32 is anticipated in bar 21. Lastly, the semitonal progressions in bars 37-9 refer back to bars 5-6 of the first movement and, indirectly, to the *Tristan* quotation.

A word or two on Berg's arrangement of the second, third and fourth movements for string orchestra. As already mentioned, the suggestion for this came from the Universal Edition which was bringing out a series of chamber music works in a version for full string orchestra including Schoenberg's Sextet, op. 4 and String Quartet no. 2, op. 10. Writing to Webern on 10 August 1927 Berg told him of this suggestion and said that he was thinking of the second, third and fourth movements. 'Do you think that *possible*? Perhaps with a few alterations in the instrumentation? (There where the cello goes up too high?) I shall be needing your advice *very* much!! Please give it to me *first* briefly *by letter*, and later orally!! Please!!' Webern replied on 24 August to the effect that he did not think the third movement (Allegro misterioso) suitable and suggested instead 'I., II., IV and VI(!) ...'[33] Berg however stuck to his original scheme.

By and large his transcription reproduces the original unchanged, except that the addition of double basses made certain minor alterations necessary. The basses not only reinforce the celli, and, occasionally, the violas, but play solo certain thematic passages and sometimes underpin the harmony. Once

---

[33] U. von Rauchhaupt (ed.). *Schoenberg, Berg, Webern* etc., p. 117.

or twice they introduce new figurations set against those of the celli. There are also simplifications of runs and Berg makes use of *divisi* for all five string groups which enhance the sound image of the original quartet. Very wisely, Berg writes *tacet* for the double basses in the Scherzo part of the Allegro so that when they enter in the Trio ecstatico, it is with redoubled force.

ELEVEN

ORCHESTRAL MUSIC

THREE ORCHESTRAL PIECES, OP. 6

We recall that the Three Orchestral Pieces, op. 6, arose out of a suggestion by Schoenberg to write a suite of several 'character' pieces, and this is to be seen not only in the titles – *Praeludium, Reigen* and *Marsch* – but more intrinsically in the entire tone and attitude of the music. In op. 6 Berg turned from the aphorisms of opp. 4 and 5 to the more congenial large-scale form that he had first attempted in the piano sonata, op. 1, and notably in the String Quartet, op. 3, and which he now applied to the orchestral medium. Yet, with the exception of the first trombone in an extremely high register, none of the youthful extravagances Berg had indulged in the score of the Altenberg Songs is present in this purely orchestral work, though the size of the orchestra employed[1] is even larger than in the songs. This fact may be interpreted as an intention to emulate Schoenberg and Webern in their use of mammoth forces in the original version of such works as the former's op. 16 and the latter's op. 6. The Three Orchestral Pieces was the first work in which Berg adopted his teacher's signs for denoting leading and subsidiary parts (H͞, N͞); Schoenberg had first used them in the fifth piece of his op. 16. Needless to say, Berg's compositional technique in op. 6 is, as in his preceding works, based on Schoenberg's developing variation and thematic integration; what was perhaps new was the accumulation of melodic-rhythmic fragments in the introduction whose theme-generating potential unfolds in the main body of a movement. In style and spirit the three pieces owe something to Mahler, particularly the Mahler of the Third Symphony, the two *Nachtstücke* of the Seventh, and the finale of the Sixth.[2]

Berg evidently conceived op. 6 as a cycle, with a crescendo in both mood and tempo from the *Langsam* of no. 1 to the *Leicht und beschwingt* in no. 2 and *Mässiges Marschtempo* in no. 3. In a remark made for the programme note for the first performance of the complete work at Oldenburg in 1930, Berg pointed out that the three movements of op. 6 approximated to a four-movement symphony, in that the *Praeludium* represented the first movement,

---

[1] The scoring is for quadruple woodwind, six horns, four trumpets, four trombones, and contrabass tuba, an array of percussion and a full complement of strings.

[2] A detailed discussion of these Mahler influences on Berg will be found in Redlich, *Alban Berg*, p. 93 ff.

the *Reigen* combined scherzo and slow movement, and the *Marsch* stood for the finale. This is further evidence of the extent to which the cyclical design of the classical sonata dominated his formal thinking. For this Oldenburg performance he retouched the original orchestration, which he found too 'thick' (notably that of the *Marsch* which even now is overscored in certain passages), and also made some tempo and dynamic alterations in the first two pieces.[3] Although *Reigen* was completed last (June 1915), it forms with the *Praeludium* a unity balanced by the much longer *Marsch*. As if to underline this unity, Berg quotes the 'angry' trumpet figure of the first movement (37-8) very softly on the violas of the second (5-6), to say nothing of other similarities. Moreover, in the revised version for Oldenburg the composer indicated that the first two pieces can also be played together, without the *Marsch*.

The *Praeludium*, into which Berg worked material from his abortive Symphony, describes an extended < >, with the climax in bars 35-8. What must have been novel for the time, though Mahler anticipated it in his Third Symphony,[4] is the *bruitism*, that is, the rhythmic noise generated by percussions without fixed pitch at the beginning and end, to which Berg adds in bar 4 a 4-note chord on the drums as the intermediary stage between noise and music (Ex. 29). The first eight bars return at the close in retrograde – the composer's first example of his predilection for using the crab for the repeat of a previous section. Out of this indefinite nebulous beginning there emerges on the bassoon (6-8) the first of the several ideas of the piece, which really starts in bar 9 with the *Klangfarben* chord on G, each of its six notes being given to a different instrument, which ushers in the main part of the music. The central section is dominated by the development of a theme derived from the opening bassoon idea and rather Mahlerian in its plastic shape, which eventually leads to the climax (35-8) with its expressionist *Ballung*, or explosion, in which Berg combines diminution and augmentation. The recapitulation opens (like the exposition) with the six-note chord anchored on D, but now scored homogeneously for strings only. And, to fashion the link with the next movement closer still, Berg cites, in addition to the afore-mentioned quotation, the tremolando string theme near the opening of *Reigen*. Both these quotations seem to have sprung from a poetic idea, the nature of which, however, we do not know.

The *Reigen*, which Berg later declared to be an orchestral study for the Inn scene of *Wozzeck* (II, iv), is in the main an Austrian waltz in tripartite form (20-100) preceded by an *alla breve* introduction (1-19) and closing with a slow section (101-21). All its material is to be found in the introduction, to be reactivated and reshaped in the developing waltz variation. The waltz is in

---

[3] A minor point: the first trombone in the *Praeludium* was originally notated in the alto clef, but is now in the tenor clef.

[4] I, 8 bars before 13.

Example 29

Berg's characteristic *rubato* style and occasionally recalls Johann Strauss, as for instance in the wide leaping figure at 'Schwungvoll, fast roh' of bars 49-51. The return of the introduction is marked by a canon between woodwind and first violins of the opening figure, and the muted horns and trumpets have the last say, sounding 'wie aus der Ferne' that recalls Mahler.

The link with Mahler becomes strongest in the *Marsch*; indeed, its godfather seems to have been the finale of Mahler's Sixth Symphony. Both composers appear to have interpreted the march as the symbol of an inexorable, cruel fate,[5] and concrete evidence of the elder composer's influence is seen in the fact that Berg, too, resorts to hammer strokes as the expression of a catastrophe. Yet, while the Mahler movement is on an epic scale, the Bergian piece concentrates the tragedy into 174 bars.

When Berg showed Adorno the score of the *Marsch*, the latter remarked that it must sound as if Schoenberg's Five Orchestral Pieces and Mahler's Ninth Symphony were played together.[5a] Berg was overjoyed at this remark which in deliberate exaggeration defines the bewildering complexity of the piece. Indeed, Berg himself described it as the most complex of his orchestral scores. The difficulty is twofold. There is, first, the extraordinary density of the texture, reaching its maximum in contrapuntal passages in which several

[5] The first to see in the march rhythm the embodiment of a poetic idea, namely life as an interminable and sad wandering on earth, was Schubert.

[5a] Pierre Boulez, in a sleeve-note to his recording of the Three Orchestral Pieces, op. 6 (CBS 72614) holds that the *Marsch* is the most 'immoderate' piece in the musical literature of the period, adding that in it can be sensed 'almost demented intoxication of the dramatic gesture, a hysteria in declamation swelled out to an unbearable din' ('la pièce la plus demesurée de la littérature musicale dans cette periode – on y sent une ivresse presque démente du geste démonstratif, je dirais une hystérie dans la declamation, s'enflant jusqu'à l'insoutenable clameur').

themes are superimposed on one another (67 ff.; 115 ff.; 121 ff.). This constitutes a major difficulty for the conductor, who must clearly differentiate between leading and subsidiary parts and accurately observe the dynamic markings, even having to adjust them in certain places. Secondly, an aspect of this complexity is Berg's continuous development of his material almost from the opening bars which recalls Mahler's technique of constant kaleidoscopic changes of motives in the course of a symphonic movement. The *Marsch* is certainly Berg's most daring excursion into chaos, but organised chaos, into which one may be able to read, with the necessary stretch of the imagination, something like sonata form: Introduction (Tempo I, 1-32), Main Section (Tempo II, 33-52; Tempo III, 53-90), Development (*Allegro energico*, Tempo III, 91-126), Reprise (127-54), and Coda (155-74). Bars 62-5 introduce a *grazioso* which, in the context of this otherwise wildly agitated and even sinister piece, seems as strange and unexpected as a similar passage in the finale of Mahler's Sixth. Incidentally, the motive of falling seconds (79-83) will reappear in *Wozzeck*, 1, 2 at the soldier's hallucinatory remark: 'Hörst du, es wandert was mit uns da unten!' – a hint perhaps at the meaning of the music. The hard core, as it were, of the whole piece is the fierce march (*Allegro energico*), which is ushered in by a mighty fanfare on four trumpets. The density of the texture gradually increases and the *Höhepunkt* or climax is reached in bar 126 in the three *ff* hammer strokes. The effect is a highly dramatic one: the hammer strokes destroy, as it were, the complex polyphony, the music continuing now with a simple two-part stretto. It is possible to see in this last section the beginning of a much compressed recapitulation – a return that is psychological rather than actual.[6] The coda (155) is based on thematic reminiscences and becomes gradually slower and slower, when suddenly in bar 171 the speed changes to Tempo III, with the brass fanfares of the third march leading finally to a high B flat on the upper woodwind, *ppp*, which is answered *fff* by E on the bass, reinforced by a hammer stroke.

Linear counterpoint is predominant in the *Marsch*. There are pointers to tonal elements such as the prolonged pedal on F (111-24) and D (155-59), and, if it is permissible to include the whole-tone scale in the tonal orbit, it occurs once or twice in both its modes.

It would require a study in itself, with a well-nigh forbidding number of music examples, to illustrate in detail the ways and means by which Berg made the three movements of op. 6 relate to one another both thematically and harmonically. The result of such a minute examination could easily be a dry-as-dust musical anatomy, which was the case in a recent book on Berg's music, and which can serve no other than a purely statistical purpose. Two examples of the relationship between the first two movements have already

---

[6] Compare the similar treatment of the recapitulation in Bartók.

been noted (p. 144). Suffice it to point out two more linking all the three movements. The opening bassoon theme of the *Praeludium* (6-8) reappears in a variant in the bassoon-trumpet theme of the introduction to the *Reigen* (2-5), which in turn produces an offshoot in the main waltz theme (bassoon-trumpet, 19-24). The second example is the cello figure in the *Marsch* (1-8) which is another version of the introductory waltz theme, and thus looks back to the opening of the *Praeludium*.

CHAMBER CONCERTO FOR PIANO, VIOLIN, AND THIRTEEN WIND INSTRUMENTS

None of Berg's works suggests to the same degree a master craftsman's delight and joy in the exercise of his technical resourcefulness and skill as the Chamber Concerto does. As he said in his Open Letter to Schoenberg: 'Not only the soloists (and the conductor!) have a chance of displaying their brilliance and virtuosity, but for once also the author'. It is his only major opus to be free of his otherwise pervasive sense of tragedy; indeed, one might almost say that it had been conceived in the spirit of a divertimento – he himself spoke of the 'light tone of the whole'. But it would not be *echt* Berg without an implied programme, at which he hints in the Open Letter when he speaks of 'how much friendship, love and a world of human and spiritual relationships I have smuggled into these three movements'. Stylistically it is a remarkable amalgam of classical, romantic and modern elements. There are contrapuntal artifices, there is the constructivism and tendency to thematic integration of the Schoenberg school, and there is the poetic symbolism of a Schumann and Brahms. And all this is achieved despite Berg's self-denying ordinance to relate length, form, design, instrumentation and so on, to the number 3 and its multiples, thus making the work a suitable birthday present for Schoenberg on his fiftieth anniversary as well as providing a document of a twenty-year-old friendship between him, Webern and his former teacher. As is the custom in German-speaking countries on birthdays and similar festive occasions, Berg in his dedication refers to 'Aller guten Dinge (sind drei)' – 'Of all good things (there are three).' This number may be said to have been the *fons et origo* of the music.

To begin with, there are three motives formed by the musical letters in the names of Arnold Schönberg, Anton Webern and Alban Berg, which stand as the motto at the head of the score and are to be played by three instruments – piano, violin and horn, respectively.

In the German alphabet there are nine musical letters, all of which except F occur in the name Arnold Schoenberg, which thus contains all the musical letters in the full names of Webern and Berg – a most appropriate symbol of the relationship between the three musicians, to say nothing of the hierarchical order in which the three motives appear in the motto, an order not only

Example 30

dictated by the master-pupil relationship but also by the respective ages of the composers: Schoenberg, fifty years; Webern forty-one years; and Berg thirty-nine years. Needless to say, these three motives play a very important part in the structure of the material, notably those of Webern and Berg, while the 'Schönberg' motive is used rather in the nature of a quotation, and remains unchanged for most of the work.[7] The extent to which the number three and its multiples determine the formal and instrumental design of the Chamber Concerto, conditioning also (as do 10 and 23 in the Lyric Suite) the bar length of themes, individual movements and the total length of the work, can be read off the table on p. 149, given by Berg in his Open Letter to Schoenberg.

Also the harmonic style of the Chamber Concerto is threefold – tonal, atonal and dodecaphonic (but not yet serial). As is the case with *Wozzeck*, free atonality prevails, yet there are tonal enclaves or insertions, such as the drone-like bass resting on F sharp minor (25-7), the violin arpeggios in major, minor and diminished sevenths (451-9), and the suggestion of the tonality of C in the very last bar. In the atonal context a succession of perfect

---

[7] The device of using the musical letters in names seems to go back to the Flemish polyphonists. Bach used it in connection with his own name, and the cryptograms of Schumann and Brahms belong to the same order.

fourths – the interval considered to be destructive of the major-minor system with its superimposed thirds – takes on a 'tonal' feel, as it does for instance in the bass of bars 16-19 *passim*. As to the twelve-note structure, all themes of the work contain the notes of the chromatic scale in a special order, but it has to be stressed that Berg still treats these themes, after their initial statement, not in a strictly serial manner.

The total number of instruments employed is 15 (3 × 5) – the same as in Schoenberg's Chamber Symphony, op. 9; but Berg replaces his master's string quintet by the solo piano and solo violin, and adds a second flute and a trumpet and trombone to the wind orchestra. Also the metronome markings of the three movements are all divisible by 3, and there are the three cryptograms each played by a different instrument (piano-violin-horn). Though Berg does not mention it in his 'Open Letter', the number 5 also plays a significant part in the work which was evidently a discreet allusion to Schoenberg's 50th (5 × 10) birthday. Thus, the motto both at the opening

I	Theme	Var. I	II	III	IV	V	Number of bars
Tema con Variazioni	in the basic shape		retrograde	inversion	retrograde inversion	basic shape	
	(Exposition)	(First reprise)	(Development)			(Second reprise in canon)	
	bars: 30	30	60	30	30	60	240–

II		*Ternary*			*Retrograde*		
Adagio	A₁	B	A₂	A₂	B	A₁	480–
			(inversion of A₁)		(mirror form of preceding B)		
	bars: 30	12 39	9 30	30	9 39	12 30	240–

960

III = I + II	Introduction (cadenza for violin and piano)	Exposition	Development	Second reprise (Coda)	
Rondo ritmico con Introduzione			(da capo)		
	bars: 54	96	79	76	305–
		Repeat: 175			175–

480–

and the close of the Concerto takes up five bars; the first movement consists of a theme and *five* variations, and the opening theme of the Adagio and its corresponding retrograde extends to five bars; finally Berg's constructive rhythm RH has five reiterated notes (see Ex. 34).

The Chamber Concerto is, incidentally, the first of Berg's two scores – the second is that of the Violin Concerto – in which transposing instruments are notated as they sound.[7a] There is a marked difference between Schoenberg's Chamber Symphony and Berg's Chamber Concerto. The former is a pronouncedly romantic piece and has a symphonic character subtilised and intimate, however, like Wagner's *Siegfried Idyll*, while the latter is dominated by the *concertante* principle and aims at virtuosity, not only with the two soloists but also with the orchestra. At times the texture is extraordinarily dense, notably in the second movement, in which Berg's linear counterpoint results in an especially intricate web of sound. And though the composer strictly differentiates between leading and subsidiary parts, an orchestra consisting exclusively of wind instruments can never be toned down to the degree of softness of which strings are capable. Moreover, a *p* on a trombone always sounds louder than a *p* on, say, the clarinet or oboe. There is little doubt that in choosing a wind orchestra for the Chamber Concerto Berg modelled himself on Stravinsky's *Symphonies of Wind Instruments* (1920) and *Octet* (1923). Another feature worth mention is the occasional introduction of *Klangfarbenmelodie* as, for instance, in bars 145-7 or 645-51, in which Berg distributes the constituent notes of a theme over a group of different instruments, though he never goes as far as Webern in his fragmentation of colour. It should be added that Berg visualised separate performances of the individual movements, and for that purpose provided special endings for the first and second. In 1935 he arranged the Adagio as Trio for violin, clarinet, and piano.

The opening movement, a 'Tema scherzoso can variazioni', in which the piano is the solo instrument, combines sonata and variation. The theme is so constructed as to suggest a sonata exposition: 1st subject, 1-15 (3 × 5 bars), 2nd subject, 16-24 (3 × 8) and closing group, 25-30 (3 × 10). As was Berg's practice since the Piano Sonata, op. 1, each of these three main sections has its own tempo – Leicht beschwingt (Tempo I) – Schwungvoll (Tempo II) – Meno allegro (Tempo III). And similar to the main themes of the *Praeludium* and *Reigen* of op. 6, the variation theme of the Chamber Concerto is shown *in statu nascendi* only gradually achieving its final shape:

[7a] The scores of the *Sieben frühe Lieder*, *Der Wein* and *Lulu* were published with the transposing instruments notated in the traditional manner, though in his autograph scores Berg notated them as they actually sound. A possible explanation for this discrepancy may be the conservatism of orchestral players of the time, who much preferred the old method of notation, a fact which Berg's publishers seem to have taken into account.

Example 31

(Cor Anglais)

The *Reihe* or serial element is here present in so far as Berg repeats the order of the notes of the 30-bar theme in every one of the five variations, with the whole movement consisting of six (3 x 2) sections. The variations implement the theme's sonata design – no. 1 is the first repeat of the exposition, nos. 2, 3 and 4 represent the development and no. 5 the recapitulation. Though the *scherzoso* character of the theme is maintained throughout, each variation has its own texture and tempo and seamlessly links with the next. Variation 1 is for piano solo, and its keyboard style seems to recall Chopin's, notably in bars 46-58. If I see a development in the following three variations this must not be understood in the sense of a thematic working-out, but largely as a contrapuntal treatment of the theme in terms of the old scholastic devices.[8] Thus Variation 2 is the retrograde of the theme and has the character of a slow waltz (the Viennese in Berg could not be suppressed!), with the melody mostly reserved for the orchestra, while the piano opens with the typical 'ump-ta-ta' of the waltz accompaniment. In bars 91-7 there occurs a three-part stretto between the upper woodwind, the horns and the lower woodwind whose comic effect is greatly enhanced by the *staccatissimo*. Another jesting gesture is slyly introduced into bars 111-12 when the violinist, who is otherwise completely silent in this movement, plucks the open strings as though testing their tuning. Variation 3 is based on the inversion of the theme and is a muscular, forward-driving piece, with an extremely massive, compact piano part prophetic of today's tone clusters. Variation 4 brings the theme in the inversion of its crab, transforming it into fleeting, scurrying figures. In bars 166-9 Berg combines the original and the inverted form of the 'Schönberg' motive. Variation 5 returns to the form and the original tempo of the theme, two bars in 3-4 time corresponding to one bar of the 6-4 theme. It is a playful, humorous piece, with gay *gruppetti* embellishing the three 'name' motives.

Example 32

Picc.   Flute

If in the preceding variations canonical treatment was only intermittent, the final variation is entirely based on it. In fact it is a canon between orchestra

---

[8] Webern's developments are almost entirely based on these devices.

and piano, in which the latter enters with the theme eight bars after the former but gradually shortens the distance through abbreviations and reductions of rests, until it catches up with the orchestra in bar 209; at Meno allegro the piano is already nine bars ahead and wins the race in bar 230, while the orchestra does not arrive at the goal until bar 240.[9] It is in this bar that Berg negotiates the transition to the second movement in a special way by combining two dynamic extremes: while orchestra and piano end *fff*, the solo violin enters imperceptibly *ppp*, with the first note of the Adagio theme, a procedure recalling a screen technique whereby the beginning of the next scene is faded into the end of the preceding scene.

The Adagio shows the composer's lyrical gift at its full stretch, as witness the rich and sustained melodic invention and its expressive warmth and ardour. The scoring is most variegated and the relationship between soloist and orchestra points forward to the Violin Concerto. It also provides an excellent example of Berg's predilection for correspondence and symmetries achieved by contrapuntal means. The form is ternary, A_1-B-A_2, in which A_2 represents the inversion of A_1, and the whole is then repeated in the retrograde. The point at which the music begins to run backwards is marked by twelve mysterious 'midnight' strikes on the low C sharp of the piano (358-63). As already mentioned, all the Adagio themes (one in A, and three in B) show twelve-note structure. The theme of A_1 extends, like the variation theme of the opening movement, to 30 bars (3 × 10), and Berg's 'trinity of things' is also manifest in the way he scores this section: solo violin (241-60) – woodwind (260-5) – (mainly) brass (265-70).

Section B itself is ternary, consisting of a prelude (271-82), a main part (283-321), and a postlude (322-30), each with its own theme and tempo. As to the prelude, it has two features worth mentioning: a three-part fugato, the first two entries of which are a fifth apart, as in tonal music, and the juxtaposition on the violin of whole-tone, diatonic, chromatic and quarter-tone steps. The last recalls Hába's microtones, but Berg, in marked contrast to the Czech composer, does not use them functionally but to intensify the colouring of the preceding chromatic steps. The most important part of B is the central section based on an expressive *Tristan*esque cantabile idea which is, significantly, first given to the warm-toned, sensuous clarinet:

Example 33

[9] A similar 'chase' takes place in the canon duet between Lulu and the Painter in I, i of the opera.

This section abounds in canonical writing, a particularly striking example of which is bars 303-8 in which Ex. 33 appears in three different note values: crotchets (trumpets and trombone), quavers (horns and clarinet), and semi-quavers (bass clarinet and bassoon). This central section also contains the climax (314-15) in which Ex. 33 reappears in inversion. In its contrapuntal density (Berg adds three more parts to the texture) the passage recalls the climax before the recapitulation of the *Marsch* in op. 6. B is, moreover, the section in which the composer first introduces his constructive rhythm, RH (297):

Example 34

a device of which he had already made use in *Wozzeck*, subjecting it like a melodic motive to augmentation (306-7) and crab (420-4). The iron rigidity with which this rhythmic pattern is employed in the Adagio stands in strongest contrast to the rubato style of the music, an antithesis that may have been of special significance to the composer.

As already remarked, the second half of the Adagio is a palindrome of the first half, the music retracing its steps from A_2 via B to A_1. Yet it is not a 'mechanical' retrograde, Berg partly writing an exact mirror image and partly a freely treated crab. The crab or palindrome has given rise to some philosophical speculations about Berg's general application of the retrograde which I find difficult to accept. With the exception of twelve-note music, the crab has been employed in other styles far less frequently than the remaining 'automatic' devices of inversion and canon,[10] and this has tempted one of Berg's biographers[11] to claim that its application was for him of symbolic significance, a technical means with which he tried to square the circle, as it were, and solve such problems as 'banning the transience of time, the undoing of temporal happenings, escaping the reality of the modern speed record and revolutionary upheavals' which, it is suggested, weighed on him like an incubus and from which he sought to free himself. All of which he tried, according to this biographer, to achieve by the use of the retrograde! As we see, much can be made of the retrograde in conceptual thinking. But as a purely aural experience it does not strike the ear as a 'going back' or return to the 'point of departure', but on the contrary as a forward motion in time. There can be very few listeners who, uninformed and following a performance without a score, would be able to recognise Berg's original in its

[10] Mozart found it necessary to write over the Trio of his Canon Minuet in his C minor Serenade (K. 388), 'Canone al rovescio'.

[11] Redlich, *Alban Berg*, pp. 156-7.

crab form. It is like a landscape which appears to the eye quite different if one returns for the first time on the same road on which one had advanced.

The finale is a Rondo ritmico opening with an introduction which is in the character of a cadenza for the two solo instruments which are given free reign to display their virtuosity. But this cadenza is strictly thematic and anticipates Berg's highly original idea of combining the material of the first two movements in the rondo. Already in the first ten bars the composer's extraordinary skill is seen in the way in which he fuses the opening of the variation theme with the first Adagio idea, the RH, the 'Schönberg' and 'Berg' motives and the arpeggiato chord A-E-G-B flat (487), in which the notes are common to all three 'name' motives. The main movement is actually designed as a sonata rondo in which the sonata element lies in the division of the music into an exposition (535-629), development (631-709) and coda (710b-85), Berg demanding a repeat of both the exposition and development. The rondo element, on the other hand – and therein resides part of Berg's remarkable ingenuity – is represented, not by a periodic return of a melodic ritornello but of rhythmic patterns in which he distinguishes three kinds: a main rhythm (RH) a subsidiary rhythm, and a motive-like rhythm, which, as he says in his Open Letter to Schoenberg, 'appear in the most manifold variants (expanded, shortened, augmented, diminished, in stretto and crab, and in all conceivable metric displacements and transposition etc. etc.)' and are impressed on the melody notes[12] of the leading and subsidiary parts, and through their rondo-like recurrence achieve a thematic unity which can compare with that of the traditional rondo. An example to stand for many similar ones is bars 571-3 in which the coda of the variation theme of the first movement appears in the RH of the second movement. Equally interesting is the manner in which Berg combines the materials of the first and second movements in the finale. Here too he upholds a trinity which, as we have seen, is basic to the work as a whole:

(a) free contrapuntal combination of parts corresponding to one another as, for instance, in bars 481-3 which bring together bars 1-2 (first movement), 297 (RH second movement) and 241-2 (second movement).

(b) the successive juxtaposition of individual phrases and little sections in quasi duet form as, for example, in bars 697-709 which combine 171-3 (first movement), 431-2 (second movement), 174-6 (first movement) and 433-8 (second movement).

(c) the exact summation of whole passages from both movements, as in bars 550-65 in which 16-20 (first movement) is set against 283-6 (second movement).

[12] This procedure is not dissimilar to that of the *talea* in the isorhythmic motet. From Berg's Open Letter we know that his model was Schoenberg's Serenade, op. 24, in which themes and motives of the Finale (no. 7) are subjected to the rhythm of the *Marsch* (no. 1), thus establishing a relationship between the opening and the closing movements.

The finale is indeed a *tour de force* of rhythmic and thematic ingenuity, comparable to a kaleidoscope in which the little squares are constantly changing their order and shape.

There is a concluding stretto (738-80) which drives everything before it at breakneck speed and closes on a *ff* chord (a dominant harmony on D) with which the finale might well have ended. But Berg has a surprise up his sleeve in the form of a five-bar epilogue in which the three 'name' motives of the motto – 'Arnold Schönberg' on the trombone, 'Anton Webern' on the muted horn and 'Alban Berg' on the trumpet – are softly intoned, as though bidding farewell to one another. The music ends with a dominant ninth on G (solo violin) suggesting an implied C tonality.

THE VIOLIN CONCERTO

It would be ludicrous to suggest that without the tragedy of the early death of Manon Gropius in April 1935, the Violin Concerto would not have come into being. As already stated, Berg had accepted Krasner's commission as early as February of that year, yet remained uncertain as to the general form and character the concerto should take. His indecision, I suggest, may have been due to the fact that he was not, as Schoenberg and Webern were, a composer to whom the writing of 'absolute' music came easy. For him music had to be 'about' something, it had to have a content closely linked with life and human experience. Significantly, it was the traumatic shock of Manon's death which fully released the springs of his imagination and made the work what it is – unusual in form, irresistible in its poignancy of feeling and immediate in its impact on the listener. (I still recall the effect it had on me when I first heard it in London in the spring of 1936.) In genre it is a symphonic concerto such as Beethoven and Brahms had written, but in intention and character it is a symphonic poem conveying a portrait, as Berg saw it, of the young girl in Part I, and of her suffering, death, and transfiguration in Part II.[13] In this context it is interesting to observe that, like Berlioz in his *Harold in Italy* and Elgar in his own Violin Concerto, Berg made the solo instrument the symbol for his protagonist. Indeed, as in Elgar, her soul is 'enshrined' in the solo violin, and another interesting parallel is the fact that, like the English composer, Berg removed the solo cadenza from its orthodox place in the first movement to the third.

The work is, as has already been pointed out, the first concerto to be written in twelve-note style and is based on the series:

---

[13] It is perhaps significant that of all the works of Richard Strauss, in whom the mature Berg had lost all interest, it was only *Death and Transfiguration* for which he preserved his erstwhile liking. (See letter to his wife of March 1934.)

Example 35

It incorporates as additional material a Carinthian folk tune and a Bach chorale. Berg thus continues a characteristic tendency of his which was to resort to 'ready-made' material, a tendency which first started in his name-inspired motto of the Chamber Concerto, continued in the Zemlinsky and *Tristan* quotations of the Lyric Suite, and, finally Wedekind's street song in *Lulu*.

Ex. 35 illustrates Berg's endeavour to assimilate tonal with serial elements at its most striking. The row is built up, in its first nine notes, of minor and major thirds which imply the tonalities of G minor, D major, A minor, and E major, to say nothing of the secondary sevenths it contains. The first two notes are important in so far as they represent the tonics of the two 'keys' or harmonic poles between which the concerto oscillates – G and B flat, with B flat being finally established as the 'real' key of the work. One might, indeed, say that the Violin Concerto shows 'progressive tonality'. It is conceivable that the immense popularity of the concerto with the public may partly be due to its tilt towards the traditional major-minor system. Berg was writing a concerto for violin which explains the arpeggio structure of the row in which the odd notes (1, 3, 5 and 7) take into account the open strings while the even ones (2, 4, 6 and 8) lie in the instrument's first position, as can be seen from the opening of the solo part (bars 2-5). In short, Berg built his row with the same consideration for the natural facilities of the violin as did the classical composers when they chose the keys of G, D, A or E for their violin concerti. The last four notes of the series form a segment of the whole-tone scale which is identical with the opening motif of the Bach chorale (Ex. 40). We know from a letter to Schoenberg of 28 August 1935 that this was not intended but merely coincidental, for the idea of using a chorale came to Berg only in the course of working on the concerto when the basic row was already in existence. Yet this mere coincidence happens to result in a most subtle poetic symbolism, which is that the idea of ultimate deliverance embodied in the chorale is present in the concerto from its very beginning. Needless to say, Berg frequently uses his series and its variants like antecedent and consequent of a theme or period and, as in the Chamber Concerto, the Lyric Suite and the concert aria, *Der Wein*, there are thematic relationships and correspondences between the movements.

Before we enter upon a detailed discussion of the concerto, something must be said in general about the relationship between soloist and orchestra, the instrumentation and other germane matter. The work differs in no way from what, since Beethoven's time, has been called a symphonic concerto, in which the orchestra plays as important a part in the elaboration of the thematic material as the soloist. In a twelve-note composition this is perhaps a superfluous remark to make, but it also implies that Berg exploits to the full both a give-and-take and dramatic opposition between soloist and orchestra. The violin part is a *tour de force* of technical virtuosity bristling with such difficulties as triple and quadruple harmonics, left-hand pizzicati and even a four-part canon in the unaccompanied cadenza. Yet there is nowhere any impression of technical display *per se*; on the contrary, as in the concerti of Beethoven and Brahms, all difficulties are intimately connected with the substance of the music – indeed, they spring directly from the violin's peculiar nature. There is, moreover, an admirable balance between expressive lyricism on the one hand and dramatic writing on the other. Berg uses a large orchestra, including a saxophone, three clarinets and bassoons, four horns, two trombones and a bass tuba, not to mention four timpani and a number of percussion without definite pitch. Yet these forces are employed in a way which allows the violin, while always deeply involved in the musical happenings, to assert itself itself as a solo instrument with remarkable ease. Berg's orchestral sonorities display a high degree of translucency and he never neglects one of the fundamental principles of good scoring, which is letting in enough 'air' into the textures.

The Concerto resembles a four-movement symphony, yet contains no sonata movement, though the Allegro of Part II was originally planned as such. Due to its underlying programme, it shows an uncommon formal design. The work is divided into two Parts and the movements follow one another in the unorthodox order Andante – Allegretto – Allegro – Adagio. To open and close with a slow movement has been anticipated by Mahler in his Ninth Symphony, and it is not beyond the bounds of possibility that Berg may have thought of this work when deciding to give his concerto the character of a Requiem, remembering perhaps his erstwhile impression of the Symphony's first movement with its 'premonition of death'. Each of the two Parts forms an emotional unity, with the strongest possible contrast between them – that between life and death.

Part I. First Movement. *Andante*

Introduction	A	Bridge	B (*Un poco graz.*)	Bridge	A	Introd.: Transition to *Allegretto*
(1–10)	(11–27)	(28–37)	(38–76)	(77–83)	(84–93)	(94–104)

The movement is ternary (A-B-A) but is made more symmetrical by forming a *Bogen* or arch in which from the central section B the music retraces its steps back via the Bridge and A to the Introduction. This evocative, dream-like Introduction suggests that the soloist is testing the tuning of the four strings and then playing himself in in the following arpeggios. Both from the imaginative and the technical point of view these opening ten bars are a real introduction and show the freedom of Berg's treatment of his row.

In the solo part he first introduces its odd notes (1, 3, 5, 7), then the even ones (2, 4, 6, 8), then again the odd ones, and it is not until bar 8 that he adds the remaining notes 10, 11 and 12. Bar 10, which conceals a regular dominant seventh, leads by way of a cadence to the main portion of the movement, which begins in a clear G minor. Out of a progression of low-lying, dark-hued harmonies, formed by telescoping the series into chords, there rises, like a sudden ray of sun, the solo violin with the original version (Ex. 35), the chromatic tail end of which, *x*, will play an important part throughout:

Example 36

pp, ma espress.

This 'sigh' seems like the first, very faint warning of the tragedy to come in Part II. If section A may be said to stand for the tenderness and loveliness of Manon, section B, marked 'un poco grazioso', seems to evoke her charm and grace but as if seen through a veil – note the 'schattenhaft' in bar 47. Partial canons are characteristic of this section. The repeat of section A begins in something like invertible counterpoint, the solo violin now playing the bass of the corresponding passage (84-87 = 11-14), and finally leads to the Introduction. Both sections are shortened and altered in the scoring. The seamless suture of the 'sigh' motive (Ex. 36) with the arpeggios of the opening, forms the transition to the next movement.

Part I. Second Movement. *Allegretto*

A_1	quasi Trio I	Trio II	Trio I (shortened)	A_2	A_3	coda
(104–36)	(137–54)	(155–66)	(167–72)	(173–207)	(208–28)	(229)

The second movement evokes the girl's youthful *joie de vivre* and vivacity, with an exuberant outburst in Trio I. It is ternary – a Scherzo with two Trios – and the Scherzo itself is tripartite (a_1, a_2, a_3–*b*–a_1 a_2 a_3), with the three *a*'s related to one another in character: *scherzando* (104-9), *wienerisch* (110-13) and *rustico* (114-17). The 'Viennese' music shows the euphonious thirds as well as the leaps of the typical Strauss waltz, while the 'rustic' section contains yodelling figures:

Example 37a

Example 37b

Quasi Trio I ('Subito un poco energico') suggests in its upward and downward leaps and the solo violin's triple stops a mood of unrestrained high spirits, reaching its climax in the thundering waltz rhythm on the brass (147-50).

Trio II ('Meno mosso'), by contrast markedly lyrical, is based on a gently rocking theme in which the tail figure (Ex. 36) appears in diverse variants. The repeat of Trio I is much abbreviated and, four bars after the return of A_2 (bar 176), the implied waltz rhythm of the previous 6-8 becomes now explicit in the 3-8 metre. Moreover, the phrasing is now in regular two and four bars, which Berg always applies when wanting to stress the *volkstümlich* character of the music, as he does in *Wozzeck*. In bar 214 begins the Carinthian folk tune, 'come una pastorale', provided with the key-signature of G flat, and in a suggestive scoring (horn, two trumpets):

Example 38

The original of this tune was published in a collection of Carinthian folksongs (Vienna, 1892) the text of which was quite *risqué* in its sexual allusions. Its key and tempo are different from Berg's.[13a] The soloist first counterpoints it with the whole-tone segment of the series in the retrograde and then imitates – an aptly rustic touch, this – the 'over-blowing' of wind instruments, a device used by wind players to produce, by increased lip

[13a] Herwig Knaus, 'Berg's Carinthian Folktune', *Musical Times*, June 1975, p. 187.

pressure, harmonics instead of fundamentals; Austrian folksingers achieve the same effect in the yodel by changing from chest voice to falsetto. The coda ('quasi stretta') is largely based on the thundering waltz figures of Trio I, with the solo violin reinforcing this exuberant mood with the series in arpeggios. The movement ends in a clear G minor, telescoping the first four notes of the series into a repeated chord of the seventh.

Part II. Third Movement. *Allegro*

A_1 B A_2
(1-42)   (43-95)   (96-135)

With the ternary Allegro we enter the sphere of suffering, torment, agony and final death. The music is harsh, cruel and highly dissonant. Significantly, in Part II: bar 23, entry of RH on the four horns; bar 207 (9 × 23), a ghost-like reminiscence of the Carinthian folktune on the muted violins; the total bar number in Part II is 230 (10 × 23). A_1 is binary opening with a 'rubato, like a free cadenza' (1-22), followed by a 'molto ritmico' portion which is dominated by Berg's sinister RH:

Example 39

On the orchestra the rhythm is sounded twelve times, after which the soloist takes it over and plays it seven times, the exacting triple and quadruple stops seeming to enhance the brutality of RH.

In section B we hear for the first time the opening of the whole-tone phrase of the Bach chorale (notes 9-12 of the row) but in the retrograde ('liberamente', 43). This section is also binary and is largely based on reminiscences from Part I which flit by like a dream.[14] B culminates in a solo cadenza whose second half is a four-part canon (78-89) based on the opening of Trio II.[15] A short bridge passage (90-5), recalling the arpeggios of the introduction and the 'Viennese' of the Allegretto of Part I, leads to A_2 which is a repeat of A_1, but with the 'rubato' greatly shortened and the 'molto ritmico' extended. The transition to the last movement is formed by bars 125-35, the opening of which represents the great climax of the work – the catastrophe – when a nine-none chord in RH on the whole orchestra is hammered out *ff*, to a most shattering effect. This transition is a *locus classicus* in Berg's art of a gradual preparation for what is to follow. The orchestral chord gradually collapses, shedding successively one note after another, while at the same time the soloist, beginning on the low B flat (126), adds

[14] *a* (woodwind 44-53) comes from Trio II while *b* (54-77) begins with the 'scherzando' of the Allegretto of Part I (solo violin, 160-1).

[15] Berg provides an *ossia* for this difficult canon in which the two lower parts are to be played by a solo viola.

progressively a note to his part until we hear a four-note motive which reveals itself as the anticipation of the chorale opening. Another interesting feature is the fact that the music rests on a bass pedal on F (from bar 97 to 136), the dominant note of B flat, the 'key' of the chorale which opens the final movement. Apart from providing a good example of Berg's bond with tonality, this long sustained pedal seems to me to possess also a poetic significance. It is as though with this pedal Berg wanted to indicate that the thought of deliverance and ultimate peace for Manon's soul is already *in statu nascendi* before and during the 'catastrophe'.

Part II. Fourth Movement. *Adagio* (136-230)

Chorale (136-57)
Var. 1 (158-77)
Var. 2 (178-97)
Carinthian folktune (198-213)
Coda (214-30)

The chorale comes from the Bach Cantata no. 60, *O Ewigkeit du Donnerwort* (1732), which Berg found in a collection of chorales published in 1920.[16] The chorale melody is by Johann Rudolf Ahle (1625-73), to words by F.J. Burmeister, and is set by Bach in four-part harmony:

Example 40

Es   ist   ge - nug: Herr, wenn   es   dir   ge - fällt,

Berg transposed the Bach original a semitone up, to integrate it with the key of B flat, the 'tonality' of the Adagio. What seems to have decided his choice of this particular chorale was undoubtedly its opening words 'Es ist genug! Herr, wenn es Dir gefällt, so spanne mich doch aus!' – a prayer for deliverance from the suffering on this earth. Berg's treatment of the chorale suggests a liturgical response in that its 'versicles' are sung alternately by the 'minister' (solo violin) and the 'congregation' (orchestra). In the orchestral segments Berg retains Bach's harmonisation, with its striking whole-tone melody in the opening (Ex. 40). These segments are scored for woodwind only, thus producing an organ-like effect, and, as in Bach, the counterpoints

[16] H. Roth (ed.), *60 Choralgesänge*, Munich, 1920.

to the soloist are derived from the chorale. It should be noted, incidentally, that while Bach closes in the tonic, Berg ends in the relative minor, and it is not until we arrive at the 'echo' passage (155-7) that we hear B flat clearly established as the tonic.

In Variation 1 ('Misterioso'), which starts with a canon between celli and harp, the various 'versicles' of the twenty-bar long chorale are transposed to diverse 'keys' (E, B, B flat, F sharp etc.), with the soloist entering in bar 164 with a poignant lament as counterpoint to the chorale; from bar 170 he is doubled by the orchestral solo violin, thus heightening the lyrical intensity of this passage and at the same time making the lament the leading part of the polyphonic texture.[17] Variation 2 ('Adagio') employs a similar transpositional procedure, but brings the chorale in inversion and culminates in bars 184-90 in a stretto between the upper brass and low strings. At the same time a passage marked 'appassionato', leads to the great *Höhepunkt* of the Adagio (186), the solo and orchestral violins and violas soaring up in a Puccinian unison. This dramatic outburst subsides in the last nine bars of the chorale, its cadential phrase (in inversion) being stated again in a stretto, a passage that corresponds to the conclusion of Variation 1. There lies an ineffable pathos in the subsequent reminiscence of a snatch of the Carinthian folktune heightened by the wraith-like scoring, with the orchestral violins playing *pp, non vibr.* The folktune is recalled 'as if from afar' and in a much slower tempo than at its first appearance in the Allegretto of Part I.

The coda shows a notable shortening of the chorale melody.[18] At 'Molto adagio' begins the transfiguration, with the music dissolving into ethereal, disembodied sound. The chorale's final four-note phrase is repeated three times (solo violin – trumpets – horns), each repeat being an octave lower and marked 'amoroso (religioso)'. At the same time the basic series counterpoints this with five ascending transpositions (D – D flat – C – A flat – D flat), rising from the lowest depth of the solo double bass to the G, three and a half octaves above middle C, on the solo violin. A last reminder of the chorale is introduced by two muted horns (229) which intone its opening whole-tone phrase in inversion. The final two bars recall the soloist's arpeggios with which the work began; note their striking scoring – first violins followed by double basses! The music closes on the B flat triad with added sixth which at once brings to mind the ending of *Das Lied von der Erde*.

This Adagio seems to me to be a masterstroke of musical symbolism, in that, after the torn, fragmented texture of the 'catastrophe' (Allegro), the music takes on a more sustained and harmonically far less discordant character, the ultimate peace of Manon's soul being suggested by a tonal chord!

[17] In a footnote in the score Berg indicates that the public be made aware 'audibly and *visibly*' of the soloist's leading role in this passage.
[18] Bars 214-19 are for the woodwind only, corresponding to the instrumentation of the Chorale's first statement.

TWELVE

THE OPERAS

WOZZECK

The author of the play which Berg set to music in his first opera is so extraordinary a figure that a sketch of his life and achievements will, I trust, not to be found amiss. Georg Büchner (1813-37) was the eldest and most precocious of four children of a medical practitioner at Goddelau in Hesse. With the exception of Georg who died young, they all achieved a considerable reputation in their lifetime. There was Karl, a member of the Reichstag; there was Luise, a noted novelist and one of the earliest fighters for women's rights, and there was Ludwig, a physician and Darwinist philosopher who aroused great controversy with his once celebrated book *Kraft und Stoff* (1855), and whom we shall meet when we come to discuss the editorial history of his brother's play. Georg studied natural science, philosophy and medicine at Giessen and Strasbourg universities and in 1836, when only twenty-three years of age, became a lecturer at Zurich University, but died in the following year.

Büchner was a unique combination of a fully trained and accomplished scientist, a fanatical revolutionary and an outstanding writer and dramatist bursting on the German theatre like a flaming meteor, though it seems that, after *Woyzeck*, he intended to give up his literary career and devote himself entirely to science. In his choice of dramatic subjects containing a socio-political message, he stood close to a literary movement of the time, *Das junge Deutschland*, to which Heine belonged and of which Karl Gutzkow, a friend and protector of Büchner's, was a leading member. It was a movement which demanded of its followers a politically committed attitude in their writings, of which Büchner's *Dantons Tod*,[1] *Leonce und Lena*, and *Woyzeck* are typical examples. Brought up in the narrow-minded, bigoted and paternalistic milieu of his native Hesse, the young Büchner reacted by becoming a political extremist and follower of the ideas which had found their way into Germany in the wake of the French Revolution; indeed, *Dantons Tod* deals with imaginary incidents of the Revolution. In 1834 Büchner founded a secret Society of Human Rights and in the same year wrote a political pamphlet, *Der Hessische Landbote*, clandestinely distributed all over the country, which opened with the battle cry, 'Peace to the humble dwellings,

[1] This play was set to music in an opera (1947) of the same title by the Austrian composer, Gottfried von Einem.

war to the palaces!' and in which he advocated the violent seizure of power from the bourgeois by the peasants and workers. Supported by figures and statistics, this pamphlet gave a precise analysis of the miserable conditions in which the lower classes lived. Büchner may be said to have been a Marxist *avant la lettre*, for he expounded ideas which thirteen years later Marx and Engels advanced in their *Communist Manifesto* of 1847. Büchner's subversive activities finally got him into trouble with the authorities, and in 1835, a warrant was issued for his arrest. He had to flee and sought refuge in liberal Strasbourg, then French, where he completed his studies. It was probably at Strasbourg that he wrote *Leonce und Lena*, a comedy with a strong satirical slant on politics; his dramatic fragment, *Woyzeck*; and the unfinished novel, *Lenz*, whose hero was Goethe's friend from his student days at Strasbourg, Reinhold Lenz, a typical *Sturm und Drang* poet who became insane in early youth.[2] For Strasbourg University Büchner wrote in French his thesis, *Sur le système nerval de barbeau* (1836).[3] After giving a test lecture at Zurich University on cranial nerves, he was installed as *Privatdozent* there, but died of typhoid infection on 19 February 1837.

Büchner had a fiancée, Wilhelmine Jaeglé, the daughter of a Strasbourg pastor, who survived him by forty-three years. Devoted to his memory, Wilhelmine never married, and it is conjectured that whatever writings of Büchner's were in her possession, she destroyed shortly before her death in 1880, including the manuscript of his last play, *Pietro Aretino*. (Some literary scholars assume that it was burnt in a fire in the Büchners' house at Goddelau.) There is also the rather unlikely suggestion that Büchner made a fair copy of the complete *Woyzeck* whose whereabouts, if it ever existed, are unknown.

Woyzeck is based on an actual murder case tried before the Leipzig court from 1821 to 1824 which at the time caused an extraordinary sensation, because it was apparently the first time in German legal history that the defence raised the question of diminished responsibility of the culprit on account of his supposed insanity. This was some twenty years before the McNaghten Rules were introduced into English criminal law. The gist of the German case is as follows:

On the evening of the 12 June 1821 the barber Johann Christian Woyzeck,[4] forty-one years of age, driven by insane jealousy, stabbed his

[2] Lenz's play *Die Soldaten* (1776), which strikingly anticipates Büchner's expressionism in *Woyzeck*, was made the subject of an opera of the same name by the German composer, Bernd Alois Zimmermann (1965), who adopted some of Berg's musico-dramatic procedures of *Wozzeck*.

[3] *The Nervous System of the Barbel*. Büchner seems to have had full command of the French language and translated Victor Hugo's *Lucrèce Borgia* and *Marie Tudor* soon after their publication in France.

[4] The name suggests a Wendian origin, the Wends being a Slavonic people who for centuries were settled in Saxony. During the trial it was stated that Woyzeck's father never learned to speak German properly.

mistress, the forty-six-year-old widow Woost, to death, was tried and finally condemned to death. It was a clear case of *crime passionnel* complicated by the fact, however, that doubts had arisen about Woyzeck's state of mind at the time of his crime. Prompted by press reports to that effect, the court decided to have the culprit examined by an eminent forensic expert, Dr J. Ch. A Clarus, whose conclusion was that the accused was in full possession of his mental faculties before, during and after the murder of the widow. The execution was fixed to take place at Leipzig in November 1822 when the court received information from a private source that in fact Woyzeck had shown symptoms of insanity in the years before his crime. The execution was stayed and the court instructed Dr Clarus to make a second and equally prolonged examination of Woyzeck which merely confirmed his erstwhile findings, whereupon Woyzeck was beheaded on 27 August 1824. In the same year Dr Clarus published his findings in a medical journal[5] which was read in the Büchner household, the playwright's father being a contributor to it. Clarus's report makes it clear that Woyzeck was a borderline case who in modern times, even before the abolition of capital punishment, would have been sent to an asylum for criminal lunatics.

That Büchner had studied this report very carefully emerges from the fact that his play contains incidents and turns of phrases to be found in Dr Clarus's deposition. Woyzeck had led an unsettled life, drifting from one occupation to another, being by turns a wigmaker, barber, soldier, bookbinder, tailor and manservant. From his thirtieth year onwards he began to show intermittent signs of abnormality such as paranoia, visual and auricular hallucinations, apathy, depression and withdrawal symptoms. Thus he imagined himself to be persecuted by a 'secret society', the Freemasons, heard inner voices, had strange visions and was in the habit of talking to himself. Moreover, at times he would spend days and nights in open fields. Yet, as witnesses at the trial confirmed, he was, when not visited by such abnormal symptoms, a reasonable person with common sense – neither Büchner's nor Berg's hero is a fool – well behaved, modest and obliging. When people said to him, 'Du bist ein guter Mensch', he would contradict them because of his guilty conscience at having deserted his mistress, by whom he had had a child. It was largely when under the influence of alcohol, in which he indulged frequently, that he became aggressive and violent. A Jew in whose service he was for a time once said to him after such a fit of aggressiveness: 'Kerl, du ist verrückt und weisst es nicht' – 'Woyzeck, you are mad and do not know it'. He had several

---

[5] His report is fully reproduced in *Georg Büchner. Sämtliche Werke und Briefe. Historisch-kritische Ausgabe mit Kommentar*, by Werner R. Lehmann (Hamburg, 1967), vol. 1, pp. 487-549. In the following pages all references to Büchner's play are, if not stated otherwise, to this edition, an edition which fully meets the most up-to-date standards of literary scholarship and textual criticism.

mistresses, one of whom, a certain Wienberg, bore him a child – she becomes
Marie of both play and opera – but her infidelities made him desert her,
which seems to have been the cause of his first deep depression. Woyzeck was
of an extremely jealous disposition and, suspecting that both Wienberg and
the widow Woost were going out with other men, he physically assaulted
them on several occasions. Some time before the murder Woyzeck had a
vision in which he saw Woost at a dance with a rival, heard the sounds of
dance music and her excited cries 'Immer drauf, immer drauf!'[6] At the
interrogation by Dr Clarus he was able to recall every single detail connected
with his crime. Thus, in a Jew's junk shop he had bought a dagger,[7] which
suggested premeditation, and was fully aware of what he had done. After the
murder he wanted to throw the dagger into a pond outside Leipzig, and
contemplated suicide, as he had already done on several previous occasions.
At the moment of the murder he was in such a state of agitation that he
stabbed recklessly at his victim, inflicting on her seven different wounds. It
should be added that Woyzeck's motive for killing his mistress was not
exclusively jealousy, but also the fact that she despised him for his miserable
poverty.

   This then was the raw material which Büchner developed, altered and
expanded into an extraordinary play. The scientist in him knew the
importance of documented facts, while the playwright in him bent these facts
to his own artistic purposes. What attracted him so forcefully to this murder
case was the fact that he perceived in it potential material for a strikingly
dramatic illustration of his views as political and social reformer, namely,
that the lower classes, the poor, inarticulate and underprivileged, symbolised
in his hero and Marie, suffer untold miseries and deprevations at the hand of
bourgeois society, a society that tries to keep the masses under its thumb in
order to exploit them for its own selfish advantage. The rich versus the poor –
this is one of the mainsprings of Büchner's drama. Woyzeck puts it
reasonably enough to the Captain when he says: 'Wir arme Leut. Sehen Sie,
Herr Hauptmann, Geld, Geld. Wer kein Geld hat!' High morals and virtues
are easy to practise when one is rich, 'Aber ich bin ein armer Kerl'. 'Wir
arme Leut!' is indeed the motto of both play and opera; its musical setting
constitutes in the latter one of the most important leitmotives. If Woyzeck
lives in sin with Marie and the child he has had by her, if he allows himself to
be used as a guinea-pig for the experiments of the crazy doctor – this is, very
largely, because he is the product of the social set-up of his time – he is the
victim of his social environment. The real culprit in this tragedy, Büchner
implies, is not the accused, but the accusers who stand in judgment over him.

   Like the historical character, Büchner's Woyzeck is mentally disturbed

---

[6] Cp. Marie's hectic 'Immerzu, immerzu!' in Berg's opera (II, 4).
[7] Scene 15 of the play, but omitted in the opera.

and shows signs of incipient insanity, but his state is due not merely to a natural disposition, but also to the treatment and the experiments to which he is subjected by the Captain and the Doctor, who thus maim his personality and are the cause of his disintegration. The motive of mental derangement was evidently so important to Büchner that in two drafts of the play he places the scene in an open field at the very beginning,[8] a scene in which the soldier has various hallucinations – he sees a head rolling, feels the ground under him trembling, which in his paranoia he ascribes to the machinations of the dreaded Freemasons, and so on. It was evidently Büchner's intention to introduce Woyzeck right from the start of the play as an abnormal character,[9] in order to puzzle the spectator and, by prompting him to ask questions which will find their answers in the course of the drama, to heighten his interest in that character. What are these answers? First, that Woyzeck's weak mind is further cruelly weakened by his two tormentors, the Captain and the Doctor, who are the representatives of higher authority, in short, the Establishment; that Marie is the only being on this earth to give substance and meaning to his life; third, that her infidelity with the Drum-Major leads to the complete collapse of his ego, in which state he murders her and then drowns himself; and fourth, that poverty, abject poverty, lies at the root of the whole tragedy.

It is interesting to observe that in the first draft the play centred on the sexual drama between Woyzeck and Marie, with only mere hints at its social message, a message which Büchner elaborated in his second draft.[10] In other words, following the actual murder case, Büchner at first dealt with the 'love and jealousy' aspect, which he subsequently combined with the accusatory social theme. Indeed, without this theme the play would have hardly been more than a straightforward melodrama in the Grand Guignol manner: a mentally disturbed and jealous soldier kills his mistress and then himself – tableau! It is, I believe, the fusion of three different elements – poverty, sexual jealousy and insanity – and their consequences for the 'hero', which make *Woyzeck* the extraordinary play it is. It has of course no hero in the classical sense, for Woyzeck is most of the time a passive character to whom things happen. His superiors treat him as a dumb animal, he is cuckolded by his mistress, and the life is almost beaten out of him by the Drum-Major. Driven to the verge of insanity, he murders Marie as if in a trance, and his own end seems to be caused more by accident than an act of volition. In short, Woyzeck is an anti-hero and one of the earliest examples of a dramatic

---

[8] In Berg's opera it is I, 2.

[9] This seems to have been a characteristic dramatic device of Büchner's which he had used previously in his novel *Lenz* and the play *Leonce und Lena*, where soon after the opening occur sentences which at once cast doubts on the mental state of the main characters.

[10] See Prolegomena to Lehmann, *Georg Büchner*, p. 54.

type which became so characteristic of the expressionist German theatre of a later period.

The Captain and the Doctor are of the same ilk – grotesque caricatures of their normal prototypes and, theatrically, descendents of stock figures of the *commedia dell'arte* – the Spanish Captain and the Bolognese Doctor. Büchner's Captain is, comparatively, the less dehumanised figure of the two: a mixture of joviality and malice, he treats his batman in a good-natured but abrasively condescending manner.[11] The Doctor, on the other hand, is as mad as a hatter, obsessed by fixed ideas, the most important of which is his dream of achieving fame and immortality through his experiments with Woyzeck, whom he advises to cultivate also a fixed idea of his own. The Doctor is said to have been intended by Büchner as a caricature of one of his professors at Giessen University, a certain Wilbrand, and this comes out particularly strongly in the Courtyard Scene (omitted in Berg), in which the Doctor produces Woyzeck to his students to show them the successful result of his experiments on him.[12] There was, incidentally, an inhuman doctor at the officers' training camp at Bruck an der Leitha while Berg was there, and it does not need much imagination to sense that the composer's personal experiences with him coloured his musical portrait of the operatic character. What Woyzeck, the Captain and the Doctor have in common, however, is their complete alienation from the world of the normal, yet with this difference that, while his superiors are wholly unaware of it and, indeed, feel smug and secure in their complete isolation, the soldier is vaguely conscious of it and suffers under it.

The Drum-Major, on the other hand, has his feet firmly planted in reality but with a vengeance – flamboyant, vain and a complete extrovert, he is the personification of male sexuality at its most virulent – in fact, he is a human stud.[13] Andres is evidently introduced into the play as a foil to Woyzeck – he represents normality of the most naïve kind.

Marie is the only character in both play and opera who is drawn, more or less, in the round. She is a normal woman of natural healthy instincts, whereas all the other main characters are heavily slanted in a single direction in the typical expressionsit manner. Like Woyzeck, she belongs to the *Lumpenproletariat*, of which she is fully conscious – 'Ich bin nur ein armes Weibsbild' is the conclusion she draws from comparing herself with the 'rich ladies' with their elegant cavaliers. She loves her child, but at the same time it constantly reminds her of her sinful relationship with the soldier. For she

---

[11] That the soldier shaves the Captain in both play and opera is an allusion to the real Woyzeck's one-time occupation as a barber.

[12] This character seems to foreshadow the type of Nazi doctor who carried out inhuman experiments on inmates of concentration camps during the last war.

[13] See his words to Marie: 'Wir wollen eine Zucht von Tambour-Majors anlegen – we will start a breed of drum-majors'. (Scene 6 of play; I, 5 of opera).

is, basically, a deeply religious woman (Bible scene) – even 'moral and, as one might say, chaste'.[14] She also realises that her affair with the Drum-Major is a betrayal of Woyzeck – 'Ich bin doch ein schlechter Mensche. Ich Könnt' mich erstechen – I am a bad woman. I could kill myself with a knife', she exclaims, after yielding to the Drum-Major. She yields because she has a sensual nature and also because she becomes more and more frightened by Woyzeck's increasingly strange behaviour and seeks an escape from her fear to an extrovert, cheerful and perfectly normal character who, in addition, flatters her feminine vanity and sense of pleasure by making her a present of a pair of earrings and taking her to a dance. But her view of life, generated by her poverty, is a nihilistic one – 'Ach! Was Welt! Geht doch alles zum Teufel: Mann und Weib und Kind' – 'Oh, this world! Everything goes to the devil: man and woman and child!' (Scene 4 in play; II, 1 in opera). At the same time, she is a courageous creature who knows how to defend herself. 'Rühr mich nicht an!' – 'Don't touch me!' she shouts in rage at the Drum-Major (Scene 6 of play; I, 5 in opera), and when Woyzeck tries to lay hands on her, she pushes him away with her furious 'Lieber ein Messer im Leib als eine Hand auf mich!' – 'Better a knife in my heart than lay a hand on me!' (Scene 8 of play; II, 3 of opera).

It is worth noting that Büchner makes a distinction between the language of the low characters and that of the Captain and Doctor. The former speak a mixture of Hessian and Alsatian dialects, the latter something like High German. To stress that the play deals with the common people, people of the folk, Büchner introduces fragments of eight folksongs (in Berg there are six), one or two of which are taken from the collection, *Des Knaben Wunderhorn*.[15] It should be added that in the first draft the two protagonists are at first called Louis and Margareth and later Franz and Louise.

Woyzeck is, as already intimated, a precursor of the German expressionist play of the first two decades or so of the twentieth century, as may be seen in several of its features. Büchner concentrates on inner, psychological states, states which are mostly rooted in the dark, shadowy and ultimately irrational part of human nature – 'Der Mensch ist ein Abgrund' exclaims the soldier. Secondly, there is the typically expressionist distortion of the characters towards the abnormal and the pathological, to which treatment the real Woyzeck lent himself particularly well – hence the feeling of a nightmarish dream in both play and opera. Moreover, Woyzeck speaks very often in clipped staccato sentences which, combined with his odd behaviour, create the impression of his being 'gehetzt' ('driven') to which the Captain refers several times and which is so graphically caught in Berg's leitmotif. Like

---

[14] A. H. J. Knight, *Georg Büchner*, Oxford, 1951, p. 139.
[15] Marie's folktune, 'Mädel, mach's Lädel zu!' is Alsatian and was published by Büchner's friend Stober in *Elsässisches Volksbüchlein* in 1842.

Dantons Tod, Woyzeck is what the Germans call a *Stationendrama*, that is, a drama in which the sequence of scenes is not dictated by a strict dramatic logic – the action does not develop in a coherent manner, but unfolds in a seemingly casual and haphazard way and is intended to project for the most part the phases in the development of a character. Büchner's play reads like a film scenario, with little causal nexus between the individual scenes, and it may be that in this Büchner followed Shakespeare and the Goethe of *Götz von Berlichingen*, which in its turn looks back to the English dramatist's loose scenic structure. It will for ever remain doubtful in which order Büchner exactly envisaged the sequence of his twenty-seven scenes. In fact, some scenes can be arranged in a different order of sequence from that of the original fragment, as has been done in various editions of the play, since Büchner in his drafts neither numbered his scenes nor grouped them into acts. From all this it follows that *Woyzeck* is not a 'well-made' play, yet in spite of this or perhaps because of it, the human message its author wanted to convey through it, comes over with a tremendous impact.

Büchner left three sets of drafts, all of them in a fragmentary state, and two of them – they are the major drafts – showing lacunae in several places. The first draft is a folio containing twenty-one scenes; the second consists of a single quarto sheet, with only two scenes – the Doctor's courtyard and the final scene between Woyzeck, the child and the idiot; the third draft, also in quarto, has thirteen scenes.[16] This last draft began as a fair copy, but as Büchner progressed his handwriting becomes all but entirely illegible because of the difficulties he experienced in deciding on the later course of the drama and its ending. It has been conjectured[17] that Büchner intended to close with a scene in the court in which Woyzeck, having been condemned to death, turns the table on his judges and delivers most violent accusations against the state and society, similar to Büchner's attacks in his political pamphlet of 1834. He had already written such a scene in the Tribunal Scene in *Dantons Tod* (III,4), but it is highly improbable that he would have repeated it in *Woyzeck*, whose protagonist is shown as such an intellectually inarticulate creature.

In 1850 Dr Ludwig Büchner brought out his brother's *Nachgelassene Schriften* but omitted *Woyzeck*, partly because of the difficulty he encountered in deciphering a great deal of the manuscript, partly because he felt disconcerted by what he called its 'cynicisms' and 'trivialities'. This we gather from his correspondence with the first editor of Büchner's collected works, Carl Emil Franzos (1848-1904), whose edition of the play Berg used as the basis of his libretto. Franzos, a German writer of Jewish-Polish origin,

---

[16] In this and in the following remarks I base myself on the Hamburg edition.
[17] Fritz Bergemann (ed.), *Georg Büchner. Werke und Briefe*, Wiesbaden, 1953, p. 366.

acquired from Ludwig all the available material[18] of his brother, with the professed aim of resurrecting a writer whom literary scholars had so far almost completely neglected. Franzos's edition appeared in 1879,[19] and was, as far as *Woyzeck* was concerned, a sheer labour of love. For Franzos was faced with a double task of immense difficulty. First, he had to decipher Büchner's handwriting, which for the most part was microscopically small, frequently illegible and faded. By using a chemical preparation – a mixture of distilled water and sulphuric ammonia – Franzos succeeded in bringing the ink of the manuscript up again. But a much tougher nut to crack was to establish a dramatically logical order in the sequence of the scenes which, as Franzos described it, was in Büchner's original 'wholly erratic: the catastrophe was followed by part of the exposition, then came a mere sketch of the closing scene, followed by that scene with which the play might well have opened ...' As regards the sequence of scenes, this was, however, a difficult thing, since there existed not the slightest indication of it.

'Besides necessary considerations for the content, I was guided also, wherever possible, by another, aesthetic consideration. It was my endeavour to group the two elements of which *Wozzeck* consists – the grotesque and the tragic – in such a way that the effect of the latter should not be impaired by the former'.[20]

In trying to obtain further material for his Büchner edition, Franzos addressed himself to Wilhelmine Jaeglé who replied with the following letter:[20a]

Honoured Sir,   Strasburg, 2 April 1877

In your esteemed letter of 17 February you speak of the moral duty I have to further the edition of Büchner's work by making available such papers of his as are in my possession.

To this I have the honour to reply to you that I feel no moral duty at all to make the said papers public; some of these concern only me personally, others are incomplete abstracts and unfinished notes. The memory of Georg Büchner is too dear to me to make me wish to expose anything of his that is unfinished, to the criticism of literary reviewers. Having been prevented by serious illness from replying to you earlier, I have had to postpone it until today.

I would be obliged, esteemed Sir, if you would permit this explanation to suffice to you in future.

---

[18] This material was bought up by the Insel-Verlag in 1918, and deposited by them in 1924 in the Goethe-Schiller Archiv at Weimar.

[19] *Georg Büchner. Sämmtliche Werke und handschriftlicher Nachlass. Kritische Gesamtausgabe*, intro. and ed. Carl Emil Franzos, Frankfort, 1879.

[20] Postscript to the play in the Franzos edition, p. 203.

[20a] Reproduced in *Georg Büchner: Werke und Brief*, ed. Fritz Bergemann, Wiesbaden, 1953, p.

(Does not Wilhelmine Jaeglé's rejection of all further enquiries into Büchner's manuscripts forcibly recall Helene Berg's strange behaviour in the matter of the last act of *Lulu*, when she placed a total embargo on the act? In both cases some two-score years had passed since the deaths of their menfolk. It seems that the thought never crossed their minds that the men to whose memories they were so devoted could never be their exclusive property, but as artists of genius belonged to the world at large. How very different was Constanze Mozart's conduct in the matter of the torso of her husband's Requiem Mass! Far less devoted to his memory than were either Wilhelmine or Helene to their respective fiancé and husband, and prompted largely by mercenary considerations, Constanze first asked Eybler and then Süssmayr to complete the work. Without Constanze's cupidity the odds are that the Requiem Mass would have remained unknown. To anticipate, Friedrich Cerha was no Süssmayr to Berg's Mozart, since his task was chiefly one of completing the orchestration of Act III of *Lulu*, rather than providing entirely new numbers, as Süssmayr did.)

To come back to Franzos. Judged by modern standards of literary scholarship, he was no more than a well-meaning amateur. As proved by later editions, notably the Hamburg edition, which prints Büchner's three drafts next to one another and enables one to see which scenes and/or sentences of the first draft the author included or omitted in the chronologically later draft, Franzos's claim that his edition was 'a literally faithful reproduction of the wording of the manuscript' is far from the truth. He arbitrarily added sentences to, and excised others from, the original text, without indication that these were his own emendations and, moreover, he misread a good many words (just as did later editors) of which 'Wozzeck' for 'Woyzeck' is one of numerous examples; Büchner's correct spelling of the name was not restored until Georg Witkowski's edition of 1920. Again, Franzos's edition of the play opens with the scene between the Captain and Wozzeck in which later editors followed him, thus going completely against the playwright's clear intention, as seen in both the folio and quarto drafts, which begin with the scene in the open field.[21] As to Woyzeck's death, Büchner does not say 'ertrinkt' – 'drowns' – and thus seems to leave the question open whether the soldier drowned by accident or by design. But recalling Dr Clarus's report which mentions that the real Woyzeck attempted suicide on several occasions – once he intended to drown himself while bathing – it is evident that Büchner had a real suicide in mind, and this was also Berg's interpretation. But it was Franzos who added the stage direction 'ertrinkt' to the text, an addition which has been described as amounting to 'almost a forgery'.[22] But if a forgery, it was one made in the

---

[21] In Franzos this is Scene 6 and in Berg, I, 2.
[22] Knight, *Georg Büchner*, p. 166.

right direction, proving that Franzos, who knew nothing of the murder case, was led by a sure dramatic instinct.[23]

To sum up. As a critical editor of the original text, Franzos was certainly a bungler. But extenuating circumstances can be pleaded on his behalf, which were the condition in which he found Büchner's fragment and which made a correct reading in many places impossible. This is shown in all later editions (including the Hamburg edition), all of which show variants of certain words and even sentences. As it is aptly put by George Perle: 'Scholarly impartiality will necessarily give way to suggestive evaluations based on plausibility, prejudice and even unconscious word-associations. The resulting emendation of the original text may be even more problematic than the deliberate emendations of a less scholarly editor.'[24] Whatever we may now think of Franzos's efforts, he has the undeniable merit of having resurrected a masterpiece for the spoken theatre, given it a viable dramatic shape and thus initiated a fruitful dialogue between Büchner and the later expressionists. Equally important, his edition was the direct cause of a unique musical masterpiece springing from it – Berg's opera, which occupies a place entirely its own in the history of the modern music drama. It is one of those extremely rare cases in which the different persons of poet and composer seem to have merged into a single and wholly organic entity, as witness, for instance, Mozart and Da Ponte in *Figaro*, Debussy and Maeterlinck in *Pelléas* and Strauss and Hofmannsthal in *Der Rosenkavalier*. Moreover, *Wozzeck* is not merely an operatic entertainment in the accepted sense, an occasion for aesthetic enjoyment, but a most challenging work confronting the spectator with situations that arouse his social and, beyond it, his moral conscience. As the painter, Georges Braque, said, 'art is meant to be disturbing'. Like *Fidelio*, *Wozzeck* reactivates our ethical personality, which it achieves, through music's mysterious power to speak directly to our emotions, in a more immediate manner than Büchner's play. (For a seemingly unfathomable reason Wozzeck und Marie sprang suddenly into my mind when I first saw in Florence Masaccio's famous fresco, *The Expulsion from Paradise*.)

Before discussing the libretto, it will be necessary to clear up the question of whether Berg based his text exclusively on the Franzos edition of the play or whether he consulted the slightly improved version by Paul Landau, published in 1909. In May 1926 there appeared in *Melos* a substantial article on *Wozzeck* in which the author, Rudolf Schaefke, stated that the composer

---

[23] The murder case was not brought to public attention until 1914, when the *Literarische Echo* published a short article by Hugo Bieber, entitled 'Wozzeck und Woyzeck'. This was soon after the Vienna production of the play. That Berg knew of this article emerges from letters to Schoenberg where he often refers to 'Woyzeck'. That he eventually retained Franzos's spelling was evidently for phonetic reasons, since in a vocal setting 'Wozzeck' is preferable to 'Woyzeck'.

[24] George Perle, 'Woyzeck and Wozzeck', *Musical Quarterly*, 53, no. 2, April 1967, p. 200.

had also used Landau's edition. Berg corrected this with his own hand, as may be seen from this reproduction:

Example 41

Ein Vergleich des Operntextes mit diesen „Woyzeck"-Editionen zeigt, daß Berg die Ausgabe Landaus vorgelegen hat. Schon damit rückt sein „Wozzeck"

Moreover, Reich, who affirms this, declares that the composer compared Franzos's edition with other later editions only *after* the work was completed.[25] Yet the sequence of certain scenes in the opera suggests that Berg must have consulted the Landau version.[26] In this version the first four scenes are identical with those in Act I of the opera, while in Franzos the scenes, 'Freies Feld', 'Maries Stube' and 'Studierstube des Doktors' follow one another as nos. 6, 7 and 8. Again, in the Franzos version the so-called 'Jewel' scene is placed as no. 4, in the exposition of the drama, whereas in both Landau and Berg it opens Act II, the development of the play. Finally, in the Franzos version the scenes, 'Kaserne', 'Kasernenhof' and 'Wirtshaus' do not follow one another (nos. 12, 16 and 17) whereas in Landau they are grouped together as nos. 15, 16 and 16a; this evidently prompted Berg to compress them, for reasons of dramatic economy, into the single scene no. 5 of Act II. All this speaks strongly in favour of assuming that Berg *did* use the Landau version as well as the one by Franzos. This assumption is further confirmed by the fact that at the Vienna production of Büchner's play in May 1914, the Landau version was performed. This is attested by a *Regiebuch* or producer's book used at the Wiener Kammerspiele and now deposited in the Theatre Collection of the Österreichische Nationalbibliothek.[26a] The mystery of why Berg absolutely denied having resorted to the Landau version (see Ex. 41) becomes more impenetrable still when we find that at one time he considered the Franzos version as unsuitable for his conception of music-drama.[26b]

The first problem for Berg was how to transform the 'open drama' of Büchner into a 'closed' libretto as needed for an opera. Although the essential 'film script' character of the play still shines through, notably in the first two acts, Berg did succeed in achieving a more or less dramatically logical sequence of scenes by reducing the twenty-six scenes in Franzos to fifteen in the opera and dividing them into three acts each consisting of five scenes. Apart from dramatic considerations, this 3 x 5 scene disposition may well have been due to his predilection for numerical correspondences, to say

---

[25] Reich, *Alban Berg* (Eng. ed., p. 118.)

[26] See Gerd Ploebsch, *Alban Berg's 'Wozzeck'*, Strasbourg, 1968, pp. 16-17.

[26a] Personal communication from Nicholas Chadwick.

[26b] See 'Die von Berg in der Textvorlage festgelegten musikalischen Formen', by Rosemary Hill, *50 Jahre Wozzeck von Alban Berg*, ed. Otto Kolleritsch, Graz, 1978, p. 27.

nothing of the fact that Schoenberg's *Pierrot Lunaire* is similarly arranged in 3 × 7 poems, which may have served Berg as a model. The libretto of *Wozzeck* is of an almost classical shape, in marked contrast to the play, with an Exposition (Act I), a Development (Act II) and the Catastrophe (Act III). The situations are concise and self-evident[27] and the tension is built step by step until it is released in a shattering climax. Compression was Berg's chief means of heightening the dramatic character of the play. He thus eliminated completely some scenes of the original such as 'The Booth', 'The Grandmother' and 'The Jew's Junk Shop',[28] telescoped Büchner's Käthe and the Innkeeper into Margaret, and Andres and another soldier into a single character, replaced the Two Citizens by the Captain and Doctor (III, 4), and excised superfluous repetitions in the dialogue, thus simplifying the language and obtaining the utmost concision in the verbal utterances. Büchner has twenty-three speaking characters – Berg eleven singing characters. In parenthesis, for all his realistic presentation of the situations in the opera, Berg shrank back from what Ludwig Büchner euphemistiaclly called the 'cynicisms and trivialities' of his brother's play. In II, 5 he suppressed the Drum-Major's line, 'Ich will ihm (Wozzeck) die Nas ins Arschloch prügeln – I will thrash your nose into your arsehole', and in I, 4 he altered the Doctor's 'gepisst' into the innocuous 'gehustet', which makes complete nonsense of Wozzeck's reply, 'Aber, Herr Doktor, wenn einem die Natur ankommt! – But, Herr Doktor, when forced to that by nature!'.

To the very few stage directions in Büchner, Berg added a considerable number of his own, such as the indication of the time of the day at which various incidents take place (morning, afternoon, evening and night), and he gives precise instructions as to the visual aspect of a given scene, pointing, for instance, to such symbolic nature phenomena as the sunset in I, 2 and the different positions of the moon on the night sky in III, 2 and 4. Indeed, *Wozzeck* represents a higher form of *Gesamtkunstwerk* than Wagner's, a work in which the whole stage apparatus – singing, acting, facial expression, gestures and movements, scenery, lighting, rise and fall of the curtain – is pressed into the service of the drama. And, while allowing the producer every freedom in staging the opera in his own individual manner, Berg demands that the action be put across in a realistic, clear, unequivocal way. The only scene which is not to be treated in a realistic style is the Tavern Scene (III, 3) which, on account of its eerie, shadowy character, requires no more than a mere suggestion of the locale.[29] To sum up, Berg's work on the libretto of *Wozzeck* (and even more of *Lulu*) was a creative act and perhaps as important

---

[27] In this Berg recalls Puccini, who spoke of 'l'evidenza della situazione'.

[28] The composer regretted the omission of this scene, forced on him by dramatic considerations.

[29] Alban Berg, *Praktische Anweisungen zur Einstudierung des 'Wozzeck'*, in Reich, *Alban Berg ...* (1937), p. 170.

to him as its musical setting.

Having achieved unity and coherence in the libretto, Berg's second and incomparably more exacting task was to set it to music of equal consistency and unity, music which, on the one hand, would reflect the physical and emotional happenings on the stage in the most immediate and telling manner and, on the other, would be dictated by the laws of musical architecture pure and simple. While the action determines the music's character and tone, it is musical laws which govern its structure and development. This twin aspect of music in opera is the mark of every born musical dramatist; it makes *Wozzeck* a supreme example of *dramma per musica* in the modern theatre, for Berg manages to resolve the dialectics between *parola* (in the widest sense) and *musica* into a complete synthesis. But the way in which this synthesis is achieved goes far beyond the Wagnerian music-drama and was at the time something quite novel. For Berg seeks to find in the text the suggestion for which kind of musical form is to be chosen for a given scene, or, to put it differently, he tries to discover parallelisms between the action of a given scene and the paramount characteristics of a musical form – a procedure which may be defined as the use of musical forms in the service of dramatic symbolism. Two scenes spring immediately to mind. One is the scene between the Doctor and Wozzeck (I, 4) in which the obsessions and fixed ideas of the two characters are symbolically represented by a passacaglia, the outstanding feature of which is variations on a fixed and constantly recurring theme. The other scene is that between Marie, the Child, and, later, Wozzeck (II, 1) which suggested to Berg the choice of sonata form with three themes, and the action of which allowed an interpretation in terms of exposition, development and recapitulation. The table below shows the symbolic relationship between the individual scenes and their musical forms in *Wozzeck*:

Scene	*Music*
ACT I	
Exposition	
(Wozzeck in his relation to the world round him):	Five character pieces:
Scene 1: Wozzeck and the Captain	Suite
Scene 2: Wozzeck and Andres	Rhapsody
Scene 3: Wozzeck and Marie	Military March and Lullaby
Scene 4: Wozzeck and the Doctor	Passacaglia
Scene 5: Marie and the Drum-Major	Quasi Rondo
ACT II	
Development	Symphony in five movements:
Scene 1: Marie, the Child, later Wozzeck	Sonata movement
Scene 2: The Captain and Doctor, later Wozzeck	Fantasy and Fugue
Scene 3: Marie and Wozzeck	Largo
Scene 4: Garden of an Inn	Scherzo
Scene 5: Guard-room in the Barracks	Rondo con introduzione

ACT III

Catastrophe and Epilogue	Six Inventions:
Scene 1: Marie and Child ('Bible' Scene)	Invention on a theme
Scene 2: Marie and Wozzeck (Death of Marie)	Invention on a note
Scene 3: A Tavern	Invention on a rhythm
Scene 4: Death of Wozzeck	Invention on a hexachord
Orchestral Interlude	Invention on a key
Scene 5: Children playing	Invention on a regular quaver
	movement

I have said before that Berg's major problem in *Wozzeck* was how to achieve in the music the same coherence and unity as characterise his libretto. Why this great concern with the unifying formal element? It seems that this was to counteract the almost overwhelming chaotic richness of invention which had to be channelled and coerced by intellectual discipline, that is, by a tight organisation of the musical material. The means by which the composer achieves this organisation all fall under the general head of constructivism, which was a major feature not only of Berg's own musical thinking but of the Schoenberg School as a whole.

Let us first examine the large-scale organisation of the opera. To begin with, Berg perceived the three acts as constituting a ternary scheme (A_1-B-A_2), in which A_2 is of course not a musical recapitulation of A_1; their correspondence with each lies in their architecture – both consist of more or less loosely arranged closed forms: character pieces in Act I and Inventions in Act III. Act II, on the other hand, is musically translated into an organic, more coherent dramatic symphony – it is the act in which the development or *peripeteia* of the drama occurs; not to mention the fact that it is at once weightier and longer than each of the two outer acts.

As to the closed forms, the difficulty was how to give them unity, consistency and articulation without using the form-building means of tonal music. Berg's great merit in *Wozzeck* was to have been the first to write a full-length opera in the atonal style, a style characterised by an extreme fluidity and randomness, but in which certain recurring melodic, harmonic and rhythmic configurations act as points of reference or as landmarks in the music. Thus we find that each act closes by way of cadence on the same chord which might be termed the 'tonic chord' of the opera, yet on each of its three occurrences this principal chord appears varied in shape, texture and orchestration dictated by the character of the finale scene of each act. This eight-note chord rests on the perfect fifth G-D, while its upper notes oscillate between augmented and perfect fourths; encapsulated in it is the tritone B-F or F-B which pervades the entire opera as the symbolic interval for the tragedy.

Apropos of Berg's use of closed forms from instrumental music in an opera. This in itself was not an entirely novel device. It was used by Mozart in *Die Zauberflöte* in which choral variations accompany the scene of the 'Two Men at Arms'; by Wagner in *Die Meistersinger*, where we encounter a fugue in the Prügel Scene of the second-act finale; and by Verdi, who resorted to fugue in the battle scene of *Macbeth* and the finale of *Falstaff*. In all these instances the character of the scene determined the choice of the musical form for which it was the symbol. The novelty about Berg's procedure was the application of it to all the fifteen scenes of *Wozzeck*, and the use of so great a variety of different forms. And since it was the text that suggested the choice of a particular form, there is an extremely close interlocking between scene and music. This is in marked contrast to such neoclassical operas as Hindemith's *Cardillac*, Shostakovich's *The Nose* and Stravinsky's *Oedipus Rex*, in which there is no such organic link, drama and music deliberately unfolding on two different planes. The point about *Wozzeck* is that while the musical forms are inspired by the text, Berg guarantees their independence as music pure and simple. He seems to have had this in mind when in an article[30] he asked the rhetorical question: 'Is it not enough to compose beautiful music to good theatre or, better, to compose such beautiful music that in spite of it good theatre results from it?'

Wozzeck might be called a 'number' opera in marked contrast to the *durchkomponiert* symphonic type of the Wagnerian music drama, were it not that Berg links the individual scenes by interludes which, apart from the practical necessity of allowing time for the scene changes, have purely musical functions to fulfil – to provide continuity by either being a symphonic transition between two scenes, or the coda to the preceding scene, or an introduction to the following scene, or both together. In other words, the interludes link disparate scenes in a gradual manner or, by being all but non-existent (as for instance between the fourth and fifth scenes of Act I), stress strong contrasts by almost juxtaposing two consecutive scenes. Berg once said to Ernest Ansermet that the device of using interludes was suggested to him by Debussy's *Pelléas et Mélisande*, just as the micro-structure, which invested each scene in that opera with a different character, gave him the idea of using a variety of instrumental forms in *Wozzeck*.[31] Another and equally close model was Schoenberg's monodrama, *Erwartung* (1909), written in the same free atonal style as Berg's opera and consisting of four scenes which are linked by a short *Verwandlungsmusik* or transformation music. No post-Wagnerian opera composer could dispense with the leitmotive and Berg was no exception. Yet in *Wozzeck* he does not use this device as pervasively as in *Lulu*, and, with the exception of some interludes in

---

[30] 'Das Opernproblem: "Pro mundo",' *Neue Musikzeitung*, Stuttgart, 1928, reproduced in Reich, *Alban Berg* ... (1937), p. 174.

[31] See H. H. Stuckenschmidt, 'L'influence de Debussy en Autriche et Allemagne', in *Debussy et l'évolution de la musique au XXe siècle*. Edition du Centre National de la recherche scientifique, Paris, 1965, p. 258.

which certain leimotives are treated in symphonic fashion, they are as a general rule employed in the manner of the pre-Wagnerian 'reminiscence'. Though the leitmotives are closely associated with certain characters, situations and even verbal utterances, Berg at times changes their erstwhile dramatic connection and thus their significance. Nevertheless, for all his freedom in their use, the composer succeeds in establishing with them a framework of relationships on both the dramatic and musical level, which is another of his means of creating unity and coherence. There are some twenty leitmotives which are employed throughout the opera, while others are merely of 'local' importance, being confined to a single scene such as the passacaglia theme (I, 4) or the two 'moon' motives (III, 2 and 4).

The motto of the whole opera is the phrase:

Example 42

Wir   ar - me Leut!

first uttered by Wozzeck in bar 136 of I, 1.[32] (It is interesting to note that also in Manfred Gurlitt's *Wozzeck* [1926] the setting of 'Wir arme Leut!' is one of the opera's main motives.) Other significant leitmotives in Berg's work are Wozzeck's 'gehetzt' (Ex. 49), Marie's 'Plaint' (Ex. 47) and Open Fifth, A-E, and the Drum-Major's military motive (Ex. 53). Berg sometimes produces a kaleidoscope of different 'reminiscences' closely ranged together as, for instance, at the opening of II, 3 and III, 2. It is very largely in the interludes where Berg, unhampered by the action and its dialogue, gives music its head and, as already remarked, subjects his leitmotives to symphonic treatment *à la* Wagner, altering their intervals and rhythms and combining them contrapuntally.

A noteworthy feature of *Wozzeck* is the clear distinction made by the composer between art music and the *volkstümlich* or folk element. In tonal music this dichotomy is easily achieved, but how is it to be presented in an atonal work? Simply by a recourse in the *volkstümlich* portions to the characteristic of the tonal style. Thus the melodies of the various folksongs in *Wozzeck* show regular and symmetrical two-bar phrasing (often in sequence) and preference for the fourth and whole-tone progressions, while the harmony is characterised by the 'primitive' third and especially the fourth. This contrasts tellingly with the surrounding atonal music, with its irregular 'prose' phrases in the melody and the dissonant intervals of the harmony. I quote the openings of Andres's folksong and Marie's Lullaby which clearly show the *volkstümlich* two-bar phraseology and the fourth as a prominent

---

[32] Its treatment in the opera is not dissimilar to that of the 'Fate' motive in *Carmen*.

interval (Ex. 43a, b). The distribution of art music and *volkstümlich* music over the opera is a characteristic feature of it. 'High' style (sonata, symphony, variation and fugue) enters into a marriage with 'low' style (folksong, ländler, polka, waltz and military march) allowing for a singularly wide range of expression in *Wozzeck*.

Example 43a

Das   ist   die   schö-ne   Jä - ge-rei,   Schie - ssen steht   Je - dem frei!

Example 43b

Mä- del, was fangst du jetzt   an?   Hast ein klein Kind und kein   Mann!

In the vocal treatment of *Wozzeck* (as of *Lulu*) Berg avails himself of all the possibilities of which the human voice is capable both as a singing and speaking organ, using traditional as well as novel vocal means. A number of lyrical passages show a cantabile style and the composer was of the opinion that they could readily be sung in a *bel canto* manner.[33] Most of the opera is, however, in a half-arioso, half-declamatory style of which Wozzeck's Air (I, 1) is an instructive example. There is also frequent resort to parlando, a particularly effective instance of which is at the end of I, 4 where the Doctor, after his ecstatic outcry, 'Immortal!', suddenly changes to a matter-of-fact attitude and drily asks Wozzeck to show him his tongue. Except for about a dozen bars, there is no recitative in the opera. Berg replaces it in two ways. One is the melodrama and the other is *Sprechstimme* or rhythmic speech used by Schoenberg in *Die Glückliche Hand* and *Pierrot Lunaire*,[34] in which the vocal line is to be delivered in strict rhythm and at a fixed pitch, yet in speaking tone.

It will be opportune to insert here a few general words on *Sprechstimme* or *Sprechgesang* since it plays an important role in Berg's two operas. *Sprechgesang* has been a problem ever since Schoenberg introduced it into the last part of his *Gurrelieder* and afterwards employed it exclusively in some later works the first of which was the melodrama, *Pierrot Lunaire* (1912). I have yet to hear a performance, live or recorded, in which the reciter observed the accurate

[33] Alban Berg. 'Die Stimme in der Oper', in *Gesang*, Year Book of the U.E., Vienna, 1929, repr. in Reich, *Alban Berg ...* (1937), p. 164.

[34] In his preface to the score of *Wozzeck* and *Lulu* Berg especially refers to these two works in connection with his use of *Sprechstimme*. Incidentally, it occurs already in the third part of Schoenberg's *Gurrelieder*, and Humperdinck employs it in the incidental music to *Die Königskinder* (1897), where the Broom-Maker's Child speaks a line in strict rhythm and fixed pitch.

musical pitches of the *Sprechgesang* for any length of time. To reproduce the musical rhythm presents no difficulty whatever. It is Schoenberg's own instruction (Preface to *Pierrot*) as to how this cross between singing and speaking is to be achieved that has caused confusion in the minds of the executants: the reciter is to start on the notated musical pitch but must at once allow his speaking voice to fall or rise to the next note and so on. What invariably happens is that the reciter, if she is a singer (not an actress) either falls into actual singing expressly ruled out by Schoenberg, or contents herself with the merest approximation to the notated pitches; usually it is a mixture of both.

Now Wagner, Strauss and Puccini would never have thought of such a device as *Sprechgesang*, for they were too deeply steeped in the art of pure singing as to contemplate so hybrid a form of vocal delivery. Boulez remarks somewhere that Schoenberg's device did not spring from contact with practical reality but was the result of his speculative thinking about extending the means of vocal expression. In his own performances of *Wozzeck* and *Lulu* Boulez rightly allows his singers a considerable measure of freedom in the execution of speech-song, and Schoenberg himself developed over the years an attitude that suggests that he found *Sprechgesang* and the demand for accurately maintaining the notated pitches really incompatible. For example, in a letter to Berg (14 January 1913) in which he explains the execution of speech-song in the *Gurrelieder*, he writes that the pitch notation here is 'by no means to be taken as seriously as in the *Pierrot* melodrama' – the different pitches are to be understood as only '*Lagenunterschiede*', that is, as differences between high and low registers. 'No intervallic relationships!' In the Preface to *Pierrot*, on the other hand, he states that it is the reciter's task to transform his part into speech-melody paying good attention to the notated pitches. The reciter must never adopt a 'singing' delivery. Yet in 'Gebet des Pierrot' (no. 9 of the cycle) he states in a footnote that the reciter is to produce the notated pitches 'nur andeutungsweise' ('only vaguely' or 'fleetingly'). And, lo and behold! in a recording of *Pierrot* made under his direction, with Erika Wagner-Stiedry (a Viennese actress) as reciter, the correct pitch notation was ignored almost throughout, Frau Wagner occasionally going in a different direction in her delivery from that of the notated speech-song line. We gather from an extremely well-researched paper by Peter Stadlen[34a] that, according to the composer's brother-in-law, Rudolf Kolisch, Schoenberg repeatedly declared towards the end of his life that the notated pitches of *Sprechgesang* in *Pierrot* must be avoided because they do *not* fit the music! What is more, in his *Ode to Napoleon* (1942) and *Survivor from Warsaw* (1944) Schoenberg used for the

---

[34a] 'Schoenberg und der Sprechgesang', given at the first Congress of the International Schoenberg Society in Vienna in June 1974, *Publikationen der Internationalen Schoenberg Gesellschaft* (Vienna, 1978), pp. 202-12. English version: 'Schoenberg and the *Sprechgesang*', *Music & Letters*, January 1981, pp. 1-11.

reciter's part a single line above and underneath which he placed the notes of the speech-melody thus merely differentiating between 'high' and 'low'; which seems to me the best way of coping with *Sprechgesang* in *Wozzeck* and *Lulu*. Stadlen suggests that true speech-melody can be achieved if the reciter eschews the singer's vibrato, and he adduces as evidence recordings of *Pierrot* made by Marie-Thérèse Escribano (Turnabout) and Helga Pilarczik (Ades). I have had no occasion to hear these records, but I heard Miss Pilarczik in a live performance as the Woman in Schoenberg's monodrama *Erwartung* which has straightforward singing. The singer displayed an enviable freedom in singing the correct notes!

To my knowledge *Sprechgesang* has never been attempted in English and French, and in Italian only once by Dallapiccola in his opera, *Volo di notte* (Florence, 1940). This leads me to assume that the peculiar effect of *Sprechgesang* is closely bound up with the phonetic property of the German language and would in no other language create the impression intended by Schoenberg.

Berg applies the *Sprechstimme* in the greater part of the opera and in certain scenes (I, 2: III, 2 and 4) achieves with it an extraordinary, fantastic, almost unreal effect. *Sprechstimme* also makes for greater clarity in the enunciation of words, which the composer called jestingly 'bel parlare'. He goes a step farther than his one-time master in that he erects a kind of half-way house between *Sprechstimme* and normal singing, more often used in *Lulu* than *Wozzeck*, for which he invented a special sign – a note with its stem crossed in the middle as, for instance, in the opening of Marie's prayer (fugue):

Example 44

Und knie-te   hin   zu sei-nen   Fü-ssen

Wozzeck's passage in I, 2 (237-42) shows all three possibilities in juxtaposition – rhythmic speech, half singing and normal singing which serves to generate a crescendo of expression.

The orchestra of *Wozzeck* is a large one, including quadruple wind (quintuple clarinets)[35] and a huge array of percussion, but Berg's treatment of it is diametrically opposed to that of Wagner, Strauss and the Schoenberg of the *Gurrelieder*. His style of instrumentation, foreshadowed in the Altenberg Songs and anticipated by his master in *Erwartung* and *Die glückliche Hand*, is that of chamber music – he significantly called *Wozzeck* a '*piano* opera' –

[35] It was for the Oldenburg production (March 1929) that Erwin Stein made, under the composer's direction, a reduced version of the score, notably in respect of the woodwind, which renders the opera suitable for performance in smaller theatres. Incidentally, Stein also made a reduced version of the score of Schoenberg's *Gurrelieder* (1920).

confining the full orchestra almost exclusively to the interludes, while in the actual scenes he mostly resorts to a tutti only when the characters are not singing, as, for instance, in the fights in I, 5 and II, 5. The scoring is partly geared to impressionist sound mixtures (I, 2; III, 4), but mostly serves to trace out and clarify the thematic lines of the texture, Berg strictly differentiating between leading parts, subsidiary parts and pure accompaniment. We shall refer to special orchestral effects in the analysis of the individual scenes.

Like all Berg's music, *Wozzeck* is a *rubato* work in which the basic tempo of a given scene suffers almost constant *accelerandi* and *ritardandi*, in tune with the ups and downs of the emotional situation on the stage. Notable exceptions to this rule are those scenes in which 'mechanical' music is played – the Military March of I, 3, the stage music of II, 4 and the out-of-tune piano of III, 3. A characteristic trait of Berg's changing tempo is to derive the new speed almost mathematically from the preceding one; in other words, he creates a relationship between the original and changed tempo. Thus, in I, 4 the passacaglia theme is crotchet = 36-40 while the first three variations are exactly double this speed, i.e. crotchet = 72-80. Again in the 'Jewel' scene (II,2) the tempo increases progressively by exactly ten crotchets per minute:

Introduction	: crotchet = 80
1st subject	: crotchet = 90
2nd subject	: crotchet = 100
Closing group	: crotchet = 110

As we see, even in the matter of tempo changes, Berg seeks to establish a definite relationship which, I believe, partly sprang from his concern for correspondences, and ultimately from his preoccupation with number symbolism.

The following pages do not aim at a comprehensive discussion of the individual scenes – this would require a monograph, already provided by two French authors[36] – but confine themselves to pointing out the salient musico-dramatic features and certain characteristics of a purely musical nature.

The first act, representing the exposition of the drama, consists of five largely static scenes serving to characterise Wozzeck's relation to the people who, with the exception of Andres, will play a varying role in his tragedy – the Captain, Marie, the Doctor and, indirectly, the Drum-Major – while at the same time different aspects of Wozzeck's personality are revealed, most important among them being his disturbed state of mind which, as already said, Büchner saw as largely a consequence of the treatment meted out to him.

[36] Pierre Jean Jouvet and Michel Fano, *Wozzeck d'Alban Berg*, Paris 1953, 2nd ed. 1964.

Scene 1. The Captain's room. Wozzeck is shaving the Captain. Early morning.

The scene shows the Captain obsessed by certain ideas – the slow ordered progress of life, the passage of time, the antithesis between eternity and the present moment, and so on. The conversation with Wozzeck moves casually from one topic to another – hence Berg's choice of a Suite which consists of a number of loosely arranged little pieces – Prelude, Pavane, Gigue, Gavotte, Air, and a repeat of the Prelude to round off the scene. The Prelude, ushered in by three bars of introduction[37] later to return, brings the Captain's leitmotive suggesting his fidgety nervous manner:

Example 45

In each movement of the Suite Berg attaches to the main orchestra a group of obbligati instruments as a further means of dramatic characterisation. In the Prelude it is five wood-wind instruments[38] whose persistent movement in semiquavers and demisemiquavers serves to illustrate the Captain's unceasing chatter. His 'Langsam, Wozzeck, langsam!' (5-6) – perhaps the epitome of his life philosophy – is accompanied by the cor anglais in a composed slowing down on the note D flat, the same note on which later Wozzeck sings his stereotyped, automaton-like 'Jawohl, Herr Hauptmann!', suggesting his submissive nature. When the Captain refers to Wozzeck's age and tells him that he still has thirty years to live,[39] working out how much this is in terms of months, not to speak of 'days, hours and minutes', the horns play a wedge-like motive which grows from a minor second to a perfect fourth (17-21), and which is related to a similar figure associated with the Doctor's obsessions in I, 4. For the Captain's bombastic speech about the contrast between 'eternity' and a 'moment in time', Berg chooses ironically the dignified old form of the Pavane, reinforcing this characterisation by the particular choice of obbligato.[40] At the mention of 'eternity' (32-3) the harp, together with first horn and bass tuba, describes a circle of fourths descending to the lowest depths evidently to suggest the infinity of time, while the earth turning round itself is caught in gyrating triplets on the woodwind. After Wozzeck's last 'Jawohl, Herr Hauptmann!' (50) Berg inserts a full stop, indicated by a four-note chord consisting of the fifth G-D

[37] Berg said that the roll on the side-drum intended to stress the crescendo between the two opening chords, appeared to him, when he first heard it, an astonishingly simple yet most effective means to characterise the military atmosphere of the opera.

[38] Oboe, cor anglais, clarinet, bass clarinet and bassoon.

[39] In the play and the opera the soldier is thirty years of age, while the historical Woyzeck was forty-one at the time of his crime.

[40] Three timpani, side-drum, bass-drum and harp.

of the opera's cadential harmony and the symbolic tritone F-B. The bridge to the Gigue is formed by a cadenza for the solo viola, a section which at the Captain's words 'Wozzeck, Er sieht immer so verhetzt aus!' brings in the voice part a hint (in inversion) of Wozzeck's leitmotive (Ex. 49). Berg's choice of the expressive solo viola is an ironically sentimental comment on the Captain's unctuous 'Ein guter Mensch tut das nicht'. In the brilliant Gigue the Captain, making derisive fun of the soldier, begins with a question about the weather which Wozzeck answers with 'Schlimm, Herr Hauptmann! Wind!', illustrated by scurrying passages on the three obbligato flutes and violins. He then says that the wind blows from 'south-north' confirmed by Wozzeck's 'Jawohl, Herr Hauptmann' (on D flat), which sends the Captain into side-splitting laughter graphically caught in the obsteperous triplets on the four muted horns and trumpets. The Gigue is followed by another cadenza for solo contra-bassoon, evidently chosen to characterise the self-important moralistic stance the Captain now adopts;[41] this cadenza represents a much abbreviated variant of the first cadenza. The Captain now proceeds to accuse Wozzeck of immorality on account of his being the father of a child born 'without the blessing of the church'. Berg casts this sermon by way of a caricature in the form of a Gavotte with an obbligato of four trumpets. The Captain's opening phrase. 'Er hat keine Moral' is trumpeted out 'like a fanfare' and freely imitated by the trumpets. When he first mentions the illegitimacy of the child, his tone is most emphatic, but when he quotes the regimental chaplain he falls into a sanctimonious cantabile which is heightened by an organ-like accompaniment, 'quasi plein jeu' of all the woodwind and brass. There follow two Doubles or Variations of the Gavotte, the first for Wozzeck, the second for the Captain. Wozzeck's is of a lyrical character and has as obbligato the four soft-toned horns. In strongest contrast to this is the Captain's Double in which four muted trombones, ff, form the obbligato to express his anger and utter confusion at the soldier's curious reply, his voice squeaking (on the high A flat-A-C), and thus showing that he has lost all control of himself. Due to Berg's compression of the Gavotte in the two variants, their repective length is progressively halved: 12-6-3 bars.

The lyrical core of the first scene is Wozzeck's ternary Air in a slow 3/2 time in which the obbligato instruments are, significantly, the strings. It is in this solo piece that we first hear the motto, 'Wir arme Leut!' (Ex. 42), which recurs in it several times in various transpositions – once in a stretto at the unison between solo violin, solo viola and solo cello (145-6), to accompany Wozzeck's words about the virtues of the rich. When he refers to the misery of people like himself in 'this and the other world', the fateful B appears in the bass to be followed by C sharp (or D flat) as the symbol of his submission. The Captain, somewhat taken aback by this outburst, tries to

---

[41] Bar 112 contains the stage remark: 'setzt sich in Positur' – 'strikes an attitude'.

pacify him, 'Schon gut, schon gut! Ich weiss; Er ist ein guter Mensch'. These words mark the beginning of the repeat of the Prelude which in bars 157-70 becomes a free palindrome of the bars 6-14, thus following the dialogue which returns to the topic of the opening. The ensuing interlude is a summing-up of the preceding scene and may be said to be a symphonic development of its main material in the order: Pavane, Gavotte, Gigue, Air[42] and Prelude; the bass pedal on C sharp (191-200) seems like an anticipation of the *Hauptrhythmus* (RH) of III, 3. The music reaches its climax in a violent tutti whose last chord (200) is quickly dampened in preparation for the next scene, which takes us into a completely different sphere.

Scene 2. An open field outside the town. Late afternoon. Andres and Wozzeck are cutting sticks in the bushes.

In this scene nature phenomena such as sunset and dusk, in themselves meaningless, exert a strange influence on Wozzeck's mind and assume for him a significance expressed in his visual hallucinations and paranoiac fear, which are thrown into strongest relief by the normality of Andres, who counters Wozzeck's fantasies with his gay folksong, 'Das ist die schöne Jägerei!' For the most part this is an eerie scene and like a premonition of III, 2 and 4. Berg called the music for it a 'Rhapsody' which, I take it, refers not to any freedom of form, which here obeys strict rules and is closely structured, but to the alternation of heterogeneous ideas – on the one hand, a chordal motive and a chromatic four-note figure, and on the other Andres's folksong (Ex. 43a):

Example 46a

Example 46b

The three chords (ex. 46a) whose progression Berg compared to that of tonic, dominant and subdominant in tonal music, are meant as a 'nature sound' and will reappear in the chorus of the snoring soldiers in II, 5. Together with Ex 46b they represent an impressionist means of evoking the prevailing atmosphere of the scene. In form this Rhapsody could be described as

[42] The violins enter in bar 191 with the motto, 'leidenschaftlich und drängend'.

sonata-like, with an exposition of the three ideas (201-22), a development of Ex. *a* (223-45) and the folksong (249-69), a second development of Ex. *a* (269-98) and a coda (299-329). 'Development' must here be understood with a grain of salt, notably of Andres's song which represents a more elaborate repeat, with the voice-part enriched by *coloratura*. Ex. *b* is the cement with which Berg holds the different sections together. In bars 271-8 he quotes the creeping passage from the *Marsch* of the Three Orchestral Pieces, op. 6 (79-83). In this scene the composer makes use for the first time of *Sprechgesang*, which seems to me to add to its nightmarish quality. Bar 302 ff. brings the chordal motive (Ex. *a*) in the crab and introduces on the strings a theme of suggestive beauty which has some affinity with Wozzeck's 'Misery' theme (Ex. 57). The coda continues into the interlude in which we hear two Austrian military calls – 'Zum Gebet' (horn and trumpet, 313-16), and 'Abgeblasen' (clarinet, 317-18), fragments of Andres's folksong 'as if from the distance', and echoes of Ex. 46*b* in the basses. Into the last bars of the coda sounds the opening, off-stage, of the Military March of the next scene.

Scene 3. Marie's room. Evening. Marie, with the child on her arm, stands at the window to watch the soldiers pass by. Margret and later Wozzeck

The beginning of this scene is to show Marie's admiration for the Drum-Major, who marches by at the head of his military band and greets her in passing while she waves to him, thus hinting at the relationship between the two. Except for the opening five bars of the Trio sung by Marie to the words 'Soldaten, Soldaten, sind schöne Burschen!', the military music (scored for wind and percussion only) provides the background for the conversation between Marie and her neighbour Margret, who taunts Marie about the great interest she shows in the Drum-Major, whereupon Marie in fury slams the window shut, so that the repeat of the March is no longer heard.[43] The main part of Scene 3, for which the preceding may be taken as a kind of introduction falls into three sections: Marie and her child – Marie and Wozzeck – Marie alone again. The opening of the first section introduces an important leitmotive which, according to Berg's lecture, stands for Marie 'bemoaning her wretched life':

Example 47

---

[43] The same device is used in Act II of Puccini's *Tosca*.

When shortly before the end of this scene Marie bursts out into the despairing cry, 'Wir arme Leut!' – her only utterance of this phrase – it is, significantly, not set to the motto sung by Wozzeck at the beginning of his aria in I, 1 but to the first bar of Ex. 47, so as to convey her desperate need to be released from the tie to the soldier, which is clearly seen in her subsequent words, 'I cannot bear it' and her sudden rush to the door.[44] While she rocks the child, the strings and subsequently the trumpet (369-70) play gently swaying triplets which seem to anticipate the triplets in the final scene of the opera. There follows her Lullaby, the characteristic fourths of which appear already in the preceding harp and celesta passage and, harmonically, in the 6/4 chord underpinning it. The Lullaby falls into two parts, the first opening with 'Mädel, was fangst Du jetzt an?' which is a slow siciliano in 6/8 (Ex. 43*b*), while the second, beginning with 'Eia popeia' – the cradle song proper – is a ländler in 3/4. The two parts are then repeated with different words and slight variations in the music which finally leads to an exquisite, sustained phrase of descending major and minor thirds ranging over more than two octaves:

Example 48

Lau – ter   küh – le Wein   muss es   sein!

(A most poignant reminiscence of Ex.48 is in the last scene of the opera, just before the Children say to Marie's Child: 'Du! Deine Mutter ist tot!') The Lullaby ends on the open fifth A-E which, Berg said, conveys Marie's 'aimless and indefinable attitude of waiting which will find its final solution only in death'. Indeed, it is heard as the last motive after her murder. In the Lullaby, however, it enters when Marie remains 'deep in thought', and what she is thinking of is revealed in fragments of the Military March. Her reverie is abruptly broken off by Wozzeck's appearance at the window. This part of the scene is the only place in the whole work where Berg dispenses with a closed musical form and resorts to the *durchkomponiert* style on the basis of leitmotives in the manner of Wagner. Wozzeck's 'gehetzt', hinted already in the Captain's part in I, 1, is caught in this motive:

---

[44] See George Perle, 'Representation and Symbol in the Music of *Wozzeck*', *Music Review* 32, no. 4, November 1971, p. 288.

Example 49a

Example 49b

which is always associated with his being haunted by pathological fear. There follow a number of 'reminiscences' – all to do with his hallucinations and frightful visions in I, 2, but altered in rhythm and instrumentation. Without giving a look to his child, Wozzeck hastily departs to his 'gehetzt' motive, now presented as a free inversion of its crab (Ex. 49*b*). This 'distortion' of the original seems to point forwards to Marie's, 'He will crack up with these thoughts!' Deeply disturbed by his behaviour, especially by the fact that he completely ignored the child, and fearing the increasing darkness in the room – in bars 462-6 we hear the 'Fear' motive on the two horns (seconds) – Marie bursts into her desperate cry, 'Ach! Wir arme Leut! I'll bear no more. I'm terrified!' and rushes out; a variant of the 'Fear' figure treated in stretto accompanies her exit. The short interlude vividly depicts her agitated state of mind and uses material from both Scenes 2 and 3 reaching the climax in bars 476-9 where her 'plaint' theme appears in a three-part stretto, with the third part (bass) representing the inversion of it. The music gradually subsides and leads to four bars preparing for the entry of the passacaglia theme of the next scene.

Scene 4. The Doctor's Study. A sunny afternoon. Doctor and Wozzeck.

This is an extraordinary scene both dramatically and musically in which two characters confront each other who have nothing in common but an obsession with certain ideas. The Doctor, a grotesque parody of the medical profession, is more an abstraction than a human being of flesh and blood, and one of his fixed ideas is to achieve immortality through his mad dietary experiments on Wozzeck. It is perhaps not without significance that the Doctor's leimotive does not appear until Variation 13, when he says to the soldier, 'Wozzeck, Er kommt in's Narrenhaus' – 'You'll end in a madhouse' by which Berg may well have wished to indicate that the Doctor is also ripe for the lunatic asylum. The soldier, on the other hand, is an all too human being, weak in his mind and suffering from apocalyptic visions, which are *his*

fixed idea. To represent the two Berg could not have chosen a more
appropriate form than the passacaglia.[45] It is, admittedly, treated in an
unconventional and highly original manner, notably in some of the later
variations, where the notes of the theme are buried in the harmonic texture,
but since the principle of an ostinato is sustained throughout, it is difficult to
see why Berg's particular treatment should 'defeat his presumed purpose in
making this choice'.[46]

The passacaglia theme is (as is its anticipation in 486-7) built up of all the
twelve notes of the chromatic scale and thus, most remarkably, foreshadows
Schoenberg's twelve-note method which, at the time Berg was working on his
opera, was still in an experimental state. Yet it is important to stress that the
variations are not treated in anything resembling that method, the note
sequence of the theme being not binding for the rest of the music:

Example 50

Redlich has shown its resemblance to such ancient passacaglia themes as
that of Bach's for organ in C minor,[47] and it is also noteworthy that it
contains no fewer than five tritones and that it ends on the leading-note to the
opening note, thus describing a circle, which ensures an organic link between
its repeated statements. Its first statement is rather unusual in that it is cast
in the form of a cello recitative, to be played 'with much rhythmic freedom',
above which the Doctor's voice part wends its serpentine way:

Example 51a

Was er-leb' ich, Woz-zeck?   Ein Mann ein Wort?   Ei, ei, ei!

Example 51b

Geb' ich Ihm da-für   al-le   Ta-ge drei   Gro-schen?

[45] He was much pleased when, long after the completion of *Wozzeck*, he looked up the article
'Passacaglia' in Riemann's musical dictionary and found that the word is synonymous with 'follia'
(madness or *idée fixe*) which is one of the oldest forms of ostinato.

[46] Perle, 'Representation', p. 304.

[47] *Alban Berg*, p. 128.

Note the dessicated, clipped parlando with its rests and the curious accentuation of Wozzeck's name on the second syllable (Ex. *a*). Ex. *b* will stand for the Doctor's mad 'science' and/or 'theory'.

This passacaglia is the first instance of Berg's predilection for number symbolism – here the number 7. The theme is seven bars long and there are twenty-one (3 × 7) variations. Fourteen (2 × 7) variations extend to seven bars each; of the remaining seven variations, four relate to 7, in that nos. 7, 10 and 12 each consist of a single bar in 7/4 time, and no. 18 is fourteen (2 × 7) bars long. But the Variations 19 and 20 have bar lengths which are multiples of 3 (9 and 18 bars resp.). The significance of the number 7, a 'holy' number which we shall encounter again in the 'Bible' scene (III, 1), eludes me in this scene; it may have been associated with a meaning wholly private to Berg. The twenty-one variations – a parallel to the 3 × 7 poems in *Pierrot Lunaire* – can be grouped into three sections. The first (Variations 1-12) is generally devoted to the fixed ideas entertained by the Doctor and Wozzeck; the second section (13-18) centres on the Doctor's diagnosis of Wozzeck's illness – 'aberratio mentalis partialis, second species' – and the third (Variations 19-21) begins with an enumeration of the Doctor's do's and don't's for the soldier, and culminates in the praise of his theory and his ecstatic outburst about immortality.

Variation 1 rests on a pedal D – the last note of the theme, which is almost entirely given to the muted first horn. Variation 2 has the theme for the most part on the xylophone (an original orchestral stroke, this). In Variation 3 the chemical constituents of 'mutton'[48] are set to repeats of the first eleven notes of the theme in the order 1-2, 1-2; 3-4, 3-4, 5-6, 5-6 and so on. Having lost his temper, at the end of Variation 3, because of Wozzeck's failure to control the action of his diaphragm, the Doctor checks himself in Variation 4 and observes that his pulse 'hat seine gewöhnliche Sechzig', Berg's metronome marking at this passage changing from 'crotchet = 63-66' to 'crotchet = 60'. Variations 5 to 12 are almost entirely given up to Wozzeck's fixed ideas. Variation 5, in which Wozzeck contrasts 'character' and 'structure' with 'nature', is dominated by his 'gehetzt', to which is added in bar 528 Marie's Open Fifth and the opening of the Military March; while in Variation 6 the muted trombones suggest the 'dark world' in Wozzeck's confused philosophising. In Variation 7 the theme is telescoped into dyads or two note combinations (two horns) and is juxtaposed with its mirror. In Variation 8 his mention of Marie's name elicits from the solo violin and, subsequently, the solo viola, her 'Plaint', and, as he makes a few long steps with outstretched arms, this gesture is caught in the rising fourth of the voice part. Variations 9

---

[48] Berg replaced Büchner's 'Hammelfleisch' and 'Erbsen' with the more common Austrian words 'Schöpsenfleisch' and 'Bohnen', which was the staple food of the Austrian Army and also reflects the composer's own experience as a soldier. See Kurt Blaukopf 'Autobiographische Elemente in Alban Berg's *Wozzeck* in *Österreichische Musikzeitschrift*, 9, 1954, p. 155.

and 10 form a pair in that they are written in invertible counterpoint, the
bass and treble of the one variation being turned upside down in the other. In
Variation 11 in which Wozzeck speaks of the 'toadstools', Berg quotes the
corresponding music from I, 2 (227-31). The 'Linienkreise, Figuren' of
Variation 12, suggested to Wozzeck by the toadstools, are mirrored in a
'geometrical' system of rising and falling whole-tone progressions in the voice
part, celesta, harp and two solo celli, the two string instruments tracing out
the shape of a rhomboid. (The whole-tone scale, because of its absence of a
tonal centre, is eminently suited for the suggestion of a circle.) Noteworthy,
too, is the partial canon of the passacaglia theme on trumpet and oboe.
Variation 13 finally introduces the Doctor's leitmotive on the first violins:

Example 52

counterpointed by the voice-part with a theme whose E minor tonality seems
to be associated with madness, which is confirmed by other passages in that
'key' in Variation 14 and in II, 4. The Doctor's sadistic glee in ascribing to
Wozzeck 'eine schöne fixe Idee' brings a 'quasi slow waltz' – a delightful
ironic touch. In Variation 14 the Doctor's 'aberratio mentalis partialis' is set
to a wedge-like theme as though to suggest his growing elation at his
diagnosis culminating in his E minor outburst, 'Sehr schön ausgebildet!'.
With Variation 15 the tempo begins to quicken from Allegro to Presto in
Variation 19 and Prestissimo in Variation 20 which introduces the
apotheosis of the 'science' or 'theory' motive Ex. 51*b*. Finally, in Variation 21
the Doctor's 'Unsterblich', set to the first five notes of the theme, is
counterpointed by a chorale-like version of the whole passacaglia theme
(grandioso!) followed, in strongest contrast, by the Doctor's matter-of-fact
request to Wozzeck to show him his tongue. To clinch this absurdly
grotesque scene, Berg demands that the curtain be at first dropped very
quickly and then suddenly slowly

Scene 5. Street before Marie's house. Dusk. Marie and the Drum-Major

Marie's seduction by the Drum-Major is to be seen as the direct cause of her
death, and this link between Eros and Thanatos is with much psychological
finesse shown in the frequency with which in this music of sensual desire the
fateful B and the tritone B-F occur. The interlude leading up to it is a real
introduction establishing as it does all the main material, except for the
Drum-Major's own leitmotive which is not sounded until the rise of the
curtain:

Example 53

The musical form of this scene represents a free rondo to mirror the to and fro of the stage action. The ritornello whose 'affettuoso' refers to Marie, expresses her desire in a theme which, significantly, recalls the opening of the Military March:

Example 54a

Example 54b

the figure *x* of Ex. *a* (E flat clarinet!) seeming to convey her burning sensuality, while Ex. *b* stands for the Drum-Major's aggressive virility. Four sections may be discerned in the music of the actual scene. The first (667-76) shows Marie naïvely admiring her erotic ideal and closes with her 'Pride' motive, at the words, 'Ich bin stolz vor allen Weibern!' In the second section (677-84) the Drum-Major boasts of himself in a little arietta which also ends on the 'Pride' motive. The imminence of Marie's falls seems to be indicated by a chromatically descending bass, from D to the F below the stave. In the third section (687-99) the Drum-Major makes his first and unsuccessful advance on Marie, leading to a fight between them (four-part stretto of Ex. 53), and culminating in a most agitated trumpet fanfare continued by Marie in her outcry 'Rühr mich nicht an!', a passage which down to the number of words and the general pause in the orchestra, at once recalls Leonore's highly dramatic 'Töt erst sein Weib!' in *Fidelio* (Ex. 55).

In the fourth section (700-15) the Drum-Major makes his second attempt on Marie, to which she yields and the two rush into her house. The music of this section is of particularly marked savagery and leads to the climax in bar

712, in which the 'Pride' motive and one of the Drum-Major's 'sexuality' themes combine. The curtain descends slowly on the opera's Principal Chord whose bass G-D formed the pedal to the preceding transformation music.

Example 55a

Rühr mich nicht an!

Example 55b

Töt   erst   sein   Weib!

Having characterised Marie already in I, 3, Berg in this scene concentrates more on the Drum-Major, whose overwhelming masculinity fascinates Marie to such an extent that she almost loses her identity under his spell, seen in some wide intervals in her voice-part, such as are characteristic of the Drum-Major's (672-5, 698, 709).

While Act I presented, with the exception of Scene 5, static tableaux for which Berg designed a number of self-contained, closed music forms, Act II has a more forward-driving character – Wozzeck's jealousy grows more intense with the passing of each scene – and a closer sequence of the dramatic events which Berg interpreted musically in terms of a five-movement symphony.

Act II, Scene 1. Marie's Room. Sunny morning. Marie, the Child, later Wozzeck.

The music for this scene is in the form of a sonata movement chosen by Berg (*a*) because the three themes of the exposition personify the three characters on the stage and (*b*) because this most organic of instrumental forms, in which one theme grows out of the preceding one and is made to flow quite naturally into the next, seemed to the composer best suited to symbolise the very close relationship of the characters. He referred to this scene as 'Schmuckszene' or 'Jewel Scene' since a pair of earrings, a present from the Drum-Major to Marie, plays an important part in it. They are a source of pleasure and flatter Marie's vanity, but at the same time they become for Wozzeck concrete evidence of her infidelity. (Büchner clearly modelled this scene on the Schmuckszene in Goethe's *Faust*, Part I.) As she looks, self-admiringly, into a broken mirror, there unfolds the first subject of the sonata which has something caressing and tender about it; antecedent and conserquent together extend to exactly sixteen bars,which may have been intentional as a characterisation of Marie's nature. It is noteworthy that in this opening it is the orchestra which plays the leading part, while the voice-part is subsidiary. In the bridge passage (29-42) which runs freely backwards (36), the child stirs for the first time and this disturbs the mother, arousing in her a guilt feeling – for the boy is the child of the man whom she has betrayed with the Drum-Major. Her admonition to the child to be still and close his eyes is really intended to silence her own conscience. The second subject (43-53) is Marie's song about the gypsy lad who will lead her by his hand to his native land, at which point we hear, significantly, the Drum-Major's leitmotive. Marie sings it with a mixture of 'mock-sinister and reckless expression'. Its fourths relate it to Marie's folksong in I, 3, while the brilliant solo violin and the vocal ending with its portamento and ornamentation imitate the typical manner of gypsy music. The closing theme (55-9) anticipates Wozzeck's motive at his entry at the end of the repetition of the exposition. This repetition, varied and much contracted, introduces in its conclusion a low-lying whole-tone motive in three-part canon on muted trombones, which relates to Wozzeck's 'Misery' theme (Ex. 57) in the next scene:

Example 56

In the development, both the dramatic and the musical characters are engaged in a fierce fight. In the first section (96-108) Marie's 'Earring' motive, in a remarkable variant, is interrupted by the 'Wozzeck' theme (101-5). In the second section (109-15), in which the soldier turns to the sleeping child, Berg horizontalises the minor seconds of the exposition's bridge passage in a delicate scoring for four muted solo violins and celesta. Wozzeck, having seen drops of perspiration on the child's forehead, remarks with bitterness; 'nothing but toil under the sun, sweat even in sleep', and bursts into the motto, 'Wir arme Leut!', the voice-part being doubled by three trombones in unison which drown the rest of the orchestra. In the third section (116-27) Wozzeck, 'in a completely changed tone of voice' says to Marie, 'Da ist wieder Geld', handing her over his scanty earnings from the Captain and the Doctor, the entire passage resting on a sustained pedal formed by the C major chord, which key was Berg's symbol for the trivial nature of money.[49] The recapitulation (128-39) is confined to the first twelve

---

[49] This seems to have been the view held by Schoenberg and his two disciples of tonality during their atonal period. It strongly contrasts with Schoenberg's later dictum in America that 'There is still a lot of good music to be written in C major'. See article, 'Schoenberg', in *Grove's Dictionary of Music and Musicians*, 5th ed., vol. 7, London, 1954, p. 519.

bars of the exposition, with dark orchestral colours, in contrast to the bright palette used in the opening of this scene. In it Marie. seized by utter despair, burst into the highly dramatic phrase, 'Ach, was Welt!', with its high A, B flat and B while the orchestra (139) condenses the fateful tritone B-F (here F-B) and Marie's Open Fifth into a single chord.

The interlude, scored in such a way as to produce a violent, explosive and even brutal sound picture, represents a symphonic comment on the three main themes of the sonata movement, taking account of Marie's gypsy song (151-9) which was ignored in the first development. The music is marked off as a unit standing entirely by itself, by two harp glissandi, the first going downwards, ff (opening) and the second going upwards, pp (end) and leading straight into the next scene.

Act II, Scene 2. A street. Daytime. Captain and Doctor, later Wozzeck

Like I, 4, this scene is pure parody and further serves to show the relationship between Wozzeck's two tormentors, a relationship absurd and ludicrous, which is brought out already in the opening words of their dialogue. Berg's sense of irony is further seen in the fact that the Doctor's gloomy prognosis for the Captain is in waltz tempo! As to the musical form of this scene, the composer chose a Fantasy and Fugue with three sharply defined, self-contained subjects to indicate the unrelatedness of the three characters with one another, which, as Berg said in his lecture, demanded a strict fugal treatment, contrasting strongly with the previous scene in which the close relationship between Wozzeck, Marie and the Child was expressed in the organic form of a sonata movement.

According to the text, the Fantasy falls into four sections:

A (171-200): Encounter of Doctor and Captain.
B (201-47): the Doctor's diagnosis of, and prognosis for, the Captain[50]
C (248-71): the Captain's reaction
D (272-85): Wozzeck's entry and his reception

For the actual encounter Berg combines contrapuntally the Doctor's motive with that of the Captain, both of which begin with a major second suggesting that the two men are birds of a feather; this in fact is exploited in the following music in which the two motives are varied, inverted, superimposed[51] and so on. The farcical, almost *outré*, character of what may be called a duet, is manifest in a number of details, notably in the Captain's part, some of which may be mentioned here. Thus his difficult breathing is

---

[50] B itself is divided into three sections each centring on a point in the Doctor's findings.
[51] Cf. Berg's similar treatment of the half-series in the Lyric Suite.

suggested by the many rests of his part,[52] there is his falsetto at moments of extreme agitation and the diminishing bar lengths (4-3-2-1) when he refers to people who died of sheer fright (262-5). Of the Doctor's dry, clipped manner of speech we have already spoken. To this must now be add his head voice and asinine braying when he delivers his prognosis of the Captain's life expectancy (216-20). 'Four weeks' is the time span he gives to his patients: when he utters these words with particular emphasis (199), Berg changes from the previous 5/4 to 4/4 and accompanies the voice-part with four trumpets. The last part of the Fantasy begins with Wozzeck's entry to his 'misery' theme, in a characteristic scoring for four muted trombones and timpani and marked 'Schwer':

Example 57

This was probably the theme to which Berg refers in a letter from Trahütten to his wife (7 August 1918). Describing his return home after seeing her off on a brief journey, he writes: 'I myself walked uphill very slowly, resting frequently "according to regulations" and finally, as I proceeded with heavy steps, there occurred to me – though I was not intending to work – a long-sought idea for an entry of Wozzeck'. (In the same letter he speaks of his identification with the hero of his opera, see p. 19.)

Berg treats Ex. 57 in an interesting manner in some of its subsequent appearance: he splits it into an upper and lower half and combines them in rhythmic displacement (276 and 281), or he uses the whole-tone top line by itself (313-17), presses it into a stretto (329-31) or allows it to be followed by its bass (332-7).

In the Fugue (286) the Captain and the Doctor taunt Wozzeck with more or less overt allusions to Marie's infidelity with the Drum-Major, which has a traumatic effect on the soldier. Each of the three themes has its proper exposition, after which they are combined so that from bar 317 we have a fugue with three subjects, with the Captain's and Doctor's motives sometimes inverted. It is the most strictly worked polyphonic piece in the opera yet, for all that, it closely follows the twists and turns of the text. Its strictness is relaxed in the more lyrical bars 326-9 in which the Captain

[52] The asthmatic Schigolch in *Lulu* is similarly characterised.

reminisces 'molto cantabile' about the amorous stirrings of his own youth (combination of the original and inversion of his motive), but suddenly alters his tone when he sees Wozzeck growing 'deadly pale', at which point the soldier's theme (Ex. 57) enters in a suggestive scoring for flutes and pizzicati violins, *pp*, 'without expression'. The Fugue peters out in trailing woodwind figures derived from the Captain's motive, which lead to the introduction to the next scene.

Act II, Scene 3. Street before Marie's house. A gloomy day. Marie, Wozzeck.

This central scene represents the turning-point of the drama, for Marie's mention in it of a knive suggests to the insanely jealous Wozzeck the idea, admittedly very vague at this juncture, of murdering her. The music takes the form of a ternary Largo – the slow movement of Berg's dramatic symphony. One of its paramount features is the use of a chamber orchestra of fifteen players exactly as in Schoenberg's Chamber Symphony, op. 9, to whom Berg wished thereby to pay his tribute in this central piece. Apart from the introduction, the chamber orchestra is largely reserved for Wozzeck's utterances, while Marie is associated with the main orchestra. This orchestral dichotomy seems to me to have been dictated by the particular psychological situation obtaining in this scene. Marie here is the superior character: she does not defend herself against Wozzeck's accusation, on the contrary, she provokes him by boldly admitting her infidelity; while a cuckold is always in a weaker position *vis-à-vis* a woman sexually attracted to another man. It is, I believe, this contrast which prompted Berg to use the two orchestras.

The preceding interlude is a true introduction containing in the cello and horn solo the main theme of which I quote the opening:

Example 58

f molto espress.

It is a darkly coloured, sombre theme perfectly in character with the atmosphere of this scene, its opening C sharp seeming to point to the knife, that is, the murder of Marie in III, 2, plus a number of reminiscences from the music of Wozzeck, Marie and the Drum-Major pointedly woven into its further course. Moreover, it is significant that, except for the soldier's expansive phrase 'wie die Sünde', *Sprechgesang* is used throughout.

As the curtain rises, Marie is seen standing at the door of her house

waiting (open fifth!) and absorbed in thought. As in a previous situation, the
nature of her thought is defined by the orchestra, which plays the opening of
the Military March 'as if from afar'. Wozzeck arrives with his 'gehetzt'
motive, and the scene is set for a violent confrontation in which at one point
Wozzeck comes very near to making a physical assault on Marie. As already
said, the music is in ternary form. In the first section (375-87), virtually a
monologue so characteristic of Büchner's Woyzeck, the soldier taunts his
mistress with bitterly sarcastic words. In the second section (387-97), a
duologue, he points, in an access of savage jealousy, to the spot where the
Drum-Major stood in I, 5. Marie replies provocatively. To his, 'You with
him!' she insolently retorts, 'And what of it?' whereupon he loses control
completely and raises his hand against her, but is held back by her cry:
'Rühr' mich nicht an! Lieber ein Messer in den Lieb als die Hand auf mich',
the first sentence being set in almost the same manner as her identical verbal
phrase in her scene with the Drum-Major (I, 5). Her second sentence starts
on a repeated C sharp accompanied by a descending chromatic motive
standing for the 'knife':

Example 59

In this second section the chamber orchestra irrupts without reference to the
tempo of the main orchestra (393), in illustration of Wozzeck's paroxysm of
rage. As Marie leaves, he stares after her, repeating her words, 'Lieber ein
Messer', (on C sharp!) which I take to be the moment when the idea of her
murder first rises into his consciousness. This marks the beginning of the
third section (398-405), in the course of which Wozzeck is made to express
the quintessence of Büchner's expressionism 'Der Mensch ist ein Abgrund,
es schwindelt einem, wenn man hinunterschaut ... mich schwindelt' – 'Man
is an abyss, it makes one giddy looking into him ... I'm giddy'. Wozzeck
leaves, but the curtain stays up for a few more bars to show the empty stage –
a subtle theatrical touch – while the two orchestras play in alternation a free
continuation of Ex. 58 (which had re-entered in 398). The curtain slowly
descends to the same trailing figures which we heard before the opening of
the scene, now resting on F sharp, the dominant of the fateful note, and
stated in retrograde.

*Act II, Scene 4. Garden of an inn. Late evening. Crowd of young men, girls and soldiers,
Marie, Drum-Major, Wozzeck, Andres and Idiot.*

This is the 'grand opera' scene of *Wozzeck*, proving Berg's eye for a vivid stage spectacle as well as his instinct as musical dramatist. The latter is seen in the immense skill with which he manages to operate a huge apparatus comprising, soloist, chorus, stage band and main orchestra. (There is little doubt that here Berg took for his model the Venetian orchestra and the gypsy band in Act II of Schreker's *Der ferne Klang*, and it may well be that the chorus of snoring soldiers behind the curtain in the next scene of Berg's work may have been inspired by the off-stage chorus in Act II of the Schreker opera). Berg thus ensures an unforced yet dramatically most effective fluctuation between the entertainment provided by the dancing crowd, the two Journeymen and the Hunting Chorus on the one hand, and Wozzeck's personal drama on the other. Moreover, its general effect is heightened by its marked contrast with the previous scene. There we had a sombre, gloomy atmosphere with only two soloists, here we have a crowd scene, generally gay and even exuberant, with ländler and waltzes recalling a popular feast on the village green. Another feature worth noting is that at the rise of the curtain we have the impression that the spectacle has been in progress for some time, which serves to intensify its impact on the spectator.

The music for this scene represents the Scherzo of Berg's symphony, but it is a much extended Scherzo (in the manner of Schumann and, notably, Mahler) which actually consists of two Scherzi and two Trios, which are then repeated, but in so varied a form that one is tempted to speak of a psychological rather than a real repeat.

Exposition	*Recapitulation*
Scherzo I: Ländler (412-47)	Scherzo I: Stage Band (592-64)
Transition (448-55)	Trio I: Melodrama (605-36)
Trio I: Song of the two Journeymen (456-80)	Trio II (637-42)
Scherzo II: Waltz of the Stage Band (481-559)	Transition (643-69)
Trio II: Hunting Chorus (560-89)	Scherzo II (670-84)

Scherzo I opens with a slow *Ländler* which sounds like an expressionist version of the Waltz in Act, I, 3 of Weber's *Der Freischütz*. This melodic distortion is matched by a harmonic distortion created by bitonality: the tonic of the *Ländler* (G minor) is telescoped with its dominant (D major) (424) and then its submediant (E flat major) (429). In his lecture Berg said that he deliberately aimed at this musical confusion in order to suggest the drunken state of a tavern band. The middle section of the *ländler* introduces the opening of Ochs von Lerchenau's famous waltz from Act II of *Der Rosenkavalier*, which Berg intended as a homage to Richard Strauss whom he greatly admired in his youth. (Strauss, who attended the first Vienna performance of *Wozzeck* on 30 March 1930, demonstratively left his box at hearing it, which deeply hurt the composer's feelings.) The section alludes to the opening of the minuet in the stage-music at the end of Act I of *Don Giovanni*, which is introduced by a *Heurigenkapelle* consisting of at least seven instruments.[53] As to Berg's combined use of stage band and main orchestra, Redlich has pointed out that it recalls Strauss's treatment in Act III of *Der Rosenkavalier*, in which the off-stage band plays the actual waltz music while the orchestra in the pit is reduced to a basically accompanying part.[54] In Berg's scene this is largely true of the Scherzo II and the Melodrama, but when the two orchestras combine, as in the recapitulation of Scherzo I, the main orchestra regains its thematic importance.

A *locus classicus* of Berg's extreme economy in handling his material in a non-serial work is the ingenious use he makes of the Transition (447-55) to Trio I. Its rising and falling arpeggios distributed alternately over four horns and four trombones – a most striking piece of orchestration – provide the harmonies for Trio I (456-79) and, more importantly, anticipate the bombardon melody (with some omissions and alterations in the note sequence) of the Chorale (604-33) in the Melodrama.

Trio I is devoted to two seedy and drunken Journeymen – the first sentimental and maudlin, the second gay and buoyant. The first has the 'Drunkenness' motive, a phrase that for me has the faint flavour of a Viennese street-song, and will be whistled by Wozzeck in the next scene with dire consequences for him:

Example 60

Und mei-ne   See - le stinkt nach Brannte - wein.

In Scherzo II the dancing, interrupted by the two Journeymen's 'performance', is resumed again to the music of the stage band, which plays a waltz of the traditional Viennese type consisting of a chain of short waltzes. This is perhaps the most dramatic portion of the scene. For in it Wozzeck enters to his 'gehetzt' motive and sees Marie and the Drum-Major dance past him. What with the close embrace of the couple and Marie's frenetic cries, 'Immerzu! Immerzu!' which he immediately imitates and which for him seems to have become a universal formula reducing the whole world to a dark sexual round-dance, Wozzeck's jealousy is whipped into such a pitch that he is about to attack them, when the band stops playing and the couples leave the dance floor. It is, incidentally, in the Scherzo II that Berg operates his logical reminiscences to particularly telling effect, such as for instance the 'Knife' motive which to Wozzeck's enraged words, 'Everything twists and

---

[53] Two fiddles, clarinet in C, accordion, two guitars and bombardon. The fiddles are tuned a tone higher than normal violins so as to produce a special effect, exactly like the solo violin in the Scherzo of Mahler's Fourth Symphony.

[54] *Alban Berg*, p. 119.

turns in lechery, Man and Woman and Beast.', continues its chromatic descent to the G below the bass stave, recalling a similar progression in the 'Fall' of Marie of I, 5.

Trio II is formed by an unaccompanied six-part Hunting Chorus in 7/4 which is unusual in its structure. There are two sections (interrupted by Andres's folksong), the melody of which consists of a scale motive starting on the 'white keys' and closing on a 'black key' chord;[55] in the second section the latter is replaced by a 'white key' harmony. The simplicity of this chorus and the brisk tempo at which it is to be sung seem to generate an outdoor air. Between the two sections Andres sings a folksong which is about a daughter who has thrown herself into the arms of 'coachmen and stable-boys' – probably inserted by Büchner (though in a different scene), for its allusion to Marie. The melody is *ländler*-like and the guitar accompaniment of three superimposed fourths adds to the song's *volkstümlich* character in Berg's sense.

In the recapitulation, Scherzo I is almost literally repeated but in 'a different musical surrounding' (Berg). By this is meant the opening key of E flat minor (as against the G minor of the exposition), the cross-rhythm between the main orchestra (5/4) and the stage band (3/4), and the markedly sombre colour of the orchestration (trumpets and trombones), all intended to characterise Wozzeck as he sits brooding on a bench. The utter melancholy of this part of Scene 4 puts one in mind of Schumann's triptych, *Der arme Peter*.

With the Melodrama which stands for the recapitulation of Trio I, Berg turns to sheer burlesque. This is a parody sermon preached by the first Journeyman on the purposefulness of God's creation, and takes the form of a five-part Chorale, the scoring of which for the *Heurigenkapelle* and with the *cantus firmus* on the bombardon, represents the musical aspect of that parody. Of the derivation of the Chorale from the Transition (447) we have already spoken, but some of its details deserve special mention. Thus, the first nine notes of the Chorale form a canon at the octave with the voice part. And each of its several sections has its own instrumental image: when, for instance, the Journeyman starts with an enumeration of the various professions, this is mirrored in a short stretto between voice, guitar, clarinet and fiddles (614-16); the tailor is accompanied by bleats best known from *Die Meistersinger*, while a march characterises the soldier. Indeed, Berg's parodistic handling of the Chorale recalls that in Stravinsky's *History of the Soldier*.[56]

In contrast to the exposition, in the recapitulation Trio I is followed immediately by Trio II, which merely hints at the Hunting Chorus and Andres's song. With bar 643 begins the retrograde of the Transition (447)

---

[55] Compare the division of the series into white and black key notes, in the first movement of the Lyric Suite, and the Athlete's two chords in *Lulu*, Ex. 73a (p. 231).

[56] He seems to have been fond of using it for the purpose of caricature, e.g. the Chorale of the Prince and the Marquis in *Lulu*.

which marks the entry of the Idiot. That Berg uses the crab for his appearance may well have been to suggest the 'reverse' world of the Idiot. To the E minor chord of the stage band's accordion – the key of Madness – and a roll on the muted side-drum evoking the sound of a child's rattle, the Idiot presses close to Wozzeck and whispers to him 'I smell, I smell blood!', which is the first time that this pregnant word is uttered in the opera. Wozzeck's reaction is to repeat it in the Idiot's inflexion, just as in the preceding scene he repeated Marie's 'Lieber ein Messer!' It would seem that the thought of murdering her has now been brought to the threshold of his conscious mind, until in the next scene it surfaces and becomes a firm decision. The main orchestra consisting of the brass only, introduces a violent rhythmic ostinato marked by semitonal *appoggiature*, in which the almost ubiquitous C sharp becomes the symbol for blood. It is to this orchestral ostinato that Wozzeck sings, *ff*, the highly significant words, 'Mir wird rot vor den Augen' – 'I see red before my eyes'. The transitional music clinches the scene with a symphonic treatment of previously heard material. In its ferocious rhythm it suggests a true *valse infernale*, the whirling mass of Wozzeck's 'Man and Woman and Beast!'. Another noteworthy feature is Berg's ingenious rhythmic displacement in the top line in which a melodic ostinato increases in length,[57] until it leads into the Chorus of snoring soldiers in the next scene.

Act II, Scene 5. A Guard-room in the Barracks. Wozzeck, Andres and other sleeping soldiers. Drum-Major. Night.

The closing movement of Berg's dramatic symphony is a Rondo marziale prefaced by a slow introduction, in which is heard from behind the curtain a chorus of snoring soldiers. The composer interpreted this as another 'nature sound' – hence his use here of the three chords of I, 2 (Ex. 46a), transposed a tritone up, which form the harmonies of a five-part chorus with an expansive top line. The fact that snoring has never before or since been conveyed in music makes this imaginatively conceived passage unique in all opera.

Wozzeck cannot sleep: he is pursued by memories of the inn, has hallucinations identical with those he had in the Open Field of the first act, and sees a 'broad knife' before his eyes, all of which is reflected in the music in apposite 'reminiscences'. The entry of the Drum-Major marks the beginning of the rondo, Berg choosing this form because in idea the fight

---

[57] The basic metre of this Transition is 3/4, against which Berg first sets the four-note figure F-E flat-D-F which, through the addition of a quaver rest, forms a 5/8 metre (692-6). Then comes a six-note ostinato extended by a quaver rest to a 7/8 (697-703). This increase suddenly culminates in a configuration in a 15/8 metre (728-31), with the rhythmic shift ending in bar 736, in a 7/8 metre.

between the Drum-Major and Wozzeck is essentially identical with the fight between Marie and the Drum-Major in the 'Seduction' Scene, I, 5. While in the earlier scene the outlines of the rondo were somewhat blurred and indistinct, in the later the articulation is clear and well defined, with four entries of the rondo ritornello and two episodes which are all but identical, since in both the Drum-Major pulls out his bottle and drinks. The ritornello seems to catch very succinctly the image of this drunken brute:

Example 61

The opening fourth appears to be associated with his sexual prowess, for when he enumerates, a little later, the attraction of Marie's body, this is done to four fourths. Similarly, when he leaves to the phrase 'Was bin ich für ein Mann', this is set to three steeply ascending fourths – a true 'phallic fanfare' as the two French authors call it.[58] What enrages the Drum-Major is Wozzeck's refusal to drink from the bottle and his contemptuous whistling of the first Journeyman's 'Branntewein' tune (Ex. 60). The fight itself proceeds to a canonical treatment of Ex. 53, in a savage orchestration in which the four trumpets and four trombones are most prominent. As Wozzeck lies half strangled on the floor, the woodwind and celli intone the 'Wir arme Leut!' motto to mark his utter humiliation.[59] The Drum-Major leaves noisily whistling Ex. 60 while Wozzeck, his face bleeding, staggers to his plank, sits down, stares into the void and repeats Marie's whole-tone phrase, 'Einer nach dem Andern!', from II, 3. In this coda (806) the principal chord of the opera gradually dissolves, to end on a single note B (harp, tam-tam, *pp*) as if to indicate that Wozzeck's mind is now made up to murder his mistress.

Act III, which bring the dénouement of the drama, is saturated in dark, oppressive colours. Night reigns in the first four scenes, serving to heighten the nightmarish, almost unreal character of the stage happenings. The idea of harnessing the five scenes musically to Inventions was partly dictated by the necessity of using, for the sake of variety, musical forms different from those employed in the first two acts, and partly by the particular nature of this act. For the problem here was to avoid a slackening of the tension, after Marie's murder, and it seems this was largely responsible for Berg composing a series of loosely ranged but in themselves closely unified pieces,

[58] Jouvet and Fano, *Wozzeck d'Alban Berg*, p. 206.
[59] The motto is first heard in this scene in bar 776 (fourth trombone).

in each of which a different musical aspect is treated in a greatly intensified variation technique. For these Inventions are nothing else but variations in which the material is attacked, as it were, from every angle available to the composer in the early 1920s – melodic, rhythmic, textural and instrumental. (I am convinced that Berg, had he written the opera in the 1950s, would have applied total serialism to it and added in the Inventions variations of pitch, dynamics and duration.) With the exception of the first variation, which maintains a close link with traditional procedures, the remaining five were entirely new at the time *Wozzeck* was written and are testimony to the composer's original formal thinking.

Act III, Scene 1. Marie's Room. Night. Candlelight. Marie turns the pages of the Bible. The Child.

This is a completely static scene which neither in Büchner nor Berg advances the action of the drama. Indeed, it might even be deemed superfluous were it not that its significance is not of a dramatic but psychological order. For one thing, it adds an important new trait to Marie's portrait in showing her as a remorseful and deeply religious woman. For another, it projects her changing state of mind as she reacts in a markedly subjective manner to the various objective passages in the Bible. It is this subjective element which invests this scene with an intense ego-bound quality, and is an example of Büchner's anticipation of twentieth-century expressionism.

Before we go into details, one general feature has to be mentioned – the role played by the number 7 in this Invention. We encountered this for the first time in I, 4, but in III, 1 the number symbolism is applied on a much larger scale, with the 'holy' 7 standing for the religious feeling – so eloquently expressed in this scene. The theme and five of the variations are each seven bars long; the exceptions are the two-bar Variation 2 and the five-bar Variation 6, but their respective metres add up to 7 or a multiple of it: $4/4 + 3/4 = 7/4$ in the first variation, and $2 \times 4/4 + 3 \times 2/4 = 14/4$ in the second. There are seven variations in all, the whole extending to 70 bars. Moreover, each of the two subjects of the closing double fugue consists of 7 different notes and the length of the fugue is 3×7 bars. The prevailing metronome figure is crotchet = 56, i.e. 8×7. It is a measure of Berg's compositional skill that, as in the Lyric Suite, the number determinant – an extra-musical, mathematical factor – is organically worked into the music, without the slightest feeling of constricting the composer's imagination.[59a]

Marie's recitation of the Bible passage and her subsequent agonised

[59a] The far-fetched suggestion has been made that Berg's choice of the number 7 as a constituent factor in the composition of the 'Bible' scene was influenced by the 'seven keys' in Paul Dukas's opera, *Ariane et Barbe-Bleu* (Paris, 1907) which Berg may have heard in Vienna in 1908.

outcry are reflected in the two halves (antecedent[60] and consequent) of the theme, separated by a bitonal chord (D major and the Neapolitan E flat major), which is of importance in the variations:

Example 62a

Example 62b

Example 62c

Note how the objective nature of the Bible quotation is caught in a four-part stretto and the *Sprechstimme* while Marie's subjective reaction is a sung passage. Her phrase 'Herr Gott, Herr Gott! Sieh mich nicht an!' may be said to be a variant of the violin figure, Ex. 62c. It should be added that the theme compresses into its seven bars altogether four different ideas – two principal ones (antecedent and consequent, Ex. 62a and c) and two subsidiary ones. In the following variations Berg subjects the theme to such radical transformations – intervallic (melodic) and rhythmic changes, transposition of its four constituent elements and even total omission of the two principal ideas (as in Variation 7) – that a detailed analysis of these alterations would be beyond the scope of this chapter. Variation 5 is exceptional in that it is in an unequivocal F minor with the appropriate key-signature;[61] the return to tonality here is intended to conjure up the 'once upon a time' atmosphere of the fairy-tale that Marie is telling her child, and that anticipates his own fate.[62] The typically romantic colour of the orchestration – strings divided into soli and tutti, and horn, *p, dolce*, is noteworthy. The last two bars of this variation constitute at the same time the first two bars of Variation 6, in

---

[60] It recalls the opening of the 'Wahnmonology' in Act II of *Die Meistersinger*.

[61] Cf. the key-signature of Wedekind's *Lautenlied* in the Variations of Act III of *Lulu*.

[62] Berg greatly shortened this fairy-tale, which in Büchner is told by the grandmother to a number of children in an entirely different scene.

which Marie wonders why Wozzeck has not come – 'gestern nit, heut nit'; at this point the trumpets play a variant of the soldier's 'gehetzt' motive. In Variation 7 Marie hastily turns the pages of the Bible to find the story about Mary Magdalen, Berg omitting in it the two principal ideas (Ex. 62a and c), since they are to form the two subjects of the following fugue. A long pause by way of a colon sets off the continuous series of variations from the self-contained fugal piece which repesents the spiritual climax of the whole scene. In it Marie entreats Christ to have mercy upon her, as he had on the sinner in the Bible.

The fugue is strictly thematic, with no free interludes between the three expositions, which may be interpreted as a reflection of the emotional intensity of Marie's prayer. The first exposition is of Ex. 62a and has five entries. Note the poignant effect achieved in the voice-part by the chromaticism at the words 'Tränen' and 'Salben' and by the climax, 'Heiland, du hast dich ihrer erbarmt' ('Saviour, you have had mercy on her'); two bars later (59-61) Berg introduces four clarinets in unison(!). The second exposition is of Ex. 62c and has four entries. The third exposition (63-7) combines the two subject in a stretto so as to achieve an increased urgency of expression. This last exposition represents the coda of the fugue which, from the second half of bar 64, becomes the transition music closing on the bitonal chord (Ex. 62b), now of a pale, etiolated colour (four trumpets, *dolcissimo* and muted violas followed by celesta and harp). At the rise of the curtain on the next scene, the double basses[63] add a low octave on the 'fateful' B.

Act III, Scene 2. Forest path by a pond. Dusk. Marie and Wozzeck.

This scene is as short as the related one before Marie's house in Act II, but with the sinister atmosphere now intensified to one of at first muted, then stark terror. The musical link with that earlier scene is established by the opening bassoon solo which comes from the same tree as that of the cello solo at the beginning of II, 3. Berg harnesses the scene to an Invention on the note B, which is ubiquitous as the symbol of Marie's death from start to finish. The note (the last one in C major!) appears in all conceivable forms – as a bass or inner pedal, in the treble, in several octaves and in diverse registers and sonorities. One of its most dramatic occurrences is at Marie's last cry, 'Help!', when it leaps down over two octaves to reiterated drum strokes on the same note (103).

The music of this scene seems to unfold in a free rhapsodic manner, with an apparent improvisatory flow of themes and motives, but the text

---

[63] *Wozzeck* uses double basses with five strings (C-E-A-D-G) the lowest of which is tuned down a semitone to B (Act III, bar 67) and stays so over the whole of the scene of Marie's murder, until bar 121. We recall a similar *scordatura* of the cello in the finale of the Lyric Suite.

articulates it into two main portions. In the first (itself divided into four
sections), Wozzeck tells Marie to sit down and then taunts her with her
beauty, goodness and fidelity. Dropping his irony, he kisses her and
expresses for the first time his love for her. Seeing her trembling because of
the night dew, he whispers to himself the sinister words: 'He who is cold, no
longer feels the cold'. The second portion begins with the rising of the red
moon 'like a blood-red iron' (Wozzeck) and culminates in the murder of
Marie. Perhaps the most important of the new material is the theme of the
rising moon – an ascending figure treated in a short nine-part stretto between
the voice, the four trombones and the four trumpets (all muted). At the
moment of Marie's death images of her life flash rapidly through her mind;
this is revealed to us by the psychological master-stroke of sounding in the
orchestra in quick succession all the musical figures associated with her – the
'Seduction', the 'Lullaby', the 'Earrings', the 'Military March', the 'Plaint'
and finally the 'Open Fifth', the last indicating that her 'aimless waiting' has
at last found its solution. Almost the whole of this passage unfolds over the
drum pedal B! The thirteen-bar transition to the next scene could be
described as the restatement of a theme after its last variation – here the note
B after its adventures in the Invention. This transition is unique in opera, for
not only is the essence of the previous murder scene distilled into it, but never
before or afterwards has the face of naked terror been conveyed by means
apparently so simply yet so shattering in their effect. Two crescendi on B –
that is all. But the first of these crescendi is built up in a subtly sophisticated
way combining a rhythmic canon with an increasing dynamic volume. Wind
and strings play the B below the treble stave – a note available to virtually all
the instruments of a large orchestra – each group introducing the same
rhythmic pattern, but in a canon at the distance of a crotchet:

Example 63

These successive entries heighten the dynamic effect of this passage, and thus intensify the first crescendo to a far higher degree than is the case in the second crescendo passage (117-21), in which the entire orchestra including percussion play the B *tremolo* in four octaves. Ex. 63 shows the *Hauptrhythmus*[64] or main rhythm hammered out by the bass drum, which is to form the basis of the following scene and is the symbol of Wozzeck's guilt. Moreover, the lower hexachord in bar 6 of the example anticipates the harmonic formula on which the Invention on a Chord of the fourth scene is built.

The question arises why Berg selected B rather than another note of the chromatic scale as the musical symbol for death. There are several answers to it. The first has already been mentioned – the availability of the B below middle C on practically all the instruments of a large orchestra. Secondly, B forms the lower note of the tritone B-F which, as Perle[64a] has shown, plays the role of a tone centre in the opera and seems to symbolize Wozzeck's tragedy. Thirdly, on the ascending scale, C (= Life) is spatially farthest away from B (= Death) which may be interpreted as an example of Berg's subtle musical symbolism. Furthermore, a highly interesting article[64b] relates the note B to the key of B minor in musical history. The author cites Bach's B minor Mass and Beethoven's dictum that this key was a 'dunkle Tonart' (dark key), then points, in Weber's *Freischütz*, to Kaspar's daemonic song. 'Hier im ird'schen Jammertal', in B minor and finally to Wagner's recourse to this key in the music of Alberich, Hagen and Klingsor where it suggests 'curse', 'revenge' or 'murder'. The technical model for Berg may have been Debussy's *Pelléas et Mélisande* (Act III, bars 1-41) and the intermittent pedal on B in *Nuages*.

Act III, Scene 3. Low tavern, dimly lit. Night. Wozzeck, Margaret and Crowd.

Apart from the setting which creates a fantastic, dream-like atmosphere, the effect of this scene lies in the contrast between a crowd of youths and girls gaily dancing to the music of a Quick Polka strummed on an out-of-tune piano, and Wozzeck's desperate attempts to conceal and master his guilt-feelings by drinking, singing and dancing with Margret.

This is the scene in which Berg, for the first time in his career, tries to impose a rhythmic pattern on his melodic and harmonic material. As already mentioned in the discussion of the finale of the Chamber Concerto, this device was used in the *talea* of the isorhythmic motet and something similar is found in such classical works as Beethoven's Fifth Symphony and Schubert's *Wanderer Fantasy*. With Berg it becomes a characteristic feature of his mature style. It must be stressed, however, that this rhythmic configuration is not

---

[64] Not yet indicated by RH as it is in the finale of the subsequent Chamber Concerto.

[64a] The Musical Language of *Wozzeck*', *Music Forum I* New York, 1967, pp. 204-59.

[64b] Josef-Horst Lederer, 'Zu Alban Bergs Invention über den Ton H', *50 Jahre 'Wozzeck'*, op. cit., pp. 57-67.

employed by him in the manner of a stereotyped ostinato, but is subjected to metrical changes and contrapuntal artifices – augmentation and diminution of its note-value, rhythmic displacement, fugato, canon and stretto – all of which are dictated both by the necessity of introducing variety into its handling and the need to characterise the changing situations on the stage. Of particular interest are those passages in which RH appears simultaneously in several different metric shapes, such as Wozzeck's folksong, 'Es ritten drei Reiter',[65] or the brief section, bars 180-6. The vocal turmoil reaches its climax towards the end of the scene, after blood has been found on Wozzeck's hand, and is generated by Berg's close canonical treatment of the solo and choral voices. This continues into the orchestral transition, which prepares for the entry of the basic hexachord of the next scene.

Act III, Scene 4. The same as Scene 2. Moonlight. Wozzeck, later Captain and Doctor

Wozzeck here is shown as standing on the borderline between normality and insanity, the latter finally engulfing him completely. At first he is fully aware of reality: driven by fear that his crime might be discovered, he has come to find the murder knife and dispose of this evidence. But already the croaking of the toads in the pond frightens him, he shouts 'murder!', and when he stumbles on Marie's body, he has the macabre vision that the knife wound is a 'crimson cord round the neck'. (This motive has been taken by Büchner from the 'Walpurgisnacht' in Goethe's *Faust*, 1.) Normality returns for a brief moment when he looks for the knife and throws it into the water. The red moon breaking suddenly through the clouds marks the beginning of Wozzeck's total and irreversible madness. He is seized by a paranoiac fear ('aber der Mond verrät mich' – 'but the moon betrays me'), thinks that he has thrown the knife not far enough into the pond and in searching for it has the hallucination that the water has turned to blood from which he wants to wash himself clean, wades into it further and drowns.

Berg, with admirable economy and resourcefulness, conveys these changes in the physical and psychological situation by means of an Invention on a chord which is the lower hexachord of Ex. 63. Looking closer at it, it seems that some of the constituent intervals are not adventitious but chosen for their dramatic symbolism. Thus, the minor third B flat-C sharp stands for 'knife', 'murder' or 'blood' as becomes clear from the verbal context,[66] while the perfect fifths B flat-F and C sharp-G sharp seem to refer to Marie lying

---

[65] It is a subtle point in Berg's verbal treatment of this folksong that Wozzeck omits the word 'Bahr' (bier) which is to rhyme with 'klar', as 'bier' would at once conjure up the image of the dead Marie. Instead of which he sings 'Verdammt', but it is the two solo violins which supply the missing word with Marie's Open Fifth (A-E).

[66] Bars 221, 250, 252, 253, 270, 278 and 282.

dead by the pond. In other words, the hexachord not only symbolizes Wozzeck's death, but also includes his crime and the victim of the crime; the whole tragedy seems encapsulated in it. As with the Invention on a Note and on a Rhythm, in this Invention the hexachord undergoes an almost infinite variety of changes – inversion, division, regrouping, horizontalisation of its notes, and alterations in register and orchestral colours. Like the 'Open Field' (I, 2), this scene is an atmospheric piece *par excellence*; but Berg does not rely on colour *per se* in the impressionist manner – he tries to harness such effects to a thematic idea, that is, the basic hexachord. Needless to say there are a number of reminiscences.[67]

The music of this scene is in ternary form determined by the treatment of the hexachord. In section A (220-66) the hexachord remains in its original shape, that is, its root rests on a single degree of the chromatic scale (B flat), or it is inverted. It is in A that the majority of the reminiscences occur, with the 'Guilt' rhythm pointedly recalled at Wozzeck's words, 'Sie werden mich suchen' – 'they will search for me'. With section B (267-301), which starts soon after the appearance of the moon, the hexachord begins to move to other degrees of the scale (C sharp, E, F sharp, E flat etc.), which movement seems to me to suggest that Wozzeck now loses all sense of reality and drifts on a sea of frightening phantasmagorias which end with his death. As the waves close over him, the orchestra illustrates this in ascending chromatic side-slippings of the hexachord, a passage which echoes a similar passage in whole-tone progression in Schreker's *Der ferne Klang*, III, 9. It is also likely that, when composing this scene, Berg had the end of Schoenberg's *Erwartung* at the back of his mind; here too we find sustained chords and a downward and upward chromatic movement (423-6). The gradual quietening of the water Berg conveys through a composed rallentando, the hexachord altering its note values from semiquaver quintuplets to quadruple semiquavers, triplets, syncopated triplets, crotchets, and finally minims. In bar 302 the hexachord returns to its original form and is held as a pedal (on two solo violins, two solo violas and two solo celli) till the end of the scene, when through the addition in the bass of the note A, it becomes the dominant of D minor, which is the key of the following interlude.

Soon after the beginning of the chromatic side-slips, the Captain and Doctor appear on the scene. For once they are not shown as grotesques but as more or less normal human beings. They are frightened by the eeriness of the place with its water and mist, and mistake the croaking of the toads for the sound of a drowning man. Berg recaptures this croaking in a wind passage in which four ostinati combine in a polyrhythmic counterpoint of remarkable effect – Ex. 64 (p. 212).

[67] Bars 237-8 and 278-83; 'gehetzt'; 241-54: 'Waltz', 'Drum-,Major', 'Earrings' and 'Immerzu!'; 252-4: 'Guilt' rhythm.

It is, incidentally, amusing to note that in this scene the Captain and Doctor have exchanged their characteristic attitudes to time: now it is the Captain who wants to hurry away while the Doctor wishes to stay!

Transition: Invention on a Key

This is the most important of all the twelve interludes of the opera – an epilogue on the death of Wozzeck, in which the composer steps out of his role as an objective narrator and reflects (comparable to 'The Poet speaks' in Schumann's *Kinderszenen*) on the life and ultimate fate of the poor soldier, addressing the audience as the 'representative of mankind' (Berg). The special position of this interlude is seen in the fact that it is the only one which introduces a theme not heard before in the opera:

Example 65

Example 64

It comes from Berg's abortive symphony of 1912, which accounts for its marked Mahlerian stamp (as indeed the whole of the epilogue belongs to Mahler's world); Berg incorporated it in the *Wozzeck* music at the suggestion of his wife. Though he described this interlude as a 'thematic development of all the important musical characters related to Wozzeck',[68] there is, with the single exception of the 'Seduction' motive, no reference to Marie. The explanation for the omission of her various leitmotives lies in the fact that they will dominate, very soon after, the last scene of the opera. In this Invention the key of D minor is in the course of the piece gradually so widely expanded that only towards the end we hear it clearly re-established (365-71).

Like the *Trauermusik* in the third act of *Götterdämmerung*, the epilogue of *Wozzeck* is a poignant threnody passing in review all the musical 'characters' (except that of Marie) associated with the protagonist. Its form is ternary, with section A (320-45) largely based on Ex. 65, the emphatic motive of which, *x*, is particularly poignant in its effect. With bar 337 the opera's chief leitmotives enter, beginning with the three chords and Andres's folksong of I, 2 and Wozzeck's 'gehetzt' from I, 3. Section B (346-64) introduces the 'Doctor', marked 'furioso'(!) followed by the 'Captain', which is combined in the bass with the passacaglia theme (349-51), as if Berg wanted thereby to indicate that 'aberratio mentalis partialis' is not only confined to Wozzeck. The Andante recalls motives from the 'Seduction' and the Drum-Major's figure from I, 5 and culminates in a two-part stretto thundering out the 'Wir arme Leut' motto on the four trombones and the upper woodwind. The harmonic tension reaches its apex in a twelve-note chord to find its immediate resolution in the D minor of section C (365-71). This brings Wozzeck's 'Misery' from II, 2 (Ex. 57) above the fundamental cadential steps V-I (D minor), the whole passage being overwhelming in its orchestration, with the top-line scored for quadruple upper woodwind, quadruple horns and trumpets, and upper strings. The epilogue closes on the D minor chord with added ninth, *pp*. A completely new colour is introduced with the arpeggio on clarinets and harp which leads to the last scene.[69]

Act III, Scene 5. In front of Marie's house. Bright morning. Sunshine. Marie's Child and other Children.

After the catharsis of the epilogue there follows the only scene of the opera in which reigns the reality of normal, everyday life as represented by playing children, who, as children will, show utter unconcern for and complete

---

[68] Redlich, *Alban Berg*, p. 326.

[69] There is a little-noticed Schoenberg quotation in this Interlude: in bars 338-9 the upper celli, doubled by three bassoons, introduce a melody from the 'Lied der Waldtaube', 'der König öffnet Toves Sarg', from the *Gurrelieder*, which is a fitting quotation in this poignantly sad piece.

indifference to human tragedy. Marie's child who is told by one of the other children that his mother lies dead on the path by the pond, happily continues to ride its imaginary hobby-horse singing 'Hopp! Hopp!', and after a moment's hesitation follows its playmates to the pond. This latter motive was Berg's own invention and adds an almost unbearable poignancy to the whole scene.

For the music to this scene the composer chose an Invention on a regular quaver movement. It is in fact a *perpetuum mobile* formed of quaver triplets, most probably to suggest the continuity of normal life.[70] The orchestral palette used takes account of the world of children by omitting low-lying instruments and giving the harp and celesta a prominent part to play. Altogether the sound is of the utmost delicacy and transparency. In the opening nursery rhyme and the 'Hopp! Hopp!' of Marie's child, Berg's *volkstümlich* fourth is much in evidence. The first time the child sings this word (380-1), the voice-part is doubled by the solo oboe which sounds like a toy trumpet, the second time (385-6) it is doubled by the xylophone recalling a child's rattle. Marie's motives predominate in this last scene. There is the chromatic 'Knife' (375-8); there is the sadly beautiful end-phrase of her Lullaby (377-8) played by a muted solo violin, 'sehr ausdruckvoll'; there is her 'Aimless Waiting' above the sinister dyad F-B (379-80), her 'Plaint' (381-2) and, finally, the opening of her Lullaby (386-7). In the last three bars the Principal Chord is sounded, with the fifth G-D on the muted strings and its oscillating middle part on four flutes and celesta(!) the latter seeming to go on for ever, as in the finale of the Lyric Suite. As Berg explained,[71] the music does indeed go on and in idea leads back to the beginning of the opera, which thus comes full circle.

Three Fragments from 'Wozzeck'

In marked contrast to the *Lulu Symphony* (pp. 266ff.) the *Three Fragments from 'Wozzeck'* concentrate on the portrayal of a single character – Marie, and follow in the order in which they occur in the opera. The first piece comprises the Transition Music from I, 2(302) to I, 3 which is followed by the complete Scene 3 containing Marie's Lullaby. The whole is one bar longer than it is in the opera. The second piece is Marie's 'Bible' scene, III, 1, in which the voice part has two *ossia* – in bar 28, G sharp is substituted for the harmonic on the high C, and in bars 38-9, Berg leaves it to the singer to sing the original or the line (largely) a minor third above it. The third piece opens with III, 4, bar

---

[70] In this invention Berg may well have been influenced by Debussy, who wrote a similar triplet movement in IV, 2 of his *Pelléas et Mélisande*, notably in the section in which the child Ynold speaks of the arrival of the 'little lambs'. Also III, 14 of Schreker's *Der ferne Klang* contains passages of a similar rhythmic pattern.

[71] Redlich, *Alban Berg*, p. 313..

284, after Wozzeck has drowned, continues into the Invention on a Key (Intermezzo), and closes with Scene 5. The short Children's chorus and the 'Hopp! Hopp!' of Marie's boy may be sung by the singer of Marie. Except for the very minor alterations mentioned above, the three pieces are completely identical with their operatic version.

In conclusion it is worth mentioning that Berg thought at first of *Wozzeck* as the first part of a trilogy of which the remaining two operas were to have been *Vincent* and *Wolfgang*, and the whole symbolizing 'Knecht' (Serf) – 'Freund' (Friend) – 'Herr' (Master). But nothing came of this idea.

LULU

From his early years Wedekind displayed an interest in the psychopathology of sexual love and, indeed, the first idea for his two Lulu dramas, *Erdgeist* and *Die Büchse der Pandora*, was suggested to him by the series of gruesome murders committed in the East End of London in 1888 and 1889 by Jack the Ripper. In other words, the end of his tragedy was in Wedekind's mind long before he conceived the actual plays. He began to study scientific literature on the physiology and psychology of the sexual instinct such as Krafft-Ebing's *Psychopathia sexualis* and the writings of Lombroso, Charcot and Montegazza, all mentioned in an early and little-known play of his, *Das Sonnenspektrum*. Wedekind's second incentive came from a French pantomime, *Lulu, Clownesse danseuse* (Paris, 1888), by Félicien Champsaur, which he saw in the French capital in 1891 and which greatly interested him on account of the author's conception of erotic love. The pantomime was an apotheosis of the sensual beauty of the female body, presented in a grotesque action in which no less a person than the German philosopher Schopenhauer is one of the three characters. The moral the playwright wished to be drawn from it was that if a man wants to know a woman's soul he must love her body and not treat her as an object to be coldly dissected and analysed as Schopenhauer does. What Wedekind took over from this pantomime was the general motive of the sensual lure of the female body, the name and also the dancing profession of Champsaur's heroine. These were the data which inspired him to a wholly original and for its time most daring, drama into which he worked contemporary events including, as we have seen, the murders of Jack the Ripper and the Hamburg cholera epidemic of 1892.

Wedekind's first version was a single drama entitled *Die Büchse der Pandora*, 'A Monster Tragedy in Five Acts', which he began in 1892 and completed in 1895. His publisher (Lange), however, refused to bring out the last two acts (the Paris and London scenes of Berg's Act III) for fear of difficulties with the German censor because of the lesbian Countess Geschwitz and the lust murder at the end, and he therefore published only the first three acts of the play, calling it *Der Erdgeist* (1895). In 1903 a second edition entitled *Lulu*.

Dramatische Dichtung in zwei Teilen was prepared, but only Part I could be issued, entitled *Erdgeist*; for the tenth performance of this Wedekind wrote the present 'Prologue of the Animal Trainer'. Part II (*Die Büchse der Pandora*) came out in 1904 with a new publisher (Cassirer), for whom the author provided an opening act (Berg's II, 2) thus turning it into a three-act play. This publication involved both Wedekind and Cassirer in a series of court cases all of which went against them. *Pandora* could not be staged in public during Wedekind's lifetime, but only in private productions before an invited audience, which explains why the Vienna production of 1905 by Karl Kraus, which Berg saw, was a hole-and-corner affair at the tiny Trianon Theater in the Nestroyhof in the second district (*Leopoldsstadt*). It was, incidentally, in this production that Wedekind's future wife, Tilly Newes, played Lulu, Wedekind himself appearing as Jack and Karl Kraus as the Negro Prince Kungu Poti. In 1913 Wedekind published a version of the two plays compressed into a single drama, which, in order to pacify the censor, omitted the last scene with Countess Geschwitz and Jack.

Among Wedekind's major plays such as *Frühlings Erwachen, Der Marquis von Keith, Schloss Wetterstein, Franziska*, and *Tod und Teufel*, the two Lulu dramas occupy a special place. They are sex tragedies *par excellence*, a ferocious battle in the Nietzschean sense between the sexes and ultimately a conflict between spirit (man) and flesh (woman). (In a sense the Lulu dramas are also, prophetically, an illustration of the key role that sex, or, more generally, libido, was to play in the Freudian theory of the unconscious.) On which side Wedekind stood is clear from what he wrote in his essay, *Uber Erotik* – 'flesh has its own spirit'. At the same time the two plays are an arraignment of German society in Wedekind's time – this is the likely reason why to a modern public they may seem to date – for its hypocritical morality, which allowed a woman sexual liberty in the matrimonial cage, but regarded her as a prostitute and outcast if she indulged it outside marriage. Lulu ignores these moral conventions; she will never be the property of a man and feels entirely free to choose for a lover only the man who appeals to her senses. 'Auf Kommando *lieben*, das kann ich nicht!', she says to Dr Schön in *Erdgeist*, a revealing passage which Berg, strangely, omitted from his libretto. Wedekind, however, does not advocate equality between the sexes in every respect. He does not write a blueprint for suffragettes or the present Women's Liberation movement, which would have horrified him, since he was fully aware of the physiological and biological barriers separating man and woman. What he does propagate is total freedom for women in all sex matters. In order to drive home this message he conceived Lulu as the embodiment of the female sex instinct – an elemental force ever since Eve. And just because she represents an elemental force – an earth spirit – she unwittingly destroys everyone, man and woman, who comes into close contact with her. Wedekind's conception of a *femme fatale* is thus the total opposite of Goethe's conception of the woman as expressed at the end of Part II of his *Faust*. Lulu is not an immoral creature but an amoral one. Beyond good and evil, she is as innocent as the flame of a candle to which moths are attracted and burn themselves to death. Her mission in life is succinctly described in the Animal Trainer's Prologue: 'Sie ward geschaffen, Unheil anzustiften, zu locken, zu verführen, zu vergiften, zu morden, ohne dass es einer spürt' – 'She was created to do evil, to tempt, seduce, poison and murder, without anyone feeling it'. As long as Lulu remains true to this mission, no harm can befall her. Even after her downfall has begun, she refuses to give in and sell herself. When in the Paris act the Marquis Casti-Piani offers her a post' in a high-class Cairo brothel, as she is down on her luck, she retorts: 'Ich tauge nicht für diesen Beruf' (I am not suitable for this profession) and later and far more forcibly, 'Und wenn ich mich gegen meine Erkenntnis versündige, fühle ich mich am nächsten Morgen an Lieb und Seele beschmutzt und brauche Wochen, um den Ekel, den ich vor mir empfinde, zu überwinden' – 'And when I have sinned against what I know of myself, then next morning I feel besmirched in body and soul and need weeks in order to overcome the disgust I feel at myself'. Finally, towards the end of her dialogue with the Marquis, Lulu exclaims in great agitation, 'Ich gehe mit dir nach Amerika, nach China, aber ich kann das Einzige nicht verkaufen, das je mein Eigen war' – 'I go with you to America, to China, but I cannot sell the only thing that has ever been my own'.

Up to her final scene Lulu remains a wholly autonomous being, completely untouched by her surroundings and, as the feral creature she is, she puts up a tremendous fight for her self-preservation. It is not until she reaches the bottom of her 'career' – in the slums of London's East End – that she sins against 'what I know of myself' and therefore can no longer be the master of men over whom she has always cast her baneful spell. She becomes a subservient creature, going on the streets in order to earn money for Alwa and Schigolch. How she feels about it, she makes crystal clear in her phrase, 'Gibt es etwas traurigeres in der Welt als ein Freudenmädchen?' – 'Is there anything in the world more sad than a prostitute?' (In Berg these words have been transferred to Alwa). This change is the only development she undergoes in the plays and the opera, or, rather, they reveal a facet of her personality hinted at in her great monologue in the final act of *Erdgeist* – *Lied der Lulu* in the opera. Up to the end of Act III of *Pandora's Box* or Act III, sc. 1 of the opera, she is an Angel of Destruction, spreading sexual terror wherever she goes, a terror reminiscent of Juliette's in the Marquis de Sade's novel of that name. There is also an interesting parallel between Lulu and the heroine of Bizet's *Carmen*. Both are *femmes fatales* and both die a violent death at the hands of their lovers. But Carmen dies because she remains true to herself to the very end, while Lulu dies because she does *not* remain true to herself, being forced against her own nature and will to become a prostitute.

Lulu is like a character in a fairytale, or better a myth, which Wedekind underlines by calling the second Lulu play after an episode in Greek mythology. (Berg himself considered her the counterpart of Don Juan, another character who, though originally historical, became a myth, and he was greatly pleased when after the Prague performance of his *Lulu Symphony* a critic referred to Don Juan in discussing the work.) Lulu has neither father nor mother – her origin is uncertain as is her name – Mignon or Nelly or Eva or Lulu – the last, with its childlike sound, being perhaps the most apt for her. Nana, the heroine of Zola's eponymous novel (1880) comes to mind. Her name shows the same baby-like repetition of the same syllable. She was a prostitute whose sexual magnetism was such as to wreak havoc on Partisan society of her time.

None of her satellites – Dr Schön, Alwa, the painter Schwarz and Countess Geschwitz – understand her true nature. The only one who does is Schigolch, as mysterious a figure as Lulu. Once her lover and now her protector and a kind of father-figure, Schigolch is rich in practical experience and always ready to come to her rescue whenever she is in an extreme situation – most effectively in the Paris act (III, 1 in Berg) where he disposes of the dangerous athlete Rodrigo.[72] How profound the insight of this gutter philosopher is into Lulu's nature comes out in what he says about her in the London act (III, 2 in Berg), after she has gone on the street for her first client: 'Die versteht ihre Sache nicht. Die kann von der Liebe nicht leben weil ihr Leben die Liebe ist' – 'This woman does not know her metier. She cannot live from love because her life is love'. There is dramatic irony in the fact that Schigolch is the one who, by sending her on the streets to earn money for him and Alwa, is the indirect cause of her murder. He is the only man who is immune to Lulu's destructive powers and hence stays alive.

The male counterpart to Lulu is Jack the Ripper. In him, too, the sexual instinct is so virulent that for its satisfaction it must destroy. Sexual possession of a woman means for him her murder, just as for Lulu sexual possession of a man means his moral and physical annihilation. There is, incidentally, in Lulu herself that half-conscious desire to fulfil herself by dying at the hands of a lust murderer. In Act I of *Pandora* she says to Alwa: 'Mir träumte alle paar Nächte einmal, ich sei einem Lustmörder unter die Hände geraten' – 'I dreamt every other night or so that I fell into the hands of a lust murderer.'[73]

Dr Schön, next to Lulu the most important character in *Erdgeist* and in the first half of the opera, closely related to her in that, like her, he is incapable of love, is dominated by his sexual instinct and does not know what devotion,

---

[72] Schigolch appears already in one of Wedekind's early plays, *Elins Erweckung*, where he is the 'mentor' of a postitute, just as the bogus Marquis Casti-Piani returns in a later play, *Tod und Teufel*, in which he ends his shameful life by suicide.

[73] Compare Effie's suicide in *Schloss Wetterstein*.

gratitude and loyalty are. Yet, while Lulu is primitive and a creature of sheer instinct, Dr Schön is highly sophisticated and educated, a man of brains and will-power with the intelligence of a beast of prey – hence his identification with the 'tiger' in the Prologue and in III, 2 of Berg's opera with Jack the Ripper. In short, he is a *Gewaltsmensch* who walks over corpses to gain his ends. It is perhaps because of this brutality that Lulu, after shooting him, says that he was the only man she loved, though this is self-deception and her real affection is for Schigolch. As long as Schön believes in his powers, he is the master of Lulu. He took her under his protection when she was a girl of twelve selling flowers, clothed her, provided for her and finally made her his mistress. But he refused to marry her because a man of his social standing cannot marry his mistress. He wants to marry a girl of a respectable family because he still adheres to the conventional code of the society to which he belongs. But he has now passed the zenith of his life and has no longer his erstwhile power to resist Lulu. His disintegration begins with the 'Letter' scene in *Erdgeist* (I, 3 in Berg's opera) which leads to his marriage with Lulu and culminates in his paranoia in *Pandora* (II, 1 in Berg). Lulu shoots him because, as she says to Alwa, Schön wanted to force her to kill herself (this sentence is omitted in Berg's text). What Wedekind wished to illustrate in Schön was a 'spiritually robust and inflexible energy and brutality which ... comes to grief through the exceptional nature of a primitive woman. I wanted to show how conscious thought, which is always and in all circumstances overestimating itself, loses in the battle against the instinctive.' So much for Schön.

His son Alwa is, in marked contrast to his brutally realistic father, an idealist. In Wedekind he is a writer and as such used by the playwright as mouthpiece for some of his own ideas. Thus in I, 1 of *Pandora* Wedekind puts the following view on literature into Alwa's mouth:

> The curse of our young literature is that we are all far too literary. ... Our horizon does not extend beyond the boundaries of our professional interests. In order to get back again on the path to great, imposing art, we would have to move as much as possible among people who have never read a book in all their life and who are guided in their actions by the simplest animal instincts. In my *Erdgeist* I have tried to work according to these principles with all my strength.

In Wedekind Alwa is the author of the play *Erdgeist*. Berg changes him into a composer with whom he identifies to a large extent and whose very opera we are watching. This comes out in I, 3 where Alwa says that an interesting opera could be written about Lulu; at which point Berg quotes the opening chords of *Wozzeck*, just as Mozart quotes from his *Figaro* in the banquet scene of *Don Giovanni*, and Wagner the *Tristan* motive in Act III, Scene 1 of *Die*

Meistersinger. Alwa is an elegiac character and a weakling. He first adores Lulu as a higher being, but gradually begins to feel the sensual attraction of her body and finally comes under the sway of her demonic power of destruction: 'Richte mich zugrunde! Ich bitte Dich, mach ein Ende mit mir!' – 'Destroy me! I beg you, finish me!'. Through his love for Lulu he becomes morally corroded, sinks lower and lower, loses his former dignity, gambles away his last penny and is finally kept by Lulu. His only desire now is for a 'beefsteak and a cigarette and then die'. In a last flicker of moral courage he tries to defend Lulu against the Negro but is killed. It should be added that Berg somewhat toned down Alwa's moral disintegration, stressing the artist's ardent admiration of Lulu as his ideal of beauty, just as Lulu becomes in Berg's hand a somewhat different character from the Lulu of Wedekind. More will be said about this point later.

The Countess Geschwitz, whose first appearance in the last act of *Erdgeist* (II, 1 in the opera) is an ill omen for Lulu's fortunes, is the very opposite of the heroine. She is a lesbian who feels most deeply for Lulu, and is always ready to sacrifice herself for her. That Wedekind invented such a highly improbable escape of Lulu from the prison hospital, with the Countess deliberately infecting herself with cholera to make this escape possible, indicates, I believe, the measure of self-sacrifice of which she is capable; to say nothing of her death in a vain attempt to defend Lulu against Jack the Ripper. In the drama, though not in the opera, she is the only character who engages the spectator's compassion and moves him. And she moves him all the more because Lulu has not a spark of sympathy for her sufferings; on the contrary the Countess is an abomination to her because of her perversion. Here is her remark to the Countess in *Pandora*: 'You were not finished in your mother's womb, neither as a woman nor as a man. You are not a human being as the others are. For a man there is not enough in you and for a woman you got too much brain in your pate. That's why you are mad.' (See Act III, sc. 1 of the opera).

In his 1906 preface to *Pandora* Wedekind said that the central tragic figure of the play is not Lulu but the Countess, yet this is not borne out by the actual drama in which in each of the three acts Lulu remains the protagonist with the Countess representing one of her satellites. Wedekind later confessed to his foremost biographer[74] that what he had written in the Preface was said in order to mislead the judges of the court who had banned all public performances of the play on account of the representation of a prostitute and her death at the hands of a lust-murderer, but strangely, not because of the appearance on the stage of a sexual pervert. Wedekind, however, was the first playwright, to my knowledge, who has introduced a lesbian into a play and he did it in order to show the tragedy and the untold

---

[74] Artur Kutscher, *Wedekind: Leben und Werk*, Munich, 1964, p. 127.

agonies of a pervert, inviting the compassion and mercy of all those not cursed with an unnatural sex instinct. Moreover, to throw into the sharpest relief the stigma of ridicule and hate a pervert may evoke in normal people, Wedekind invented the character of the *Kraftmensch* and *Springfritze*, Rodrigo Quast, prototype of the uneducated and vulgar who have only mocking sneers for what in Wedekind's time was considered a most unfortunate creature to be shunned by society. The athlete is the natural antagonist of the Countess and with his snide remarks tries to hurt her to the quick. He is a rare mixture of boastfulness with cowardice, bad manners with snobbery, base feelings and sentimentality and, moreover, represents male virility *per se* which makes him cousin to the Drum-Major in *Wozzeck*.

The Painter (Schwarz) is a mediocre artist who obtains fame only through the press publicity given him by Schön. His only merit is to have painted Lulu's Pierrot portrait – the symbol of Lulu at the height of her career which follows her wherever she goes. In the last act it reflects the complete turn of her fortunes by showing that 'around its edges the colour has peeled off' (Alwa) and that it has 'extraordinarily darkened' (Schigolch). The Painter suffers from an inferiority complex *vis-à-vis* Lulu because of his low origin as compared with that of his wife: 'Ich komme aus den Tiefen der Gesellschaft. Sie ist von oben her' – 'I come from the depths of society, she from on high'. All he seeks to obtain from Lulu is the homely happiness of a *petit bourgeois*. Banal and at the same time naïve, the Painter has no inkling of Lulu's true nature. 'Er sieht nichts. Er sieht mich nicht und sich nicht. Er ist blind, blind, blind' – 'He sees nothing. He does not see me nor himself. He is blind, blind, blind ... ' Lulu exclaims to Schön. The Painter's marriage to Lulu has its counterpart in Georg Tresman's marriage to Hedda Gabler, the man-eating monster in Ibsen's play.

The remaining three characters of the large cast can be limned in a few sentences. The Marquis Casti-Piani of *Pandora*, II and Berg's III, 1 is a most odious creature. A former convict, he is now police informer, blackmailer, procurer and lover of Lulu rolled into one who, incidentally, has infected Lulu with a venereal disease to which she herself is immune but which she has transmitted to her other lover Alwa. Prince Escerny, an Africa explorer who in Berg (I, 3) has no name proper and remains a shadowy, episodic figure, is treated more fully in Wedekind. He is a masochist who wants to be dominated by a woman and, in total ignorance of Lulu's nature, wishes to marry her and offer her 'quiet happiness in the noble seclusion' of a country villa. Lastly there is the Schoolboy (Hugenberg) who is portrayed as something like a young hero, full of contempt for the world and, like Countess Geschwitz, prepared to sacrifice himself for Lulu. But, when in the Paris act of *Pandora* (III, 1 in the opera) Alwa quite casually informs Lulu of the Schoolboy's suicide in the prison, she scarcely takes notice of this piece of news.

As we see, Wedekind offers us a panoramic view of society, his 'Circus', to show how universal Lulu's fascination is. Whether aristocrat (Countess, Prince Escerny), middle class (Schön, Alwa), plebs (Rodrigo) or underworld (Schigolch, Marquis, Jack) – all are, in spite of individual differences, devotees at Lulu's shrine. In their reaction to her fatal spell, each figure characterises himself and adds at the same time another touch to the portrayal of the heroine. Moreover, the manner in which they speak is a further means of characterisation, and in this context it is worth mentioning what Wedekind himself said about the language of the heroine: 'In the description of Lulu I attached importance to the way in which the words she speaks paint the body of a woman. With each of her remarks I asked myself if it served to make it young and beautiful.' In the opera this finds its equivalent in the voice of Lulu which is a coloratura soprano, the voice of a young woman. Another feature of Wedekind's dramatic technique is the so-called 'aneinander vorbei reden' (speaking at cross-purposes), but here meant to denote a dialogue in which the one character takes no heed of what the other says and continues, automaton-like, with his or her own speech. Berg recaptured this most aptly in the duet between Lulu and Schön, I, 2, 589-86.

In an important letter to Schoenberg of 7 August 1930, Berg summarises his conflation and adaptation of Wedekind's two plays as follows:

> Of the opera I can tell you that I am still in the first act. Apart from composing in 12-note technique which does not allow me to work swiftly, it is the libretto that holds me up so very much. For its arrangement goes hand in hand with the composition. As I have to cut four-fifths of Wedekind's original, the selection of the remaining one-fifth causes me enough trouble. How much more trouble when I try to adapt what I have selected to the musical structures (large and small) and to avoid destroying Wedekind's particular language in the process! ... In spite of this clinging to detail, the libretto as a whole has, of course, been quite clear to me for a long time. This applies to the musical proportions as to the dramatic structure.

Berg then proceeds to give Schoenberg the outline of the scenario in relation to the two Wedekind plays which I reproduce with slight modifications:

	Wedekind *Erdgeist*	Berg	
Act I	The Painter's studio. Dr Goll, Lulu's husband, has a fatal stroke.	Act I,	Scene 1

Act II	House of Lulu and her second husband, the Painter, who commits suicide.		Scene 2
Act III	Dressing-room in the theatre. Dr Schön promises Lulu marriage.		Scene 3
Act IV	Schön's home in which he is shot by Lulu. She is arrested.	Act II,	Scene 1
	After a year in prison Lulu is freed by Countess Geschwitz and returns to Schön's home.		Orchestral Interlude

	Wedekind	Berg	
	Die Büchse der Pandora		
Act I	Schön's home (scene as before). Lulu becomes Alwa's mistress.		Scene 2
Act II	Gambling casino in Paris. Lulu and Alwa have to flee.	Act III,	Scene 1
Act III	In an attic in London.		Scene 2

Berg then continues:

> The interlude which bridges the gap between the last act of *Erdgeist* and the first act of *Pandora*, is the central point of the whole tragedy in which after the ascent of the preceding acts (or scenes) the descent of the following scenes is indicated by the retrograde. (By the way, the four men who visit Lulu in her attic have to be impersonated by the same singers who represent the men who become Lulu's victims in the first half of the opera – but in reverse order.)

The 'four-fifths' which Berg omitted from Wedekind's original included the opening two scenes of *Erdgeist*, which are merely preparatory to the action proper; their excision allowed the composer to plunge directly into the middle of things. Furthermore, he cut out the playwright's general, and frequently polemical, observations on art, literature and society and concentrated on the story line. In addition, Berg made some alterations in the dialogue, transposing sentences to obtain a better verbal logic and also achieve parallelisms dictated by musical considerations as, for instance, in the first recapitulation of Schön's sonata in I, 2. In Wedekind virtually all characters without distinction bear proper names; in Berg only the chief characters have proper names – Lulu, Dr Schön, Alwa, Countess Geschwitz and Schigolch – while the subsidiary ones are referred to merely by their profession or social rank – The Medizinalrat (Dr Goll), the Painter

(Schwarz),[75] the Prince (Prince Escerny), the Marquis (Casti-Piani), the Athlete (Rodrigo Quast),[76] the Schoolboy (Hugenberg) and so on.

Berg's method of adapting Wedekind's original was different from that he applied to *Wozzeck*. There he set, with just a few modifications, the text as he found it. In *Lulu*, however, he was forced to cut a very considerable amount of the original text, and what remained unfolded not separately from the music; on the contrary textural arrangement and composition went hand in hand, as Berg wrote in the afore-mentioned letter to Schoenberg. It was the same method Schoenberg used in *Moses und Aron*, where the text was fixed in its definitive form 'only during the composition, some of it even afterwards. This proves an extremely good method.[77] In the discussion of the Schön sonata and the Alwa rondo we shall see how Berg set about it to make text and music interact to the advantage of both.

Let us for a moment consider the reason which prompted Berg in his letter to Schoenberg to speak of the impersonation of Lulu's four clients in the last scene by the same singers who enact her victims in the first half of the opera (Acts I and II, 1), but in reverse. In the final version of the libretto Berg dropped the idea of a reversed order and, moreover, reduced Wedekind's four clients to three by eliminating the Swiss *Privatdozent* Dr Hilti, whose implied academic title 'Professor' he transferred to Hunidei – in the opera a nameless non-singing role. In the play Dr Hilti speaks in Swiss-German dialect which was probably one of the reasons why Berg dropped this character. The correspondences between Lulu's victims and her clients are now as follows:

Medizinalrat (speaking role)	= Professor (silent role)
Painter	= Negro
Dr Schön	= Jack the Ripper

In Wedekind there is no suggestion of the doubling of these roles by the same actors. This idea seems, on the face of it, to have been Berg's own, though there is a slight hint of it in Wedekind, when Jack, after killing Lulu and Geschwitz, says cynically, 'Das war ein Stück Arbeit! ('This was some job!'), which is a literal repeat of Schön's phrase said to the Painter after he has told him about Lulu's past.[78] Berg's idea could only be realized because of

[75] Though the Painter plays an important role in I, 1 and 2, Berg, strangely, did not consider him a main character – possibly because his activity is, unlike that of the other protagonists, confined to only two scenes.

[76] The cast list of both the full and vocal scores had originally 'Rodrigo, ein Athlet'; in the body of the opera he is merely called 'Athlet'.

[77] Letter to Berg of 8 August 1931. *Arnold Schoenberg. Letters*, p. 151.

[78] It is indeed characteristic of Wedekind's style to have a phrase which was first uttered by one character, later repeated by another character, *e.g.* Alwa's 'In Paris ist Revolution ausgebrochen' ('Revolution has started in Paris') (I, 2) which is reiterated by Schön in II, 1. Similarly, when in the Prologue the Animal Trainer describes the beasts of his menagerie as 'real wild animals', this is echoed in Alwa's comment on the wild shouts of the audience

his conflation of the two Wedekind plays, thus creating the dramatic unity of his libretto. But who was the real author of Berg's idea to double certain roles? It is possible that he took his cue from Offenbach's *Tales of Hoffmann* in which the poet's four loves are sung by the same soprano and the four villains by the same baritone. But it is my strong belief that it was the interpretation which Karl Kraus put forward in his speech at his production of *Pandora* in Vienna in 1905, a speech he later reprinted in his periodical, *Die Fackel* (June 1925) of which Berg was an assiduous reader, and subsequently in a collection of essays.[79] This interpretation had for one of its main points the following observation: that the drama is the 'tragedy of the hounded grace of woman, eternally misunderstood' and that in the last act 'the great retribution has begun, the revenge of the world of men which makes bold to avenge itself for its own guilt.[80] It was this 'great retribution' which Berg wanted to convey by having the same artists impersonate Lulu's three victims and her three clients, who act out their revenge by first degrading and finally murdering her. This was a most striking piece of dramatic symbolism which is paralleled in the music – for extended portions associated with the Medizinalrat, the Painter and Schön return again in the last scene with the Professor, the Negro and Jack, a fact which makes this last scene function as a musical recapitulation,[81] and which has greatly facilitated the completion of the opera with the help of Berg's short score for Act II (p. 259).

Incidentally, Puccini, in his *La Bohème*, anticipated Berg's recapitulation when in Act IV he draws, with very few exceptions, on motives, themes and leitsections of Act I, a procedure he called 'logical reminiscences'. In both these cases this has the effect best expressed in Dante's 'Nessun maggior dolore che ricordarsi del tempo felice nella miseria'; though with Lulu, her 'time of happiness' can only be interpreted in a Pickwickian sense.

Another pairing of roles is that of the Animal Trainer in the Prologue and the Athlete in the opera – both are circus performers! But it is interesting to note that the Animal Trainer is allotted the Alwa series (Ex. 71a), Berg thus indicating the ideological identity of circus performer, author and himself, i.e. Animal Trainer = Alwa = Berg. There are also triple roles assigned to the same performer, which Berg introduces merely as a matter of economy and convenience:

---

watching Lulu's ballet performance, 'it sounds like a menagerie when food is brought to the cages' (I, 3).

[79] *Literatur und Lüge* (Vienna, 1929).

[80] Whether Wedekind accepted this interpretation is not known, but it seemed to have been implied in his expression of gratitude to Kraus for his 'unforgettable production' of the drama (preface to *Pandora* of 1906).

[81] See George Perle, '*Lulu*: Thematic Material and Pitch Organisation', *Music Review*, November 1965, p. 278.

1. Prince – Manservant – Marquis
2. Medizinalrat – Banker – Professor
3. Wardrobe Mistress – Schoolboy – Groom

Berg, however, acknowledges in the music an element extrinsic to the drama, in that the men of the first group are linked by a Chorale (Ex. 86 and 87) and those of the second group by an identical motive of thirds. Only the members of the third group, with the Schoolboy and the Groom being *Hosenrollen* and sung by the singer of the Wardrobe Mistress, have no material in common.

The ethos of *Wozzeck* and *Lulu* may be said to be identical – both operas speak of profound compassion, the first for the underprivileged, the second for the social outcast. In their strong anti-Establishment message they are disturbing, provocative music-dramas calculated to *épater les bourgeois*. *Lulu* is a female *Rake's Progress* and may even be called a 'morality play'. Yet in style and technique they differ in several important respects.

To take the text first. The Büchner original is a text without form which Berg's ordering dramaturgy transmuted into a drama with a proper beginning, middle and end. The Wedekind originals, on the other hand, were articulated, rounded plays, yet with discursive and anecdotal features, which Berg had to eliminate in order to make the two plays suitable for an operatic libretto. Again, in *Wozzeck* we have fifteen short, loosely ranged scenes of a cinematic character, each of which Berg treats as an independent musical unit. In *Lulu*, on the other hand, there are seven long scenes allowing room for a consistent development of character on a much broader, more spacious scale than in the earlier opera. Berg seems to have had this consistent, large-scale development of the main characters in mind when he spoke of the 'durchzuführende Gesamterscheinung' or 'total phenomenon to be put across'. While in *Wozzeck* the scene is the determining factor of the musical form, in *Lulu* it is the character which inspires the form chosen. Thus Dr Schön is associated with an extensive sonata movement to indicate the major importance of this character (Act I), Alwa is symbolised in a rondo (Act II) and Lulu by vocal forms, and near the bottom of her career, in a Theme and twelve Variations (III). The subdivisions of the sonata and rondo do not, as we shall see, follow one another successively but are interrupted by other 'alien' musical forms which make *Lulu* more complex in the musico-dramatic structure than *Wozzeck*, and are an expression of the difference between the Büchner and Wedekind plays. Moreover, the later work is more of a singers' opera than the earlier one, containing such typical vocal forms as aria, song, arioso, canzonetta, duet and ensemble. Thirdly, the orchestral forces employed in *Lulu* are, with the exception of the jazz band in I, 3, smaller than in *Wozzeck*, and show a pronounced transparency of texture calculated to let the singing voice through without any difficulty and strain. Fourthly and lastly, *Lulu* is in serial technique; this constitutes the major stylistic difference from the earlier opera and will occupy our exclusive attention in the next few pages.

There is an important letter to Schoenberg, of 1 September 1928, in which Berg has this to say about his manipulation of the twelve-note row in *Lulu*:

> I am not confining myself to a *single* series, but derive from *this* at once a number of *other* forms (scale and chromatic forms, third and fourth forms, progressions of three- and four-note chords, etc. etc.) each of which I consider as an independent series and which I *treat* like one (with its inversion and retrograde); but always with the proviso that, in case this should not be sufficient, I would construct a *new* series, similar to the manner in my Lyric Suite in which the series underwent some minor modifications (through *transposition* of a few notes) which was then, at any rate, very stimulating for my work.

I believe that this gives in a nutshell the various novel ways in which Berg treats the basic series in *Lulu*, aiming to enlarge its thematic potential by altering the original sequence of the twelve notes, or using only segments of it independently, or rotating the series and choosing certain notes at regular distances to derive new series. In other words, with the exception of Wedekind's *Lautenlied* in Act III, the total material of the opera is derived, directly or indirectly, from an *Ur-* or Basic Series. It is in the manifold manipulation of the Basic Series that Berg demonstrates a well-nigh limitless ingenuity, an ingenuity foreshadowed in his treatment of the row in the Lyric Suite, and going far beyond anything in Schoenberg or Webern.

The Basic Series (BS) of the opera stands for Lulu as the ideal of sexual desire for all men, irrespective of their individual character and social status:

Example 66

Just as in the drama she is the central figure round whom everything revolves, so in the music BS is the matrix out of which all leitmotives and leit-harmonies grow. (Incidentally, the relationship between the two halves of the series is that of a tritone – B flat-E an interval absent from the *successive* note sequence of BS.) Through segmentation of BS into four three-note chords (see the above letter), Berg arrives at the motive of Lulu's 'Pierrot Picture' which plays so important a part throughout the opera, notably in II,

2 and III, 2 where it serves as a pathetic reminder of the heroine's better
days:

Example 67a

Example 67b

Apart from symbolising the picture, Ex. *a* also stands for Lulu as the subject
of the painting and the Painter as its author, while Ex. *b* (bass line of Ex. 67*a*)
expresses her tender beauty. By horizontalising the three parts of these
chords Berg obtains a scale motive (see his letter), investing it with a dance-
like rhythm and associating it with Lulu's destructive charm and grace:

Example 68a

Example 68b

It is, significantly, first heard in the Animal Trainer's Prologue, at his
phrase, 'Sie ward geschaffen, Unheil anzustiften ...' Lastly, Lulu as an
Erdgeist or Earth Spirit, as an elemental force of nature, is projected in a
series of successive fourths[82] seemingly derived from BS in this way:

Example 69a

---

[82] Cf. the fourth in the 'nature sound' of the opening movement of Mahler's First Symphony.

Example 69b

The Prologue opens with Ex. 69*b*, and one of its most dramatic occurrences is in the duet between Lulu and the Marquis in III, 1, in which she refuses to accept a 'post' in a brothel as a professional prostitute. As a rule, however, Berg uses only one or two segments of it by itself as, for instance, in the orchestral Interlude between II, 1 and 2.

While Lulu is characterised in at least four different ways, the other characters have only a single theme or motive associated with them. Next in importance to the heroine is Dr Schön, whose series results from rotating BS several times and omitting from it, first, one note, then two notes, and finally three notes, reversing this operation and repeating the whole process until a new twelve-note series is obtained (Ex. 70*a*).

Dr Schön's series frequently adopts the thematic shape Ex. 70*b* to characterise the *Gewaltsmensch* or the predatory animal, the 'tiger' of whom the Animal Trainer speaks in the Prologue, where Ex. 70*b* appears for the first time; note its leap a tenth upwards. Significantly, after Schön's death it will not recur again in that shape until the entry of his double, Jack the Ripper, in III, 2.

Example 70a

Example 70b

Alwa's series is gained by extracting every seventh note from the rotating BS, beginning with the first note.

Example 71a

Example 71b

1   2   3   4   5   6   9 8 10 11 12
                                         7

The thematic articulation of Alwa's series (Ex. 71b) dominates the rondo and lends it a marked elegiac character. It is to be noted that the first three notes of both the Schön and Alwa series form a 6/4 chord in major and minor respectively, the two modes being Berg's means of characterising the contrasting natures of father and son, as he does for instance in the juxtaposition of the two chords in II, 1 (Ex. 88). This is an example of the composer's use of traditional harmony in a serial work to serve a dramatic purpose, and confirms what Schoenberg wrote about a conversation he had with Berg about the subject of keys, in which the latter said that he did not think he could dispense with the employment of major and minor in order to achieve contrasts of characterisation.[83]

Countess Geschwitz is associated with a series which is gained by extracting every fifth note of BS. But this series (Ex. 72a) is never used for Berg subjects it to several precompositional operations:

(a) he rotates it so as to make it begin with the note 10 (Ex. 72b)

(b) he extracts from this new series the notes 5 and 9 (Ex. 72c)

(c) he places these notes as a dyad at the beginning of the series and divides the remaining ten notes into two five-note segments (Ex. 72d)

(d) he re-orders these segments into a 'black key' and 'white key' configuration (Ex. 72e)

Example 72a

1   2   3   4

Example 72b

10   11   12   1   2   3   4   5   6   7   8   9

Example 72c

1   2   3   4   5   6   7   8   9   10   11   12

Example 72d

Example 72e

Geschwitz is mostly represented by Ex. 72*e*, its pentatonic tendency being, possibly, intended to suggest her lesbian nature. The line is usually thickened out by parallel fifths to obtain a quasi-impressionist effect. (Act II, 5-6 *et passim*, 605-8; Act III, 888-9 and 1123-7). The verticalization of the segments produces two tone-clusters used by Berg to characterize the Athlete, the stark juxtaposition of the 'white key' and 'black key' chords evoking his coarseness and brutality:

Example 73a

Example 73b

Example 73c

His brutality is also conveyed by the manner in which these tone-clusters are to be played: with the fist and the forearm pressed down on the white and black keys of the piano. In addition, the Athlete has his own series, the first half of which is derived from the odd-numbered and the second from the even-numbered notes of the basic row (Ex. 73*b* and *c*), but its use is far more restricted than that of the tone-clusters. The close resemblance of Ex. 73*a* with Ex. 72*e* (black and white keys) is utilized by Berg to striking effect, in those dramatic episodes in which the Athlete and Geschwitz confront each other with extreme hostility, as in Act II, 2 and Act III, 1.[84]

As for Geschwitz's derived series, Ex. 72*b* appears, for example, in inversion in Act II, bars 4-5 and 9-11, in the orchestral Interlude (*Ostinato*), bar 673 and, more frequently, in Act III where she gains in dramatic importance. Ex. 72*d*, also inverted, occurs in Act III, 2, in the monologue in which Geschwitz contemplates suicide; here the dyad lies in the bass while the ten remaining notes unfold in two-note chords (1152-55) above it. The close of the opera is dominated by Ex. 72*d*, as in bars 1174-79, in her *Nocturne* (1279 ff.), and, most poignantly, in her apostrophe to the dead Lulu.

We recall that in his letter to Schoenberg Berg spoke of chromatic forms derived from the basic series and transpositions of some of its notes so as to enlarge the thematic scope of the original series. Schigolch's chromatic leit-motive is the result of these two operations carried out on the half-series which leads to two-part formations such as we encountered in the third movement of the Lyric Suite:

Example 74a

Example 74b

Example 74c

---

[84] We recall what Wedekind said about the relationship between these two characters.

Schigolch makes his first entry (I, 2) with the inversion of Ex. 74*b*, while Ex. 74*c* occurs already in the Animal Trainer's Prologue at his phrase, 'Sie sehen auch das Gewürm ...' In its creeping chromatic progression it is most suggestive of this shady figure from the underworld. Perle, who calls Schigolch's leitmotive a trope, sees in its chromaticism a 'symbol of Lulu's background' and, beyond it, the 'ultimate source of the tone material of the work itself'.[85] The Schoolboy's series Berg obtains from an ingenious manipulation of the notes of BS, which looks like interlocking Chinese boxes (Ex. 75).

The Medizinalrat, who is even less than episodic and almost a super, has, strangely, also his own leitmotive, while the Painter has, in addition to the 'Picture' figure, two more motives which are, however, not as explicit in their representation of this character as are most of the leitmotives associated with other personages of the drama. There remains the Marquis, who appears only in III, 1; but he has his own series, the derivation of which we shall discuss in connection with the Prince's chorale.

Example 75a

BS on C 1   5   9   2   6   10   3   7   11   4   8   12
        (1) (2) (3) (4) (5) (6) (7) (8) (9) (10) (11) (12)

Example 75b

1   2   3   4   5   6   7   8   9   10   11   12

Wedekind saw his two Lulu dramas in the symbolic terms of a circus performance – hence the Prologue of the Animal Trainer who introduces the main characters or, rather, exhibits them by the names of various animals in his menagerie.[86] Berg, who wrote the Prologue last, indicates by the leitmotives he attaches to the animals which characters of the opera they represent. Thus the 'tiger' is identified with Schön and his double Jack the Ripper (21-3), the 'bear' with the Athlete (24-5), the 'monkey' with the Marquis (28-31), the 'vermin' with Schigolch (34-6), the 'reptiles' with the Medizinalrat (36-8), the exotic 'crocodile' with the Countess Geschwitz (39-42), the 'snake' with Lulu (43-73) and Alwa with the Animal Trainer (74-5). The 'camel' is musically not identified with a character, but since the Animal Trainer refers to this animal as standing 'behind the curtain', it may be

[85] *Lulu*, Thematic Material, p. 285. Incidentally, Ex. 74*b* hints, in its lower part, at the *Hauptrhythmus* (see below).

[86] In a Berlin production in 1926 the characters actually appeared in the Prologue in the guise of animals, some even in a cage.

assumed that it symbolises the Painter, who is seen at his easel at the rise of
the curtain on Scene 1. Yet the Painter is not entirely absent from the music
of the Prologue, in which one of his motives appears, yet it is here not
associated with him directly, but with the 'Haustiere, die so wohl gesittet
fühlen ...'; in short, he is one of these domesticated animals. The Schoolboy's
series appears twice in the Prologue, in connection with the 'bear' and the
'snake' (26/7 and 49/52), possibly a reference to his confrontation with the
Athlete and Lulu in II, 1 and 2; but the Animal Trainer does not consider
him important enough to include him among the animals of his menagerie.
As for the Animal Trainer himself, we have already mentioned the fact that
he is represented by Alwa's series indicating that Berg equates circus
performance with authorship. It should be added that the voice part
constitutes a retrograde in that the Animal Trainer begins with simple
speech and then turns to *Sprechstimme*, half-singing, parlando and full singing,
and back again in reverse order. The Circus Music accompanying the two
Sprechgesang portions denotes the shallow, meretricious ambience of such an
establishment and is used in III, 1 to convey the shady and corrupt assembly
of people in a Paris gambling place:

Example 76

Ex. 76 returns for the last time in III, 2 where, with slight variations of
harmony and tempo, it is heard as Jack the Ripper, about to leave, looks for a
towel to wipe the blood off his hands, and makes a most cynical remark
about it.

   Lasty, the Circus Music of the Prologue introduces Berg's *Hauptrhythmus* or
RH (bass of Ex. 76) which in the opera becomes his chief means of
suggesting violent death and destruction. In III, 3 of *Wozzeck* an ostinato-like
rhythmic configuration stood for the soldier's guilt feelings; in *Lulu* it
symbolises the sinister fate that befalls everyone who comes into contact with
the heroine. In the opera this rhythmic pattern is first heard at the death of
the Medizinalrat (I,1); it ·assumes great structural importance in the so-
called Monoritmica (I, 2):

Example 77

and pervades the opera throughout. Its symbolic significance is particularly strongly felt in the cadential chords at the end of each act where RH articulates the harmonies that stand, respectively, for Dr Schön, Alwa and the Countess Geschwitz. As in *Wozzeck* and the finale of the Chamber Concerto, RH is subjected, like a theme, to metric changes, stretti, inversions, augmentations, diminutions and substitution of rests for notes.

All that is missing in the Prologue is the Jazz Music (I, 3) and Wedekind's *Lautenlied* (III, 1), for the rest it is to be regarded as a thematic inventory listing the material used in the opera, and in this respect it forms a counterpart to the orchestral Interlude between III, 4 and 5 of *Wozzeck* where the material is, however, passed in review *post factum*. The Prologue is also the place in which Berg indicates the kind of orchestration he will resort to in the course of the opera in order to characterize his *dramatis personae*. Thus, the Athlete has his brutal tone-clusters on the piano (16), Schigolch is conjured up by crawling figures on the low strings, bassoons and contra-bassoon (34-5), Lulu's beauty is symbolized by the strings (43-8), and the languorous Alwa by the sentimental alto saxophone and English horn (74-5). Finally, the Marquis is projected by three solo strings – cello, viola, first violin (28-31) – which in Act III are reduced to a solo violin.

The method employed in the discussion of *Lulu* is different from that which I applied in *Wozzeck*, which I examined scene by scene because the musico-dramatic unity there was the individual scene. In *Lulu*, on the other hand, it seemed to me more apt to try to study the main characters in their *total* projection first – Berg's *durchzuführende Gesamterscheinung* – and then analyse remaining matters in each scene.

We begin with Lulu. The fundamental question to be asked is whether she is the same demonic earth spirit in the opera that she is in the two plays of Wedekind. The answer is both yes and no. No, because there is, first, the humanising effect which music imparts to any character, however inhuman and heartless; the very fact that Lulu *sings* is already an important step in the direction of her humanisation. Secondly, although in the first two acts of the opera she is on the whole depicted in the terms in which the playwright visualised her, she has, however, passages to be mentioned later, in which she shows herself capable of 'profound and poignant feelings'[87] which engage the spectator's sympathy and compassion, sentiments which are bound to increase very considerably in the final act of the opera, in Scene 1 of which Lulu confronts the loathsome Marquis in a heroic struggle to preserve her independence while in Scene 2 she embraces Jack to the alluring music of her 'Entrance' in the Prologue, a moment or two before her murder.

It is significant that, with a few exceptions, Lulu is portrayed in vocal

[87] Cf. Donald Mitchell, 'The Character of Lulu: Wedekind's and Berg's Conceptions Compared', in *Music Review*, November 1954, and a reply to it by George Perle, 'The Character of Lulu: a Sequel', in *Music Review*, November 1964.

forms, while Dr Schön and Alwa are delineated in the instrumental forms of sonata and rondo. There is, first, her Canzonetta (I, 2), sung before the Medinizalrat's corpse, with which Berg seems to have wanted to portray two different things. One is Lulu as a dancer, for which she had been trained by her balletomanic husband, and as which she is to appear in the theatre before the public (I, 3). This is conveyed by the dance-like Andantino grazioso, with its leaping melody and the gently bouncing 6/8 rhythm:

Example 78

Ex. 78 is derived from an inversion of BS on G, with the twelve notes distributed over melody and harmony. The scoring underlines the intimate character of the music. The second feature which the Canzonetta portrays is Lulu's childlike innocence and complete unconcern at the death of the Medizinalrat; significantly, Ex. 78 returns immediately after the Painter's suicide (I, 2; 868-72) and the shooting of Dr Schön (II, 1; 611-12). Lulu's next solo number is her Cavatina (II, 1) which serves to show her at the pinnacle of her career; she is now the wife of the powerful newspaper tycoon. The elegance of her home and of herself as its mistress seems to be suggested by an ostinato tango rhythm in the bass. The piece is really a duet with Schön in which Lulu declares that it was not he who married her, but she who married him. To his question what difference this makes she replied, 'A great deal, I fear, except for one thing: your love for me', which, significantly, she sings to the memorable Closing Theme of Schön's Sonata (see below).

As the outstanding portrait of Lulu must be accounted her subsequent *Lied*. Sung in the 'tempo of the pulse-beat, crotchet = ca. 80, in a determined, proud tone', it is her reply to Schön's raging outbursts and represents her credo in which she lays bare the essence of her amoral personality. The exacting coloratura passages reaching up to D on the leger line convey to me something of the unreal mythological sphere in which Lulu has her origin while, at the same time, the immense flexibility and agility of her vocal lines seem to suggest the movements of a snake.

The text consists of five sentences each comprising two clauses which form a kind of dialectic:

1. Wenn sich die Menschen um meinetwillen umgebracht haben,
   so setzt das meinen Wert nicht herab.

2. Du has so gut gewusst, weswegen du mich zur Frau nahmst,
   wie ich gewusst habe, weswegen ich dich zum Mann nahm.

3. Du hattest deine besten Freunde mit mir betrogen,
   du konntest nicht gut auch noch dich selber betrügen.

4. Wenn du mir deinen Lebensabend zum Opfer bringst,
   so hast du meine ganze Jugend dafür gehabt.

5. Ich habe nie in der Welt etwas anderes scheinen wollen,
   als wofür man mich genommen hat,
   Und man hat mich nie in der Welt für etwas anderes genommen,
   als was ich bin.[88]

This dialectic is conveyed in the music by making the second phrase the
(permuted) inversion of the first:

Example 79

The opening phrase begins with BS starting on middle C,[89] the central note
of our tone system, just as Lulu is the central character of the opera. The
second pair of sentences is set to a variant of BS, the fourth pair is based on
the 'Young Beauty' or 'Dance' motive (Ex. 68*b*), and the fifth pair returns to
BS on E and ends with the 'Earth Spirit' fourths. In other words, all the leitmotives associated with Lulu are gathered together in the *Lied*, a shortened
version of which will appear in the Concertante Chorale Variations of III, 1
in which she confronts the Marquis in a great duet.

[88] 1. If people killed themselves for my sake,
        this does reduce my worth.
     2. You knew just as well why you took me for a wife,
        as I knew why I took you for a husband.
     3. You deceived your best friends with me,
        you could not very well deceive yourself, too.
     4. If you sacrifice to me the evening of your life,
        you had in exchange the whole of my youth.
     5. I never wanted to appear in the world
        other than what people took me for,
        And I never have been taken in the world for
        anything other than what I am.
     Berg, it should be added, slightly shortened Wedekind's text.
[89] This is one of the few occasions that BS appears in its original form on C. It so heard first
in The Animal Trainer's part, in the Prologue (63-4).

There is finally Lulu's Arietta near the end of II, 1 where for the first time in her career she finds herself *in extremis*: her arrest by the police for Schön's murder is imminent. In a wildly passionate manner and betraying an unspeakable terror, she implores Alwa not to hand her over to justice; she will always, she cries, only belong to him,[90] and finally throws herself on the ground before him. The music of this Arietta takes up the 'fate' rhythm RH, the Alwa series, the 'Dance' motive, and the 'Earth Spirit' fourths which from bar 637 (voice) are accompanied by diminished sevenths cascading down in triplets and comprising the twelve chromatic notes as in bars 5/6 of the Prologue (orchestra).[91] The second time, Lulu finds herself in an extreme situation from which, however, there is no escape, is in the final scene with Jack the Ripper where her *Todesschrei* brings her 'Earth Spirit' fourths telescoped into a twelve-note chord, which is an instance of Berg's predilection for establishing logical correspondences. So much for the large-scale characterisation of Lulu.

A word or two on Berg's vocal style in the part of Lulu. Its paradigm is her *Lied* with its high *tessitura*, its long-winding *coloratura* and its top C and top D. Such exacting writing is characteristic of the whole of this role. Berg demands the impossible when in III, 1 he requests the singer to sing for four bars (257-61) on the E above the stave, which renders the words unintelligible; he has, however, added an *ossia* on the E an octave lower. (Cerha, in his expansion of the dialogue Lulu-Geschwitz, wisely avoided such vertiginous heights.) It is no exaggeration to say that the Lulu part is vocally one of the most taxing in all opera, and even surpasses, because of Berg's pervasive use of the high register, the original version of Zerbinetta's part in Strauss's *Ariadne auf Naxos*.

Also, from the acting point of view, the role demands of its interpreter great flexibility and, above all, versatility, because of the many changes in Lulu's dramatic situation to each of which she has to react in a different way. True, Lulu is of child-like naivety and directness, a creature of pure instinct untroubled by intellectual thought. (That is why Wedekind's dialectics in Lulu's *Lied* are out of character.) Nevertheless, Lulu as the Painter's mistress must be different from the Lulu who murders Dr Schön, and different again as the seductress of Alwa, and must show a completely different facet of her personality when, in the final act, catastrophe begins to close in on her.

We now turn to Dr Schön. In marked contrast to Lulu, Schön has a complex psychology, the paramount feature of which is his brutal predatory intelligence. Berg takes full account of this complexity by characterising him

[90] Her phrase, 'Ich will nur Dir allein gehören. Sieh mich an, Alwa!' extending to eleven bars, returns almost literally in the Duet with the Marquis in III, 1 where, as here, she faces the threat of being arrested by the police.

[91] Note in bars 647-8 the enormous leap downwards in the voice-part, from C sharp *in alt* to middle F, a leap of a thirteenth.

in three different forms – a sonata movement, an Arioso, and an Aria in five strophes. Of these the sonata movement – many-layered, spacious and dynamic – is of course the most important form and a very apt choice for this character. As in *Wozzeck*, II, 1, it also allows for the presentation of a clash, here the clash between Schön and Lulu, which finishes with his complete surrender to her, at the end of Scene 3 of Act I.

The whole of the sonata is largely based on Schön's series (Ex. 70*a*) and the 'leaping tiger' theme derived from it (Ex. 70*b*), which are treated in various transpositions and inversions. Berg's immense skill in adapting the music to the text, while at the same time preserving a measure of independence, can be seen in the contrast between the four sections of the exposition whose change of tempo, metre and general mood is illustrated in the following table:

Introduction (530-32)	Anticipation of Closing Theme
First subject (533-53)	Schön's relationship to Lulu: he wants to
Allegro energico in 4/4	break her spell over him and realise a long-planned marriage with a socially respectable girl.
Transition (544-86)	Lulu's relationship to the Painter: she feels
Quasi Allegretto in 6/8	completely misunderstood by him and suffers from his coarse sensuality.
Second subject (587-614)	Schön's relationship to his bride: her
Gavotte and Musette in 2/4	youth and inexperience.
Closing section (615-24)	Lulu's relationship to Schön: he is the only
Lento in 4/4	man in the world to whom she belongs.
Reprise of Exposition (625-99)	Schön's firm intention to marry.

There are several special features here that call for comment. It will be seen that in the opening two bars of the first subject Schön's theme peels off the basic series on A flat as though to suggest in a symbolic way that his whole *raison d'être* lies in his sexual servility to Lulu. At the death of Schön, the peeling-off process is reversed, in that his series is now being re-absorbed into BS (II, 1; 591-602) which means that his life is ebbing away as the third and most important victim of Lulu – a striking example of Berg's use of serial technique in the service of dramatic symbolism:

Example 80a

The Transition consists of two different sections, the first for Lulu ('Earth Spirit' fourths), the second for Schön ('Dance' motive). These are then combined in both the text and the music in a two-part counterpoint, and it is here where Berg achieves the effect of 'an einander vorbei singen' (579-86), when the stage action stops completely and a feeling of unreality steals over this duet. The Second Subject is in the tempo of a Gavotte, this dance standing for the idea of bourgeois hypocrisy as well as bourgeois respectability which Schön hopes for from his marriage to a society girl. (In *Wozzeck*, we recall, the Captain's moralising sermon to the soldier unfolds to the music of a Gavotte.) The Closing group, foreshadowed by the transposed Introduction of the sonata movement, represents the 'Love' theme of the opera deriving from a melodic-harmonic unfolding of the Schön series and articulated by the 'Fate' rhythm RH:

Example 80b

This is one of the great lyrical inventions of *Lulu* conveying, as Perle puts it,[92] Lulu's 'love' for Schön and his inability to free himself from this love, and the fatal consequences it will have for him. Again, as in *Wozzeck*, II, 1, there follows an immediate but much shortened repeat of the exposition dictated by the essential identity of the topics discussed (625-69). The continuation of the sonata into development and recapitulation does not start until the finale of I, 3 (1209). About this finale there is a highly interesting letter by Berg to Webern, of 23 July 1931, which gives us an insight into his musico-dramatic thinking in *Lulu*:[93]

> The finale of Act I ... is a development and recapitulation of a sonata movement whose exposition and reprise have occurred much earlier. Now the difficulty is (one of the thousand difficulties): to work the music, which is conditioned by *musical laws*, into the Wedekind text which is determined

[92] 'The Character of Lulu', p. 315.
[93] Reproduced in Reich (ed.), *Alban Berg. Bildnis im Wort*, Zurich, 1959, p. 60.

by *dialectical laws*, make the two coincide and span over it the powerful arc
of the action.

It may well be that, apart from dramatic considerations, the idea for this
splitting up of the different sections of a sonata movement was suggested to
Berg by Schoenberg's D minor Quartet and the Chamber Symphony, op. 9,
in which sonata exposition, development and recapitulation are separated
from one another by the interpolation of other movements.

The precondition for Berg's development section (1209-88) lies of course in
what has happened in the drama after the sonata exposition – the Painter's
suicide, as a result of which Lulu is free again to realise her paramount aim of
marrying Schön, her theatre performance or rather non-performance, and
the Prince appearing in her dressing room and courting her, which she uses
as a counter in her clever game with Schön. Needless to say, in this
development the clash between Lulu and Schön is far fiercer than in the
exposition, but it would take us too far to analyse this section in detail.
Suffice it to point out that the Schön theme, in its original form as well as in
inversions and transpositions, is predominant and is supplemented,
according to the turn of the dialogue, by the 'Love' theme (1250 ff.) and other
relevant motives including the Prince's chorale (see below), and the rhythm
of the English waltz of the preceding music. The texture grows in density
until it reaches its highest complexity in bars 1275-80, in which Schön in a
paroxysm of rage raises his fist against Lulu. The love-hate relationship
between the two[94] is conveyed with subtle dramatic irony in the last three
bars of the development, with the 'Love' theme stealing in on the strings. A
notable feature of the recapitulation is the extension of the second subject
(1304 ff.) from 28 bars in the exposition and 16 bars in the first reprise, to 52
bars. This is the 'Letter Duet' in which Schön suffers his utmost humiliation
in that he has to write, at Lulu's dictation, a letter to his bride saying that he
has to renounce her because he has not the strength to tear himself away
from the woman who has dominated him for the last three years. The length
to which Berg went to make the spectator *aurally* aware of Schön's writing of
the letter is seen in the fact that each phrase dictated to him by Lulu is
imitated in canon by an obbligato instrument, which is a striking example of
what Berg said in connection with *Wozzeck*, namely, that 'the opera
composer must accomplish the task of an ideal producer'. When Schön
interrupts his writing to confirm what Lulu has just dictated to him – that he
cannot reconcile with his conscience to chain his bride 'to my terrible fate',
Berg sets his phrase, 'Du hast ja recht!' pointedly to the elemental 'Earth
Spirit' fourths (1320-1). Schön's final phrase, 'Now comes the execution' is

---

[94] Schön, completely exhausted and sinking into a chair, says, 'Oh, oh, Du tust mir weh' –
'oh! oh! you hurt me!' to which Lulu replies, 'Mir tut dieser Augenblick wohl – ich kann nicht
sagen, wie!' – 'I am enjoying this moment – I cannot say how!'.

sung to the 'Love' theme, which confirms the assumption that it also serves to express the fatal consequences of his love for Lulu. The act ends on the repeated A major triad in the second inversion (on E), which is the telescoped version of the first three notes of the Schön series, and is articulated by the 'fate' rhythm; the chord rests on the bass pedal F. The same harmonic-rhythmic configuration opens the first scene of the second act, which contributes considerably to the musical characterisation of Schön as Lulu's husband in two important solo numbers.

The first is a monologue (Lento) in arioso style and corresponds to Lulu's Arietta after his death, both of which express a highly agitated state of mind. In this monologue (marked 'Ballade' in one of Berg's sketches)[94a] Schön, seized by persecution mania and with revolver in hand, pulls the curtains apart to see whether he is not being overheard by someone or other. The voice part opens with the inversion of Schön's series (Ex. 81a) – possibly to suggest his paranoia – while the orchestra is dominated by an ostinato formed of the last seven notes of his series in the original, which tellingly underlines his inner turmoil. The same passage returns in a slightly altered version in the last scene of the opera just before Jack the Ripper leaves.

Example 81a

Example 81b

At the point at which Schön draws the revolver which will kill him, RH cuts brutally in on piano, harp, percussion, and upper woodwind.

Schön's second solo piece is his great Aria in five strophes between the fourth and fifth of which is inserted Lulu's *Lied*. All five strophes are in

[94a] Douglas Jarmann, 'Lulu: The Sketches', Newsletter, no. 6, *International Alban Berg Society*, New York, 1978, p. 7.

Tempo furioso, with the raging Schön hurling imprecations at Lulu and finally trying to force her to shoot herself with his revolver. Each successive strophe is longer than the preceding one – 14 bars, 20 bars, 21 bars – with the fourth strophe extending to 48 bars while the fifth, which is cut short by Lulu's five shots, returns to the length of the first strophe.[95] Schön's jealous fury is aroused by discovering in the room his real and assumed rivals in his love for Lulu – Alwa, the Manservant, the Athlete and Countess Geschwitz – which is accurately reflected in the music, in which Schön's series and his 'leaping tiger' theme represent the basic material to which are added the leitmotives of the other characters. It is interesting to note that Alwa is uppermost in Schön's mind as his rival, for his son's series (Ex. 71*a*) appears at least three times in the Aria, the first time when Schön contemplates the murder of Alwa (second strophe), the second time when he refers to the Manservant who, he thinks, cuckolds him (third strophe), and the third time when, in reply to Lulu's suggestion for a divorce, he says, 'Das wäre noch übrig! Damit morgen ein Nächster seinen Zeitvertreib finde' – 'That would be splendid! So that tomorrow the next one can find his amusement' (fourth strophe), Alwa's series here indicating that he will be indeed 'the next' to enjoy Lulu's favours.

The moral disintegration of Schön, begun in the 'Letter Duet' of I, 3 and continued to an increasing degree in his Arioso of II, 1 is shown to be complete in his Aria. He is now no more than a hollow shell. Though he adopts the blustering, threatening manner of the *Gewaltsmensch* of before, in reality he is seen to be entirely powerless to impose his will on Lulu any more. In terms of the drama, he has lost his *raison d'être* and can be dispensed with. With Lulu's five shots begins the Tumultuoso which in bars 568-76 combines the Schön series with the Alwa series (orchestra), suggesting that the son will be the successor of his father in the relationship with Lulu, who at this point confesses that Schön was the only one whom she loved. In bar 587 ff. we hear the Schön series in unison on the combined strings which shortly afterwards (591-4) is, as mentioned before, being absorbed or swallowed up into the basic series, (Ex. 80*a*), which triumphantly rises, again in a unison, on the combined woodwind and harp (603-4):

Example 82

---

[95] Did Berg intend a relation between the number of strophes and the number of shots?

Schön's last words, 'Der Teufel', are uttered at the sight of the Countess who has come out of her hiding, to her characteristic sequence of fifths on the muted strings. This marks the beginning of a Grave section which introduces several reminiscences such as the opening of Lulu's Canzonetta and her tripping figure (I, 1). After her Arietta (already discussed), the bell rings to announce the arrival of the police and the curtain descends on the Orchestral Interlude. It should be added that Berg's musical equivalent for the ringing of the door bell is the fourth A flat –D flat on the vibraphone, which is treated like a leitmotive but always remains tied to the identical pitch and timbre.

We now turn to the characterisation of Alwa. As was said before, Berg used the contrast between major and minor to indicate the basic difference between the two, as is seen from their respective series whose first three notes are the determinants of these modes. On the other hand, the father-son relationship is indicated in the identical pitch content of the 'white-key' and all but 'black key' hexachords in the inversion of Schön's series and the prime of Alwa's series on A and E respectively:

Example 83

This affinity is used by Berg to relate Schön's Arioso, 'Das ist mein Lebensabend!' to its corresponding piece, Lulu's Arietta near the end of this scene in which she addresses the murdered man's son.

The Alwa of the opera is not exactly the same character as the Alwa of the two plays. This is partly due to certain omissions as well as additions in Berg's libretto, of which I cite one striking example. When in I, 3 Lulu appears from behind a screen in a ballet costume, Berg's stage direction demands that 'Alwa, almost painfully blinded by her sight, presses his hand against his heart'; in Wedekind's corresponding scene this is completely missing. But it is, largely, in the music that Berg transforms the decadent and cynical *fin-de-siècle* character of Wedekind's into a romantic *Schwärmer* and idealist, with whom the composer identified to such an extent that one is tempted to assume that he portrayed Alwa in the image of himself as a young man. No doubt Berg must have noticed the phonetic affinity between 'Alwa' and 'Alban'. (The assumption that the Wedekind plays possessed a wider autobiographical significance for the composer is supported by the fact that, like Countess Geschwitz,[95a] his sister Smaragda was a lesbian. Moreover, there was a painter in Vienna, Richard Gerstl, who belonged to the Schoenberg circle and gave the composer a few painting lessons. Gerstl later eloped with Schoenberg's first wife, Mathilda, and afterwards committed suicide in the same horrifying manner as the Painter (Schwartz) in *Erdgeist*).

To return to Alwa. An elegiac as well as ecstatic lyricism is the keynote in Alwa's characterisation, a feature which dominates his Rondo and Hymn which represent the two great romantic love scenes of the opera. Berg himself said about the Rondo that it projects Lulu 'as the artist sees her, and as she must be seen so that one can understand that – despite all the frightful things that come about because of her – she is so beloved'.[96]

Alwa's lyricism, which also affects Lulu and thus makes her different from Wedekind's heroine, is manifest in sustained legato phrases of remarkable amplitude, flexibility and pliancy:

Example 84

Ei-ne See - le, die sich im Jen-seits den Schlaf aus den Au-gen reibt.

and is matched by Berg's 'romantic' scoring in which, next to the expressive strings, clarinets, saxophone, horns, celesta, and harp are prominent.

Like the Schön sonata, the Alwa rondo is distributed over two long scenes (II, 1 and 2), but its dialogue has a markedly less dialectic character than the other piece. In fact it centres largely on Alwa, with Lulu participating in it far less than she does in her scenes with Schön. Though the rondo is formally a complex piece it is, in tune with the dialogue which expresses feelings rather than thoughts, simpler of texture and less intricate in the serial treatment than the more 'intellectual' Schön sonata. It consists of three large sections:[97] exposition, middle part and recapitulation the detailed structure of which is as follows:

[95a] In a letter to Helene of 9 March 1934, Berg says that he has little love for Geschwitz but that he must respect her and that this character causes him more difficulties than all other satellites of Lulu put together. In the event he wrote some of the finest music in the opera for this character, in Act III, 2.

[96] Reich, *The Life and Work of Alban Berg*, p. 168.

[97] It is advisable to study the rondo first in its continuous version in the Symphonic Pieces and then turn to the operatic version, with its scenic interruptions.

Rondo

II,1 (First Part)
Ritornello (243-9)
[Chorale (250-61)]
Transition (262-7)
Second Theme (268-74; Tumultuoso; 275-80)
Ritornello (variation 281-6)
[Chorale (287-97)]
Ritornello (variation: 298-305)
Transition (306-9)
[Tumultuoso (310-17)]
Closing Theme (318-28)
Codetta (329-36)

II, 2 (Middle Part)

Lulu's 'Entrance' Music (1000-4)
Second Theme (variation: 1004-9)
'Entrance Music (1010-15)
Contrasting Section (1016-37)
Episode 1 ('Picture' Music: 1016-29)
Episode 2 ('Entrance' Music: 1030-37)
Closing Theme (variation: 1038-47)
Codetta (1048-58)

II, 2 (Recapitulation)

Ritornello, Part 1 Canon (1059-65)
Transition (1065-8)
Ritornello, Part 2 (1069-74)
Closing Theme (1075-79)
Coda ('Entrance' Music: 1080-7)

Musette (1087-96)
Hymn (1097-1150)

The rondo is, inevitably, dominated by the Alwa series in various transpositions, into which is also worked the 'Picture' motive, Lulu's 'Dance' figure and her 'Entrance' Music. Although the space of a year lies between the two scenes of Act II during which Lulu was in prison, nothing has changed in Alwa's emotional relationship to her so that the continuation of the rondo – the musical symbol of this relationship – into the second scene, after her return, is fully motivated psychologically. While the exposition and middle part of the rondo are, on the whole, marked by delicacy and tenderness, the recapitulation is characterised by Alwa's growing passion, by which Lulu also is seized. Significantly, this last section is flanked by her 'Entrance' music (Ex. 67*b*) and one of her most memorable phrases in the whole opera is formed of it:

Example 85

An acute discrepancy is, however, felt between the ecstatic expression of this phrase and Berg's stage-direction for Lulu to sing it 'im muntersten Ton' (in the most cheerful tone); Wedekind here has merely 'hell' (brightly).

The transition to the Hymn is formed by a reminiscence of the Musette from the exposition of the Schön sonata, evidently because of the essential identity of meaning in the two texts. In the Hymn Lulu achieves the last triumph of her career – she persuades Alwa to flee with her 'across the frontier'. It shows Alwa at the height of his erotic ecstacy – in fact it is the 'dithyramb' of which he speaks shortly before and in which he extols the sensual beauties of her body. It opens in a flowing 12/8 metre richly scored for combined strings, piano and harp and with a voice part that seems the quintessence of Berg's lyricism.

George Perle was the first to point[97a] to Berg's significant allusion in the text of the Hymn to the Lyric Suite, an allusion that underlines the erotic implications of the earlier work. I print below Wedekind's text and Berg's modification of it:

Wedekind

Durch dieses Kleid empfinde ich deinen Wuchs wie eine Symphonie.
Diese schmalen Knöchel, dieses Cantabile; dieses entzückende Anschwellen;
Und diese Knie, dieses Capriccio; und das gewaltige Andante der Wollust.

Berg

Durch dieses Kleid empfinde ich deinen Wuchs wie Musik.
Diese Knöchel: ein Grazioso; dieses reizende Anschwellen: ein Cantabile; diese Knie: ein Misterioso;
Und das gewaltige Andante der Wollust.

Wedekind

Through this dress I feel your body as a symphony
These slender ankles: the Cantabile;
This charming swelling;
And these knees: the Capriccio;
And the powerful Andante of voluptuousness.

[97a] 'Die Personen in Bergs *Lulu*', *Archiv fur Musikwissenschaft*, November 1975.

Berg

Through this dress I feel your body as music.
These ankles: a Grazioso;
This enticing swelling: a Cantabile;
These knees: a Misterioso;
And the powerful Andante of voluptuousness.

Berg's reference to the first four movements of the Lyric Suite in the Hymn is not explicit but suggestive enough of their respective characters. This is a verbal parallel to the quotation of the opening bar of *Wozzeck* in Act I, 3 of *Lulu*.

The material used in the Hymn is Alwa's series, BS and Lulu's 'Dance' motive. A noteworthy feature of the vocal writing in both the rondo and Hymn are the high notes for soprano and tenor, Lulu reaching up to D above the stave and Alwa to top C, which intensifies of course the feeling of ecstasy. (Part of the Hymn returns in the final scene of the opera when Alwa ecstatically contemplates Lulu's picture, which has been brought to the London attic by Countess Geschwitz.) Near the end Lulu asks Alwa casually: 'Is this still the couch on which your father bled to death?', the question being in rhythmic speech so as to give added point to it; it corresponds to Lulu's statement in the exposition of the Rondo (II, 1; 337): 'I poisoned your mother.' The scene concludes on the Alwa chord in RH thus indicating that, like his father, he too has now become Lulu's victim, and will meet his death through her.

And now for a discussion of the individual scenes with their various secondary characters: the Painter, Schigolch, the Countess Geschwitz and such minor figures as the Prince, the Athlete, the Schoolboy and the Marquis.

Act I, Scene 1. A spacious but poorly furnished studio. On an easel stands Lulu's unfinished picture as Pierrot. Lulu, Painter, Schön, Alwa and, later, the Medizinalrat.

Up to the departure of Schön and Alwa the dialogue is treated in a light, conversational manner, and introduces BS on C (85-90) followed by its inversion (90-91). In bar 92, in which Alwa joins his father and the Painter, the three solo celli intone two major (Schön) and two minor chords (Alwa) while the treble represents the crab of the 'Painter' or 'Picture' motive – a *locus classicus* of Berg's concentrated musical characterisation. Lulu's request to Schön to remember her to his bride is set to her 'Dance' figure (Ex. 68*b*), suggesting that in her mind she is comparing her beauty with that of a cipher. Schön's deliberate ignoring of her request and his turning to the Painter with a criticism of the painting, brings his 'leaping tiger' theme in the bass. After Schön and his son have left begins the Introduction to the first set-piece – a two-part canon. The Introduction, with its three sections each beginning, in following the text, with the 'Picture' theme, serves to illustrate the growing fascination exerted on the Painter by Lulu conveyed in the feverish succession of tiny, mosaic-like figures in the voice part. Lulu's throwing of the shepherd's staff (a requisite for her sitting) into the Painter's face is the cue for the canon between the two based on her 'Dance' motive. He chases after her and, as this chase becomes more and more hectic, the distance between the canonical voices becomes shorter[98] until they end in unison. The coda, in which the Painter covers Lulu's hands with passionate kisses and demands that she kiss him, is a varied recapitulation of the Introduction. Note, incidentally, the subtle intrusion of RH (186-8), the first appearance of which occurred, in the actual opera, as early as bar 91, after Alwa's entry. The following scene with the Medizinalrat is treated in unpitched rhythmic speech as well as *Sprechgesang* and is dominated by this character's motive of thirds and RH. After Lulu's *Canzonetta* comes a Recitative in which the Painter discovers that the Medizinalrat, Lulu's first 'Schlachtopfer', is dead. (The same music accompanies the entry of the Medizinalrat's double, the silent Professor, in the London attic of III, 2.) Lulu's callous remark in front of her husband's corpse, 'Jetzt bin ich reich ...', the Painter finds 'grauenerregend', and in a great Duet, he subjects her to a catechism – whether she believes in truth and in a Creator, whether she has a soul, whether she has ever loved, and so on. To all this her stereotyped answer, completely in tune with her character, is, 'I don't know'. Her musical phrases increase in length at each repetition of the words until in bars 318-20 they culminate in a drawn-out coloratura. Left alone, the Painter addresses the body of the Medizinalrat in an Arioso in which his pusillanimity, his lack of moral courage and fear of overwhelming happiness are extremely well brought out. Introduced by the 'Fate' rhythm, the Arioso has for its material one of the Painter's motives, Lulu's 'Dance' figure and BS in the prime, inversion and permutation. Lulu's return from the other room in street dress is accompanied by a tripping figure which first occurred in her Canzonetta at the words, 'Er (Medizinalrat) sieht mir auf die Füsse ...', and now forms the transition to the interlude to the next scene. Like some interludes in *Wozzeck*, this one combines development and recapitulation of the previous scena. Its character is scherzo-like, with a Trio in which the preceding two-part canon of the voices is transformed into a three-part canon for the orchestra. Each of its three sections is scored for a different combination of instruments: brass, vibraphone, piano and harp – strings – upper woodwind. The metre of the Trio is 3/8 but Berg phrases the canonical voices throughout in a 7/8 rhythm, and, as in *Wozzeck*, the number seven here is of importance.

[98] We recall a similar 'chase' in Variation 5 of the opening movement in the Chamber Concerto.

Act I, Scene 2. A very elegant room in the house of the Painter. Lulu's portrait hangs above the chimney. Lulu, Painter and, later, Schön.

Schön has married off Lulu to the Painter in order to realise at last his intention of a union with an aristocratic girl (Fräulein von Zarnikov in Wedekind). The scene opens with a dialogue between Lulu and the Painter, out of which emerges a Duettino in two strophes, with the 'Earth Spirit' fourths much in prominence. In the first strophe, the Painter is shown to have lost all sense of his own identity through his servile love for Lulu – 'Ich habe nichts mehr, seit ich Dich habe. Ich bin mir vollständing abhanden gekommen' – 'I have nothing more since I have you. I have completely lost my identity.' The ringing of the bell, on the fourth A flat-D flat, announces Schigolch, whom Lulu is secretly expecting. This leads to the second strophe of the Duettino, largely a repeat of the first, but contains Lulu's visionary exclamation, 'Du! – Du!', on the high F sharp-F which is to be taken as referring to Schigolch, once her lover and now her protector and father-figure. He enters to an inversion of his chromatic motive (Ex. 74*b*), inversion being Berg's symbol for disappointment, frustration and failure; here the inversion indicates Schigolch's disenchantment with the Painter whom he had imagined looking quite differently: 'mehr Nimbus!' The music for this scena is entitled Chamber Music I, and is scored for a woodwind nonet[99] and pizzicati strings. Schigolch, a frail old man, suffers from asthma and Berg, afflicted with the same illness, does not miss the opportunity to illustrate Schigolch's difficult breathing in a realistic manner (486-8, 491-3 *et passim*). Following the text, the interchanges between the *Lumpenphilosoph* and Lulu show ternary build, preceded by a Lento introduction in which he demands money of her – the principal purpose of his visit. All three sections are based on Schigolch's leitmotive in variants. In section A_1 he remarks on the astounding progress she has made in her 'career', in section B he asks Lulu, whom he has not seen for a long time, about her present mode of life, while in section A_2 he expresses his fatherly affection for 'meine kleine Lulu'. She replies that she has not been called by that name since time immemorial, nor does she dance any more: she now is only a 'Tier' ('Earth Spirit' fourths) with which she anticipates what she later says to Schön about her marriage to the Painter. The bell rings to announce Schön's arrival, whereupon Schigolch makes his 'hasty' but 'circumstantial' departure.[100] The subsequent scene between Schön and Lulu, geared to a sonata exposition, has already been discussed.

The Finale of I, 2 comprises Schön's conversation with the Painter in the

[99] Piccolo, flute, oboe, cor anglais, clarinet, bass clarinet, alto saxophone, bassoon and double bassoon.
[100] Schön mistakes Schigolch, whom he encounters on his entrance, for Lulu's father.

course of which he reveals Lulu's shady past and his own role in it, the Painter's moral collapse, his suicide and the indifferent reaction to it of Schön, Lulu and Alwa. The scena between Schön and the Painter is musically cast in the form of a Monoritmica based on RH (Ex. 77) which, as intimated, is treated like a theme and subjected to the contrapuntal devices of augmentation, diminution and canon, the last being particularly in evidence at the Painter's suicide (748-86) – a passage scored for percussion only and reminiscent of the bruitism in the *Praeludium* of the Three Orchestral Pieces, op. 6. The Monoritmica falls into two long sections. The first extending from the Painter's entry (666) (codetta of the Schön sonata) to his suicide and the discovery of his corpse (842), represents a composed accelerando which unfolds in eighteen different metronomically fixed tempi, from very slow to very fast, and expresses the rapidly mounting tension of the stage action. The second half of the Monoritmica is a composed ritardando (843-957), such as we shall find again in the final scene of the opera, and passes, in contrast to the first half, *gradually* through all intervening tempo changes until it reaches the Grave of the opening Monoritmica. This is a supreme example of Berg's use of mere tempo changes in the service of the dramatic action. The material employed in this portion of I, 2 includes BS, Schön's series and his theme, the 'Painter' or 'picture' motive and the 'Earth Spirit' fourths. Of the many interesting details of this music I metion only two. One is the cyclical permutation of Alwa's series in bars 927-31 (4 5 6 7 8 9 10 11 12 1 2 3), the text referring to his envious words about the Painter, 'Er hatte, was sich ein Mensch nur erträumen kann'. The second detail is found in bars 897-9 in which Alwa says, 'als meine Mutter starb', set to the first half of Lulu's 'Dance' motive, the explanation of her death being provided in II, 1, where we learn from Lulu's own lips that it was she who poisoned Alwa's mother. The curtain descends on the transition to the next scene, which is a symphonic elaboration of the memorable Closing Theme of Schön's sonata into which is worked his series in the prime and inversion, and the Musette. This transition is virtually identical with the Grave section in the last movement of the Symphonic Pieces.

Act I, Scene 3. Dressing room in a theatre. On the back wall a poster which is a copy of Lulu's portrait from the previous scene. Alwa, Lulu, the Prince and, later, Schön.

Berg's resort to jazz music in this scene is on all fours with his use of it in *Der Wein*. It is to characterise a shallow, meretricious atmosphere – here the atmosphere of a theatre dressing-room. A jazz band off stage[101] plays first a

---

[101] It consists of two clarinets, an alto and tenor saxophone, two jazz trumpets, a sousaphone, three violins, a double bass, banjo, piano and percussion. There is of course a stylistic discrepancy caused by Berg's resort to jazz in a drama that takes place some twenty to thirty

Rag-time (992), then an English Waltz (1040*a*) and finally the Trio of the Rag-time (1155) which is suddenly cut off by Alwa's closing of the door, similar to Marie's shutting the window against the military march in *Wozzeck* (I,3). The final scene of Act I falls, roughly, into two halves, the first comprising a series of small formal units (melodrama and recitatives) to reflect the swiftly changing situations on the stage, while the second is devoted to Lulu and Schön (sonata development and recapitulation). Perhaps the most inspired portion of the first half is the recitative after Lulu appears from behind the screen dressed in her dance costume. Alwa is 'almost painfully blinded by her looks and presses his hand against his heart', at which point we hear for the first time his lyrical rondo theme in a melodic-harmonic configuration (1021 ff.). Another exquisite passage is Alwa's recitative after Lulu has left for the stage. He muses on her, saying that 'an interesting opera could be written about her', at which point Berg quotes the opening of *Wozzeck* as an indication of his identification with his character. Another self-quotation from *Wozzeck* occurs in the scene of Lulu with Alwa in II, 1: when he says to her, 'Ich hab' auch nur Fleisch und Blut' ('I'm only flesh and blood'), his vocal phrase is identical with Wozzeck's, sung to the same words. Alwa then outlines the scenario, with the first scene centring on the Medizinalrat (thirds in RH), the second on the Painter ('Picture' leitmotive) and the third on ... He dues not utter the name but the music is quite explicit, with Schön's series in the voice part and the 'Love' theme in the orchestra.

Enter the Prince who, though an episodic figure, has his own theme, a ten-bar *Chorale*[102] arrived at by successive statements of the Alwa, the Basic, and the Schön series accompanied by the 'Picture' and other harmonies. This synthetic chorale has 36 chords grouped in regularly increasing and decreasing number of notes (1, 2, 3, 4, 5, 6, 5, 4, 3, 2, 1):

Example 86

---

years before jazz music conquered Europe. But this is of little import and has its counterpart in *Der Rosenkavalier*, in which Strauss introduces waltzes *à la* Johann Stauss into an eighteenth-century comedy of manners. But this discrepancy should certainly not be made the pretext for moving the time of action forward to the mid-nineteenth century (as in Erté's production of the Straussian opera at Glyndebourne in 1980) or to the 1930s (as in Chéreau's production of *Lulu* in Paris in 1979).

[102] Cf. the Chorale in *Wozzeck*, II, 4, which is also attached to episodic characters. There are also other formal parallels between this scene in the earlier opera and I, 3 of *Lulu*. See Klaus Schweitzer, *Die Sonatensatzform im Schaffen Alban Bergs*, Stuttgart, 1970, pp. 222 ff.

If we range the final chords of these eleven groups together, we obtain a chord progression whose top notes form an eleven-note series which, with addition of the missing note C at the end or beginning, represents the Marquis in III, 1:

Example 87

That Berg uses the Prince's chorale as the matrix for the Marquis series is explained by the fact that the roles of the Prince, the Manservant (also accompanied by the chorale) and the Marquis are to be impersonated by the same singer. In the subsequent variation the chorale is played by the bass tuba (predominantly) and counterpointed by a concertante cello solo 'delicate and capricious' to characterise the Prince (just as a viola solo and violin solo, respectively, are attached to the Manservant in II, 1 and the Marquis in III, 1). It should be noted that the cello solo begins with a rhythmic variant of the chorale melody and is punctuated by the first seven notes of the Schön series (first horn 1127-9). The chorale itself proceeds as *cantus firmus* on bass tuba – harp – horns.

Since the considerably more important Concertante Chorale Variations of III, 1 in which the crucial confrontation of Lulu with the Marquis takes place, proceeds in a similar manner, they might be as well discussed here. The Marquis series (Ex. 87) appears in the form of a chorale which provides the theme for twelve variations. In some variations the theme lies in the bass (1, 5, 7, 8, 9), in others it moves to the treble as the top-line of chord progressions (2, 3, 4, 6, 11, 12), and is stated either in the original pitch class or is transposed to other degrees of the chromatic scale. The chain of variations is interrupted after Var. 2 when two episodes are introduced – the *Lied des Mädchenhändlers* and the *Lied der Lulu* (a much abbreviated reprise of the *Lied* of II, 1). Var. 7 is a four-part canon or *stretto* in which the entries of the last three canonical voices are concealed in the middle parts. It is, perhaps, significant that in Vars. 9 and 10, in which Lulu declares with waxing agitation (*Tempo appassionato!*) that 'I cannot sell the only thing that has ever been my own', the chorale is intoned by the trombone. Var. 12 (*Stretto*) is the shortest piece – a mere three bars which recalls similarly brief variations in the Passacaglia and Marie's 'Bible' scene of *Wozzeck*; it forms the transition to the second Ensemble of III, 1.

We return to I, 3. The commotion caused by Lulu's unexpected return from the stage culminates in a sextet[103] which is based on the theme of the Rag-time Trio. It is a piece belonging to the sphere of comic opera (like the

---

[103] Alwa, Schön, Lulu, Prince, Theatre Director and Wardrobe Mistress.

ensembles in II, 1 and III, 1) in which each of the six characters sings a different text in order to create the utmost confusion. From the second half of bar 1190 the music runs backwards, which is comparable on a larger scale to the orchestral Interlude between II, 1 and 2, and is one of the few instances in this opera of an extended retrograde. A possible explanation for the rare use in *Lulu* of this device may be the fact that while the inversions of a theme still preserve its intrinsic identity, this is totally lost in its crab form.

Act II, Scene 1. A resplendent room in Schön's home. Lulu's portrait stands on an easel. Countess, Lulu, Schön and, later, Schigolch, the Athlete, the Schoolboy and Alwa.

Lulu has married Schön and thus reached the zenith of her career, conveyed outwardly by the lavish furniture in German Renaissance style of the room. II, 1 opens with the same Schön chords in RH which concluded the last scene of Act I and begins (as I, 1) in light, conversational exchanges between the Countess, Schön and Lulu. The Countess's pentatonic leitmotive, sometimes thickened out by fifths, is the first of the four new ideas introduced into this scene, the remaining three being the Athlete's tone cluster, his series and the Schoolboy's series. The scena between these two and Schigolch is pure situation comedy (note, for instance, the bizarre voice part of the Athlete 100-10), which first unfolds in a Trio and with the entry of Lulu turns into an intermittent Quartet. There follows an amusing canon for the three men, which is a kind of lullaby in the course of which Schigolch says that he is *not* Lulu's father as the Athlete imagined him to be, to which Lulu replies 'Yes surely, I am a freak of nature', a pun on the German 'Wunderkind'. Equally comic is Lulu's coloratura about the Athlete's 'long ears', clinched by Schigolch's imitation of a donkey's braying (223). The Manservant's announcement of Alwa's arrival disperses the three male characters, each seeking a different hiding place.[104] In one of Berg's sketches this escape scene is called 'Burleske'.

The ensuing Rondo, to the sound of which the first love scene of the opera unfolds, is interrupted by the Manservant laying the table for Lulu and Alwa. He is also under her spell, as suggested by the repeat of the Chorale from I, 3, now set against a recitative for a viola solo (250-61). The second though very brief, interruption of the love scene is caused by Schön's appearance on the gallery: he sees his own son with Lulu when, significantly, Alwa's minor chord shades into his father's major chord (trombones):

---

[104] The Schoolboy concealing himself under the table recalls Cherubino's similar action is Susanna's room before the arrival of the Count in *Figaro*. There is, moreover, an affinity between the two youths in that both show the awakening of erotic desire, and both have written a poem addressed to the object of their desire.

Example 88

(This change of tonal 'sex' is strongly reminiscent of the motto in Mahler's Sixth Symphony. In both cases an harmonic device is made to bear an extra-musical, poetic connotation.) There are two more interruptions, the last being a Subito tumultuoso, in the course of which Schön descends from the gallery and brings Alwa down to earth from his erotic trance by addressing him in the same words that Alwa used to him after the Painter's suicide in I, 2. 'In Paris ist die Revolution ausgebrochen ...' (350-5). After Alwa's departure follows Schön's Aria, Lulu's *Lied*, the shooting of Schön, Lulu's Arietta and her arrest.

The curtain descends on the opening of the orchestral Interlude which links the two scenes of Act II. Berg intended this piece to accompany a silent film which was to illustrate the events between Lulu's arrest and her liberation by Countess Geschwitz from the prison hospital, such as her detention, her trial with its three witnesses (Alwa, the Countess and the Schoolboy), her imprisonment, her cholera infection and so on. For its time, the resort to a film in an opera was unquestionably a novel and interesting experiment. Milhaud employed a film in his opera, *Christophe Colomb* (Berlin, 1930) and in the same year Schoenberg completed his *Begleitungsmusik zu einer Lichtspielszene, op. 34.*[105] But opinions nowadays about the usefulness of the *Lulu* film are much divided. Apart from the fact that it introduces an alien autonomous medium that blends with the opera rather uncomfortably, it is doubtful whether the large majority of the audience really grasps the drift of the incidents it sees on the screen.[106] Moreover, the orchestral Interlude (Ostinato) lasting three minutes is too short to allow all and every incident Berg envisaged to be shown, as was proved at the Zurich première of the incomplete version in 1937. Elsewhere the film was replaced by images projecting only the main stages of what happens to Lulu between the time of her arrest and her liberation. Since the 1960s most opera houses have

[105] Karl Neumann has drawn attention to the fact that in a Munich production in 1928 of Wedekind's two plays, the producer, Otto Falkenberg, used film sequences to bridge the numerous scene changes. It is likely that Berg was influenced by this procedure too. See Karl Neumann, 'Wedekind's and Berg's "Lulu" ', *Music Review*, February-May 1974, p. 55.

[106] At the first-night of the complete *Lulu* at Covent Garden I asked members of the audience whether they had been able to follow the film incidents and relate them to the action of the opera. Of a dozen people, only two answered in the affirmative, three said they were none too sure, and seven confessed to have been much confused.

dispensed with a visual representation altogether – Vienna, Hamburg, the Welsh National Opera at Cardiff, Paris and La Scala, Milan in 1979; Covent Garden though had the film in 1981. Producers in general rightly feel that it is better to leave it all to the spectator's imagination. I, for one, prefer this as it allows me to listen, entirely undistracted, to the splendid music of the Interlude which with its scurrying fleeting passages and its palindrome constitutes the orchestral counterpart to the unique *Allegro misterioso* of Berg's Lyric Suite.

Below I reproduce Berg's film 'script'[106a]. From it, it will be seen that Berg freely indulges his obsessional preoccupation with symmetries and correspondencies (congruences) also pictorially; while the extremely detailed script forcibly suggests that it was his self-confessed inclination to pedantry (p. 20, n. 9) that persuaded him to show *visually* what the spectator can be told in the programme and what, besides, he partly gathers from the account Lulu later gives Alwa in II, 2.

The Ostinato, so called because of an almost constant reiteration of

---

[106a] 'During the Transition music a silent film is to indicate the course of Lulu's fortunes in the next year. The film sequence – in accordance with the symmetrical course of the music – should also be quasi-symmetrical (i.e. it should run forwards and backwards). To this end the events that correspond, together with their accompanying phenomena (music) should be fitted together as closely as possible. This yields the following sequence of scenes (following the direction of the arrows)':

◀ **Arrest**

The three people con-
  cerned in the arrest
Lulu in chains

On the way to her final liberation ◀

The three people concerned
  in the liberation
Lulu at liberty (disguised as
  the Countess Geschwitz)

Detention pending trial

Nervous expectancy
Dwindling hopes

Isolation ward

Nervous expectancy
Rising hopes

Trial

Her guilt
Judge and jury
The three witnesses
The judgment
Her transfer in the police
  van to the prison

Medical council

The illness
Doctor and students
The three helpers in the
  liberation
Her transfer in the ambulance
  from the prison

Prison

The prison door shuts
Initial resignation
Lulu's portrait: as a
  shadow on the prison wall

Prison

The prison door opens
Awakening of courage
Lulu's portrait: as a reflec-
  tion in a shovel

▶ One year's imprisonment ▶

scurrying semi-quaver figures, consists of two fairly equal halves (652-87 and 687-721), the first illustrating Lulu's incarceration and the second her liberation. As in the Allegro misterioso of the Lyric Suite which is also dominated by fugitive, fleeting semi-quaver figures, the second half of the Ostinato is a palindrome of the first half. The material used consists of virtually all the series and leit-motives of the opera,[107] some presented in stretto and inversion. The climax is reached in bars 677-81, with the 'Earth Spirit' fourths and the 'Dance' motive (in stretto) thundered out by the combined brass, after which the music begins to slow down and comes to a halt on a pause in the middle of bar 687. From this point onwards it runs backwards, but its character is now changed by the darkening of the orchestral timbre (muted brass and strings), to suggest the reversal in Lulu's fortunes. The Ostinato divides the opera into two exactly symmetrical halves.

In addition to the congruent elements of the main events, such as

trial	medical council
arrest	liberation

smaller correspondences of detail should also be shown, such as

revolver	stethoscope
bullets	phials
Law	Medicine
paragraph sign	cholera bacilli
chains	bandages
prison clothes	hospital smock
prison corridor	hospital corridor

etc.

Also personal correspondences, such as

judge and jury	doctor and students
police	nurses

[107] The Alwa series, Schön's major chord, BS, the 'earth Spirit' fourths, Lulu's 'Dance' figure the series of the Countess, the Schoolboy and the Athlete, the 'Picture' motive, and RH. The presence of the 'Picture' motive is explained by the fact that in the film Lulu's image is first seen as a shadow on the wall of her prison cell and later reflected in a shovel.
There exists a more detailed scenario than the one published which Berg added, on a separate sheet, to his short score. Its notable feature is that it contains bar numbers indicating the correspondence between music and film. This scenario was evidently of a later date than the published one, and was prepared before the composition of the film music but left uncorrected by Berg. This may have been the reason for the editorial decision not to print this version in the published full and vocal scores. Cf. George Perle, 'Das Filmzwischenspiel in der Oper *Lulu*', *Österreichische Musikzeitung*, **December 1981**, pp. 631-38.

Act II, Scene 2. The same as Scene 1, a year later. Alwa, Geschwitz, Athlete, Schoolboy,
and, later, Schigolch and Lulu.

Already the visual aspect of this scene shows the turn in Lulu's fortunes. The
curtains are drawn, dust covers the furniture, and Lulu's Pierrot portrait is
placed with its front against the chimney. In short, the room has not been
lived in for a long time and creates the impression of the utmost neglect.
According to the characters on the stage, the scene falls into five sections.
The first centres on Alwa, the Countess and the Athlete dressed as a
Manservant. They are awaiting the return of Schigolch to take the Countess,
in execution of her daring liberation plan, to Lulu's isolation ward in the
prison hospital.

A musical relationship between these three characters is established by the
fact that the 'white-note' and 'black-note' tone clusters of the Athlete are
identical in pitch content with the last two segments of the Countess's leitmotive, while the first hexachord of Alwa's series on E (776-8) is contained in
the Athlete's 'white-note' cluster. Berg uses this relationship at the beginning
of Scene 2, also in the section in which Alwa and the Athlete are alone. The
first section is largely devoted to showing the Athlete's coarse, vulgar nature
which contrasts so strongly with the Countess's noble character, evoked in
such exquisite phrases as this:

Example 89

Mit viel Wärme
Countess:

Sie ist herr - li - cher an- zu-schau'n als ich sie je - ge- kannt ha - be.

The second section opens with Schigolch's arrival, which is in the form of a
Largo (788) and is a varied repeat of the corresponding section in II, 1
(94 ff.), but at half its speed: 'quasi Zeitlupe' or 'slow motion' is Berg's
marking. In it the Athlete shows his contempt for the Countess in the grace-
notes attached to the main notes of his voice part (793-6) which echoes his
passage in II, 1, bars 102-4 when he carries the Schoolboy in his arms. The
third section reintroduces the Schoolboy who has come to explain to Alwa
his own plan for the liberation of Lulu. This is the Chamber Music II[108] for
wind, piano, and eight solo strings, largely based on fragments of the
Schoolboy series (834-952). Its tempo is a Vivace but grows gradually slower
and at the schoolboy's reading in the newspaper, 'Die Mörderin des Doktor
Schön an der Cholera erkrankt', it takes on the 'Wiegend' of the first scene

---

[108] The 'II' is not in the score, but it is the second chamber music after that for Schigolch in I,
2, and in view of Berg's predilection for correspondencies the duet between Schigolch and Lulu
in III, 1 may be called Chamber Music III.

(173-94). In bars 915-19 the solo cello and violin contradict the Athlete's remark that Lulu is 'buried next to the rubbish heap', by quoting variants of her 'Dance' motive. The Schoolboy is finally thrown out (his series) by the Athlete (tone clusters). The arrival of Lulu, dressed in the Countess's black dress, and leaning on Schigolch, starts the fourth section of this scene. This is a Melodrama in 8/4 (4 × 2/4) which has to be phrased in 3 × 16 bars (as in classical music), to which the vocal parts, all in *Sprechgesang*, have, most strictly, to adapt themselves. In this Melodrama the Athlete, mortified by Lulu's apparently emaciated looks, threatens to denounce her to the police and runs off. Also Schigolch takes his leave in order to buy the railway tickets to take him and Lulu over the German frontier. The fifth and last section begins with Lulu and Alwa alone introducing an outstandingly beautiful phrase derived from Lulu's 'Entrance' music in the Prologue (Ex. 85), and includes his ecstatic Hymn.

Before dealing with Act III, let me first enumerate the source material which served Friedrich Cerha for his *Herstellung* or provision of a performing version of that act.[108a]

(1) Berg's complete draft in short score or *particella* running from the beginning to the end of Act III. It contains, in varying measure, indications of the phrasing, articulation, dynamics, manner of performance and instrumentation.

(2) Sketches for it.

(3) Berg's full score for the first 268 bars. He left, after the downbeat in bar 262, three pages blank for the 'insertion of 22 (2 × 11) bars for the possible extension of Ensemble II and the clarification of the dialogue Lulu-Geschwitz'.

(4) Two large tables containing the basic series (BS) of the opera, and the derivation from it of the 'Picture' harmonies, and the series of Lulu, Schigolch, the 'Erdgeist' fourths and the diminished seventh. All these are transposed to all twelve degrees of the chromatic scale. On Table 2 the same is done with their inversions.

(5) The Variations and the Adagio completed by Berg for the Symphonic Pieces, hitherto known as *Lulu Symphony* or *Lulu Suite*.

(6) A vocal score for the last 17 bars of Act III which was evidently used for coaching the singer in the Adagio of the Symphonic Pieces.

(7) Erwin Stein's vocal score (1935-6) of the complete Act III. 60 pages of it were engraved but this was discontinued, most probably owing to the critical political situation at the time in Central Europe, with dodecaphonic music being banned as 'decadent' in Nazi Germany. Stein's vocal score, revised by Cerha, was published in 1978.[109]

[108a] See *Arbeitsbericht zur Herstellung des 3.Akts 'Lulu' von Alban Berg*, Vienna, 1979.

[109] Perle asked Stein about the state of these sketches and the possibility of completing the

Act III, Scene 1. Paris. A spacious salon. A door in the centre leads to the gaming room. Lulu's Pierrot portrait in a golden frame is let in the left wall. Lulu, Alwa, Marquis, Countess Geschwitz, Schigolch, Athlete. A big party is in progress to celebrate Lulu's (Gräfin Adelaide von ...) birthday.

Just as in *Wozzeck* there is a scene in the grand opera style (II, 4), so Scene 1 of Act III of *Lulu* aspires to grand opera, as shown by the fact that it contains three great Ensembles. They are all based on the Circus Music of the Prologue, Berg equating the meretricious make-believe brilliance of a circus with the atmosphere of a Paris *demi-monde* consisting of gamblers, pimps, blackmailers and prostitutes. According to the prevalent mood, these three twelve-part Ensembles are marked:

1. Flau (listless)   Parlando
2. Festlich (festive)   Cantato
3. Aufgeregt (agitated)   Spoken

All three Ensembles are ternary, with a contrasting middle section. Berg called the middle section of Ensemble I a 'Rhabarber-Rhabarber'[110] Ensemble in which the assembled party acknowledges the Athlete's toast in honour of Lulu's birthday. In Ensemble II the party returns from the gaming room and comments on the astonishing rise of the shares of the Jungfrau railway ('Alle Welt gewinnt'). In this Ensemble occurs the dialogue between Lulu and Geschwitz to clarify which Berg left three pages blank in the full score. It is an important dialogue, for it is the first occasion in the whole opera in which the two women define their relationship to each other. In a head-on collision Geschwitz accuses, with the utmost bitterness, Lulu of betraying her (Geschwitz's) love of her to which Lulu coldly retorts, 'Du bist kein Menschenkind wie die andern. Für einen Mann war der Stoff nicht ausreichend, und zum Weib hast Du zu viel Hirn in deinem Schädel bekommen. Darum bist du verrückt'.[110a]

---

opera from them. Stein told him that this would present not the slightest difficulty for a musician familiar with Berg's late style, and he always hoped he would be entrusted with this task. (Personal communication from Mr. Perle.)

   While understanding the reason for Frau Helene Berg's adamant refusal to permit this, I quoted to her Mozart's *Requiem*, Offenbach's *Tales of Hoffmann*, Borodin's *Prince Igor*, Puccini's *Tyrandot*, Busoni's *Doktor Faust*, and Mahler's Tenth Symphony – all works finished by other hands than their composers', without detriment to the original and accepted by a large majority of responsible musicians. Moreover, without the complete final act, *Lulu* suffered, I said, from a serious imbalance, to say nothing of its highly unsatisfactory effect as organic music drama.

   [110] This is the word which used to be spoken in German theatres by the stage crowds to evoke the effect of an animated but indistinct murmur.

   [110]a You are not a human being like the others. For a man you were not given enough substance and for a woman you have too much brain in your pate. That's why you are mad'. In Wedekind, Lulu prefaces this 'diagnosis' with, 'Du bist im Leib Deiner Mutter nicht fertig geworden, weder als Weib noch als Mann' – 'You were not finished in your mother's womb, either as a woman or as a man'.

Ensemble III shows the mortification that the announcement of the collapse of the Jungfrau shares causes to the assembled guest of the Paris Casino ('Alle Welt verliert'). Berg only wrote out the dislogue between the Banker and the Mother and the exclamation of her fifteen-year-old daughter (633-52). The rest of this Ensemble the composer indicated by a wave-line, with the marking, 'Leises Gemurmel aller' ('Soft murmur of all'). He evidently intended to compose this Ensemble in the manner of the 'Rhubarb' Ensembles I and II. These three Ensembles are balance by three Duets:

1. Lulu-Marquis
2. Lulu-Athlete
3. Lulu-Schigolch

Of these, Duet no. 1 is dramatically and musically the most important in that it fully characterises the bogus Marquis – the blackmailer, procurer and police informer rolled into one – and completes Lulu's portrayal presented in her *Lied* of II, 1. In it the Marquis threatens to hand Lulu over to the police unless she agrees to join a high-class brothel in Cairo, which she refuses – 'Ich kann nicht das Einzige verkaufen, das je mein Eigen war'.[111] and the Duet ends with her great outcry, 'Du kannst mich nicht ausliefern' – 'You cannot hand me over'. The music takes the form of twelve Chorale Variations in Concertante Style on the theme of the Marquis (Ex. 87); its derivation from the Prince's Chorale in I, 3 has already been discussed. After the second variation there are two Intermezzi, the first of which is the *Lied des Mädchenhändlers* (The Procurer's Song) sung by the Marquis and accompanied by a violin solo which is the only entirely new tune in Act III. It is Wedekind's *Lautenlied* no. 10, entitled *Konfession*, the poet's verses expressing a woman's intense desire to become a whore and who considers her beautiful body as the source of passionate sexual pleasure. The tune has the character of a monotonous, sad street ballad and might almost have come out of Brecht-Weill's *Dreigroschenoper*. It will form the theme of the Variations of the Interlude between Scene 1 and 2 of this act (Ex. 90).

After a few bars of transition, Intermezzo II follows, a shortened repeat of Lulu's *Lied* of II, 1 after which the chain of the variations continues. In Var. 9 and 10 (205-23) in which Lulu sings, 'Ich gehe mit dir nach Amerika ...', she repeats, almost note for note, the phrase of Act II, 2, 'Es ist schade um mich ...' (228-44), just before the police arrive to arrest her for Schön's murder.

Duets nos. 2 and 3 introduce, appropriately, reminiscences from previous music of which that of Lulu-Schigolch would have probably been Chamber Music III. In it Schigolch promises to dispose of the Athlete if the latter can

[111] This is musically an exact replica of her phrase, 'Ich will nur Dir allein gehören ...' which she addresses to Alwa after having shot his father, near the end of II, 1.

be induced to visit with Countess Geschwitz a third-rate hotel. This is followed by spoken dialogue between the Marquis and the Athlete which unfolds over a cadenza for solo violin and piano, not unlike the cadenza before the finale of the Chamber Concerto. In the ensuing section in which Lulu arranges a tryst between Countess Geschwitz and the Athlete at the address given her by Schigolch, Berg constantly varies the vocal treatment between *Sprechstimme*, recitative, parlando and cantabile. This section includes an important scene between the Athlete and Geschwitz who does violence to her lesbian nature by pretending, for Lulu's sake, that she adores the Athlete, and asks him to have pity on her in her love for him.

Example 90

Ensemble III follows in which everyone loses their money ('Alle Welt verliert') in the crash of the Jungfraubahn shares, and the end shows Lulu, dressed in the Groom's clothes, escaping with Alwa over the back stairs, as the Police Commissioner, who has been alerted by the Marquis, arrives to arrest her for the murder of Schön.

An orchestral Interlude provides the Transformation music to scene 2. It consists of four variations on Wedekind's *Lautenlied*, but, in contrast to the Variations from the Symphonic Pieces, they are not flanked by the Marquis's Chorale. Var. 1 starts immediately after the curtain has descended on scene 1, and Var. 4 debouches into the *Lautenlied* at the opening of scene 2. These Variations will be discussed in greater detail in the section dealing with the five Symphonic Pieces.

Act III, Scene 2. London. A garret in the East End. Alwa, Schigolch, Lulu, Geschwitz, Silent Professor, Negro and Jack the Ripper.

After the deceptive splendour of the Paris scene, the desolate sordidness of the London attic strikes with redoubled force. Lulu has reached the nadir of her career, having become a common prostitute to earn money for her companions, Alwa and Schigolch, who fled to London with her.

The scene opens with Wedekind's *Lautenlied*, which has now become the symbol of Lulu in the gutter. The tune is scored for seven woodwind[111a]

[111a] Piccolo, flute, three clarinets, bass clarinet and contrabassoon.

producing the sound of a *Werkel* or barrel organ. It is harmonized by Berg in simple major and minor chords, probably in imitation of Wedekind's own lute harmonization which employs only tonic, dominant and subdominant chords. The original tune is in C major while the operatic version is in E flat major (737-52). The model for Cerha's harmonization as well as instrumentation were the four bars 49-52 (Thema) into which Var. 4 of the Symphonic Pieces leads.[111b] Berg provides a bitonal support for the Wedekind tune in a string tremolo illustrating Schigolch's opening words in the second scene, 'Der Regen trommelt zur Parade' ('The rain is beating a tattoo'). This tremolo forms a 6/4 chord, A-E-C sharp, that is the first three notes of Schön's series (Ex. 70b), Berg subtly and ominously hinting at Schön's double, Jack, at the end of the opera.

The *Lautenlied* appears three more times in the course of this final scene: when Schigolch and Alwa crawl out of their hiding-place after Lulu and the Professor have disappeared into her room (872-42); when Alwa speaks of the venereal disease which was transmitted to him by Lulu from the Marquis (1024-47), but in the bitonal version of Var. 2 of the Symphonic Pieces; and finally when Schigolch drags Alwa's dead body away (1110-19), the music being that of Var. 3 (*Funèbre*) of the Symphonic Pieces. But neither of these last two operatic statements are exactly identical with their counterparts in the Symphonic Pieces.

Beginning with the entry of Lulu with her first client, the silent Professor, Berg conceived the whole of this scene as a composed ritardando, starting in bar 768 with Presto and ending via a number of intervening tempi in a Grave (1315), a procedure that recalls the same device in the second half of the Monoritmica of I, 2.

With the exception of Wedekind's *Lautenlied*, the music of Scene 2 is made up of reminiscences dictated by Berg's dramatic symbolism which, as was said, equates Lulu's three victims in Act I and II with the three clients who come as their avengers. Thus, Lulu's arrival with her first client, the silent Professor, recalls fragments from the Recitative and Canzonetta after the death of the Medizinalrat (I, 1). With the entrance of the Professor begins, similar to the second half of the Monoritmica (Act I, 2) a composed ritardando from Presto, through twelve tempo changes, to Grave, the latter tempo starting with Geschwitz's apostrophe to the dead Lulu (1315). With the entry of Countess Geschwitz, Berg reintroduces her pentatonic figure and the Circus Music (in combination), and as she unrolls Lulu's Pierrot portrait, the 'Picture' harmonies are heard. Alwa's fixing of the portrait on

---

[111b] It seemed a simple matter to continue Berg's harmonisation of those four bars, but difficulties arose because Cerha was faced with the choice of several possibilities, since no harmonisation of the complete *Lautenlied* was found among the Berg material. It first occurs as the *Lied des Mädchenhändlers* in Act III, 1 but in an entirely different dramatic context from Act III, 2 and, moreover, is there embedded in a contrapuntal texture.

the wall by using the heel of his shoe as a hammer proceeds to the 'Fate' rhythm RH. Soon after, there begins a vocal Quartet (960-1007). Lulu, the Countess, Alwa and Schigolch stand before Lulu's pierrot picture, each commenting on it in his or her characteristic way, with the Countess saying that it must have been painted 'long before my time'. Berg wrote out only the tenor part, 'always dominating', and merely marked the entry of the other voices which Cerha skilfully completed. Alwa's music repeats part of his Hymn (Act II, 2), from 'Diese Knöchel: ein Grazioso' to 'das gewaltige Andante der Wollust' (974-89).

The scene between Lulu and the Negro unfolds almost exclusively to a shortened version of the Monoritmica, the jazz drum in RH evidently pointing to the primitiveness of her second client as well as to the imminent killing of Alwa by the Negro. After the Negro has left, Lulu's firm decision to go down again on the street in search of another client is set to the music in I, 2 (849-74), in which she insists on leaving the room after the Painter's suicide. Schigolch comes back, bends over Alwa's corpse and drags him into another room. This marks the return of Variation 3 of the Interlude whose 'Funèbre' now reveals its significance.

The Countess re-enters and contemplates suicide, but kneeling in front of Lulu's picture changes her mind and implores Lulu to have mercy on her. It is with the 'Geschwitz' fifths (*Sostenuto*, 1146) that the Adagio of the Symphonic Pieces opens.) Enter Lulu and Jack in whose scene Berg recalls the following music: Schön's 'leaping tiger' theme (the first six notes of his series only) (Prologue); Coda of the Sonata (I, 2); Lulu's Cavatina (tango rhythm) and Schön's Arietta 'Das mein Lebensabend') (II, 1); the Interlude (II, 2/3) which is not literally repeated and in this latter version is taken over into the final movement of the Symphonic Pieces; and Lulu's 'Entrance' music (Prologue) as she embraces Jack and the two disappear into an adjoining room. In the Countess's ensuing monologue, called by Berg 'Nocturno' (*sic*), she decides to return to Germany, study law and become a fighter for women's rights. The finale begins with Lulu's *Todesschrei*[112] in which all six 'Earth Spirit' fourths are telescoped into a twelve-note chord for the whole orchestra. The *Todesschrei* has, significantly, as its root Marie's fifth A-E, the symbol of her and Lulu's 'aimless waiting which will find its final solution only in death'. This was Berg's third allusion in the opera to his *Wozzeck*. From the death cry to the end of the opera, the music is, minus Jack's voice part,[113] identical with the last thirty-three bars of the Adagio in

[112] Berg reverses Wedekind's order of the killings: Jack first murders Lulu and then stabs the Countess to death.

[113] In the opera he says: 'Das war ein Stück Arbeit!' – 'That was some job!' Washing his hands he congratulates himself: 'Ich bin doch ein verdammter Glückspilz!' – 'After all I am a damned lucky fellow'. Looking round for a towel he complains that 'Nicht einmal ein Handtuch haben die Leut!' – 'Not even a towel have these people!', and turning to the dying Countess he says: 'Mit Dir es auch bald zu Ende! – You too will not take long to die!'.

the Symphonic Pieces. The Countess's last dying words, 'Lulu, Mein Engel ...', which are incorporated in the symphonic Adagio, are set to one of the most moving passages in the whole opera:

Example 91a

In Wedekind, Geschwitz's last word is a curse – ('O) verflucht!' ('Oh) cursed!'). Berg, it is true, omits this word in order not to taint at the moment of death Geschwitz's noble character, but he does not omit the *music* for it, for her part ends with the two toneless notes C-B, set to a quaver followed by a dotted crotchet = ver*flucht*! Does this reveal a fundamental ambivalence in Berg's attitude towards this figure? The opera closes with three cadential chords: 6/4 of A major = Schön, 6/4 of A minor = Alwa, and E-A-B=Geschwitz, anchored on F and articulated by RH:

Example 91b

Berg thus ends the opera with the musical symbols of the three characters who played the most important roles in Lulu's life dying through and for her – Alwa and Geschwitz in a futile act of self-sacrifice.

From every point of view, dramatic and musical, the final scene of *Lulu* – a study in the horrific and macabre – stands unique in all opera.

Symphonic Pieces (Lulu Symphony)

In conclusion, a few words must be said about the Symphonic Pieces which Berg wrote with the same purpose in mind as the *Three Fragments from 'Wozzeck'* – to arouse interest in his opera. Berg first called the Symphonic Pieces a 'Propaganda Suite' (in a letter), later simply 'Suite' and also 'Little Symphony from the opera, *Lulu*'. It was not until June 1934 that he hit on the final title. They consist of five movements:

1. Rondo: Andante and Hymn
2. Ostinato: Allegro
3. Lied der Lulu: Comodo
4. Variations: Moderato
5. Adagio: Sostenuto-Lento-Grave.

Unlike the *Wozzeck* Fragments, which centre on Marie and follow one another in the order in which they occur in the opera, the five movements of the Symphony are ranged, not as they happen in the drama, but to show various aspects of the music of the opera. In addition, they characterise not only the heroine (*Lied der Lulu*), but also Alwa (Rondo and Hymn) and the Countess (Adagio). Berg later discovered that the five pieces accorded with his conception of a symphony (hence their collective title), notably of Mahler's Seventh, in that a big opening movement is balanced at the end by an extensive finale, while the inner three movements are to be regarded as 'character pieces'. In the *Wozzeck* Fragments Berg made scarcely any changes and this is equally true of the inner movements of the *Lulu Symphony*. The Rondo and Adagio, however, were 'edited' by the composer for performance in the concert hall, that is, he eliminated all those dramatic interpolations which in the opera originated in the action, so that these two movements are continuous in their orchestral version. Apart from instrumental alterations, Berg also provided the Rondo with an eight-bar Introduction which is based on bars 56-63 from Lulu's 'Entrance' music in the Prologue and added, in the Adagio (45-79), Schön's music from the orchestral Interlude between sc. 2 and 3 of Act I.

Of the five movements of the Symphonic Pieces four have already been discussed (Rondo; Ostinato; *Lied der Lulu* and Adagio). There remain only the four Variations to be described. They are framed on both sides by the Marquis's Chorale (Ex. 87) and have for their theme Wedekind's *Lautenlied* (The Procurer's Song, Ex. 90). The tune consists of 2 × 8 bars, the first half in C major and the second in the relative minor. This tonal scheme, transposed to other keys, is adhered to throughout. The theme is first stated by itself but is thundered out by the four horns in unison as Variation 1. In all the variations it is used in the manner of a *cantus firmus* remaining intact in the melody but undergoing harmonic and rhythmic modifications within a contrapuntal texture. In marked contrast to Berg's use of tonality in the Violin Concerto, here it seems to symbolize disintegration, corruption and putrefaction. Variation 1 (*Grandioso*) is so scored as to recall the sound of an orchestrion – a mechanical organ which can still be heard at some fairs. Its intention is to convey the meretricious splendour and tinsel elegance of the Parisian gaming casino. Variation 2 (*Grazioso*) is bitonal, the theme bearing the key-signature G flat. This variation opens with a bitonal stretto (C major against G flat major), and in bars 20-1 Berg resorts to his favourite circle of descending fifths. The music is said to reflect Lulu's loveliness against a corrupt glitter. Variation 3 (*Funèbre*) anticipates Alwa's murder at the hands of the Negro in Scene 2 of this act. The theme, in A major, lies in the bass but all feeling of tonality is destroyed by the fourth chords in the treble. Variation 4 (*Affettuoso*) represents the emotional and musical climax. The theme is treated in the manner of a *Klangfarbenmelodie*, being distributed over second violins and celli occasionally doubled on other instruments. In bar 44 the bass has the 'Fate' rhythm while the first violins introduce the open fifth of the Countess's theme (Ex. 72*e*) intoned on different degrees of the scale. In the ensuing four bars 45-48 the opening fragment of the theme reappears in E flat major resting on a string tremolo E-A-C sharp, the first three notes of Schön's series heralding the coming of Jack the Ripper. The scoring is such[114] as to produce the effect of a barrel-organ. The variations close with the aforementioned Chorale of the Marquis followed by the last bars of the *Lautenlied*. Throughout one admires Berg's orchestral imagination, which enables him to impart to each variation a distinct colour of its own.

Before turning to the posthumous history of *Lulu* the hypothetical question may be asked: if Berg had lived to complete the opera and had had the opportunity to see it on stage, which is after all the crucial test of a stage-work, might he not, in the light of it, have reconsidered certain points in the dramaturgy and the musical treatment?[115] This is not unknown with opera composers, *e.g.* Puccini, Britten, Krenek, Weill and others. The points I have in mind suggested themselves to me after a close study of the three-act version and particularly after hearing that version in Paris and London. Let me deal with them on a rising scale of importance.

There is, first, a great deal of spoken dialogue in II, 2 – dialogue between Alwa and Geschwitz, Alwa and the Athlete; finally, there is Lulu's narration in which she describes to Alwa Geschwitz's ingenious stratagem by means of which the Countess enabled Lulu to escape from the prison hospital leaving her to be imprisoned in her stead as the murderess of Dr Schön. The total

---

[114] Piccolo, flute, three clarinets, bass clarinet, contrabassoon.
[115] I was glad to find that so experienced an opera composer as Ernst Krenek is of the same opinion. See his article, 'Marginal remarks re *Lulu*', Newsletter no. 9, Autumn 1980, *International Alban Berg Society*, pp. 9-10.

duration of all this is nearly five minutes – a long span in terms of stage time. Not only do these verbal exchanges interrupt the musical flow, but they also act as a retarding factor to the action, to which their content is rather irrelevant. It might be argued that we accept spoken dialogue without much ado in the German *singspiel* and the French *opéra comique*, but then *Lulu* is a fully developed music-drama in which spoken text has no place. Moreover, the text is not couched in exalted poetic language but is prosaic, matter-of-fact and, as far as the Athlete is concerned, vulgar, which brings the spectator down to the mundane with a bump. I feel that on reconsideration Berg would have found a way of obviating the spoken sections of the text, either by choosing the form of the *melodrame* (as he does, for example, in bars 239-49 in II, 1), which would at least have anchored the words in music, or setting them in *Sprechgesang* and/or song, with an abbreviated wording of the original text.

Secondly, I wonder whether in Berg's symbolic equation of Lulu's three husbands with her three clients there is not a dramaturgical imbalance between the Medizinalrat (I, 1) and the Professor (III, 2). The scene of the former hardly registers with the audience since it is very short, extending to a mere 23 bars in which all the Medizinalrat says is 'Machen Sie auf! ... Ihr Hunde!' after which he collapses and dies of a heart-attack. True, the Professor is a silent (mimed) role, but he impresses himself on the spectator by his comic-grotesque behaviour and Lulu's reaction to it. This latter scene occupies almost a hundred bars, nearly five times as long as the Medizinalrat's scene. This striking disproportion creates a feeling that, compared with the Professor, the Medizinalrat does not have sufficient dramatic weight, which tends to render the symbolic equation of the two characters tenuous and even contrived. Now the opening act of Wedekind's *Erdgeist* contains two scenes (2 and 3), with Dr Goll (Medizinalrat), Dr Schön, Schwartz (The Painter) and Alwa, providing material on which Berg might have drawn in order to make the Medizinalrat a more meaningful figure and thus raise him to the level of his double.

Of the questionable usefulness of the film between the two Scenes of Act II I have already spoken (pp. 255-6).

We now come to the important dialogue between Lulu and Geschwitz in III, 1. This is the only occasion in the whole opera in which the two women face each other, in a head-on collision, and in which Geschwitz accuses Lulu of having betrayed her (Lulu's) passionate promises (*Beteuerungen*) made in the prison hospital, promises that induced Geschwitz to let herself be incarcerated in Lulu's place. Lulu's utterly cruel reply is: 'You are not a human being like the others. For a man the stuff was not sufficient and for a woman you have too much brain in your pate. That's why you are mad'.[116]

---

[116] Wedekind prefaces Lulu's diagnosis with 'You were not finished in your mother's womb either as man or woman', which Berg, regrettably I feel, omitted.

Now Berg set this not as a true dialogue (argument – counter-argument), as it is in Wedekind, but as a kind of duet in which the two women sing different words *simultaneously*, whereas I feel it should have been set, being a confrontation, in a similar way to the confrontation of Lulu and the Marquis in a previous scene. The duet form plus the different words make it impossible to hear the text clearly, and the text is of great importance, since it defines Lulu's attitude to her lesbian friend, and renders the latter's utterly vain attempt to defend Lulu against Jack in the last scene all the more pathetic. That Berg did feel the great importance of this dialogue is proved by the fact that he left three pages blank in the full score for the further clarification of this exchange. The difficulty of following the words of which at best only the soprano's can be heard, is heightened by Berg pitting the duet against a background ensemble of other voices which inevitably obscures the words of the two soloists. Berg was of course aware of this difficulty, as his stage direction shows.[117] But this does not resolve the difficulty which lies in the particular form given to the dialogue.

In this connection attention must be drawn to the contradiction between what Wedekind makes Geschwitz say in this dialogue and what he makes Lulu tell Alwa in her preceding narration (II, 2). In the latter she explains that her escape from the prison hospital was planned in its entirety and put into effect by Geschwitz, with all the dire consequences for the latter; whereas in the former Geschwitz tells Lulu that it was her passionate promises that persuaded her to let herself be imprisoned in Lulu's stead. This contradiction Berg overlooked.

Lastly there is the scene in the Paris gambling casino. I feel that with the notable exception of the Chorale Variations, the scene between Lulu and Schigolch and that between Lulu, the Athlete and Geschwitz, the level of inspiration has gone down. This is of course a purely subjective view, but what cannot be denied is that from a purely dramaturgical point of view the spectator receives from the whole scene the impression of some confusion, which results from the fact that, bar the Marquis, a variety of ancillary characters are introduced, and this late in the opera. They make but a fleeting appearance and contribute little to the main action. Berg seems to have had too much respect for Wedekind's text.

The posthumous history of 'Lulu'

Up to 1977 it had been assumed that of the three composers alleged to have been approached by Helene Berg and the Universal Edition with the request to complete Act III – Schoenberg, Webern and Zemlinsky – only the first was known to have accepted. The publication in 1974 of a book on

---

[117] 'The dialogue Lulu-Geschwitz apart from the others, always in the foreground, clear: outside the ensemble (*Gesamtklang*)'.

Schoenberg[118] shed for the first time some light on this strange affair. We read there that on Berg's death Schoenberg sent his widow a letter of condolence in which he volunteered to complete the orchestration of the final act. Frau Berg, deeply moved by this, replied on 14 January 1936 saying that this was the first ray of hope in her darkness. On 9 March Schoenberg received the photostats of the Berg material and the libretto of the act, but already on 11 March, two days later, he wrote to the Universal Edition saying that he was unable to carry out the work of completion as it had proved more difficult and time-consuming than he had anticipated. This was his official explanation, but in a letter to Erwin Stein on 11 March[119] he gave his real reason, which was that he interpreted as antisemitic Berg's stage direction for the Banker (III, 1), which deeply hurt him as a Jew. Apart from the Journalist calling the Banker 'Saujude!' ('Jewish swine'). which is in Wedekind, Berg makes the Banker speak 'jüdelnd' (in the libretto) and 'mauschelnd' (in the short score), which is *not* in Wedekind. Both terms are derogatory, denoting the wheedling way supposed to be characteristic of Yiddish speech. Berg had evidently added them in order to portray the Banker in an unmistakably Jewish manner.[120]

Schoenberg was prepared to ascribe these antisemitic words to what he called Berg's 'thoughtlessness', but he found it difficult to understand this at a time when the Jews in Germany were being presecuted. He remarked to Stein that this had not helped Berg to ease his way with the Nazis, implying a production of *Lulu* in Germany, and wondered whether Berg expected anything to come of it. Plainly, Schoenberg's objection to the final act of *Lulu* was not based on objective artistic criteria, but on strong personal feelings, to which he was perfectly entitled. Stumbling over the caricature of a Jewish Banker, a wholly episodic figure in that act, Schoenberg did not bother to study the music in any detail and sent his official (negative) reply to the Universal Edition only two days after receiving the *Lulu* material. A lesser reason for his refusal was that he very much doubted whether at his age (62) he could afford the time for someone else's work without detriment to his own and at the same time make a living. In conclusion he stressed that this played no part in his decision to decline the work of completion, and hoped that some other musician, instructed by Stein or Reich, would be able to finish the orchestration of the act in time – apparently for the Zurich

[118] H.H. Stuckenschmidt, *Schönberg, Leben, Umwelt, Werk*, Zurich, 1974, p. 372.
[119] Reproduced in *Österreichische Musikzeitung*, Vienna, 1977, pp. 398-400.
[120] But Wedekind gives the Banker a short soliloquy that imitates the peculiar syntax and dialectic of a Yiddish speaker of which Berg retained only the opening sentence: 'Schneid ich dir nicht die Ohren ab, schneidst du sie mir! Kann ich nicht vermieten mein Josaphat, muss ich mir helfen mit meinen Verstand; Wird er nicht runzlig, mein Verstand; wird er nicht unpässlich; braucht er nicht zu baden in Eau de Cologne!' – 'If I don't cut off your ears, you will cut off mine! Cannot I lease my Josaphat, help me must my reason! Does it not become wrinkled my reason; will it not become indisposed; will it not need to bath in Eau de Cologne!'

première in June 1937.

It should be noted that Schoenberg was not sent the photostats of the first and second acts of *Lulu*, which were indispensable for the work he was expected to do.[121]

Did Berg really show an antisemitic tendency? In his letter to Malipiero Berg speaks of the 'present tendency in Austria to glorify the Jews as martyrs' so that '*I am hardly performed*' (see p. 81), which may seem to suggest it. (Also Helene Berg, in a letter to Frau Mahler of mid-February 1934, says that 'cowardice is a Jewish speciality' – not a very tactful remark to make to the widow of Mahler and wife of Werfel). But against this slight suspicion stands the major fact that only six weeks after his letter to Malipiero, Berg informed Schoenberg (29 August 1934) that he had dedicated *Lulu* to him, to the composer whose name will forever be linked with the 'most German music'.

It has now been established[122] that after Berg's death the Universal Edition asked Webern and Zemlinsky whether they would be prepared to finish the orchestration of Act III. Zemlinsky, a man of the theatre, was at first greatly interested in this, but after two days' study of the material declined and suggested that the opera be performed as it stood. Webern also declined, saying that after the fourth bar he would not know how to go on, although there was no question of having to continue or develop a passage as Berg's draft was all but complete. Cerha is of the opinion that Webern may initially have been frightened off by the amount of work involved, work that for all his close friendship with Berg was far removed in spirit from the world of his own music. Yet, in March 1943, he expressed a wish to complete Berg's unfinished act. Krenek was also approached, and refused, but suggested Hans Erich Apostel, a former pupil of Berg and a composer in his own right who had edited the full scores of *Wozzeck* and *Lulu*. Between 1963 and 1966 Cerha had a number of conversations with Apostel about *Lulu*, in which he asked him why he, who was so intimately acquainted with Berg's style and knew *Lulu* so well from his work of editing, had not undertaken the task of completion. Apostel pleaded illness and his own creative work, mentioning also something about Berg's 'thick' orchestration. He finally said that in principle a member of Cerha's generation (Cerha was born in 1926) must do

---

[121] Before receiving the particella of the final act Schoenberg had looked through Berg's Symphonic Pieces which by then had been published. He found, as he wrote to Stein, that the bass line of the Rondo in bars 81-3 resembled the left-hand part of a piano piece, and he thought the same of the bass of the Hymn (167-82), though he felt that the latter passage ought to sound 'very characteristic and beautiful'. After receiving the operatic material Schoenberg complained to Stein that part of it was almost illegible and this, he argued, would have greatly delayed his task of realising it. Moreover, he discovered that Berg's employment of the note-row was very different from his own ('octave doublings, etc') so that the deciphering of illegible notes was made 'infinitely more difficult'.

[122] Cerha, *Arbeitsbericht* op cit., pp. 35-6.

the completion of Act III – 'we are still still too close to Berg's music ... and the generation after you will no longer be able to feel itself into Berg's world'. Although Frau Berg, after Schoenberg's refusal in March 1936, said that she saw in this the hand of Providence and would never permit someone else to complete the final act, it is true that in the early 1950s Felix Greissle, Schoenberg's son-in-law, wanted to entrust the work to Luigi Dallapiccola, but the Italian composer, to whom the *Lulu* material was never shown, refused.[123] According to Cerha,[124] there were three stages in Helene Berg's attitude to the unfinished act. The first stage extended from her husband's death to the world première of *Lulu* in Zurich on 2 June 1937. When she and the Universal Edition first heard of Schoenberg's refusal they were greatly dismayed; and, since Webern and Zemlinsky had also declined the invitation to complete the act, the Universal Edition made Frau Berg a proposition: to produce *Lulu* in Zurich as the composer had left it at his death, but with the end of Act III tacked on as a kind of epilogue, to be mimed to the music of the Adagio from the Symphonic Pieces. The publishers regarded this as merely a makeshift, a *pis aller* not to be repeated at any other theatre. The immense success of the Zurich production, however, persuaded Helene Berg that the opera was indeed viable and stageworthy as a torso, and writing to Dr Heinsheiner of the Universal Edition ten days after the première (12 June), said that while she had accepted previously the publisher's point of view in not publishing a work that was incomplete and therefore not performable, she must return to her erstwhile wish to have published as soon as possible Berg's full score 'up to the bar where catastrophe befell Alban (Lulu's last victim!), the vocal score of Act III and the complete libretto ... one simply has a duty to bring out a work of such greatness so far as it exists and must not withhold from the world the smallest fraction of it. We owe this to Alban and his grandiose creation'.

If anything, Helene was even more enthusiastic about *Lulu* in what she wrote to her 'dearest Almschi' on 24 June,[125] giving a summing-up of *Lulu* and its effect on her. She says that one can say nothing of the music, one must hear it. It has a beauty and truthfulness which efface everything hateful and repulsive in the text and leave only an unquestionable masterpiece. When she heard it for the first time, it seemed so deeply familiar to her, as though it came from her and was her own speech. There are passages in it where one feels that one is no longer on this earth. Alban has grasped the depth of two things and has understood how to give it back again: the mysteries of love and death. The beginning and end of our earthly existence. She was always prejudiced against Wedekind, but since she has heard the music everything is different. *Lulu*, like *Wozzeck*, is dear to her now. She loves it and trembles

[123] Personal communication from the late Maestro Dallapiccola.
[124] Cerha, op. cit., pp. 37-9.
[125] Newsletter no. 7, Autumn 1978, *International Alban Berg Society*, p. 9.

for it, as for a child. It is fearful thing and people don't like it when one illuminates their depths; but when Alwa sings of Lulu in tender ecstasy, 'Eine Seele, die sich im Jenseits den Schlaf aus den Augen reibt' – 'a soul that rubs the sleep from its eyes in the beyond' – Helene knows that this dream *also* had to be written, for it has its own profound meaning. She is not surprised that the opera is stageworthy as a torso. She has learned to trust in that which is called the Higher: it has all happened according to a plan. How could Alban, who had so much to say and to give, have been called away if his last work, which nothing else can touch, had not been, in some possible way, 'completed'. Even those who today face this work without understanding or with misgivings – for he was so far in advance of them – will gradually grow into it, until a time comes when people will at last know who Alban Berg was.

It is certainly a wonderful letter, though its end takes us into the realm of Higher Belief where everything seems possible, such as declaring an objectively incomplete work to be complete. From these heights we descend to the mundane and to Dr Heinsheimer's reply to Helene's letter of 12 June.

On 15 June he assured Frau Berg that, like herself, the Universal Edition was anxious to publish not only the libretto of the third act of *Lulu* but also the vocal score of Erwin Stein, who had already arranged the first two acts for voice and piano. But, he continued, what had to be considered was the great likelihood that in that case both the press and the theatres would clamour for stage performances of the whole of Act III, which would again raise the question of its completion. This contingency the Universal Edition wanted to avoid after the Zurich production. The vocal score of the first two acts was duly published, with a note saying that the vocal score of the incomplete last act would come out at a later date. This never materialized. The reason for this was Helene Berg's changed attitude to a publication of that act, which marks the second stage of this saga. We recall that already in her letter to Alma Mahler she had said that the opera was stageworthy as a torso, apparently accepting Dr Heinsheimer's reason for not publishing the final act. When in the late 1940s interest in *Lulu* began to revive, notably in Germany, and when increasing demands were made in various quarters for a completion of the unfinished third act by a composer intimately acquainted with Berg's late style, such as H.E. Apostel, Frau Berg set her face against all publication of it and finally, in 1969, placed a total embargo on the whole material of that act. This represents the last stage in her changing attitude towards it. Her reasons for the embargo were:

(1) Schoenberg, Webern and Zemlinsky, close friends of her husband, had all, after inspection of the existing material, declined to undertake the work of completion; this for her was the determining factor.

(2) Alban's artistic endeavour was always to give of his best and to bear

the fullest (*hundertprozentig*) responsibility for every note he had written, before publishing a work of his.

(3) The completion of an unfinished work which in Berg's own words needed 'gründliches Überholen' (thorough overhauling) by someone else would introduce into it an alien spirit.[126]

All this formed part of her handwritten will (23 July 1969)[127] in which she categorically laid down that 'der 3 Akt von *Lulu* darf von niemandem eingesehen werden! Ebenso darf die Photokopie bei der Universal Edition auch nicht eingesehen werden' – 'No one must inspect the third act of *Lulu*! Equally, no one must inspect the photocopy at the Universal Edition'. This was, indeed, a very far cry from her declaration in 1937 that 'not the smallest fraction of the opera must be withheld from the world'. As I intimated before, from a very narrow artistic point of view Frau Berg's objections were understandable. However, it seems that her negative attitude to the final act and the opera as a whole was strongly influenced by purely personal feelings. There was, for one thing, Wedekind's text which to a woman of her cast of mind was not only entirely alien but at first thoroughly repellent.[128] Moreover she may have, as we already hinted, perceived, consciously or otherwise, an allegorical enactment in Alwa and Lulu of the relationship between her Alban and Hanna. There is no concrete evidence for this assumption, but it may have contributed to making the third act of *Lulu* something of a *cause célèbre*. I venture to suggest that Berg's love affair with Hanna made the composer ponder deeply on the mysterious nature of sexual attraction and that this was partly responsible in 1926 for his choice of Wedekind's two Lulu dramas as the subject for an opera.

Lulu had its première in Zurich in June 1937, when only the very end of Act III was shown on the stage. The first concert performances after the war took place in Vienna on 15 February and 29 April 1949, the joint promoters being the Austrian section of the ISCM and Austrian Radio. The first post-war production was staged at Essen on 7 March 1953; Act III followed the Zurich model: Geschwitz kneeling before Lulu's pierrot painting – arrival of Lulu with Jack – Lulu's *Todesschrei* – murder of Geschwitz. All this was mimed to the music of the Adagio from the Symphonic Pieces. Up to the Paris production of 1979 this was the deplorable makeshift version in which

---

[126] When I wrote to her in September 1972 expressing my anxious wish to inspect the third-act material, Frau Berg replied (9 October 1972) saying that if a thorough analytical discussion of the sketches appeared in my book, this would 'set off an avalanche of "finishers", which would be quite useless since my embargo (*Sperre*) must remain in force without exception'.

[127] Reproduced in *Österreichische Musikzeitung*, April 1977, pp. 169-79.

[128] Berg is said to have tried, as far as possible, to shield Helene from anything equivocal, improper, indecent and trivial – he even withheld from her experiences of his own of this nature. This may explain why it was only after Helen's death that Berg's affair with a Carinthian girl and his begetting of an illegitimate daughter became known.

Lulu was performed in all opera houses.

24 February 1979 was a red-letter day in the history of twentieth-century opera in general and *Lulu* in particular. On this day – forty-four years after Berg died over it – the complete opera was staged at the Paris Opera, with a hand-picked cast under the direction of Pierre Boulez and produced by Patrice Chéreau. For Act III Friedrich Cerha, a Viennese composer and conductor, provided, on the basis of all the existing material (see p. 259), a performing version[129] which by common consent represented a most scrupulous realization of Berg's intention and thus at long last restored the dramatic balance and the imposing overall structure of the opera. From a somewhat shadowy existence, *Lulu* has finally been raised to its rightful place beside *Wozzeck* – both towering peaks of the modern music-drama. The last act is not merely a logical continuation of the action to its end, but the inevitable solution, a true dénouement, of the dramatic knot tied with such skill in the preceding two acts. Cerha's completion fulfils two other, highly important requirements – the first formal, the second moral. Berg's ingrained sense of symmetrical design, dominating all his work from the Chamber Concerto to the Violin Concerto, manifests itself with particular clarity in *Lulu*, namely in the ascent and descent of Lulu's 'career', with the pivot precisely in the middle of the opera, so that the first half has its mirror image in the second half. Berg's preoccupation with mirror images is seen also in the fact that he makes Lulu's three husbands return, symbolically, in her three clients who avenge their death on her, Schön's murder by Lulu at the end of Act II, 2 being exactly paralleled by her murder at Jack's hands at the end of Act III. Moreover, as I have already said, Lulu's three husbands are to be impersonated by the same artists as take the parts of her three clients, which gives the characters a close dramatic link. There are, in addition, musical correspondences of varying degrees of closeness between the two halves which were buried in the hitherto suppressed last act of the work.

The second important gain achieved by Cerha's completion is that when the spectator sees the last act in flesh and blood his former view of Lulu will perforce undergo a change. Up to this point one is unable to register any sympathy for the heroine, who in the first two acts appears solely as the quintessence of a *femme fatale* – even as an Angel of Destruction. Now that we see the last act unfolding before our eyes exactly as Berg visualized it, the perspective has changed and our compassion for her is aroused. Her end comes with the impact of classical tragedy: poetic justice is done to her as it is done to Don Giovanni in Mozart's opera – both go to hell and our moral conscience, so greatly disturbed, is at last set at rest.

It would be wrong, however, to allow a moral point of view to have much say in our aesthetic judgment of the opera. Yet this is exactly what a

---

[129] See Appendix B.

distinguished English critic did when he declared that 'Lulu is a worthless creature upon whom Berg lavished all the resources of his genius'. More pharisaical still is the dictum of Dr Josef Polnauer:[130] 'Wir können die Schweinereien im dritten Akt nicht brauchen' – 'We have no need of the filth and dirt in the third act' – which was his furious reply to Cerha when the latter told him of his intention to complete that act.[131]

In a work of art it is not the subject but its imaginative treatment, that is, the way in which an artist exteriorizes his ideas and feelings *about* the subject, that counts in the last analysis. Flaubert once wrote: There are no noble or ignoble subjects from the point of view of pure Art, one might almost establish the axiom that there is no such thing as a subject'. For example, in a painting it is not the *What* that appears on the canvas, but the *How* that remains the principal theme of study and debate. It is, therefore, completely irrelevant from an aesthetic point of view that the heroine of *Lulu* and her hangers-on are worthless creatures, and that its drama is a sordid and lurid sex drama – a *Monstertragödie*, as Wedekind first called his two plays, which is decked out with features from realism, surrealism, the theatre of cruelty, grotesque comedy and farce. If the plays are accepted as three-dimensional (a proposition strongly contested by hostile critics), Berg has added a fourth dimension. Music always does that. By setting the *Lulu* dramas Berg ennobled, as he did in his *Wozzeck*, the characters, intensified their passions and emotions, and deepened their psychology. He raised Wedekind's happenings to the level of a modern music-drama, which constitutes, again like *Wozzeck*, a most challenging, provocative experience for the spectator. Its excellence as a work of art resides in Berg's sovereign treatment of its dramatic aspect, in his magisterial command and organization of the musical material, both *per se* and in the service of the *dramatis personae* and their relationship with one another, and in the uniquely subtle symbolic significance with which he invests the serial technique.

Lulu (like *Wozzeck*) transcends the *données* of the libretto. Indeed, it can be argued that it reaches into a sphere in which such questions as what is the *nature* of sexuality, of sexual perversion and amorality, of human relationships, free will and predetermination, achieve a new topicality. But towering above these philosophical questions is the Aristotelian catharsis the spectator undergoes, as he watches the struggle between the individual and the elemental forces of nature, a struggle in which he is, perhaps against his will, compelled to participate very closely through the power of Berg's music.

[130] A Schoenberg pupil of Berg's generation and President of the Austrian Section of the ISCM in 1965.
[131] Cerha, op. cit., p. 33.

APPENDIX A

Berg's Letter to Schoenberg

In the Music Division of the Library of Congress, Washington, Schoenberg's heir deposited nearly 400 letters, postcards and telegrams sent by Berg to his erstwhile teacher which cover the span of twenty-four years (1911-35) – perhaps the largest correspondence in existence by one eminent composer to another. At first, frequent, prolix, docile, and full of admiration for the venerated father-figure, Berg's letters after he finished *Wozzeck* (1921) become less frequent, briefer, more factual and to the point. And while still echoing his one-time respect for the older man, Berg's former student-master relationship makes room for a more independent stance: conscious of his achievements and growing fame Berg now speaks to Schoenberg as an equal.

I reproduce Berg's longest and, perhaps, most outspoken letter to Schoenberg, written from the military hospital at Bruck an der Leitha in November 1915.[1]

November 1915

Dear Herr Schönberg

I think the best thing will be for me to repeat what I said in the letter that I wrote while I was in the Bruck hospital but never posted, filling in the gaps with the things which only became clear to me after your explanations on Wednesday. I am afraid that this will mean going in some detail over things in the not very recent past, and I must ask you to be patient and only to read this letter when you have plenty of time to spare. I hate worrying you with my personal affairs at a time when you have good reason to fear the worst – I mean military service – yourself. But I think I owe it both to you and to myself to state clearly what I call the 'situation' in which I have come to find myself during the years of your absence from Vienna. I blame this 'situation' for the fact that I continually did things which could not fail to annoy you and destroy your faith and interest in me.

As my health has got worse and I have to be in bed, I'm afraid that I must write in pencil.

It was on the journey to Amsterdam (1913) that I first noticed your dissatisfaction with me. What Stein and Webern told me later also confirmed this impression. At that time you observed a regression and remissness in my

[1] Translated by Martin Cooper.

work; and the false and malicious accounts given you by my sister and her friend forced you to the conclusion that the cause of this remissness lay in my total dependence on my own relations and those of my wife – a dependence which involved me in daily card-playing and the like. This was of course all a lie. It may perhaps be said that a certain financial dependence on my family did involve my devoting to them and their affairs time which should ideally have been devoted to composition. If I counted up at that time how much had happened during that long period – apart from my administrative work, apart from travelling (Munich, Berlin, two journeys to Prague, Leipzig, Amsterdam and two visits to the Berghof), apart from lessons on three afternoons every week, various businesslike arrangements for concerts, the final proofs of the 'Harmonielehre', apart from the brochure 'Arnold Schoenberg' (admittedly entirely my own responsibility), apart from my work on the 'Gurrelieder' (vocal score, correction of parts, the two 'Guides' and the actual performance), apart from vocal scores of the two songs from the F sharp minor string quartet, the piano arrangement, partly for four hands of Mahler's eighth symphony, the transposing of Strauss songs – *and my short orchestral songs and even shorter clarinet pieces* – ... If I counted it all up, I had to admit that two and a half years' work amounted to damned little, and that bad planning of my time was chiefly to blame. Hence my serious resolve to change things and to do better.

In the first place I must aim at complete independence as far as my wife's relations are concerned and at reducing my dependence on my mother to the financial support arising from the administrative duties incumbent on me. I must cut myself resolutely off from all family quarrels and all gossip.

Next, I must aim at improvement in all the small matters for which you rightly found fault with me – my illegible hand-writing, my unintelligible style of letter-writing, neglect of my clothes etc. Lastly, I naturally took very much to heart your criticisms of the triviality and worthlessness of my latest compositions and of the piano scores that I made of your Orchestral Pieces and the Chamber Symphony. The Three Orchestral Pieces were really the outcome of the most intense and devoted efforts to write characteristic pieces in the form you suggested, of normal length and closely developed thematically without any striving to create anything necessarily novel, but simply the best that I could do. I am in any case a slow worker, and the outbreak of war initially destroyed all desire to compose as well as doubling my repsonsibilities for finding somewhere for my mother to live and for the Berghof – otherwise I might have accomplished more. But I cannot say that, in any case I did what I could.

If I can trust the judgment of Webern and Steuermann, I think I may say that in the piano score of the Kammersymphonie I have done something good, i.e. comparatively easy to play and sounding well. All the same, my attempts at improvement proved quite ineffectual. The few reports that I had of you made it clear to me that everything that concerned me – even trivial matters – caused you bitterness. And finally there appeared solid reasons which far from raising me in your estimation – as I never ceased to hope – did but lower me still further. I mean the wretched business over the Mahler Fund[2] and the preparatory arrangements for the concert at which you conducted Beethoven's Ninth Symphony [April 1915].

There is no need for me to go over again today how it came about that all these things, which I undertook with the best intentions and the clearest of consciences, went wrong either wholly or in part. Little wonder that I had the feeling at that time of being in some way fated, so that despite my intention of improving myself and my behaviour I found myself time and again driven to seem worse in your eyes rather than better – to appear not so much a human being as a monster, totally unaware of the duties of friends towards each other and ranged *against* you rather than on your side – in fact only acting in your interests in order to assure myself a share in your immortality. Your behaviour towards me when you were in Vienna at the beginning of this summer was the natural outcome of this opinion that you had of me. I could not open my mouth without arousing your bitterness. It became quite clear in conversation that you credited me with actions with which one only credits an enemy e.g. that I was intriguing against you with Frau Mahler, who behaved tactlessly on that occasion, or that when I thanked you professionally for some piece of advice I thanked you in an *ironic* manner. I could only conclude from all this that my whole personality was alien and unpleasing to you and that you would find it preferable and least irritating if I were not continually to intrude myself on you. The most natural solution therefore appeared to be to rid you of my presence at a time when you were in any case surrounded by people and I knew, from the time of the Ninth Symphony concert, how tedious you then found it to be perpetually besieged. I must admit that this solution *coincided* with a plan that I had *already* made to go to Trahütten for a few weeks. There was no danger of this plan appearing selfish, since I took it for granted that you would be spending your summer on the Semmering [a mountain resort south of Vienna] and I should be doing nobody any service by staying on in Vienna. I had announced my intended visit to the Semmering well beforehand to Stein and yourself; and it only fell through because I had no answer, still another proof that my presence was not desired. So in the knowledge that nobody would be pleased if I stayed, and that in fact I was completely superfluous – in fact without being particularly selfish (since selfishness consists not only in doing what suits oneself but also in doing it with the idea of making it inconvenient

[2] A fund created by Alma Mahler after the death of her husband for the purpose of supporting needy musicians, for which she enlisted the help of wealthy friends. Schoenberg, then in straitened material circumstances, seems to have had some quarrel with Frau Mahler over a subsidy he expected from the Fund.

to other people, which honestly never occurred to me) – in *this* knowledge, then, I carried out the plan which I had made in the circumstances described, but in other circumstances and ones which I found most painful. There were *also* other serious reasons for carrying out my plan, which I should perhaps have got over or explained to you in good time, if I had for a moment supposed that you were in fact interested in any way.

1. It was to be foreseen that you would in any case sooner or later go to the Semmering.

2. I was anxious not to deprive my wife who was at that time badly in need of a period of recuperation in good air, since the summer was in any case half its normal length owing to my call-up.

3. I wanted to finish work on the Orchestral Pieces –
   (a) because they should have been finished already
   (b) because I had actually promised them to you, and
   (c) I did not know whether I should otherwise ever manage to finish them in view of my being called up.

4. Finally, the question of money. And there you think it impossible that I should have difficulties that are not easily overcome. But that is in fact the truth! Of course it is true that I have my regular income and in *that* sense do not need to worry. But this does not alter the fact that I cannot spend more than this fixed sum without accumulating debts that I cannot pay off in any foreseeable future. My regular income may justify the supposition that I am in a position to put *money aside*. As far as the house and everything connected with it are concerned, we are in any case living above our means and have often considered making economies in that department in order to be able sometimes to allow ourselves something extra in the way of travelling or spending the summer somewhere else, which would only be made possible by imposing economies on ourselves in some other field. You yourself are fully aware of the possibilities of actually *earning* money. It is virtually out of the question for me to obtain any sum of money, however small, from somewhere else. I have no acquaintances to whom I could turn in such a matter, and there only remains my own family. The sum my *mother* gives me in return for what I do in the way of administering the estate is already difficult for her to find, and to ask for more would be tantamount to a real imposition on her personally or on my brother and sister. *My wife's* marriage settlement cannot be touched and is administered by her parents and therefore there is no hope in that quarter; and it would be mere pipe-dreaming to count on *more* from *her* family than occasional presents to my wife, such as clothes etc. and the yearly summer holiday which involves us in no expense [at Trahütten].

These are things, Herr Schönberg, that may well not be easy for you to understand. But perhaps it would surprise you to know that I am still *today* paying off the extra expenditure involved in the trip to Leipzig and

Amsterdam; and that last summer (1914) I could only afford to take my wife to Karlsbad for the cure she needed to recover from a long-standing illness. I had to leave her there entirely alone for four weeks, in a very modest room in a cheap pension, since I could not afford to stay on with her. And that, after all, was *before* the war. This year, with inflation added and *half* our *cost-free* holiday lost in any case by my being called up, we have less money and more expenses; so that it was an absolute *necessity* to economise at least a few weeks of the summer – something that no one could deny who has the smallest acquaintance with my circumstances.

To repeat, then – since I had absolutely no feeling that you welcomed my presence and you were in any case sooner or later going to the Semmering, I accepted these four more or less compelling reasons for going to the country for a few weeks, without for a moment suspecting that I might be behaving selfishly.

A further circumstance seemed also to confirm that I was right in my supposition. My repeated and even pressing (perhaps indeed importunate) enquiry as to whether I should be in the way if I come to Breitenstein [Schoenberg's temporary residence near Vienna] remained unanswered; so that once again I could only suppose that my presence was unwelcome. Eventually, when it was almost too late, I learned that you were going to Berlin. If I had left immediately on hearing this news from Stein, I could have seen you for just one day in Vienna. The spy-business in Trahütten[3] made that impossible for me. I wrote to tell you this and at the same time sent you the completed score of my Three Orchestral Pieces in the belief that *these* at least would furnish a proof of how you were perpetually in my mind during these weeks, and I also hoped to satisfy you in this way. Once again, no answer. My only source of information was Stein and I extracted this from him by means of prepaid answer-cards. Meanwhile, in view of your moving entirely to Vienna, my wife too had written to yours to say how much she looked forward to their seeing a lot of each other in the autumn. Your wife's silence could only confirm my wife as well as myself, in supposing that scattered remarks that your wife was said to have made about mine, and that were repeated to her, really did express what you and your wife thought about her – so that there could be no question of your being friendlily disposed towards her, but at best tolerated her as my wife.

Please, Herr Schönberg, this and everything else in this letter are all real facts and not simply fantasies of mine, and I should like to give you several other examples more recent in date – I mean last Wednesday – which prove that you instinctively incline to put the worst interpretation on my

---

[3] I was unable to identify this event.

behaviour, or at least on things that concern me. When you came to Vienna [April 1915] for the performance of the Ninth Symphony, I was still confident that you did not actually dislike me and I foolishly believed that, as far as humanly possible, I had done my duty, did not in fact yet suspect that I might be intruding on you. It was therefore naturally my first thought to invite you to my house, and all the more pressingly because I thought that, on your last visit to Vienna, a dinner at my house, which turned out a failure, represented a breach on my part of the rules of hospitality. Even then, in the modest (and justified) belief that the company of my wife and myself could not be enough for you – to do you honour, in fact – we *also* invited Frau Mahler. At that time nothing had occurred to arouse any suspicion of Frau Mahler's unqualified esteem for you. That I can swear to you! I believe that you are so convinced of my poor character that you can have absolutely no inkling of just how wounding your interpretation of our inviting her was, but also how demonstrably wrong – since after all we can give a dinner party for Frau Mahler *any day* of the week, and you must yourself remember that it was only on your own request that I invited Frau Lieser, so that I simply cannot understand your now saying that we gave a dinner party for Frau Mahler and Frau Lieser and then invited *you* and *your* wife to it. [Frau Lieser was a wealthy friend of Schoenberg's who had financed his Beethoven Concert.] This automatically contradicts the accusation that you made at the time viz. that our behaviour to you and your wife implied something like a social 'rating'. The friendship between my wife and Frau Mahler developed automatically out of a simple exchange of letters and knowing each other by sight, and Frau Mahler's social position as Gustav Mahler's wife played not the smallest part in it. Frau Mahler might just as well have been the wife of some quite unimportant businessman.

Then there was another improbable but very significant occasion! On Wednesday, when Stein told you on the telephone about Bittner's crazy idea [presumably a reference to Bittner's efforts to get Schoenberg out of the army in 1915], you exclaimed as you put down the receiver, 'I can't imagine what Berg is thinking of!'

And then 'trara-Burg!' Amusing as this confusion of names may be, I am quite aware of the 'dig' that it contains, and that it is not against the *place* – which is anything but a *Burg* where people live in a 'trara' style. It is in fact one of a number of poor Alpine villages (Trahütten, Glasshütten etc.) where I have spent a number of summers, living in a simple cottage very close to nature and working hard almost the whole day ... no, the 'dig' can only have been aimed at me, because I love the place and anything towards which I show any inclination automatically arouses your spite and mockery.

Dear Herr Schönberg! I am telling you all these things not in order to warm up old stories or to reproach you in any way, which I should never be justified in doing. It is quite simply in order to ask you to put yourself for one moment in my place, and to imagine what I have gone through during these four years, watching your goodwill towards me steadily dwindling *despite* the fact that my whole concern was to do right by you. I had only to correct one mistake to find myself, without being aware of it, falling into another until at last it was borne in on me that everything on which I laid my hands or which had anything to do with me was odious to you, or at least alien; so that in the end I could only conclude that you did not want to have anything to do with a person like me – quite understandable when I look at the list of all the items that I have quoted (and others that I have not quoted) and remember that you drew up that list, as it were, when you gave me to understand that I was in danger of completely losing your interest in me. 'But how can it matter to you?' you added casually, 'in four or five years, when the war is over, there will in any case be no more interest in my music,' thus making it plain for the second time that my motives for wishing to keep or regain your friendship were the lowest and most contemptible, namely not only to assure my own immortality but to obtain a share in your success here and now, to act accordingly – a second Paul Stefan! [A Viennese critic].

It is any wonder, then, since I am in any case always inclined to think myself in the wrong and to see everything fail that I worked so passionately to achieve – that I fell into a state of utter dejection and perplexity, lost all confidence in myself and my own judgment and became so confused in my ideas, all of which seemed topsy-turvy, that I failed to do the most obvious things and omitted the most fundamental social duties. I simply *cannot* find any other explanation to offer you: I was idiotic enough not to dare to offer you my help when you moved to Vienna. It was not modesty, but quite simply fear – that an absolute natural readiness to help (no question of 'making sacrifices') might be interpreted as a heaven-sent opportunity to impose myself on you à la Paul Stefan, to offer my services and make myself indispensable by exploiting the position in which you found yourself for the moment. An additional factor was my military training which took a lot out of me in every way and made it impossible for me to think things over quietly and realise at the last moment how greatly mistaken I was. I *really* thought I was right to approach you without foisting myself on you and to wait for *you* – who after all have never hesitated to make quite clear at once what you considered proper to expect from me – to say the word which would have made it easier for me to offer my help. If when you were first here you could only once have asked casually when we could meet again, I should certainly have had the courage to ask you whether you would like to have your meals with us while you had not yet settled in. But instead of that you became increasingly cool – I *now perfectly* understand and appreciate the reason, but then I misinterpreted it. I became increasingly shy of approaching you, until finally you made it absolutely clear that you did not wish for a meeting. It would never have entered my head then to explain this by a recent neglect of dutifulness on my own part. Instead of that *I thought it was rather* the complete withdrawal of your friendship that I had so long feared – the catastrophe towards which I had been heading helplessly for years and something which, without any new push, was bound to happen.

Of course I now understand that I was wrong in this supposition, and the same is true of the mistakes and omissions in my behaviour towards you, once again caused by repeated misinterpretations and false conclusions. But none of these offences and omissions were deliberate or the result of selfishness on my part; they were the result of a total confusion caused by my inability to orientate myself in a situation in which I was groping helplessly – or if you will not accept that as valid – by sheer stupidity, which amounts to much the same thing.

I can only hope now that you are not afraid that my struggle against this is a vain one, that you will not completely give me up and that you will admit me again to your friendship. Your last invitation to come and see you again at last gives me reason to hope that this may be so. God grant that my pouring out my heart in such a long letter has not extinguished that hope.

If I can take it that you have read this letter, and if – as I hope – I have no relapse into my illness, I shall allow myself to enquire again when I can see you, unless you prefer to let me know this sooner. Since a lunatic fate is after all not to spare you from being called up, I may possibly be able to be of some use to you with my own military experiences, or at least to accompany you to the various interviews. Meanwhile, dear Herr Schönberg, I send you my warmest greetings.

Your
Berg

APPENDIX B

Friedrich Cerha's performing version of Act III of *Lulu*

Friedrich Cerha (b. Vienna, 1926) studied composition and violin at the Vienna Muskhochschule and German literature at the University. In 1958 he founded, together with Kurt Schertsik, the ensemble *Die Reihe* which was one of the first organizations in post-war Austria to specialize in and propagate contemporary music. Cerha has composed a diversity of works, among them an opera *Baal* based on Brecht's play. His intimate acquaintance with the music of the so-called Second Viennese School made him the obvious choice for the completion of Act III of *Lulu*.

Cerha worked for nearly twelve years (1963-1974) on his self-chosen task and subjected it to a revision in 1976-7, in connexion with his editing of Erwin Stein's vocal score and Berg's libretto. In 1979 he published an *Arbeitsbericht* or Work Report[1] which in its scrupulous scholarship and thoroughness is a model of its kind. In it he tells us how his interest in *Lulu* was first aroused by a performance of the opera at the Theater an der Wien in 1962 and how profoundly dismayed he was when he saw the makeshift ending of the work. After a thorough study of all the authentic source material, the most important of which was Berg's all but complete draft in short score for Act III, Cerha weighed up the pros and cons before deciding on the *Herstellung* or provision of a performing version of that act. He then goes on to discuss the multifarious problems he was faced with in the work of completion – in the first place the filling of compositional gaps and the orchestration of an act which in his numbering now runs to 1326 bars of which Berg left only the first 268 bars in full score. (Owing to two counting errors, Berg's short score extends to 1300 bars which was corrected by Erwin Stein in his vocal score to 1304 bars).

There were six lacunae to be filled, two of which are of special importance. The first is not so much a gap as a need for expansion of the existing music; it occurs at bar 262 of the full score where Berg left three pages blank, with a note saying 'Insertion of 22 bars for a possible extension of Ensemble (II) and clarification of the dialogue Lulu-Geschwitz'. Cerha's extension of 2 × 11 bars (262-84) is not a literal repetition of the existing music but a variation of it which was Berg's method of modifying a repeat. The second important gap is to be found in the Quartet of scene 2 in which Lulu, Geschwitz, Alwa and Schigolch contemplate Lulu's pierrot picture of her 'great days', each

[1] *Arbeitsbericht zur Herstellung des 3. Aktes der Oper 'Lulu' von Alban Berg*. Vienna, 1979.

reacting to it in his or her characteristic way. Berg wrote out only the part for
Alwa ('always dominating') and merely indicated where the other voices are
to enter (976-1000). In completing the missing parts Cerha followed Berg's
technique of developing a vocal phrase from the instrumental texture, but he
confessed to have proceeded here more cautiously than Berg himself might
have done. The missing text for Geschwitz and Schigolch was taken from the
Wedekind text indicated by Berg in the *particella*, but there were no words for
Lulu for whom Cerha took two sentences (slightly modified) from the
dialogue Lulu-Schön in II, 2.

A gap of some 20 bars occurs in the Ensemble III in which Berg composed
only the Banker-Mother dialogue and the daughter's exclamation after her
mother has swooned, 'Wach auf, Mama, wach auf!'. The remaining voice
parts of this Ensemble were indicated by Berg in a wave-line bearing the
remark, 'Leises Gemurmel aller' ('Soft murmur of all'), the composer
evidently intending the same 'rhubarb' effect as of the Ensembles I and II.
Cerha followed him in this, of course, at the same time modelling Ensemble
III on the structure and texture of the two preceding ensembles.
Furthermore, there is no complete music in the short score for the
Jazzschlagwerk (1088 ff). Berg notating only RH in the bass drum. Taking his
cue from the canonic statement of RH in bars 1080 ff., and the jazz music of
I, 3 (bars 749 ff. and 766 ff.) Cerha scored the passage in question for cymbal,
side drum, bass drum, tam-tam and jazz drum. Finally, the orchestration of
Wedekind's *Lautenlied* was modelled on bars 49-52 of the Variations from the
Symphonic Pieces.

According to Cerha's timing, Act III of *Lulu* lasts about 64 minutes but I
have checked this figure against the DG recording and the Covent Garden
performance in which the duration was *c.* 57 minutes. Of these about 19
minutes are taken up by the music of Berg's full score. For a further 17
minutes Cerha has referred directly back to the Variations from the
Symphonic Pieces and the transformation music between scenes 2 & 3 of Act
I, while the Cadenza for violin and piano (Marquis-Athlete) was indicated in
the *particella*. A second group lasting for about 20 minutes included passages
for which Berg had provided the model in the two preceding acts, such as
Lulu's Canzonetta (I, 2) for the scene Lulu-Professor, Alwa's Hymn (II, 2)
for the quarter, Lulu's Cavatina (II, 2) for the Grazioso, and the scene Lulu-
Schigolch for their corresponding scene in III, 1. For the rest of the music
only vague correspondences could be found and Cerha adopted a more
tentative approach to it; but such passages were few in number. Fortunately,
Berg left in full score the first 268 bars of the act including the Concertante
Chorale Variations while the orchestral Variations between the two scenes of
the act and the music for the very last scene (1146-87; 1924-1326) were taken
from the fourth and fifth movement, respectively, of the Symphonic Pieces.
All these sections, Cerha says, could not have been orchestrated by someone

else without serious risk to authenticity.

The *particella* contained only sporadic indications as to the intended orchestration. As for the phraseology, articulation and dynamics, Cerha solved this problem by going back to similar or corresponding markings in the preceding acts and Berg's full score for Act III, also taking into account other works of Berg's in order to achieve the widest measure of stylistic fidelity. On the other hand, tempo and metronome markings were precisely indicated in the short score. In two cases in the final scene – Andante (1180) and Grave (1315) – the metronome marks were slightly faster than those given for the corresponding sections of the Adagio from the Symphonic Pieces.

To sum up: with the exception of the six lacunae involving some compositional work (notably the expansion of the dialogue Lulu-Geschwitz and the Quartet) Cerha's over-riding aim was to provide (1) an authentic realization of Berg's short score, (2) carefully considered additions to the phrasing, articulation and dynamics, (3) marking of RH and leading (H) and subsidiary (N) parts, and (4) completing and editing Berg's stage-directions.

Certain quarters have raised objections to the fact that such an important task as the full realization of Act III of *Lulu* should have been entrusted to a musician of but local repute and of no marked creative personality. The argument runs that only a composer of outstanding individuality should have been commissioned to do this work. I for one take the contrary view, and am glad that both Schoenberg and Webern declined, though for patent reasons they were the first to be approached with the task. The odds are that both, because of their strong musical personalities, would have unwittingly impressed them on the work of completion and thus introduced that 'alien spirit' which was the very thing Helene Berg wanted to avoid when she imposed a total embargo on all the material of Act III of *Lulu*. Zemlinsky, on the other hand, a composer of little individuality and an eclectic, would have been far more suitable, but then he had little liking for atonal and twelve-note music which did not, however, prevent him from conducting it. Just because Cerha is a composer of no pronounced creative personality but a highly professional musician, he was able to feel himself completely into Berg's late style identifying with it with total submission, and accomplished an intricate task with the utmost fidelity to Berg's intentions. There has been a general consensus of opinion wherever the complete *Lulu* has been staged that Cerha came as near to these intentions as it at all possible for another musician. In my view, formed after hearing the opera in Paris and London and confirmed by the DG recording, there is not a single bar in Cerha's performing version that could be called un-Bergian.

APPENDIX C

Synopsis of the opera plots

Wozzeck

Act I
Scene 1: The Captain's room. Early morning

Wozzeck is shaving the Captain, who admonishes him to go about it more slowly. To do things slowly is a fundamental principle of the Captain's philosophy. He wonders what he will do with the time saved him by Wozzeck's rapid shaving. He compares eternity with the moment, boggles at the thought of the earth turning round and says that he becomes melancholy at the sight of a revolving mill-wheel. Wozzeck's reply to the Captain's remarks is a stereotyped 'Jawohl, Herr Hauptmann!'. The Captain notices that his batman looks harassed – 'A good man does not look harassed'. He then chides him for having no 'moral sense', for he is the father of a child born out of wedlock. Wozzeck answers that it is easy to be virtuous when one has money; he is a poor man (aria, 'Wir arme Leut!'). The Captain, much confused by Wozzeck's reply, dismisses him, enjoining him to walk slowly.

Scene 2: An open field behind the town. Late afternoon

Wozzeck and Andres are cutting sticks in the field. The soldier feels that the place is haunted and evil, the rising mist and the toadstools frighten him – it is all the fault of the Freemasons – and in his hallucinations he sees a head rolling on the ground. Andres, completely unconcerned, sings a folksong ('Das ist die schöne Jägerei'). As the sun sets Wozzeck has a vision of a huge fire shooting up from the earth to heaven. Darkness falls and the two men depart.

Scene 3: Marie's room. Evening

Marie, Wozzeck's mistress, stands with the child by the window and watches a military band pass by. The Drum-Major greets her and she waves back to him. Margret, her neighbour, makes a spiteful remark on Marie's behaviour, whereupon Marie slams her window in anger. She sings a lullaby to the child (Mädel, was fangst du jetzt an?'). Wozzeck appears at the window in a distraught state and tells Marie of his strange hallucination while cutting the sticks in the field. He quotes a passage from the Bible, and without sparing a look for his child he leaves for the barracks. Marie breaks out in sudden anguish and rushes out of the room.

Scene 4. The Doctor's study. A sunny afternoon

The Doctor tries out dietary experiments on Wozzeck, who thereby earns a little money for Marie and his child. The Doctor asks him whether he has been following his prescription of eating beans only – next week it will be mutton, he adds. The soldier tries to tell him of his visions in the open field, but the Doctor, impatiently brushing this aside, declares that Wozzeck has fixed ideas and is a clear case of 'aberratio mentalis partialis, second species'. The Doctor's own fixed idea is to achieve fame and immortality with his inhuman experiments on the soldier.

Scene 5: A street before Marie's house. Dusk

The Drum-Major boasts of his virility to Marie, who stands before him full of admiration. He makes advances to her and after some struggle she yields and the two disappear into the house.

Act II

Scene 1: Marie's room. A sunny morning

Marie is admiring a pair of ear-rings given her by the Drum-Major. The child is restless and she tries to calm it by singing a gypsy song ('Mädel, mach's Lädel zu'). Coquettishly she is looking in a mirror at her face adorned by the ear-rings, when Wozzeck enters unexpectedly. Marie tries in vain to hide the ear-rings and to Wozzeck's question of where they have come from, she answers that she has found them. The soldier remarks that he has never been so fortunate as to find two such together. He hands Marie the money earned from the Doctor and the Captain and departs. Overcome by deep remorse – 'I am a bad lot. I could stab myself' – she rushes off in great agitation.

Scene 2: A street. Day

The Captain and the Doctor meet and start a conversation. The Doctor frightens the life out of the Captain by remarking on his 'apopletic constitution' and on the likelihood of a stroke 'within four weeks'. Wozzeck passes by in great haste. The Captain and the Doctor detain him, taunting him with insinuations about Marie's infidelity with the Drum-Major. Wozzeck, profoundly shaken, warns them not to make fun of him and runs off, leaving the two in utter consternation.

Scene 3: A street before Marie's house. A dull day

Wozzeck accuses Marie of being unfaithful. She answers provocatively, whereupon he tries to strike her. She warns him off – 'Rather a knife in the heart than lay hands on me'. As she leaves, the soldier stares after her, pondering her remark about the knife.

Scene 4: A garden inn. Late evening

Soldiers and young men and girls are dancing a ländler and waltz to the accompaniment of a tavern band. Marie and the Drum-Major join the dancing crowd, and Wozzeck observes them in great agitation – 'Everything twists and turns in lechery, man, woman and beast'. A hunting chorus is heard, after which a drunken Journeyman launches into a long 'philosophical' sermon. The Idiot appears and, pressing close to Wozzeck, whispers to him that he smells blood. Wozzeck repeats the word 'blood' as though the thought of murdering Marie were rising up in him.

Scene 5: A guard room in the barracks. Night

Soldiers are asleep and snoring loudly. Wozzeck, awake, is haunted by the vision of a knife, hears voices coming from the wall and music of the tavern band. The Drum-Major enters, stone drunk, and whips up Wozzeck's jealousy by enumerating the attractions of Marie's body. He tries to force Wozzeck to drink from his bottle. The latter refuses and whistles contemptuously, whereupon the Drum-Major thrashes him. Wozzeck's mind is made up to kill Marie.

Act III
Scene 1: Marie's room. Night. Candlelight

Marie is filled with deep remorse at her unfaithfulness and seeks consolation in the Bible. She interrupts her reading to tell the child a sad tale about a little orphan who has no one in this world ('And once there was a poor little child'). She then turns to the story of Maria Magdalena, entreating Christ to have mercy upon her as he had mercy upon the sinner in the Bible.

Scene 2: A forest path by a pond. Night

Wozzeck and Marie have been walking through a forest and now stop by a pond. He taunts her with her beauty, goodness and faithfulness. As the moon rises blood red, he pulls out a knife and cuts her throat.

Scene 3: A low tavern. Night

A crowd of youths and young girls are dancing a polka strummed on an out-of-tune piano. Wozzeck drinks, sings, and dances with Margret in order to drown his torturing feelings of guilt. Margret suddenly notices blood on his right arm. Wozzeck rushes off, pursued by the cries of the crowd.

Scene 4: The same as in Scene 2. Moonlight

Driven by fear that his crime might be discovered, Wozzeck has come back to the pond to find the murder knife. He stumbles over Marie's body, and seeing the line of blood around her throat, he likens it to a 'crimson necklace'. He finds the knife and throws it into the water, but thinking that he has not thrown it far enough, he wades into the pond and drowns. The Captain and the Doctor pass by and hear noises as if someone were drowning. Greatly frightened, they hurry away.

Scene 5: In front of Marie's house. Bright morning. Sunshine

Children are playing. Among them is Marie's child, riding a hobby-horse. He is told by a playmate that his mother lies dead by the pond. He continues on his hobby-horse while all the other children run off to the pond. Noticing that he is alone, he hesitates and then rides off after them.

Lulu

Prologue: Before the entrance to a circus

The Animal Trainer invites the audience to step inside his circus and see his animals – a tiger (Schön and Jack the Ripper), a bear (the Athlete), a monkey (the Marquis), reptiles (Schigolch and the Medizinalrat), a crocodile (Geschwitz) and a snake (Lulu). At his command a clown brings in Lulu dressed in the pierrot costume in which she is painted in the first scene of the opera.

Act I
Scene 1: The studio of the Painter

In the presence of Dr Schön, the Painter is painting Lulu's pierrot portrait which, as the symbol of her beauty and youth, appears in every scene of the opera. Alwa, Schön's son and a composer, arrives to take his father to a dress rehearsal. He expresses astonishment at seeing Lulu for the first time alone, without her husband, the Medizinalrat. In parting Schön asks Lulu to convey his greetings to him, whereupon in repartee she begs him to give her regards to Schön's fiancée whom, she pointedly says, she does not know. The Painter and Lulu are left alone. Immensely attracted by her, he is unable to continue with his painting and pursues her all over the studio until he catches her on the divan and covers her hands with passionate kisses. The Medizinalrat arrives and, finding the door locked, breaks it down in rage. Seeing the two together, he has a stroke and dies. While the Painter goes to call a doctor, Lulu coolly contemplates her husband's body (*Canzonetta*). The Painter returns and is appalled by the indifference shown by Lulu to the death of the Medizinalrat. He catechizes her, asking whether she believes in a God, whether she has a soul and whether she had ever loved. To all these questions Lulu replies with a stereotyped 'I do not know'. While she goes into the other room to change her dress the Painter contemplates the corpse and, filled with a sudden fear for the future, prays for a little happiness for 'her sake'.

Scene 2: An elegant room in the Painter's home

Lulu and the Painter are married. With the morning post arrives a letter announcing Schön's engagement to a girl of noble birth. The door bell rings: the visitor is an asthmatic old man, Schigolch, Lulu's one-time lover and now a kind of father-figure to her. Letting him in, the Painter takes him for a beggar and leaves him alone with Lulu. Schigolch has come to ask Lulu for money – '200 marks; I don't mind taking 300'. The two reminisce on their past, when another ring announces the arrival of Schön. Schigolch leaves and Schön passing him thinks he is Lulu's father. Schön tells his mistress that she must stop her visits to him and that their long affair has finally ended. He has, he says, found two husbands for her and is supporting her present marriage financially; he must now be free to marry a respectable girl. Lulu replies that her husband's love for her is totally blind and uncomprehending. The only man who understands her, and whom she loves, is Schön. He has cared for her since she sold flowers in the streets at the age of twelve and she owes him everything.

The Painter returns, wondering what their arguments are about. Lulu leaves and Schön decides to tell the Painter the truth about his marriage: that he has invested half a million in the marriage and that he expects that the Painter will keep a stricter control on his wife. Schön hints at his own relationship with Lulu and reveals to him her past – how he had taken her off the streets and adopted her, how after his wife's death she had come between him and his fiancée and how, in order to free himself of her, he had married her to the Medizinalrat and then to the Painter. The latter collapses under these revelations and leaves, saying that he will speak to Lulu. Terrible groans are heard from the room into which the Painter has disappeared, and Schön, together with Lulu and Alwa, who has meanwhile arrived on the scene, breaks down the door with an axe. Unable to face the truth about Lulu, the Painter has committed suicide by cutting his throat with a razor. Schön calls for the police while Lulu vows that she will yet marry him (*Monoritmica*).

Scene 3: The dressing-room of a theatre

Schön has arranged a stage performance for Lulu as a dancer, in the hope that she will meet someone willing to marry her and thus make him free to marry his fiancée. As the curtain rises, we see Alwa and Lulu celebrating the success of her performance with champagne. Alwa is already deeply in love with her and while she leaves for the stage, he contemplates writing an opera with Lulu's story as the subject. Enter the Prince, an explorer of Africa and one of Lulu's most ardent admirers. He wants to take her to Africa. Lulu suddenly rushes into the dressing-room – she has caught sight while dancing of Schön and his fiancée, whose presence she considers an insult to her, and has therefore broken off her performance. Schön enters in rage, commanding her to continue with her dancing before his fiancée. A commotion ensues (*Sextet*). Left alone, Lulu, who is now completely composed, tells Schön that the Prince wants to take her to Africa. Cleverly playing on his jealousy and his inability to cut himself loose from her, she now forces him to write a letter to his fiancée, dictating to him to say that for three years he has been unable to sever himself from a woman who dominates him and that the engagement is now at an end. Schön collapses with the prophetic words, 'Jetzt kommt die Hinrichtung' – 'Now comes the execution'.

Act II
Scene 1: A resplendent room in Schön's home

Lulu has reached the peak of her career by marrying Schön and living in a palatial home.

Countess Geschwitz, a lesbian, is paying Lulu and Schön a visit. Schön detests her, feeling that the pest has entered his house. In an outburst of paranoia he tears the curtains apart to see whether Lulu's lover or lovers are hiding behind them. Geschwitz pretends to be leaving but conceals herself behind a fire-screen. It is Schön's day to go to the stock exchange but Lulu lures him into another room to make love to her. Taking advantage of Schön's supposed absence, a trio of Lulu's admirers enter: Schigolch, the Athlete and the Schoolboy. From their conversation it emerges that Schigolch is not Lulu's father – she has no father, he says, and that at one time both he and the Athlete wanted to marry her. The man-servant, also in love with Lulu, announces the visit of Alwa which is the signal for the trio to hide themselves in different places in the hall.

Alwa declares his love for Lulu and buries his head in her lap, while she casually tells him that she had poisoned his mother. Schön, who has observed the pair from the gallery, descends with a revolver in his hand and leads his son away. In an excess of rage he utters horrible accusations against Lulu (Beginning of Schön's *Aria in five strophes*), in the course of which he presses the revolver into Lulu's hand commanding her to shoot herself. She fires a shot against the ceiling, whereupon the Athlete darts up the staircase and escapes through the gallery. Schön searches for other hidden guests, discovers Geschwitz and pushes her into another room, whose door he locks. He now tries to force the revolver from Lulu, but she resists and declares that if Schön has sacrificed his old age for her, she has sacrificed her whole youth for him. She concludes by saying that she never wanted to appear other than what the world has taken her for and that the world has never taken her for other than what she is (*Lulu's Lied*). Schön attempts to direct the revolver in Lulu's hand against herself, when the Schoolboy, who has been hiding under the table, suddenly jumps and thus makes Schön turn his back to Lulu. She fires five shots at Schön.

Alwa and the Schoolboy lead the dying Schön into another room, whose door they find locked. Alwa turns the key and out comes Geschwitz; at the sight of her Schön utters his last words, 'Der Teufel' – 'The devil'. Lulu tries to escape but is prevented by Alwa, who calls the police. She implores him to save her from justice and punishment, vowing that she will be faithful to him all her life and belong only to him (*Arietta*).

The following orchestral interlude (*Ostinato*) divides the opera into two symmetrical halves and accompanies a film showing what happens to Lulu between the last scene and the next, events that cover a span of one year – her detention, her court trial, her imprisonment, her removal to an isolation hospital on account of the cholera which she deliberately contracted from Geschwitz, and her disguise as Geschwitz in preparation for her escape. In modern productions this film sequence is often omitted.

Scene 2: The room as in Scene 1 but covered in dust and shuttered against daylight, giving the impression of having been uninhabited

Alwa, Geschwitz and the Athlete are awaiting Schigolch's arrival. He is to take Geschwitz to Lulu's prison hospital. The Athlete is to marry Lulu and hopes she will have retained her former good looks, since he wants to make her 'the most graceful acrobat of present times'. Schigolch comes to take Geschwitz to the hospital where she will change places with Lulu. There follows a most unpleasant conversation between Alwa and the Athlete about money, the latter describing Alwa as the author of a 'horror opera that no decent theatre will stage'. A knock at the door is heard: it is the Schoolboy, who has escaped from a house of correction and comes with a plan to free Lulu from her imprisonment. On being told by the Athlete that she has died of cholera, he departs.

Schigolch returns with Lulu dressed in Geschwitz's clothes. Feigning utter debility, she slowly drags herself down the staircase. The Athlete is mortified to see Lulu in this state, and realizing that his plan to make an acrobat of her has come to nothing, rushes off in a fuming rage to denounce her to the police. As soon as Schigolch has left to collect the tickets for her escape to Paris, Lulu drops her pretence, becomes her former self, and explains to Alwa Geschwitz's clever stratagem for her escape from the prison hospital. They declare their love, Alwa describing in ecstatic words the sensual allure of her body (*Hymn*). Lulu persuades him to flee with her over the frontier and asks him quite casually if the divan on which they are sitting is the one on which his father bled to death.

Act III

Scene 1: A spacious hall in a Paris gambling Casino. A door at the back opens on to a gaming room. In the right corner hangs Lulu's pierrot painting

The Athlete and the other guests drink a birthday toast to Lulu, their hostess. While some of the guests leave for the gaming room, Alwa, the Banker, the Journalist and the Mother stay behind to comment on the high price of their shares in the Jungfrau Cable Railway. The Marquis and Lulu come forward and engage in a tense conversation. He confronts her with the alternatives of either becoming a prostitute in a high-class Cairo brothel or being denounced by him to the police for the murder of Schön. In either case he will receive a handsome sum of money. Lulu replies that she is willing to follow the Marquis to America or China, but she will not become a prostitute. For she cannot sacrifice the only thing that has ever been her own – her free choice of a lover. The Marquis gives her until eleven o'clock to make up her mind (*Twelve concertante variations on a chorale*). The company return from the gaming room, jubilant about their winnings, and withdraw into the dining room. Geschwitz and Lulu exchange angry words, the Countess accusing her of having betrayed her love, while Lulu declares her to be mad. Presently the Athlete corners Lulu, trying to blackmail her (like the Marquis) into giving him 20,000 Marks; otherwise he will denounce her and her crew to the police. The Groom hands the Banker a telegram informing him that the value of the Jungfrau shares has dropped to nought. Schigolch approaches Lulu with the request for money in order to support his mistress and pay for her flat. She tells him of the Athlete's threat, whereupon Schigolch promises her that he will dispose of him (the Athlete) if she will lure him into Schigolch's room in a shabby hotel where he will push the Athlete from the window into the Seine.

The Marquis accuses the Athlete of threatening to denounce Lulu, which the latter denies (*Cadenza for violin and piano*). The Marquis leaves to call the police. Lulu tells the Athlete that Geschwitz wants to spend the night with him and will pay him the 20,000 Marks he had demanded from her. She calls Geschwitz into the hall and persuades her to go with the Athlete to Schigolch's hotel room. The Countess is at first horrified at this monstrous proposition, but in her utter devotion to Lulu she consents, and taking the Athlete by the hand pretends to be deeply in love with him. She and the Athlete depart. The guests return from the gaming room. All have lost to the Banker, who, now that the Jungfrau shares have become worthless, refuses to accept them in payment of their gambling debts and wants money in cash. In a rage the Journalist throws his shares on the floor and all, except Alwa, leave in great agitation. Lulu, having exchanged clothes with the Groom, escapes with Alwa over the backstairs. The Marquis arrives with the police and discovers the deception.

Scene 2: A garret in the East End of London

Lulu has sunk to being a cheap prostitute and gone for the first time on the streets to find clients to support Alwa and Schigolch. The two men await her return and, hearing footsteps on the stairs, hide in a shed. Lulu and her first client, the Professor (silent role), come in and go across into her room. Alwa and Schigolch emerge from their hiding place and, while Alwa listens at Lulu's door, Schigolch ransacks the Professor's coat pockets for money. They hide again as Lulu and the Professor reappear. He leaves and Lulu hands Alwa the money received from the professor. Footsteps are heard again. It is Geschwitz bringing Lulu's pierrot painting with her. Alwa nails it to the wall and the four contemplate it (*Quartet*). Lulu, accompanied by Geschwitz, leaves for the streets again; Schigolch comments that Lulu does not know her métier: she cannot live from love because love is her life. In a conversation with Alwa the latter reveals that he has caught a venereal disease from Lulu, who had been infected by the Marquis. Hearing footsteps again, Schigolch returns to his shed, while Alwa stays where he is but covers himself with a rug so as to be invisible. Lulu arrives with her second client, the Negro. They argue about money. As the Negro lays hands on her Alwa comes to her rescue, but is bludgeoned to death by the black man who quickly departs. Lulu leaves for the streets again, while Schigolch drags Alwa's dead body away. Geschwitz enters slowly and nervously, after which Schigolch departs for a pub. She contemplates suicide but the sight of Lulu's portrait makes her change her mind. Lulu and her third client, Jack the Ripper, arrive and after haggling over her payment go into her room. Geschwitz considers, as if in a dream, returning to Germany and fighting for women's rights (*Notturno*). Lulu's death-cry is suddenly heard, and Geschwitz rushes to her door. Jack opens it and runs a knife into her. After washing the blood from his hands he leaves, with the cynical remark that 'these people have not even a towel' with which he can clean his blood-stained hands. The Countess addresses her last words to Lulu, 'Lulu, my angel ...' and dies over her dead body.

LIST OF WORKS

UNPUBLISHED COMPOSITIONS

73 Songs with piano accompaniment (1900-8)[1]
Double fugue for string quintet and piano (1907) (autograph lost)
Choruses for 6 and 8 parts (1907) (autograph lost)
12 Variations for piano on an original theme (1907-8) (facsimile reproduced in Redlich's *Alban Berg*)

PUBLISHED COMPOSITIONS

Seven Early Songs (Berg's date: 1907) (1905-8)
    1. Nacht (Carl Hauptmann)
    2. Schilflied (Nikolaus Lenau)
    3. Die Nachtigall (Theodor Storm)
    4. Traumgekrönt (Rainer Maria Rilke)
    5. Im Zimmer (Johannes Schlaf)
    6. Liebesode (Otto Erich Hartleben)
    7. Sommertage (Paul Hohenberg)
    Version with piano accompaniment, publ. 1928
    Version for full orchestra, publ. 1955
Schliesse mir die Augen beide (Storm) (Version I, 1907); (Version II, 1925) (publ. 1954)
An Leukon (J.W.L. Gleim) (1907) (first published in Willi Reich's *Alban Berg*, 1937)
Piano Sonata, op. 1 (1907-8) (autograph lost)
Four songs with piano accompaniment, op. 2 (1909-10) (autograph lost)
    1. Schlafen, schlafen (from Hebbel's *Dem Schmerz sein Recht*)
    2. Schlafend trägt man mich
    3. Nun ich der Riesen Stärksten überwand
    4. Warm die Lüfte (from Mombert's collection, *Der Glühende*)
String Quartet, op. 3 (1910)
Five Orchestral Songs to picture postcard texts of Peter Altenberg, op. 4 (1912).

---

[1] For list of dates and titles, see Nicholas Chadwick, 'Berg's Unpublished Songs' (op. cit.), pp. 123-5.

1. Seele, wie bist du schön
2. Sahst du nach dem Gewitterregen
3. Uber die Grenzen des All
4. Nichts ist gekommen
5. Hier ist Friede

Four Pieces for clarinet and piano, op. 5 (1913)

Three Pieces for large orchestra, op. 6 (1914-15)

Praeludium (1914)

Reigen (1915)

Marsch (1914)

Wozzeck, op. 7. Opera in three acts after the play of Georg Büchner (1914-21).

Three Fragments from the opera (1924)

Chamber Concerto for piano, violin and 13 wind instruments (1923-5)

Second movement (*Adagio*) arr, for violin, clarinet and piano (1935)

Lyric Suite for string quartet (1925-6)

2nd, 3rd and 4th movement arr. for string orchestra (1928)

Der Wein, concert aria with orchestra to poems by Baudelaire, in a German version by Stefan George (1929)

Four-part canon with text by Berg, written for the fiftieth anniversary of the Frankfort Opera House (1930)

Violin Concerto (1935)

Lulu, Opera in three acts after the plays *Erdgeist* and *Die Büchse der Pandora* by Frank Wedekind (1928-35) (orchestration of Act III completed by F. Cerha).

Symphonic Pieces (1934)

Rondo (Andante und Hymne)

Ostinato (Allegro)

Lied der Lulu (Comodo)

Variations (Moderato)

Adagio (Sostenuto, Lento, Grave)

ARRANGEMENTS OF OTHER COMPOSERS' WORK

Frank Schreker

Der ferne Klang. Vocal score with text (1911)

Arnold Schoenberg

Gurrelieder. Vocal score with text (1912)

Litanei and

Entrückung, from String Quartet No. 2. Vocal score with text (1912)

Chamber Symphony, op. 9. Piano score, possibly for four hands (autograph lost) (1913-15)

THEMATIC ANALYSES, ESSAYS, ARTICLES

(R = Reprint in Willi Reich's biography of 1937)

Arnold Schoenberg
    Gurrelieder (1913)
    Chamber Symphony, op. 9 (1913)
    Symphonic Poem *Pelleas und Melisande* (1920)
Lecture on *Wozzeck* (1929) (first published in Redlich's biography)'
Was ist atonal? Dialogue on Austrian Radio (RAVAG) (23 April 1930),
    first published in Magazine *23* (June 1936)   R
Lecture cycle on Schoenberg's music (Vienna, 1932-3) (autograph lost)
Dem Lehrer, Symposium 'Arnold Schoenberg' (Munich 1912)   R
Der Verein fur muskalische Privataufführungen in Wien, Prospect (Vienna,
    1919)   R
'Erziehung des Zeitungslesers tut not', fragment of an article of 1928,
    first published by Reich in *Melos*, July-August 1953   R
'Die musikalische Impotenz der "neuen Aesthetik" Hans Pfitzners'
    (*Anbruch*, Vienna, June 1920)   R
Warum ist Schoenbergs Musik so schwer verständlich?, written for the
    composer's fiftieth birthday (special number of the *Anbruch*,
    August-1924). English translation (*The Music Review*, Cambridge,
    August 1952)   R
'Die musikalischen Formen in meiner Oper *Wozzeck*' (*Die Musik*,
    February 1924)   R
'Offener Brief an Arnold Schoenberg' (analysis of Berg's Chamber
    Concerto) (*Pult und Taktstock*, February 1925)   R
'Verbindliche Antwort auf eine unverbindliche Rundfrage' (Year Book
    of U.E., *25 Years of Modern Music*, Vienna 1926)   R
'A Word about *Wozzeck*' (*Modern Music*, November 1927)
'Operntheatrer' (*Anbruch* 1928)   R
'Das "Opernproblem"' ' (*Neue Musik-Zeitung*, Stuttgart. 49, no. 9, 1928)   R
'Zu Franz Schuberts 100 Todestag' (*Vossische Zeitung*, 18 November
    1928)   R
'Vorstellung Ernst Kreneks' (Speech given in Vienna, 3 January 1928)   R
'Die Stimme in der Oper' (Yearbook of U.E., *Gesang*, 1929)   R
'Credo' (*Die Musik*, January 1930)   R
'*Wozzeck* Bemerkungen' (Vienna 1930; except for a new introduction
    identical with 'Pro Domo' section in article, 'Das
    "Opernproblem"' ')
Praktische Anweisungen zur Einstudierung des 'Wozzeck' (Vienna, 1930).
    English translation, *The Musical Times*, June 1968, George Perle   R
An Adolf Loos. Festschrift on the 60th Anniversary of Adolf Loos (Vienna,
    1930)   R

'Gedenkrede auf Emil Hertzka (Speech given in Vienna on 20 June
    1932   R

Zum 60 Geburtstag. Festschrift for Arnold Schoenberg (Vienna, 1934)

An Karl Kraus (Stimmen über Karl Kraus on his 60th Birthday, 28 April
    1934)   R

'Händel und Bach' (Magazine *23*, no. 20/21, 1935)   R

Zwei Feuilletons. Ein Beitrag zum Kapitel 'Schönberg und die Kritik' (Vienna
    1920) (published for the first time in Reich, 1963)

SELECT BIBLIOGRAPHY

ADORNO, TH. W.
Philosophie der Neuen Musik, Tübingen, 1949.
Dissonanzen. Musik in der verwalteten Welt, Göttingen, 1956
'Alban Berg', in *Klangfiguren. Musikalische Schriften I*, Frankfort, 1959.
'Die Instrumentation von Bergs Frühen Liedern', ibid.
'Bergs kompositionstechnische Versuche', in *Quasi una fantasia, Musikalische Schriften II, Frankfort* 1963.
Alban Berg. Beiträge 1967. Österreichische Gesellschaft für Musik, Kassel, 1967.
Alban Berg, Der Meister des kleinsten Übergangs, Vienna, 1968.

BERG, ALBAN
Letters to Schoenberg (1911-35) (unpublished).

BERG, ERICH ALBAN (ed.)
Alban Berg. Leben und Werke in Daten und Bilden, Frankfurt, 1976.

BERG, HELENE
Alban Berg. Briefe an seine Frau, Vienna, 1965; London, 1971.

BOULEZ, PIERRE
Relevés d'apprenti, Paris, 1966.
'Lulu': Analyse et commentaire, Paris, 1979.

CARNER, MOSCO
'Berg's Violin Concerto', in *The Concerto*, ed. R. Hill, Penguin, London, 1952.
'Alban Berg in his Letters to his Wife', in *Music and Letters*, July 1969.
'The Berg Affair, Venice 1934', in *Musical Times*, November, 1969.
Alban Berg. L'Homme. L'Oeuvre (rev. ed.), Paris, 1979.

CERHA, FRIEDRICH
Arbeitsbericht zur Herstellung des 3. Akts der Oper 'Lulu' von Alban Berg, Vienna, 1979.

CHADWICK, NICHOLAS
'A Survey of the Early Songs of Alban Berg' (Dissertation, Oxford 1971, unpublished).
'Berg's Unpublished Songs in the Österreichische Nationalbibliothek', *Music and Letters*, April 1971.

GREEN, DOUGLAS, M.
'Berg's De Profundis: the Finale of the Lyric Suite', Newsletter No. 5, *International Alban Berg Society*, June 1977.

HILMAR, ERNST
'*Wozzeck' von Alban Berg. Entstehung – Erste Erfolge*, Vienna, 1975.

JARMAN, DOUGLAS
The Music of Alban Berg, London, 1979.

JOUVE, PIERRE JEAN and FANO, MICHEL
Wozzeck d'Alban Berg, Paris, 1964.

KOLLERITSCH, OTTO (ed.)
50 Jahre 'Wozzeck' von Alban Berg. Vorgeschichte und Auswirkung in der Opernästhetik, Graz, 1978.

KRENEK, ERNST
'Alban Bergs "Lulu" ', in *Zur Sprache gebracht*, Berlin, 1958.

LEIBOWITZ, RENE
Schoenberg et son école, Paris, 1947; English ed., 1949.

MITCHELL, DONALD
'The Character of Lulu: Wedekind's and Berg's Conception Compared', *Music Review*, November 1954.

PERLE, GEORGE
Serial Composition and Atonality, London, 1962. 4/1978.
'The Character of Lulu: a Sequel', *Music Review*, November 1964.
'A Note on Act III of *Lulu*'. *Perspective of New Music*, Spring-Summer 1964.
'*Lulu:* The Formal Design', *Journal of the American Musicological Society*, 17, no. 2, 1964.
'*Lulu:* Thematic Material and Pitch Organisation'. *Music Review*, November 1965.
'Woyzeck and Wozzeck', *Musical Quarterly*, 53, no. 2, April 1967.
'The Musical Language of Wozzeck', *The Music Forum*' ed. William J. Mitchell and Felix Salzer, New York, 1967, Vol. 1, p. 104.
'Representation and Symbol in the Music of *Wozzeck*', *Music Review*, 32, no. 4, November 1971.
'The Secret Programme of the Lyric Suite', *Musical Times*, Aug.-Oct. 1977.

PLOEBSCH, GERD
Alban Bergs 'Wozzeck': Dramaturgie and Musikalischer Aufbau, Strasbourg, 1968.

RAUCHHAUPT, URSULA VON, ed.
Schoenberg, Berg, Webern: Die Streichquartette. Eine Dokumentation, Hamburg, 1971.

REDLICH, H.F.
Alban Berg, Versuch einer Würdigung, Vienna, 1957; London, 1957.

REICH, WILLI
Alban Berg. Mit Bergs eigenen Schriften und Beiträgen von Theodor Wiesengrund-Adorno und Ernst Krenek, Vienna, 1937.
Alban Berg. Leben und Werk, Zurich, 1963; London, 1965.

(ed.) *Alban Berg, Bildnis im Wort. Selbstzeugnisse und Aussagen der Freunde*, Zurich, 1959.

Schönberg oder der Konservative Revolutionär, Vienna, 1968; London, 1971.

REITER, MANFRED

Die Zwölftontechnik in Alban Berg's Oper 'Lulu', Regensburg, 1973.

ROGNONI, LUIGI

Espressionismo e dodecafonia, Milan, 1954.

SCHOENBERG, ARNOLD

Harmonielehre, 3rd ed., Vienna, 1921.

Style and Idea, New York, 1950.

Briefe, ed. Stein, Mainz, 1958; English ed., London, 1964.

Arnold Schönberg. Gedenkausstellung 1974 (ed. Ernst Hilmar), Vienna, 1974.

SCHWEIZER, KLAUS

Die Sonatensatzform im Schaffen Alban Bergs, Stuttgart, 1970.

STEIN, ERWIN

Orpheus in New Guises, London, 1953.

(ed.), *Arnold Schoenberg: Letters*, London, 1964.

STUCKENSCHMIDT, H.H.

Schönberg. Leben – Umwelt – Werk, Zurich, 1974.

WELLESZ, EGON

Die neue Instrumentation, Berlin, 1928.

INDEX

Works – unpublished: Double Fugue for string quintet and piano, 14; Symphony (uncompleted), 24, 25, 144, 213; Twelve variations for piano on an original theme, 14, 14n; Songs, 9, 'Traum', 5n, 62n, discussion, 93-4

Works – published: 'An Leukom', 9n; Chamber Concerto, xiii, xix, 19, 22, 30, 75n, 121, 124, 125, 128, 135, 156, 209, 209n, 235, 249n, 275; importance of number three, xix (and see discussion); Schoenberg's interest, 53; composition and dedication to Schoenberg, 28, 55; discussion, 147-55; *Five Orchestral Songs after Picture Post-card Texts of Peter Altenberg*, op. 4, 22, 25, 26, 29, 40, 45, 93, 98, 108, 111, 120, 143, first performance, 27, publication of full score, 25-6, discussion, 101-8; Four Pieces for Clarinet and Piano, op. 5, 25, 29, 45, 98, 113, composition, 25, dedication to Schoenberg, 30n, 121, first performance, 28, 48, 121, publication, 52, discussion, 120-1; Four Songs for Voice and Piano, op. 2, 4, 12n, 75n, 113, 116, 120, composition, 14, reissued, 52, orchestral version, 101, discussion, 98-101; *Lulu*, xi, xiii, xiv, xix, 6, 9, 20, 38, 39, 70, 71, 73, 76, 77, 78, 80, 84, 100n, 105, 108, 109, 112, 113, 140, 150n, 156, 175, 178, 197n, 202n; first interest in subject, 71; composition, 74-8, Lulu's *Lied* inscribed to Webern, 78n; genesis of libretto, 215-27; non-completion, 89; foreign productions, 233n, 256; posthumous history, 267-76; dedication to Schoenberg, 78, 271; Zurich première of incomplete version, 225; discussion, 215-76; Berg's available source of material for completion of Third Act, 259; filmed Interlude, 75, 255, 256, 268, film script, 256; reasons for Helene Berg's embargo on publication of Third Act material, 273; reference in Helene Berg's Will, 274; consideration by various composers to complete work, 270-1; completion of Third Act by Friedrich Cerha, xi, 172; première of completed Cerha version in Paris, 275; synopsis of opera plot, 291-7; foreign productions of completed version, 256; discussion of Cerha's Third Act, 259; Lyric Suite, xi, xiii, xiv, 19, 62, 68, 70, 75n, 80, 81, 85, 100n, 108, 110, 112n, 113, 118, 120, 148, 156, 196n, 202n, 205, 207n, 214, 227, 232, 247, 248, 256, 257; importance of number '23', xix, 43; composition and dedication to

Zemlinksy, 62-3; Adorno's comments on symbolism, 67; annotated score with secret dedication to Hanna Fuchs-Robettin, 68, 70, 123, 127, 133, 134, 135, 138; importance of (Hanna's) number '10', 123, 134, 135; vocal part contemplated, 138; performance with vocal part, 138-9; first performance, 63; performance problems, Venice Biennale, 80-2; discussion, 121-42; Piano Sonata, op. 1, xviii, 4, 85, 113, 115, 116, 117, 120, 126, 143; composition, 14; first performance, 27n; re-issued, 52; discussion, 113-15; 'Schliesse mir die Augen beide' (1907 setting), 9, 68, 107n; 'Schliesse mir die Augen beide' (1925 setting), 62n, 68, 93, 111, 124; composition, 55; dedication to Hertzka, 55, 107; discussion, 107-8; Seven Early Songs, 9, 33, 94, 97, 101, 115, 150n; composition 14; orchestral version made, and first performance, 74; discussion, 94-8; String Quartet, op. 3, xviii, xix, 15, 19, 25, 101, 113, 121, 125, 126, 143; composition, 14-15; first private performance, 27n; publication, 52; first public performance, 55-6; discussion, 115-20; Symphonic Pieces (*Lulu* Symphony), 88, 214, 245n, 251, 259, 262, 263, 271n, 272, 274, 286, 287; composition and first performance, 78; foreign performances, 85n, 88, 218, 274; discussion, 266-7; Three Pieces for large orchestra, op. 6, xiii, xviii, 18, 21 22, 24, 25, 45, 49n, 98, 153, 187, 251, 278, 280, 281; composition, 30; use of material from abortive Symphony, 25; dedication to Schoenberg, 18, 30; first performance, (incomplete), 30, 55; first complete performance (revised scoring), 31; discussion, 142-7; Violin Concerto, xiii, xiv, xv, xviii, 19, 43, 73, 82n, 107, 110, 123, 150, 152, 267, 275; commissioning by Krasner, 85-6, 155; dedication to Krasner, 87; first performance, 69, 82n, 87; piano score made by Rita Kurzmann, 85, 88; discussion, 155-62; *Wein, Der*, 63, 85, 150n, 156, 251; commissioning by Ružena Herlinger, 75; composition and first performance, 80; first Italian performance, 80-2; selection of text, 109; discussion, 108-12; *Wozzek*, op. 7, xiv, xix, 4, 9, 18, 19, 20, 21, 21n, 22, 24, 25, 26, 27, 28, 34, 44, 49, 49n, 55, 56n, 57, 62, 71, 72, 73, 75, 76, 77, 79, 81, 82, 97, 98, 108, 109, 113, 120, 121, 124, 127, 139, 144, 146, 148, 153,